MY FRIEND DAHMER

a graphic novel by
DERF BACKDERF

Abrams ComicArts, New York

ACKNOWLEDGMENTS

Thanks to my friends Mike, Kent, and Neil (especially Mike) for sharing their memories over many hours of conversation. Thanks also to Bob Ethington, who critiqued this project every step of the way. I shamelessly exploited his expertise, and his counsel was invaluable.

EDITOR: Charles Kochman
DESIGNER: Neil Egan
PRODUCTION MANAGER: Alison Gervais

Library of Congress Cataloging-in-Publication Data

Derf.
  My friend Dahmer / written & illustrated by Derf Backderf.
      p. cm.
  ISBN 978-1-4197-0216-7 (hardcover)
  ISBN 978-1-4197-0217-4 (paperback)
1. Dahmer, Jeffrey—Comic books, strips, etc. 2. Graphic novels. I. Title.
  PN6727.D466M9 2012
  741.5'973—dc23

                    2011285306

ISBN for this edition: 978-1-4197-2755-9

Text and illustrations copyright © 2012, 2017 John Backderf

Introduction copyright © 2017 Marc Meyers

Storyboards copyright © 2017 Marc Meyers (inset artwork from *My Friend Dahmer* copyright © 2017 John Backderf)

Photograph on page 8 copyright © 2012, 2017 William S. Henry. All rights reserved. Used with permission.

Photo gallery copyright © 2017 MFD The Movie, LLC

Printed and bound in U.S.A.
10 9 8 7 6 5 4 3 2 1

Abrams ComicArts books are available at special discounts when purchased in quantity for premiums and promotions as well as fundraising or educational use. Special editions can also be created to specification. For details, contact specialsales@abramsbooks.com or the address below.

ABRAMS The Art of Books
195 Broadway, New York, NY 10007
abramsbooks.com

Contents

by Marc Meyers

When I was a kid growing up in the eighties, I had a friend who lived down the street in a beautiful home set on the edge of a small lake. I never witnessed it, but I heard he would occasionally take a baseball bat into the backyard and try to hit the snapping turtles that were nesting on the edge of his property. Friends would quip that someday he'll surely become a serial killer. Yet today, according to Facebook, he's a schoolteacher and happily married with kids.

This memory stuck with me and provided the initial seed of an idea for a fictional film that would be a portrait of a serial killer as a young boy. I believed it would be fascinating to show the embryonic stage of a person who would one day become a monster.

In October 2011, I came across an advance copy of the graphic novel *My Friend Dahmer* at New York Comic Con, and I could see my idea perfectly represented in Derf Backderf's deeply personal, true story.

What are those forces in life that sculpt and define us? How do we become who we are? Why does one teenager find promise, while his friend enters adulthood broken? How well do we know our friends?

Nature versus nurture is one of our most fundamental debates. And in my film adaptation of the graphic novel, I don't provide answers, but I hope that by sharing this story, audiences might ask these questions for themselves— and in the future, hopefully, one might look at a troubled teen through a more empathetic lens.

I was committed to adapting Derf's tale as faithfully as possible. I'm forever grateful he entrusted me with his masterpiece. The author's personal narrative is horrifyingly honest, and for me it was of utmost importance to maintain that candidness in my interpretation, translating it to film. I could relate to these characters. They remind me of my own high school days growing up in a rural suburb similar to Akron, Ohio. Plus, the time line of Dahmer's family life disintegrating around him oddly mirrors my parents' divorce during the end of my high school experience.

When I was writing an early draft, Derf took me around his hometown and showed me the actual locations portrayed in the book, including the high school and Jeffrey Dahmer's childhood home. For me, location is as important as casting the right actor for a role, and I was immediately determined to film at Dahmer's real house. One might assume filming there was creepy, but that wasn't the case. The spot gave myself, the cast, and the crew a deeper connection to the actual events in our story.

After writing my screenplay, I storyboarded the entire script in three sketch pads, and incorporated many of Derf's own drawings whenever my adaptation and the source material overlapped. These storyboards were with me on set every day. Fans of the graphic novel will recognize many of its panels respectfully interpreted for the screen.

The collaboration I had with the entire cast is one of the highlights of my career. I'm very grateful for their talent, passionate dedication, and enthusiasm for the project.

I met with and auditioned around a hundred young actors for the lead teen roles of Jeff, Derf, Neil, and Mike. I knew I had to find an actor who had the versatility, depth, and physical likeness to take on the role of Dahmer; when I met Ross Lynch I quickly locked into the idea that he could carry this film. Many people thought it was a risky choice given Ross's background as an actor on the Disney Channel, but his casting felt perfect to me and my fellow producers. Originally a dancer, Ross is a consummate performer who inhabited the role from head to toe. The way he transforms, carrying his body with the stiff gait and rolled shoulders; his ability to re-create the hallway spasms; his strength of saying so much with an eye glance; his charming and persuasive qualities—all mix together to create a unique character who is compelling to watch.

I equally responded to the talents of Alex Wolff and Tommy Nelson when they auditioned in New York. I knew the role of Derf had to be a likeable and relatable counterbalance to the darker tones of Dahmer's character. And Alex has those confident and subversive qualities that Derf's own band-nerd, alpha-male character needed for our adaptation. We're so fortunate that the chemistry extended with Tommy Nelson and Harry Holzer, and that filming and being on set brought the teen actors together as real friends. Even after production ended, all of us remain friends.

My adaptation expands on Dahmer's homelife more than is portrayed in the book. As an adaptation, there's some creative license that one must take; and when my producing partners and I were developing the screenplay, it became evident that the movie needed to lean more heavily on the title character and his private life. The roles of this story required seasoned talents, and I'm so fortunate that the script found its way into the hands of Anne Heche, Dallas Roberts, and Vincent Kartheiser.

Re-creating the truly bizarre world of the suburban seventies swirling around Dahmer's teenage life was great fun. It was an era before computers entered the home, before cable TV and CNN's twenty-four hour news cycle. It was still a local life. And teens from Northeast Ohio were soaking up an incredible, varied moment in music. I'm proud that our indie film was able to include accurate period music from the area—audiences will experience songs from Akron-originated punk bands, as well as more mainstream tunes that were in rotation on Cleveland's hit radio station WMMS Buzzard Radio. I even courted the actual WMMS DJ, Denny Sanders, to lend his voice as the DJ in the film.

Many films portray an ordinary person faced with extraordinary circumstances. In contrast, this is the story of an odd and deeply troubled, truly rare individual who tries to navigate through an ordinary world. Dahmer's gradual, inevitable unraveling is horrifying, and right there in full view. This is a story of its time, but it is also sadly relevant today.

Marc Meyers
Brooklyn, New York
July 2017

Marc Meyers is a writer/director. His films have screened at film festivals around the world and have been released theatrically. *My Friend Dahmer* is his fourth narrative feature film. Previous movies include: *How He Fell In Love, Harvest* (a *New York Times* Critics' Pick), and *Approaching Union Square*. Marc lives with his wife, who is also his producing partner, and their daughter in Brooklyn, New York.

PRAISE FOR THE GRAPHIC NOVEL *MY FRIEND DAHMER*

"Stunning. Horrifying. Beautifully done." –Alison Bechdel

"A brilliant graphic novel and surely ranks among the very best of the form."
–Dan Chaon

"A well-told, powerful story." –R. Crumb

"A solid job. Putrid serial killer Jeffrey Dahmer's origins are explored in this
fine book. Dig it—it'll hang you out to dry."
–James Ellroy

"*My Friend Dahmer* will certainly quench your dark little desires."
–Chuck Klosterman

"This one's still haunting me." –Brad Meltzer

"It wasn't easy reading this book, but I'm glad I did."
–David Small

"Wow. Reading this is unlike any other reading experience I've ever had. Do it."
–Rainn Wilson

"Masterful . . . a rich tale full of complexity and sensitivity."
–*The Cleveland Plain Dealer*

★ "An exemplary demonstration of the transformative possibilities of
graphic narrative."
–*Kirkus* (starred review)

★ "A small, dark classic." –*Publishers Weekly* (starred review)

"One of the most thought-provoking comics released in a long time."
–Slate.com

"Astounding." –Lev Grossman, *TIME*

"One of the best graphic novels I've read this year." –*USA Today*

"When I was a kid, I was just like anybody else."

—Jeff Dahmer

Jeff Dahmer (left) and an unknown classmate in Revere High School, Ohio, 1978. Copyright © 2011 William S. Henry.

The Convoluted History of *My Friend Dahmer*

M Y *Friend Dahmer*, a twenty-year work in progress, started as a short story eight pages in length. I began collecting material for this book a few weeks after Dahmer's ghastly crimes became public in July 1991. I wasn't sure what I was going to do with the material, but I recognized that here was a remarkable tale—one that wasn't being told by the mainstream media that swarmed in Dahmer's wake—and my friendship with Jeff provided me with a unique perspective. Indeed, I didn't do anything with the idea for several years, but when Jeff was killed in prison on November 28, 1994, I sat down and wrote the first short story as a cathartic exercise. To you Dahmer was a depraved fiend, but to me he was a kid I sat next to in study hall and hung out with in the band room. You just can't imagine what it was like once the news of his crimes exploded, or what it's still like for me whenever I think about our friendship. So from time to time, between 1994 and 1997, I wrote several stories about Jeff when the mood struck.

The few people I showed these to urged me to finish and get them in print. That first story made it into the anthology comic *Zero Zero* in 1997 and garnered much acclaim. This prodded me to write a one-hundred-page graphic novel collecting all the stories I had written about my friend Dahmer up to that point. I spent the next three years trying in vain to sell this project.

Frustrated and stonewalled, I self-published a comic book version in 2002. A mere twenty-four pages, because that's all I could afford, *My Friend Dahmer* became an immediate cult classic. It was nominated for an Eisner Award (a rare honor for a self-published comic), translated (without permission, I might add) into several languages, and featured in three documentaries. Author Chuck Klosterman wrote about my Dahmer stories in his bestseller *Sex, Drugs, and Cocoa Puffs*. And New York University's theater department adapted and staged the comic as a one-act play.

Mature readers
DERFCITY COMICS
$2.95 USA
$4.50 CAN.
MY FRIEND
DAHMER
A TRUE STORY by derf
REVERE

But I wasn't happy with what I'd done.

The book was way too short. There was so much more to the story, loads of material I had to cut because of that twenty-four-page limit. It was also my first attempt at long-form graphic storytelling, and to be blunt, it shows. The drawing stinks, the narrative is choppy, and the timeline is a mess. The original is also a straight memoir, culled entirely from my memory and from stories my friends and I shared over the years. But it doesn't go any deeper than that. All in all, when I look back at the original comic, I see a huge missed opportunity. It should have been a major work, and instead it was just a self-published pamphlet that only a couple thousand people read. This bugged me for years, until I finally decided I was no longer going to regret this for the rest of my life. I would produce the work I had envisioned.

So what's different about this version? To start with, this is the best drawing I've done to date. My previous graphic novel, *Punk Rock and Trailer Parks,* had been my most ambitious and had pushed me to new heights as an artist and a storyteller. I've put the lessons I learned producing that book to good use here. This version was written in one monthlong session, with a clear narrative vision. It has a flow and clarity the original lacked.

Second, I went back and researched the story, the right way this time. I interviewed dozens of former classmates and teachers, pored over FBI and police files, combed through every interview Jeff gave before his death, and uncovered some surprising and never-before-disclosed revelations about his young life. The resulting work is a graphic novel that details Jeff's descent from an oddball twelve-year-old to a young teen struggling helplessly against the dark thoughts that gurgled and bubbled in his head, leading up to the exact moment when he plunged off the brink.

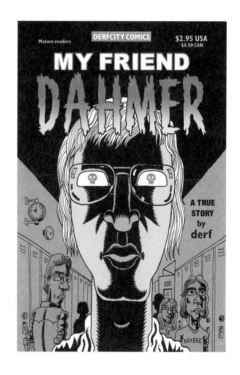

This is a tragic tale, one that has lost none of its emotional power after two decades. It's my belief that Dahmer didn't have to wind up a monster, that all those people didn't have to die horribly, if only the adults in his life hadn't been so inexplicably, unforgivably, incomprehensibly clueless and/or indifferent. Once Dahmer kills, however—and I can't stress this enough—my sympathy for him ends. He could have turned himself in after that first murder. He could have put a gun to his head. Instead he, and he alone, chose to become a serial killer and spread misery to countless people. There are a surprising number out there who view Jeffrey Dahmer as some kind of anti-hero, a bullied kid who lashed back at the society that rejected him. This is nonsense. Dahmer was a twisted wretch whose depravity was almost beyond comprehension. Pity him, but don't empathize with him.

This book probably isn't the smartest follow-up to *Punk Rock and Trailer Parks*, which was a raucous, joyful comedy. In fact, *My Friend Dahmer* is completely unlike anything else I've done, or will likely do in the future. But I just had to do it nonetheless. At long last, *My Friend Dahmer* is finished, and I'm happy with this, its final incarnation.

derf

Derf Backderf
Shaker Heights, Ohio
April 2011

Prologue

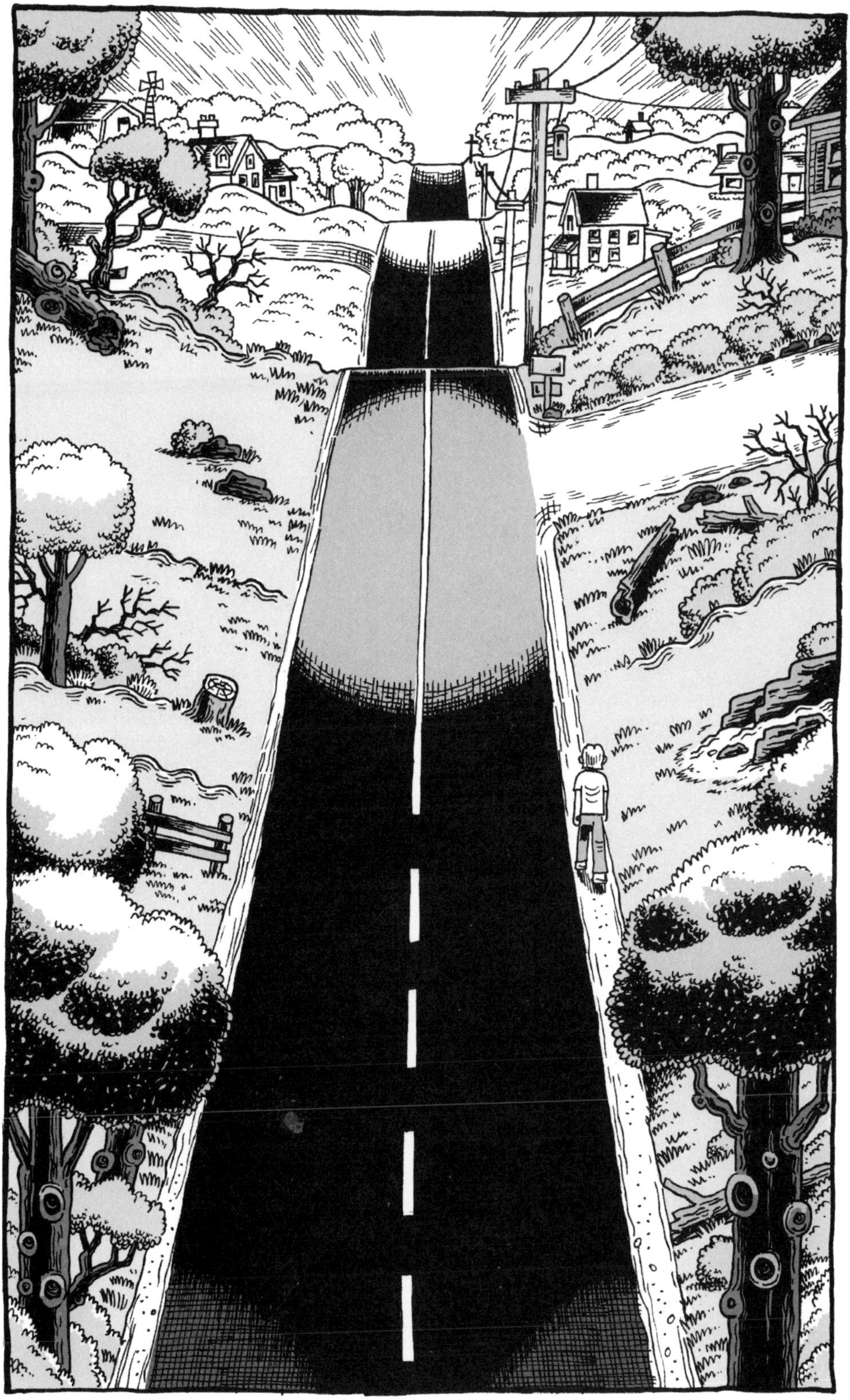

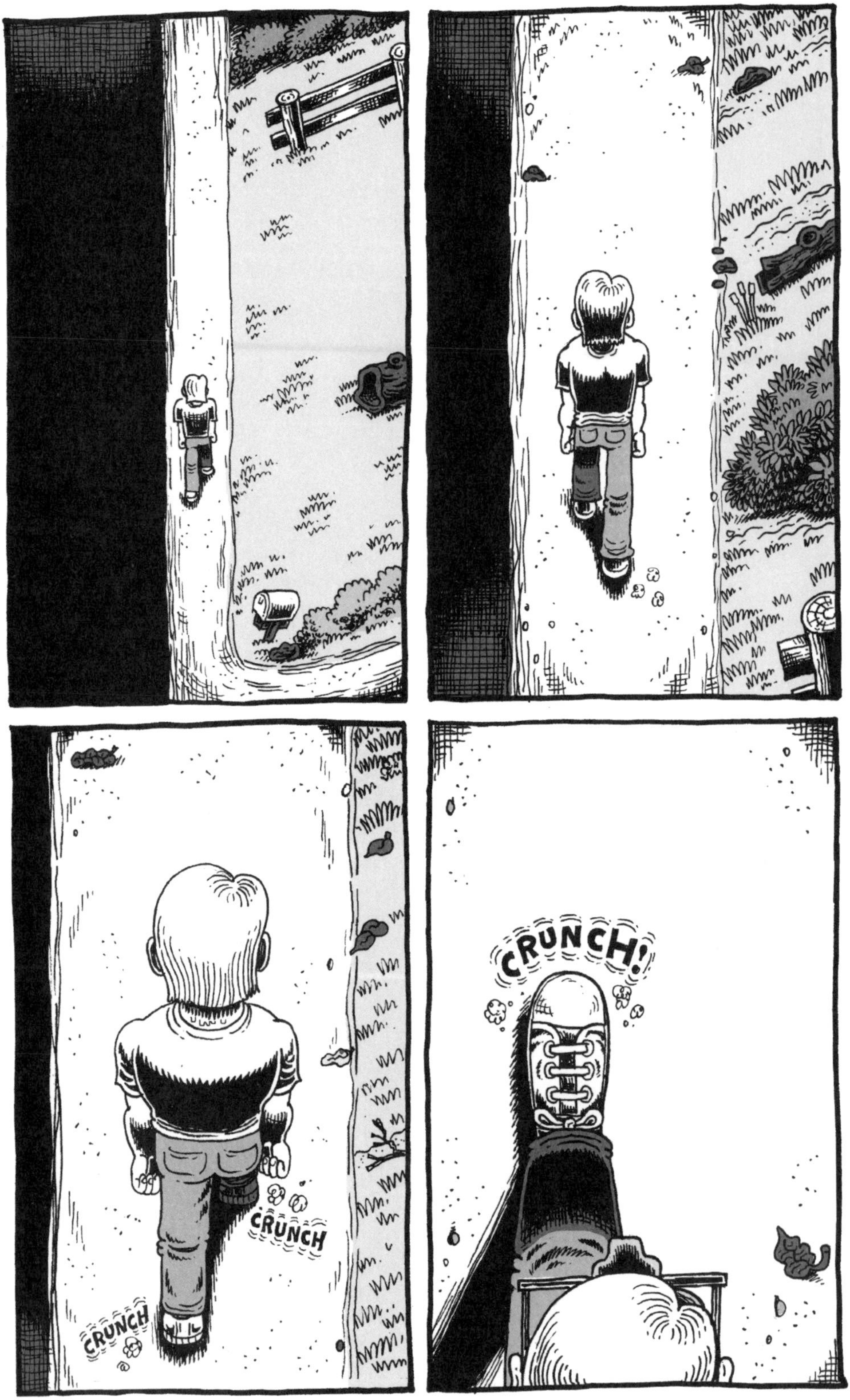
CRUNCH
CRUNCH
CRUNCH!

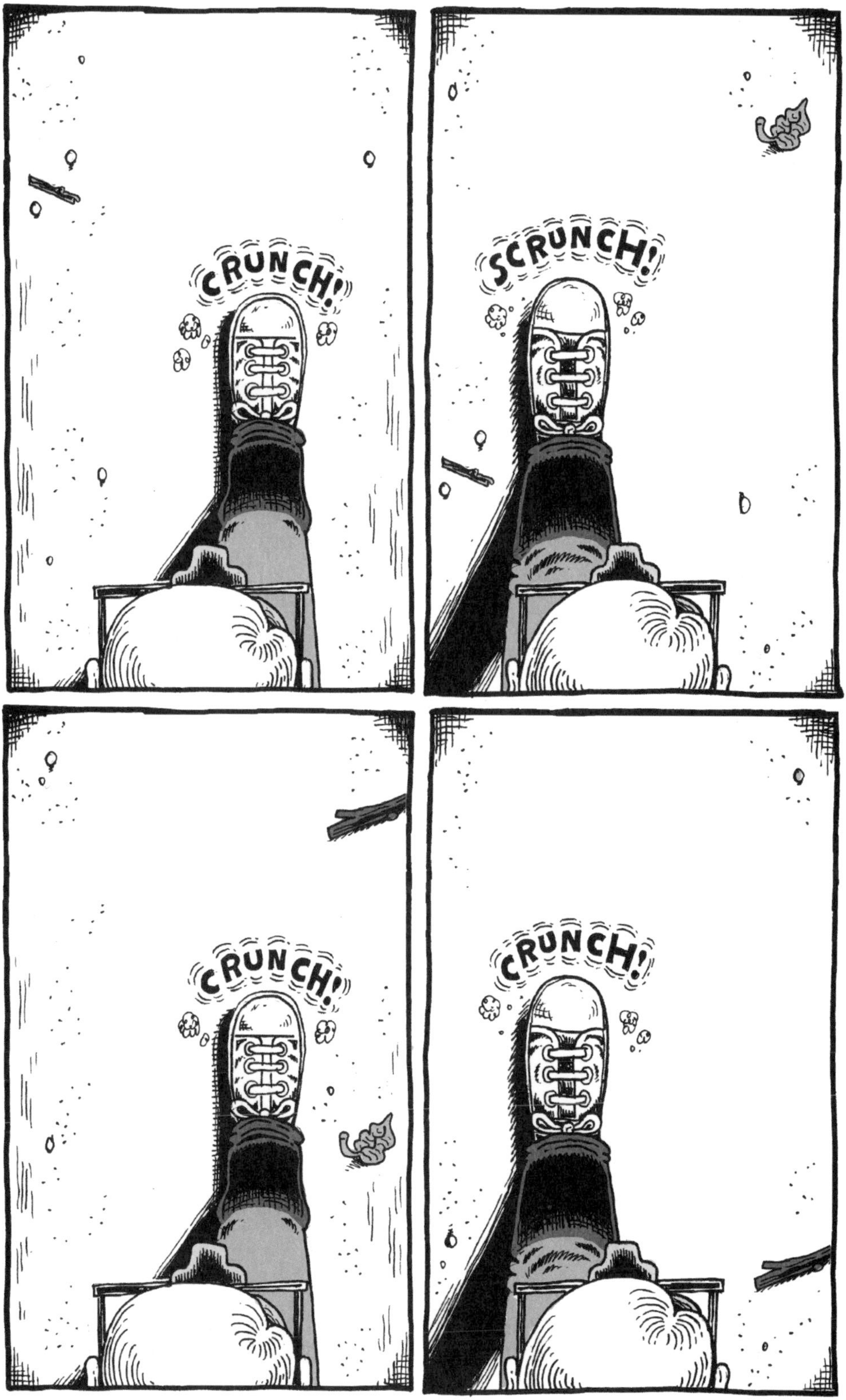
CRUNCH!
SCRUNCH!
CRUNCH!
CRUNCH!

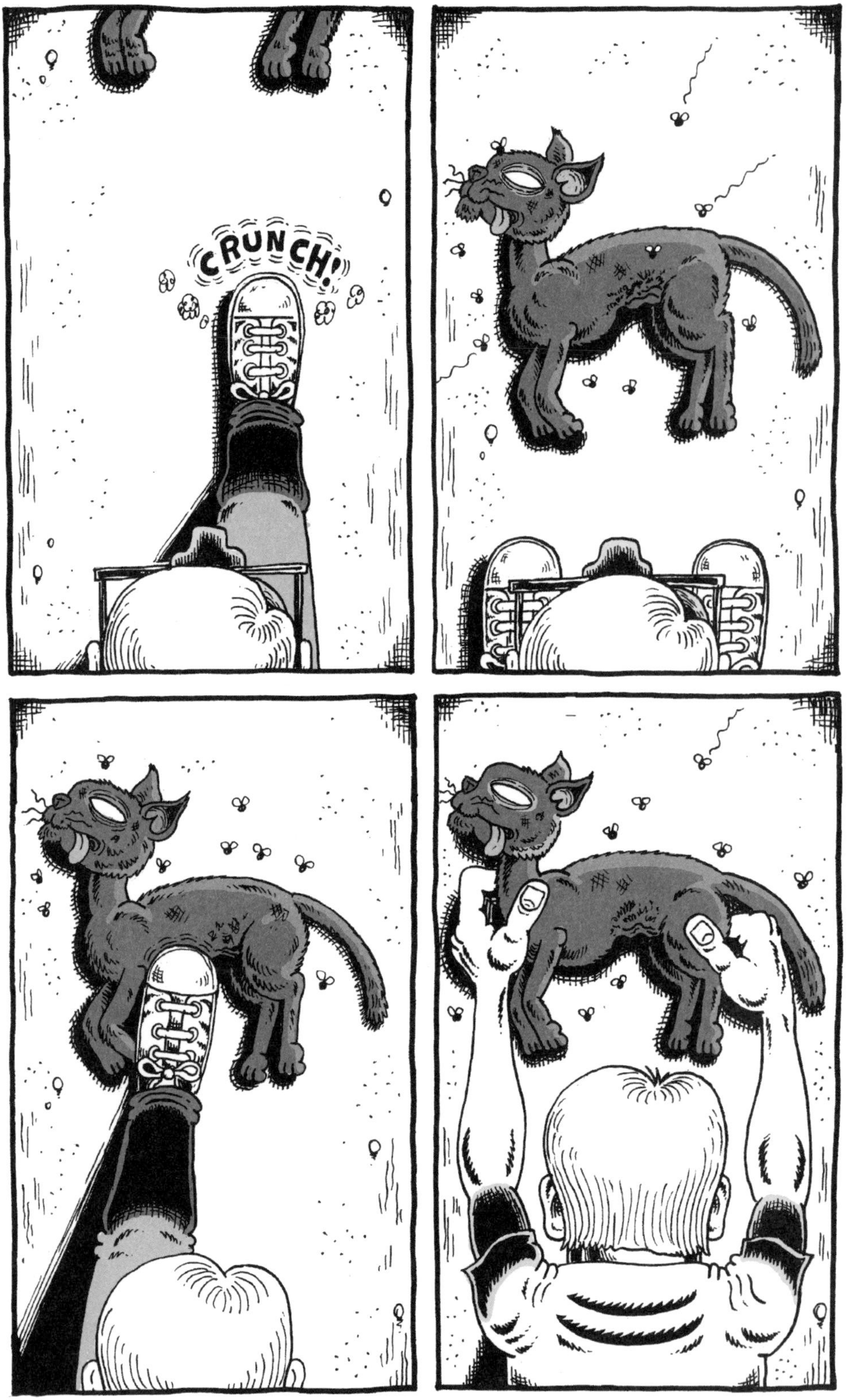
CRUNCH!

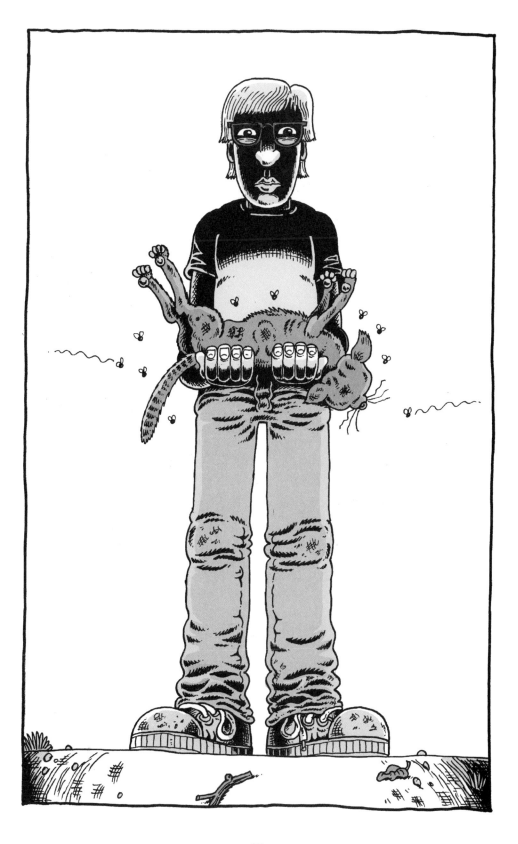

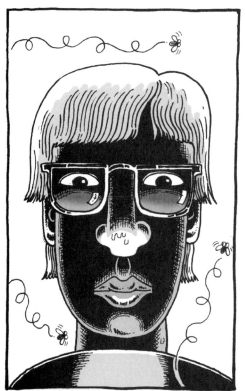

CRUNCH CRUNCH

18

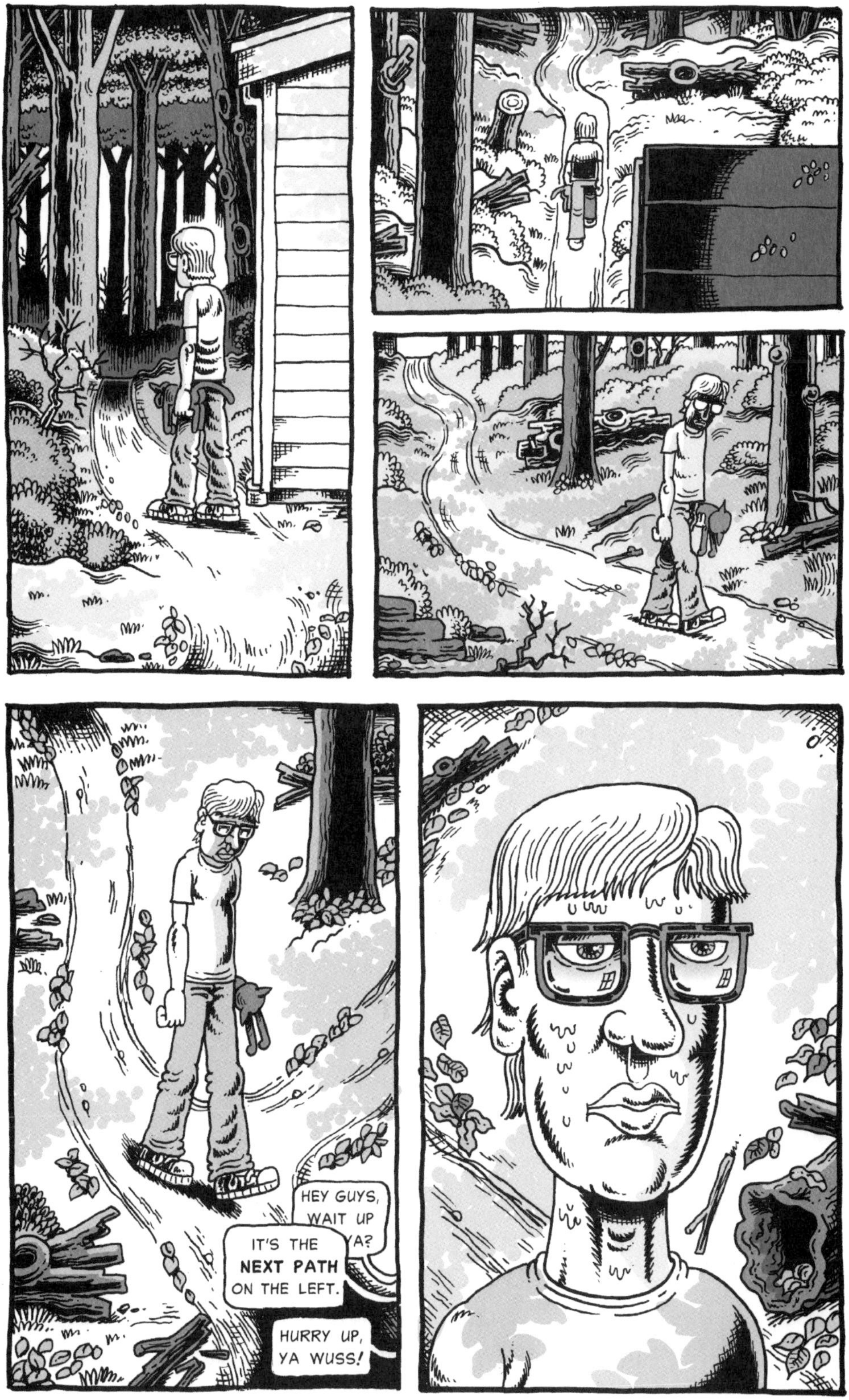
HEY GUYS, WAIT UP YA?
IT'S THE **NEXT PATH** ON THE LEFT.
HURRY UP, YA WUSS!

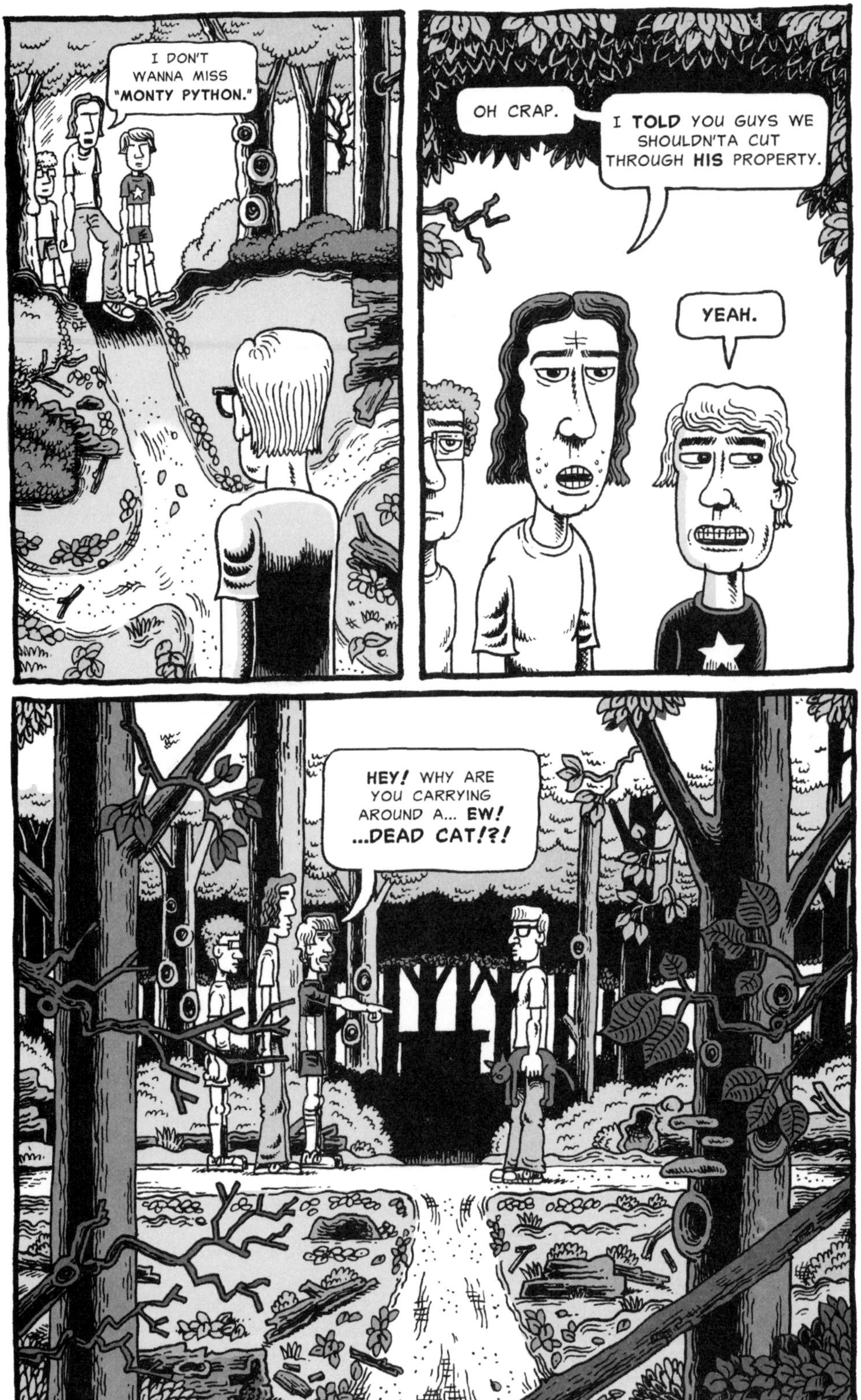
I DON'T WANNA MISS "MONTY PYTHON."
OH CRAP.
I TOLD YOU GUYS WE SHOULDN'TA CUT THROUGH HIS PROPERTY.
YEAH.
HEY! WHY ARE YOU CARRYING AROUND A... EW! ...DEAD CAT!?!

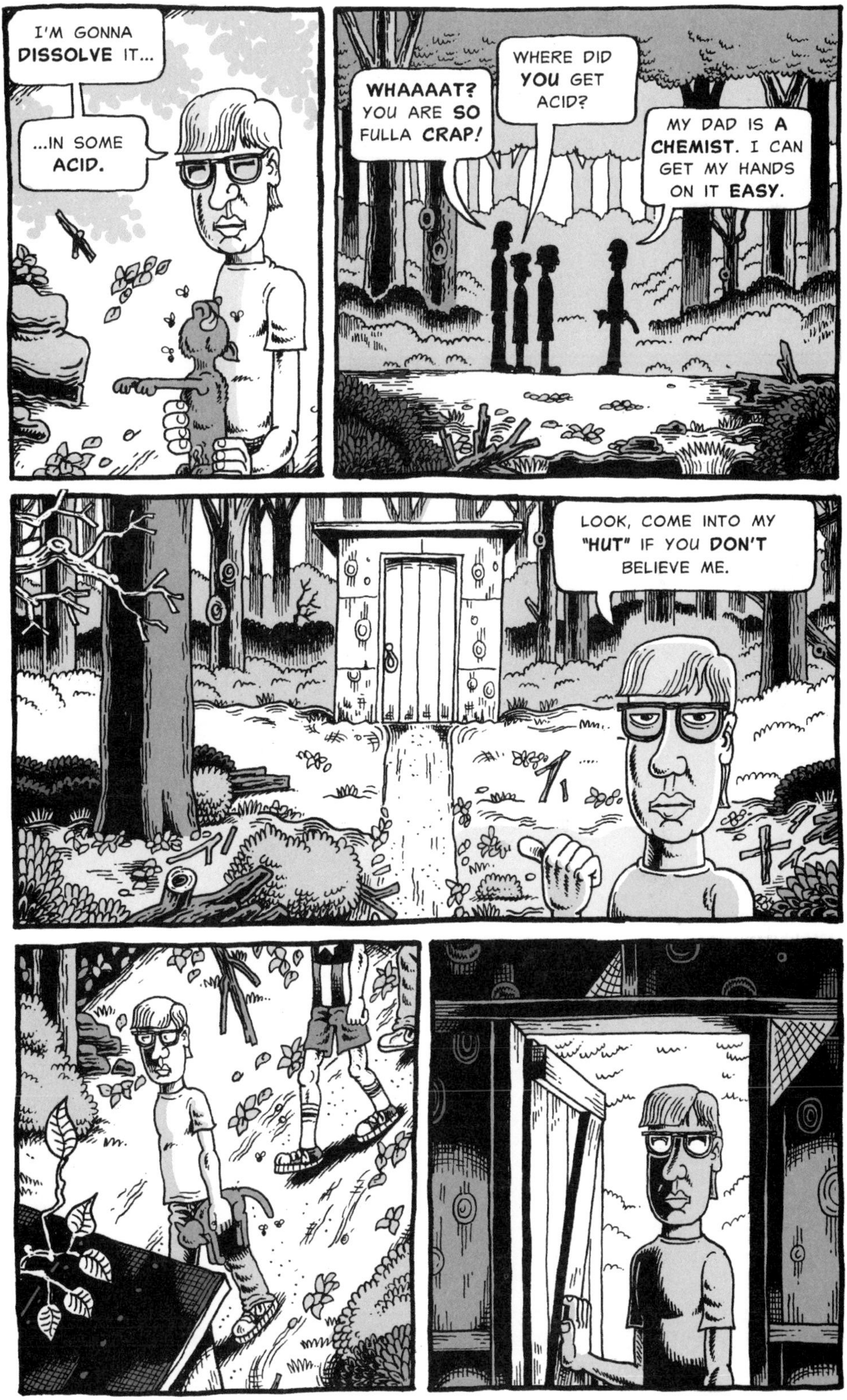
I'M GONNA DISSOLVE IT...
...IN SOME ACID.
WHAAAAT? YOU ARE SO FULLA CRAP!
WHERE DID YOU GET ACID?
MY DAD IS A CHEMIST. I CAN GET MY HANDS ON IT EASY.
LOOK, COME INTO MY "HUT" IF YOU DON'T BELIEVE ME.

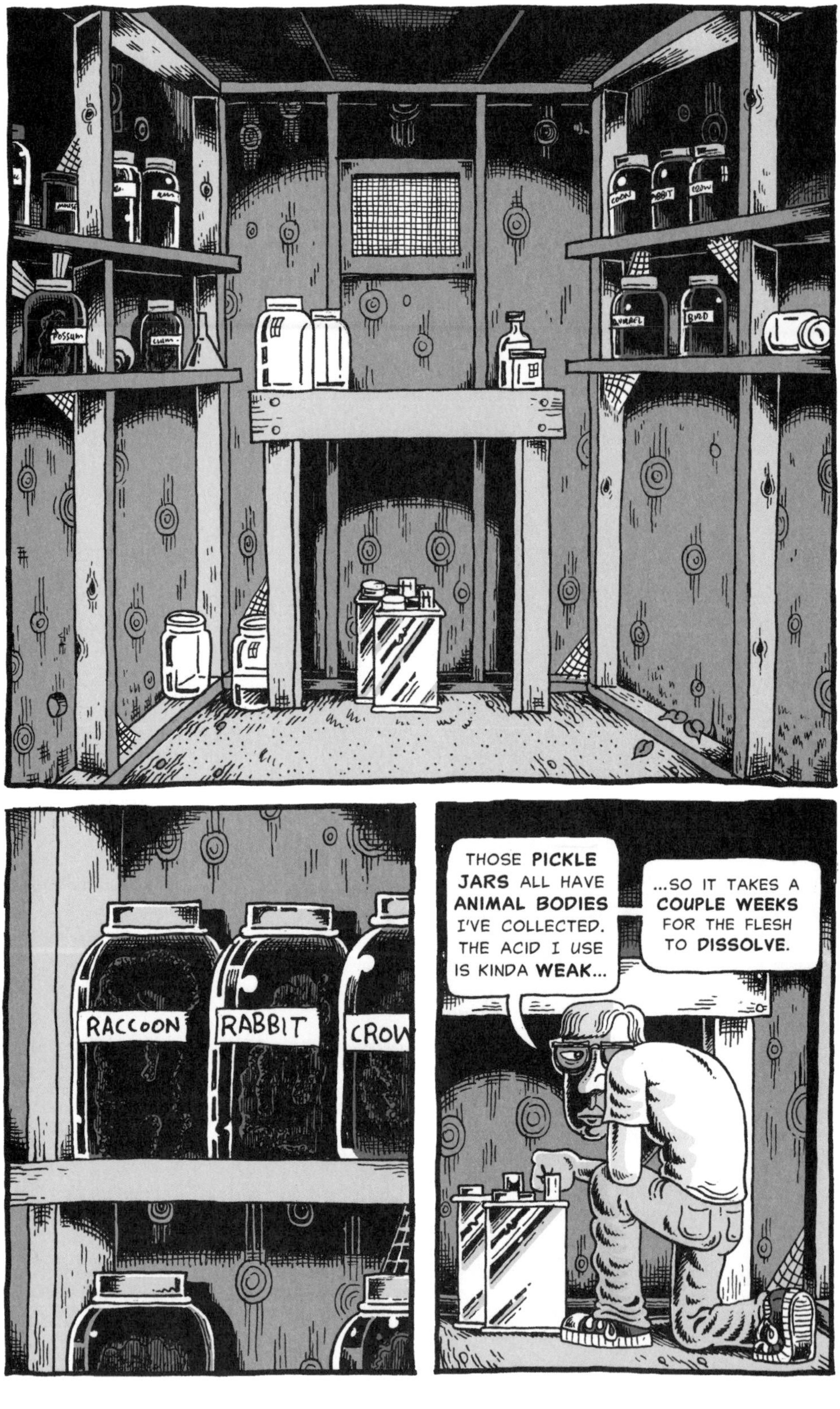
RACCOON
RABBIT
CROW
THOSE PICKLE JARS ALL HAVE ANIMAL BODIES I'VE COLLECTED. THE ACID I USE IS KINDA WEAK...
...SO IT TAKES A COUPLE WEEKS FOR THE FLESH TO DISSOLVE.

W-WHY ARE YOU DOING THIS?

YUK.

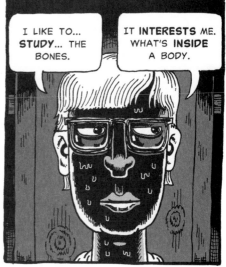

I LIKE TO... STUDY... THE BONES.

IT INTERESTS ME. WHAT'S INSIDE A BODY.

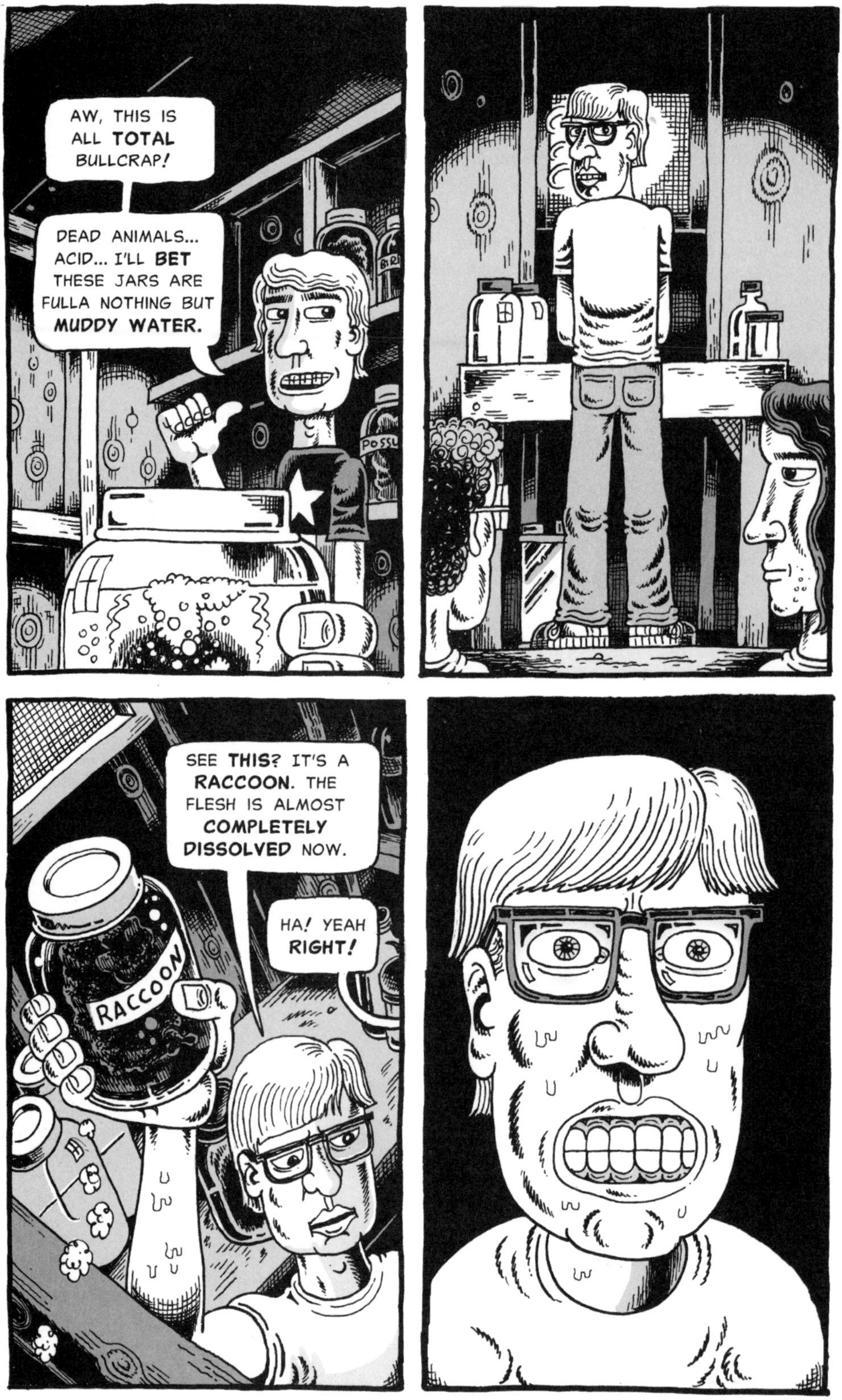
AW, THIS IS ALL TOTAL BULLCRAP!
DEAD ANIMALS... ACID... I'LL BET THESE JARS ARE FULLA NOTHING BUT MUDDY WATER.
SEE THIS? IT'S A RACCOON. THE FLESH IS ALMOST COMPLETELY DISSOLVED NOW.
HA! YEAH RIGHT!
RACCOON

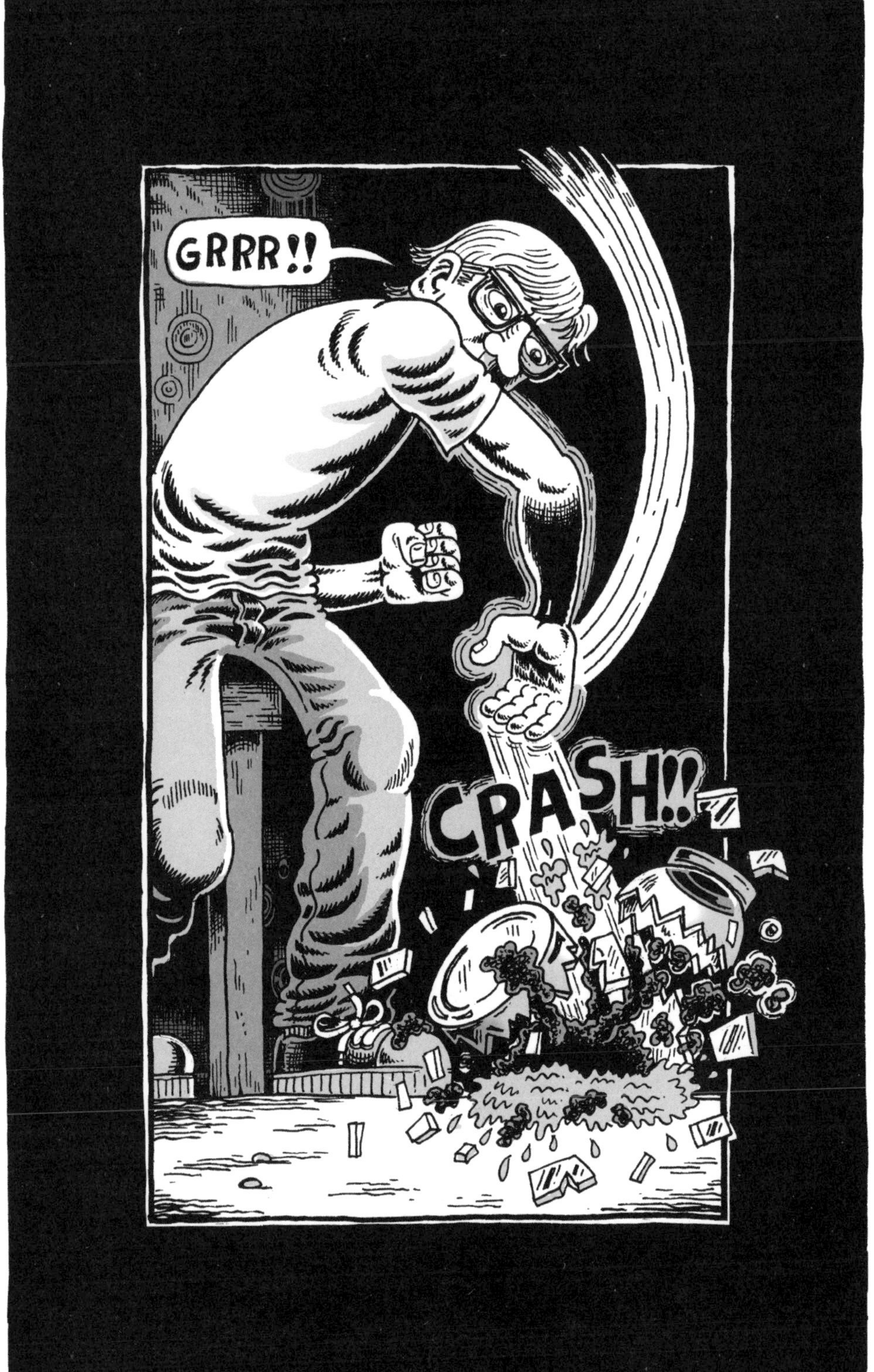
GRRR!!
CRASH!!

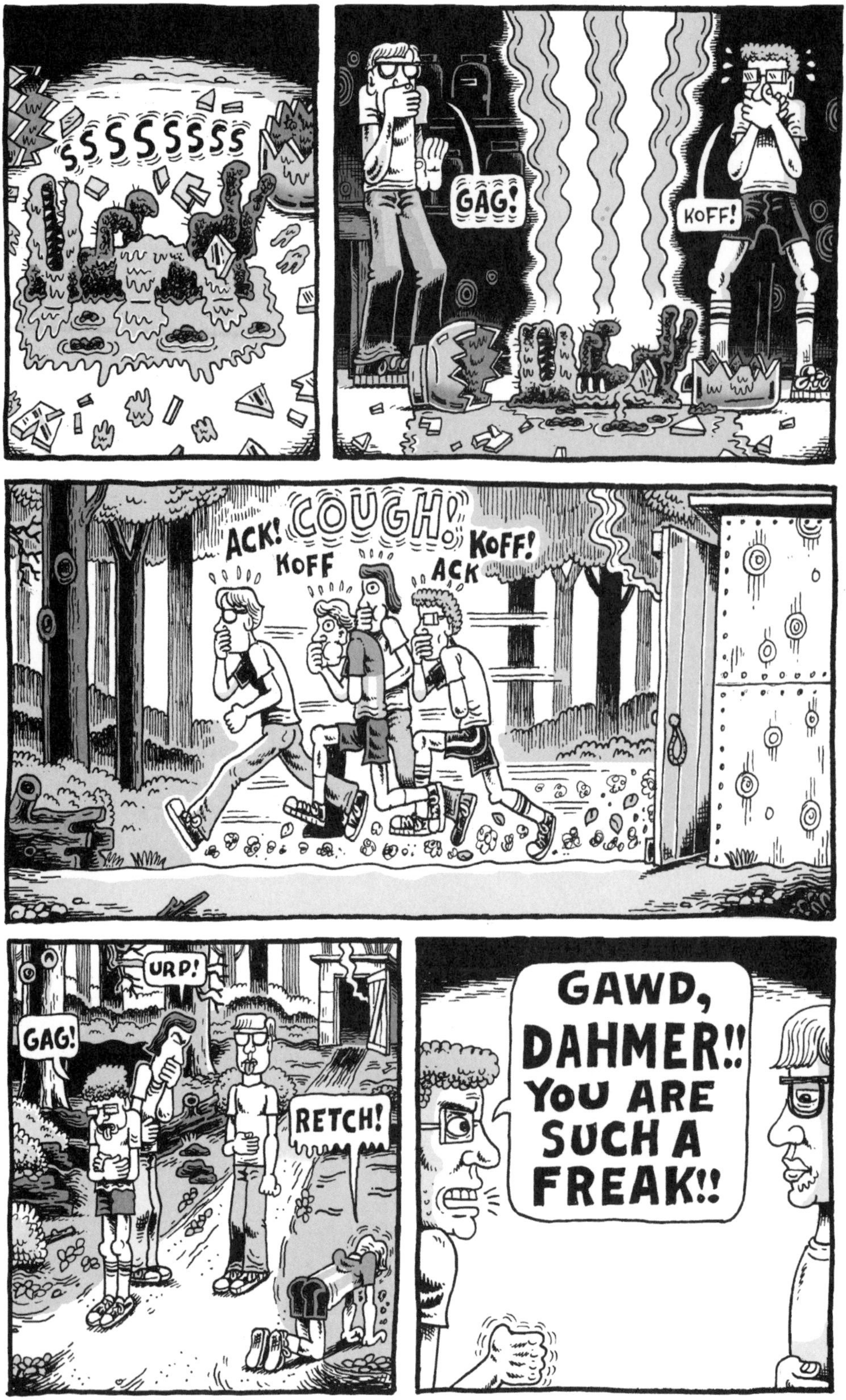
SSSSSSSSS
GAG!
KOFF!
ACK!
COUGH!
KOFF
ACK
KOFF!
URP!
GAG!
RETCH!
GAWD, DAHMER!! YOU ARE SUCH A FREAK!!

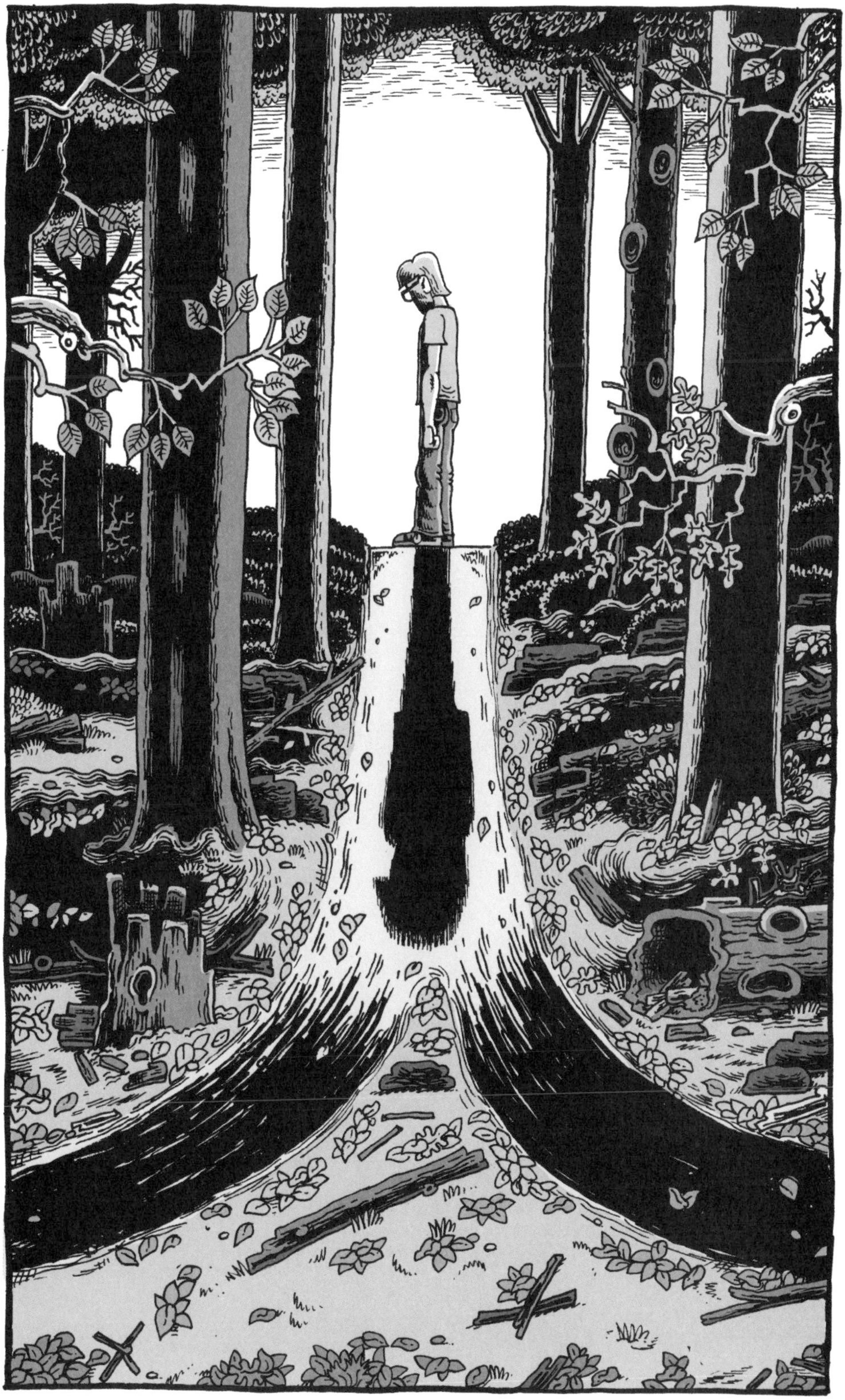

"I had normal friendships in high school . . . and really never had any close friendships after high school."

—Jeff Dahmer, interview with Nancy Glass,
Inside Edition, February 1993

PART 1

The Strange Boy

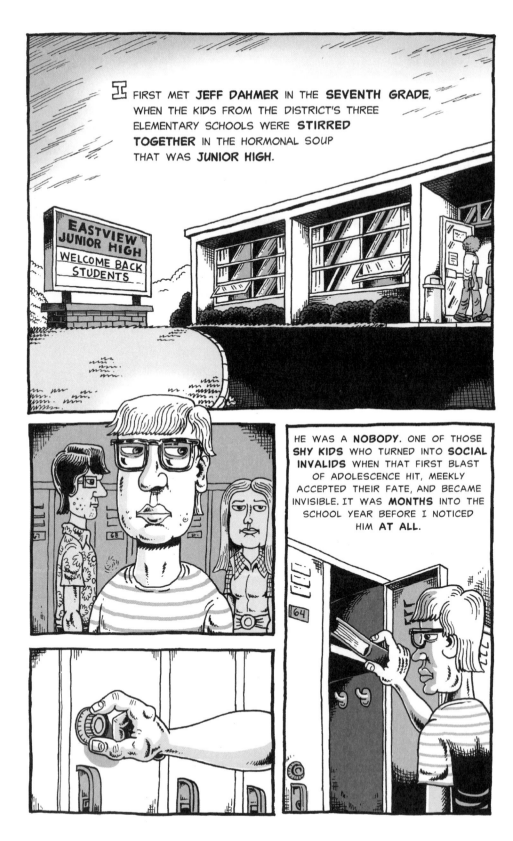

I FIRST MET **JEFF DAHMER** IN THE **SEVENTH GRADE**, WHEN THE KIDS FROM THE DISTRICT'S THREE ELEMENTARY SCHOOLS WERE **STIRRED TOGETHER** IN THE HORMONAL SOUP THAT WAS **JUNIOR HIGH.**

EASTVIEW JUNIOR HIGH

WELCOME BACK STUDENTS

HE WAS A **NOBODY.** ONE OF THOSE **SHY KIDS** WHO TURNED INTO **SOCIAL INVALIDS** WHEN THAT FIRST BLAST OF ADOLESCENCE HIT, MEEKLY ACCEPTED THEIR FATE, AND BECAME INVISIBLE. IT WAS **MONTHS** INTO THE SCHOOL YEAR BEFORE I NOTICED HIM **AT ALL.**

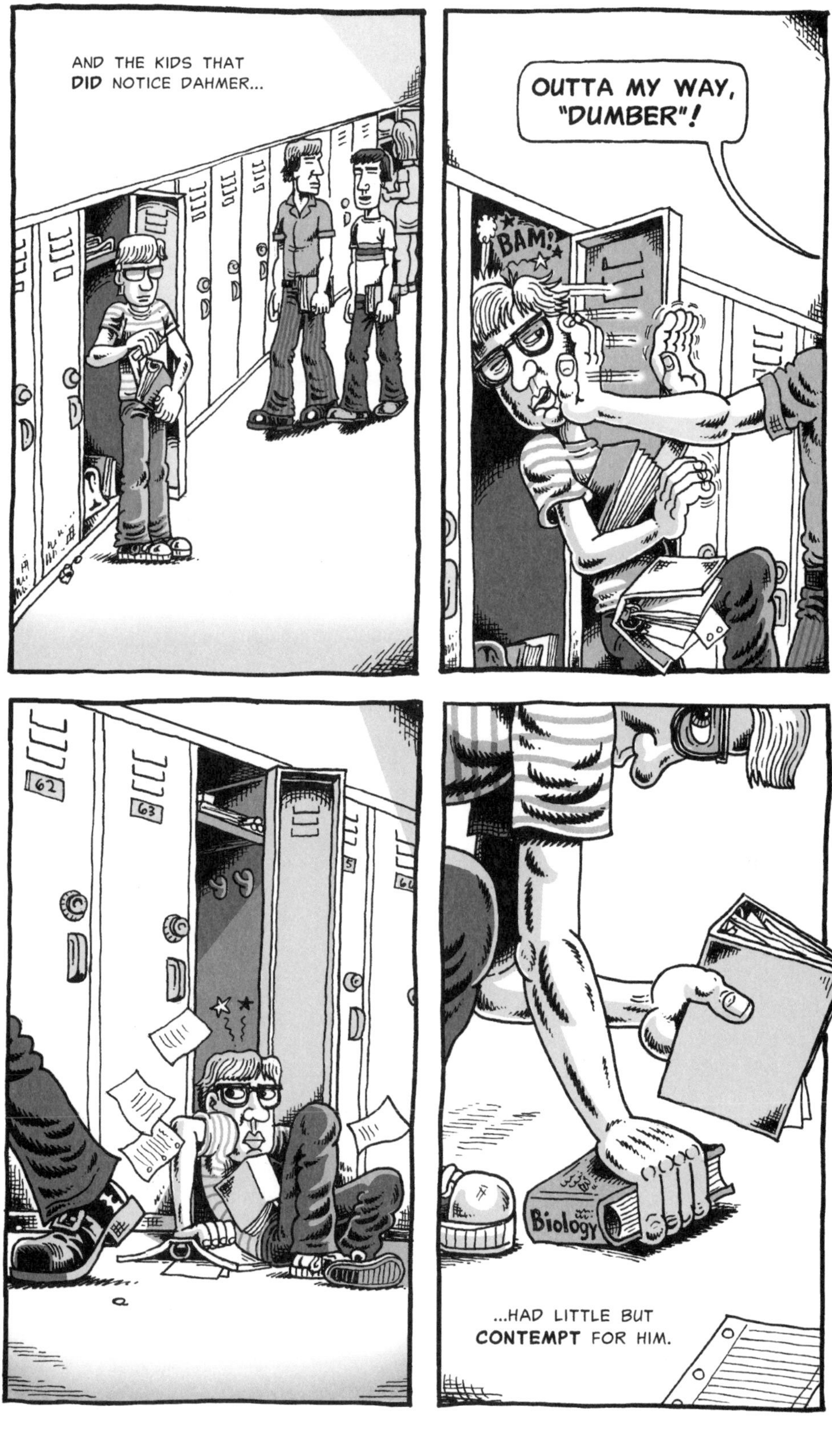
AND THE KIDS THAT DID NOTICE DAHMER...
OUTTA MY WAY, "DUMBER"!
BAM!
62
63
Biology
...HAD LITTLE BUT CONTEMPT FOR HIM.

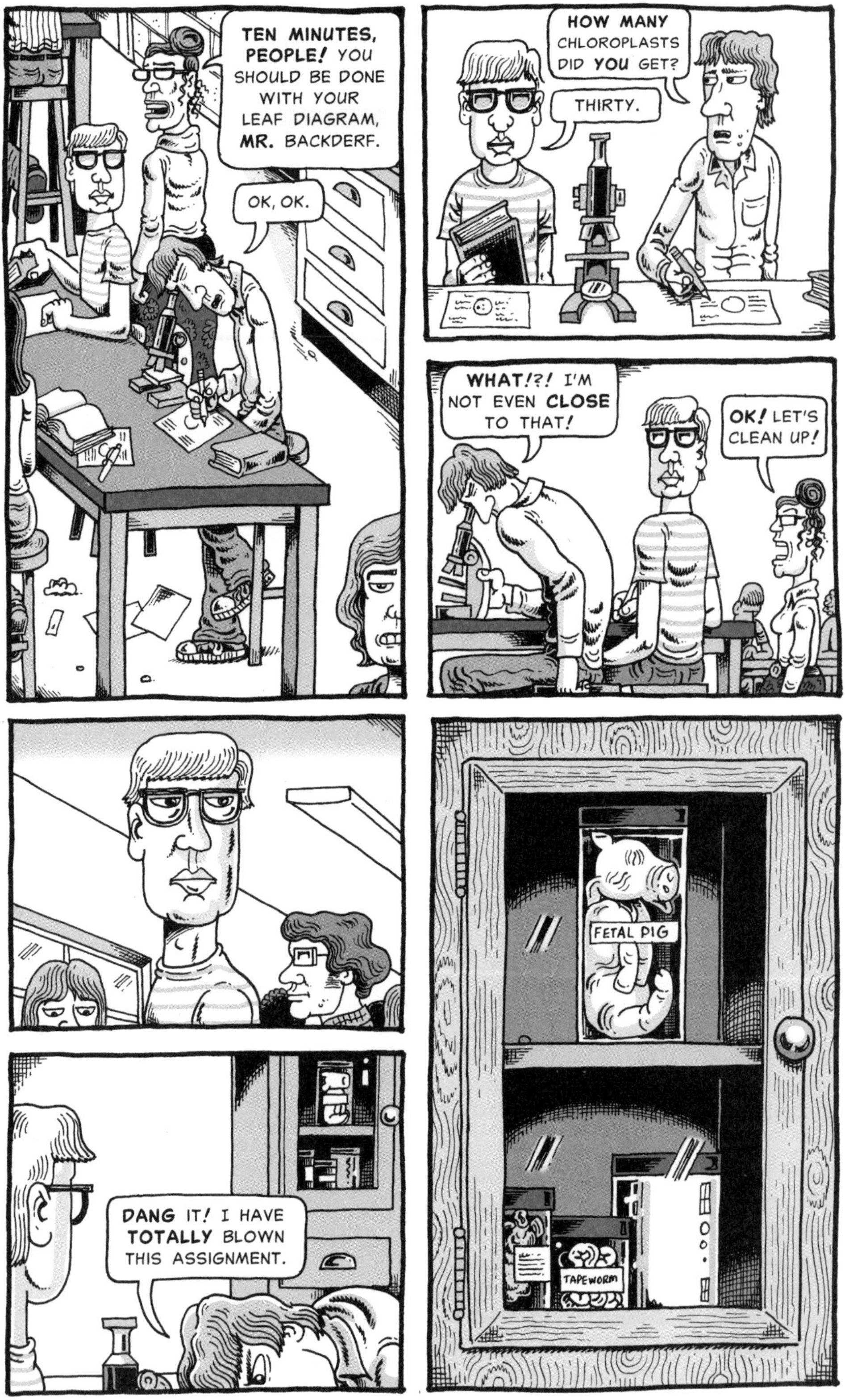
TEN MINUTES, PEOPLE! YOU SHOULD BE DONE WITH YOUR LEAF DIAGRAM, MR. BACKDERF.
OK, OK.
HOW MANY CHLOROPLASTS DID YOU GET?
THIRTY.
WHAT!?! I'M NOT EVEN CLOSE TO THAT!
OK! LET'S CLEAN UP!
DANG IT! I HAVE TOTALLY BLOWN THIS ASSIGNMENT.
FETAL PIG
TAPEWORM

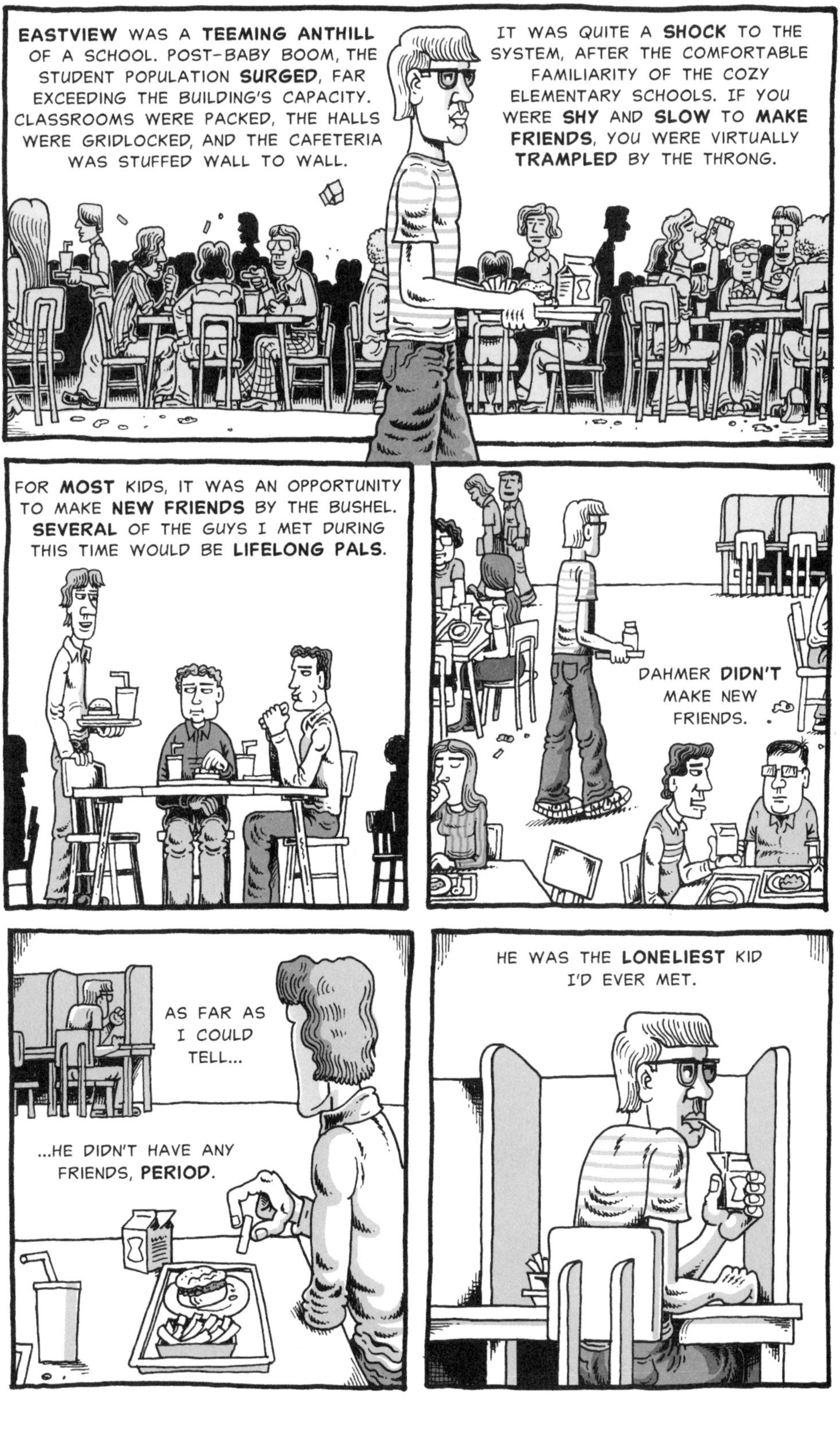
EASTVIEW WAS A TEEMING ANTHILL OF A SCHOOL. POST-BABY BOOM, THE STUDENT POPULATION SURGED, FAR EXCEEDING THE BUILDING'S CAPACITY. CLASSROOMS WERE PACKED, THE HALLS WERE GRIDLOCKED, AND THE CAFETERIA WAS STUFFED WALL TO WALL.
IT WAS QUITE A SHOCK TO THE SYSTEM, AFTER THE COMFORTABLE FAMILIARITY OF THE COZY ELEMENTARY SCHOOLS. IF YOU WERE SHY AND SLOW TO MAKE FRIENDS, YOU WERE VIRTUALLY TRAMPLED BY THE THRONG.
FOR MOST KIDS, IT WAS AN OPPORTUNITY TO MAKE NEW FRIENDS BY THE BUSHEL. SEVERAL OF THE GUYS I MET DURING THIS TIME WOULD BE LIFELONG PALS.
DAHMER DIDN'T MAKE NEW FRIENDS.
AS FAR AS I COULD TELL...
...HE DIDN'T HAVE ANY FRIENDS, PERIOD.
HE WAS THE LONELIEST KID I'D EVER MET.

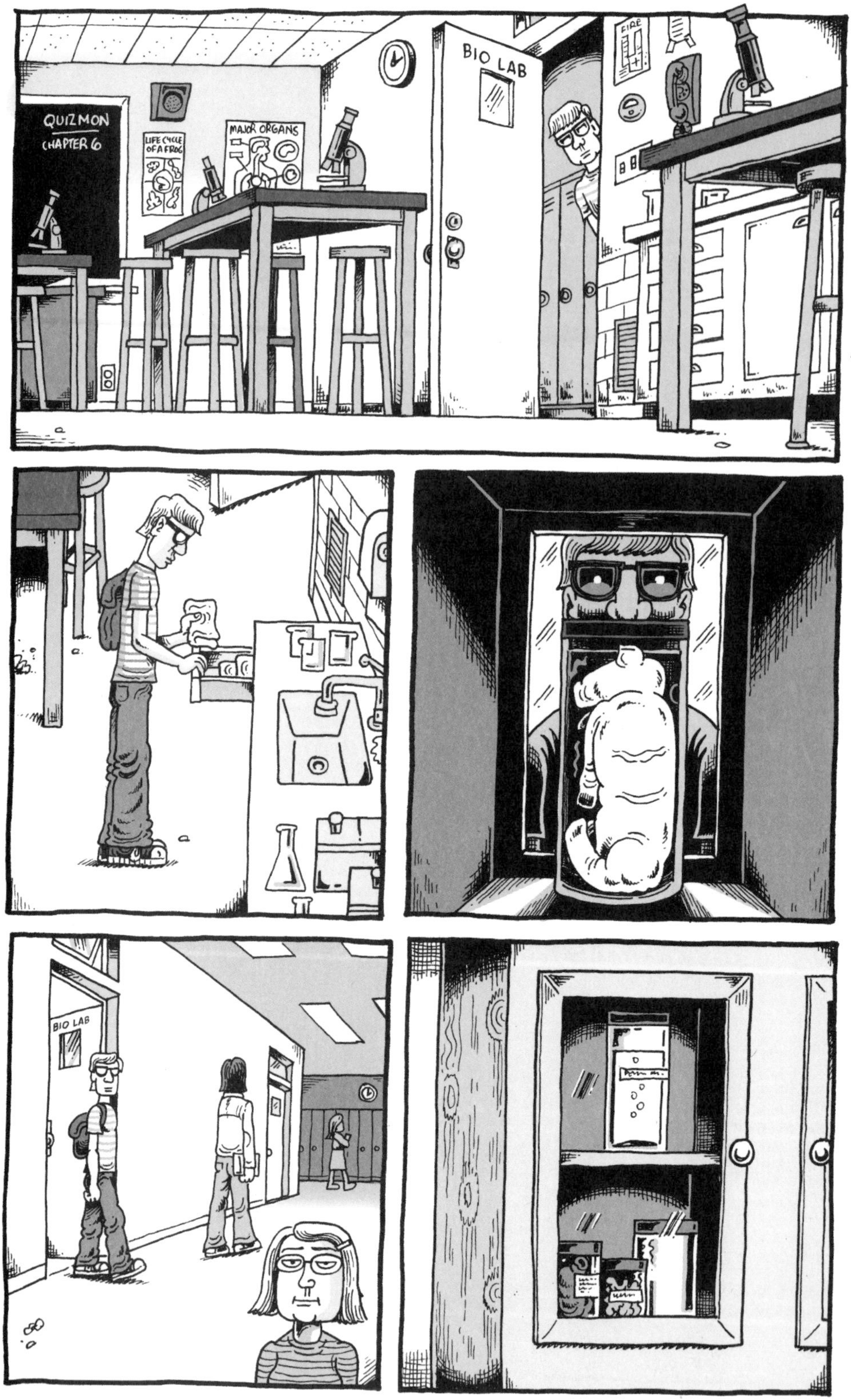
QUIZMON
CHAPTER 6
LIFE CYCLE OF A FROG
MAJOR ORGANS
BIO LAB
FIRE
BIO LAB

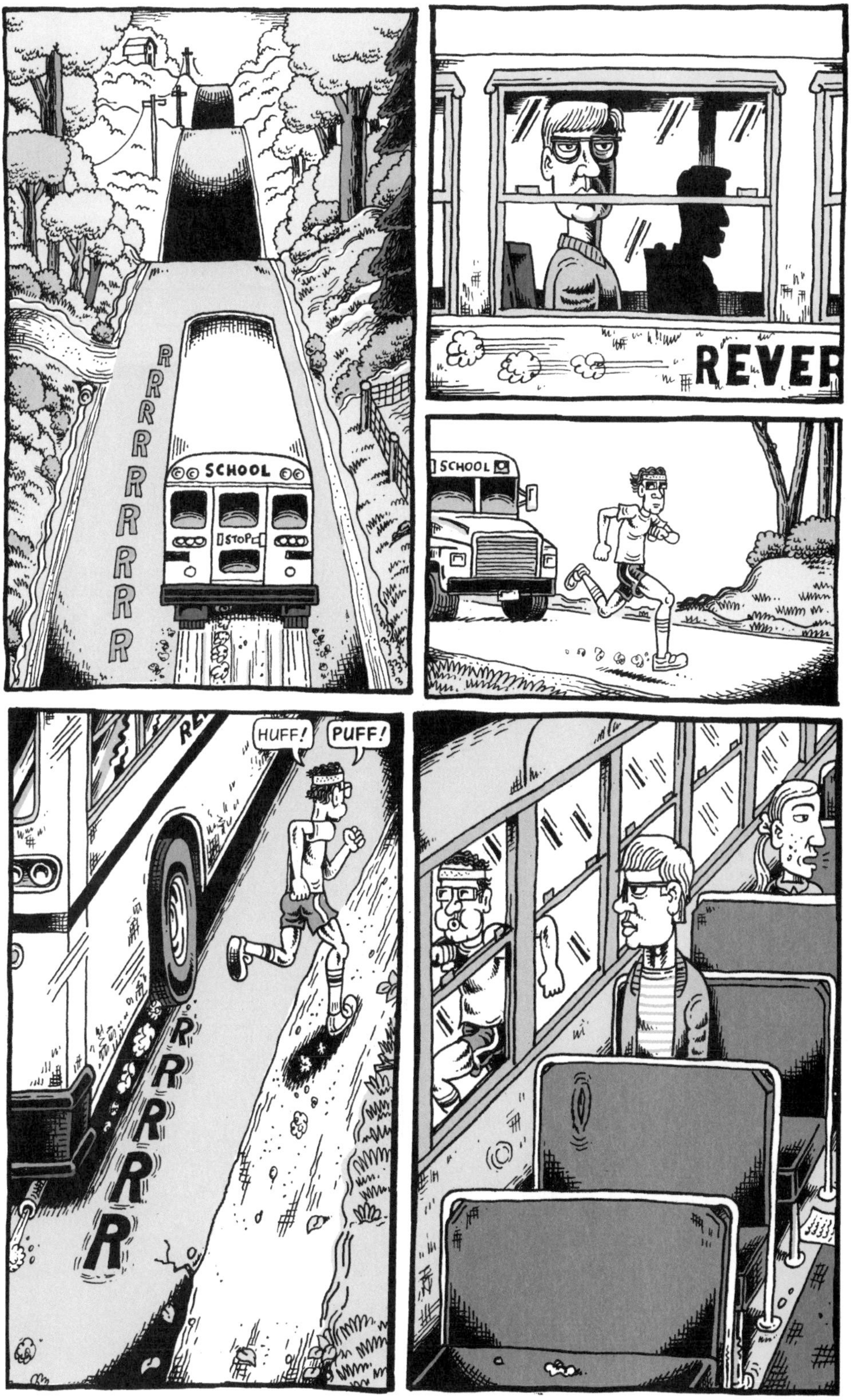
RRRRRRRRRR
SCHOOL
STOP
REVER
SCHOOL
HUFF!
PUFF!
RRRRRR

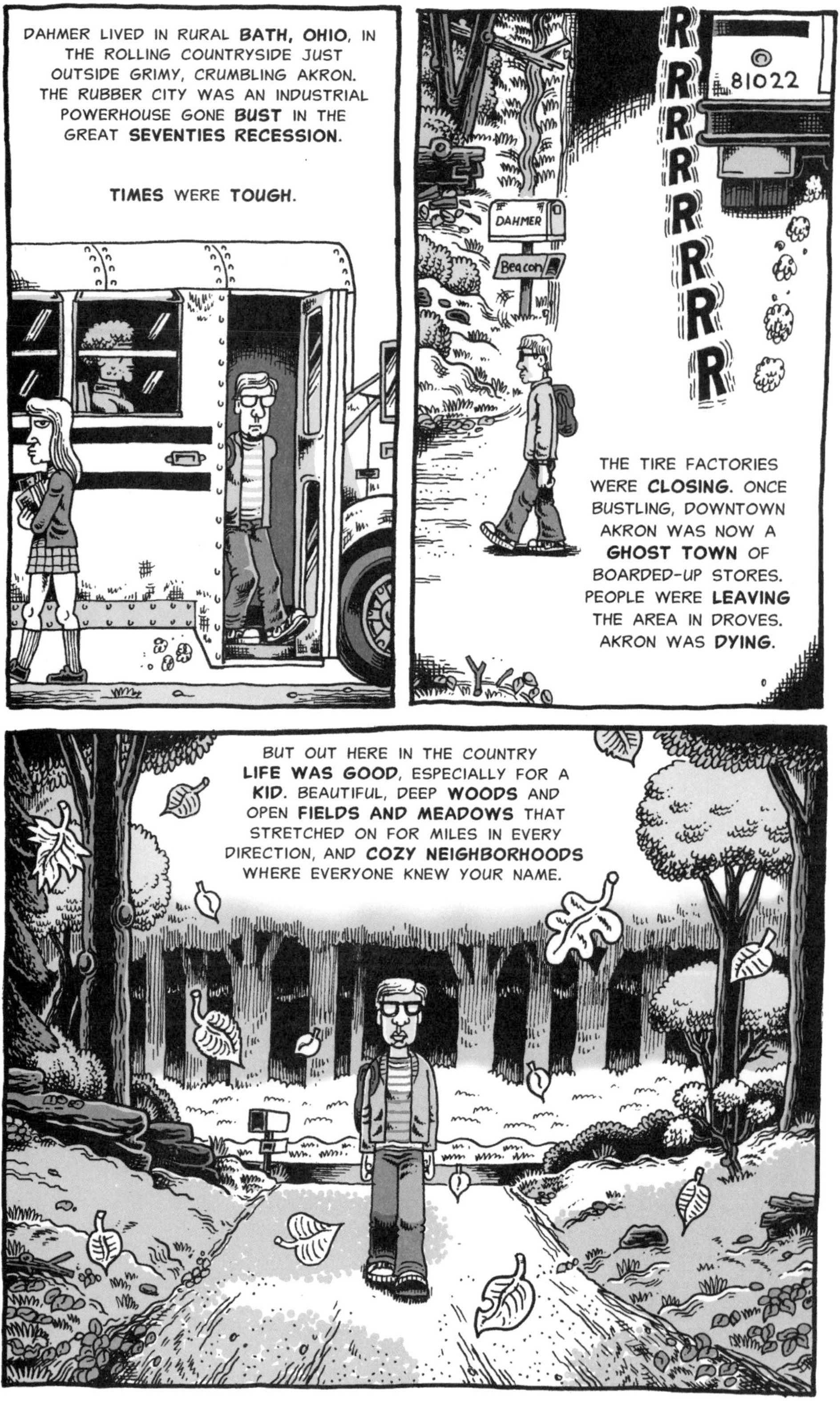
DAHMER LIVED IN RURAL BATH, OHIO, IN THE ROLLING COUNTRYSIDE JUST OUTSIDE GRIMY, CRUMBLING AKRON. THE RUBBER CITY WAS AN INDUSTRIAL POWERHOUSE GONE BUST IN THE GREAT SEVENTIES RECESSION.
TIMES WERE TOUGH.
81022
RRRRRRRR
DAHMER
Beacon
THE TIRE FACTORIES WERE CLOSING. ONCE BUSTLING, DOWNTOWN AKRON WAS NOW A GHOST TOWN OF BOARDED-UP STORES. PEOPLE WERE LEAVING THE AREA IN DROVES. AKRON WAS DYING.
BUT OUT HERE IN THE COUNTRY LIFE WAS GOOD, ESPECIALLY FOR A KID. BEAUTIFUL, DEEP WOODS AND OPEN FIELDS AND MEADOWS THAT STRETCHED ON FOR MILES IN EVERY DIRECTION, AND COZY NEIGHBORHOODS WHERE EVERYONE KNEW YOUR NAME.

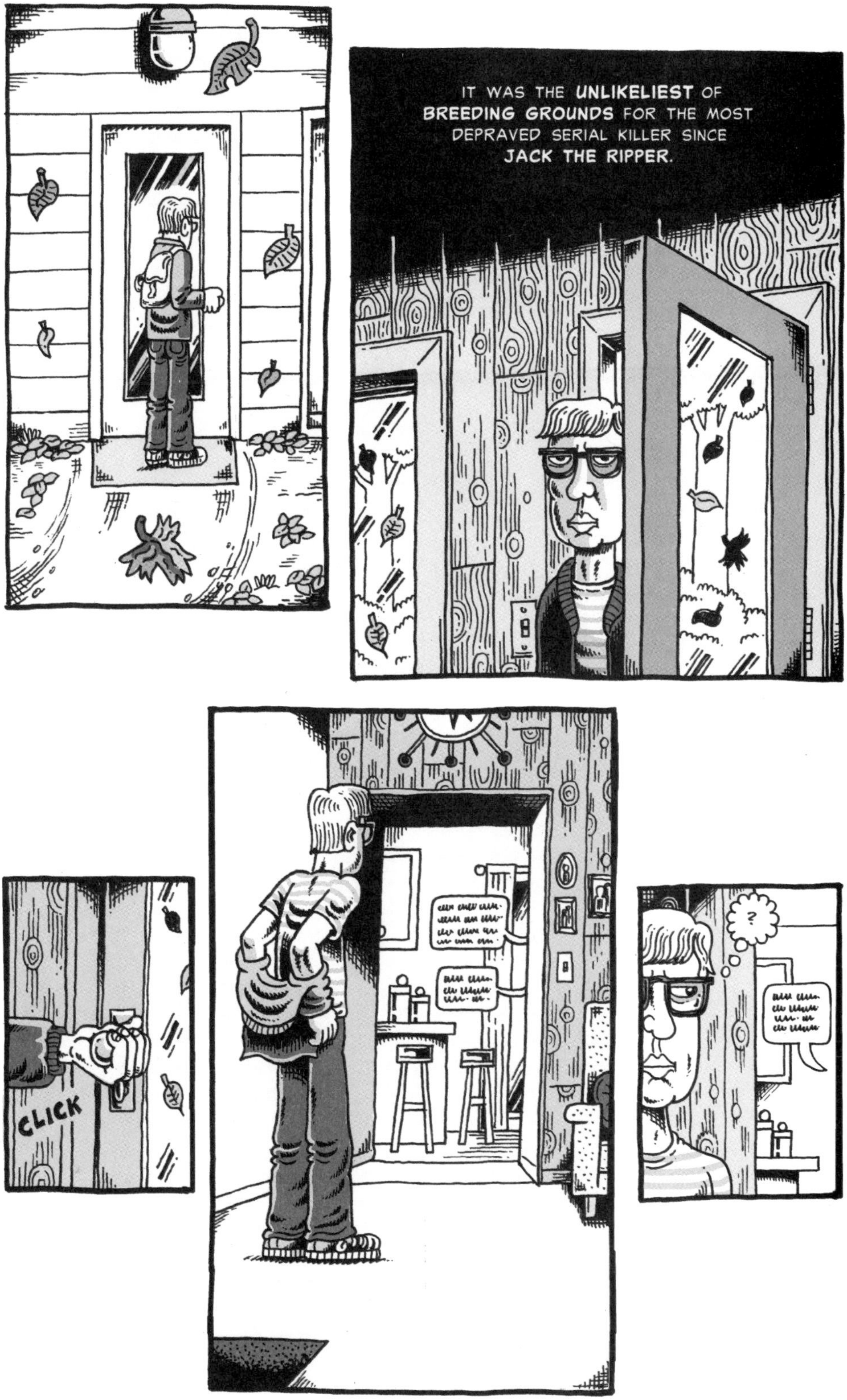
IT WAS THE UNLIKELIEST OF BREEDING GROUNDS FOR THE MOST DEPRAVED SERIAL KILLER SINCE JACK THE RIPPER.
CLICK
?

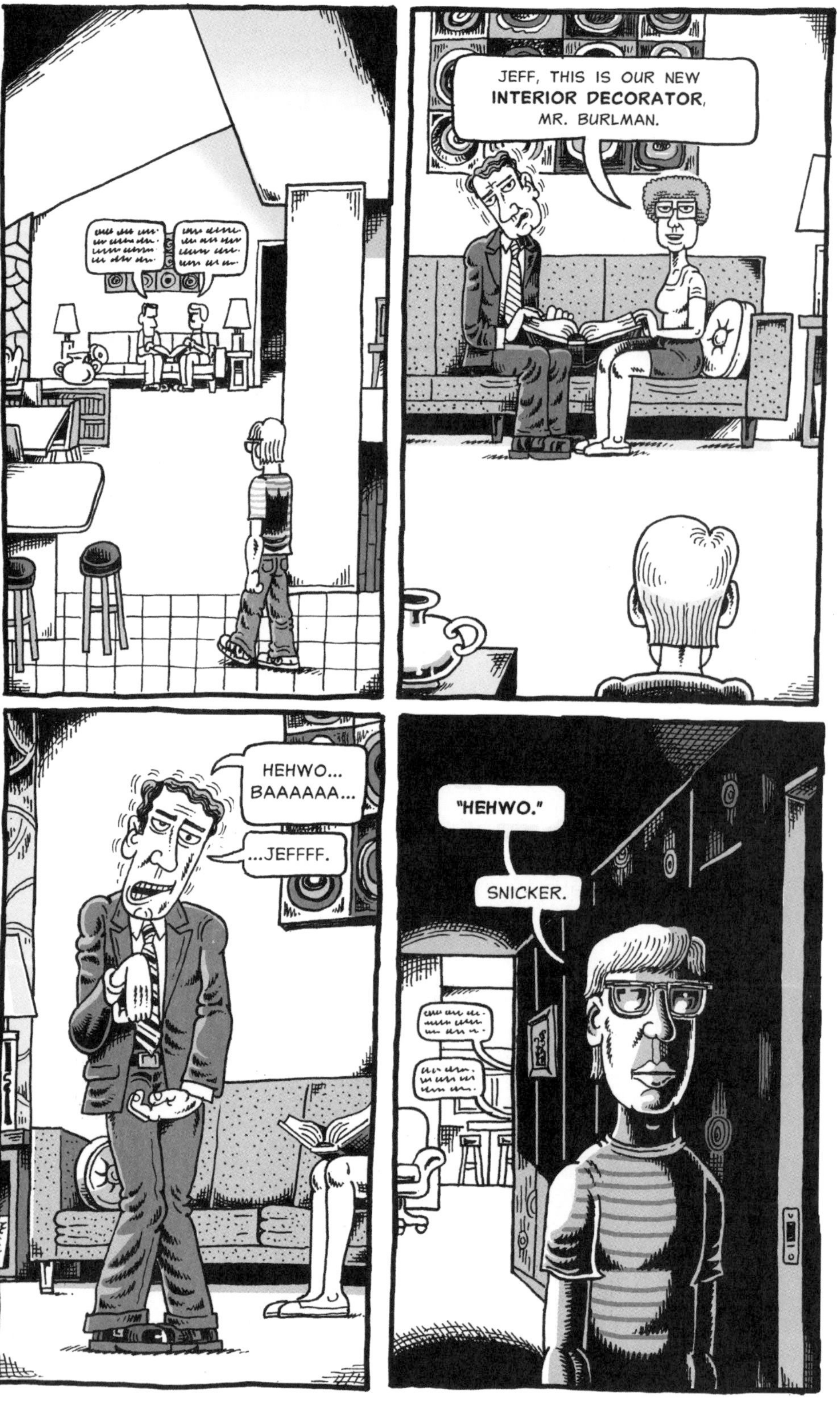
JEFF, THIS IS OUR NEW INTERIOR DECORATOR, MR. BURLMAN.
HEHWO... BAAAAAA...
...JEFFFF.
"HEHWO."
SNICKER.

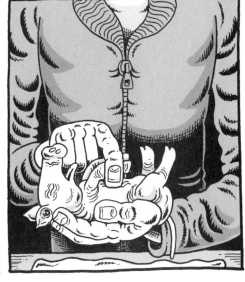

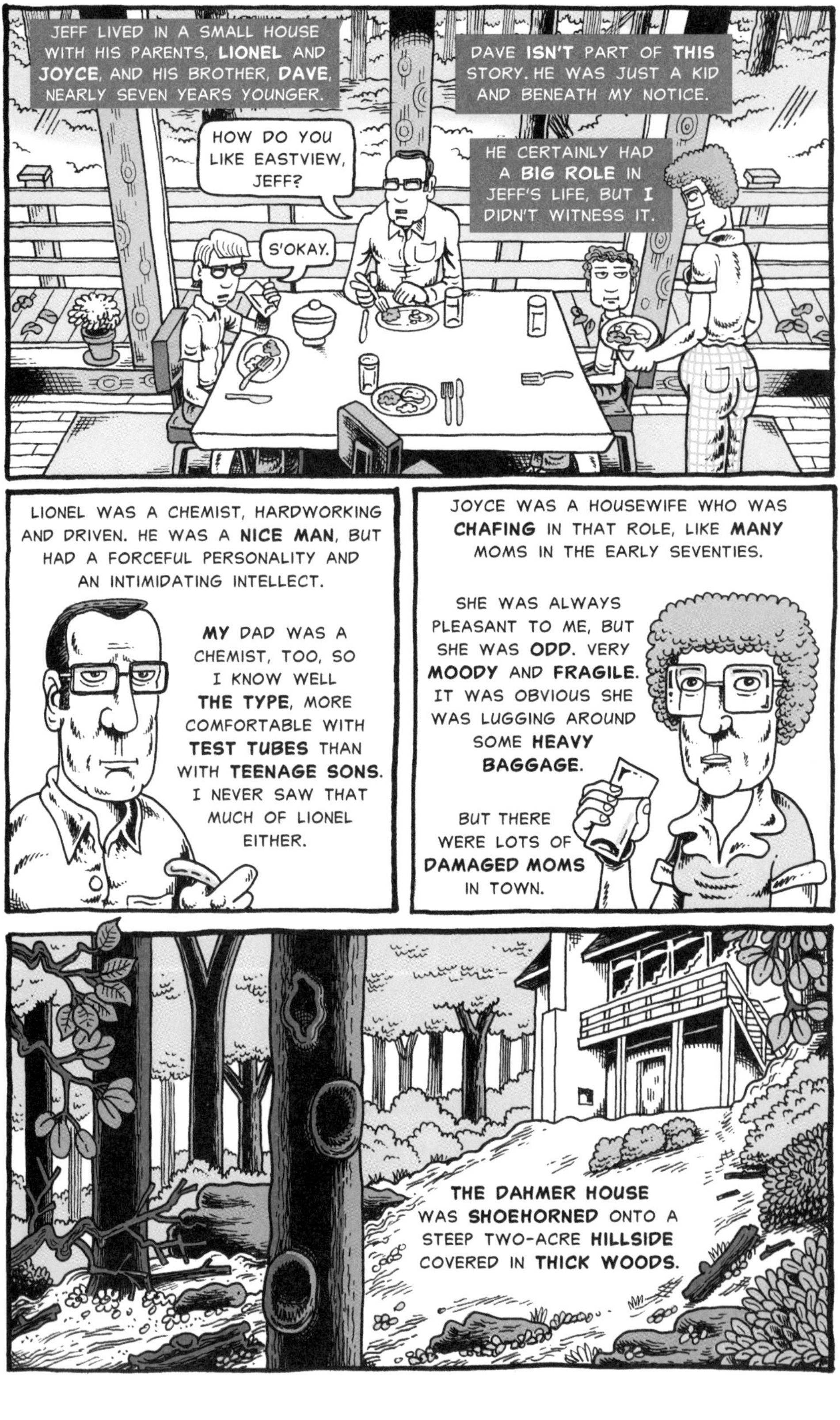
JEFF LIVED IN A SMALL HOUSE WITH HIS PARENTS, LIONEL AND JOYCE, AND HIS BROTHER, DAVE, NEARLY SEVEN YEARS YOUNGER.
HOW DO YOU LIKE EASTVIEW, JEFF?
S'OKAY.
DAVE ISN'T PART OF THIS STORY. HE WAS JUST A KID AND BENEATH MY NOTICE.
HE CERTAINLY HAD A BIG ROLE IN JEFF'S LIFE, BUT I DIDN'T WITNESS IT.
LIONEL WAS A CHEMIST, HARDWORKING AND DRIVEN. HE WAS A NICE MAN, BUT HAD A FORCEFUL PERSONALITY AND AN INTIMIDATING INTELLECT.
MY DAD WAS A CHEMIST, TOO, SO I KNOW WELL THE TYPE, MORE COMFORTABLE WITH TEST TUBES THAN WITH TEENAGE SONS. I NEVER SAW THAT MUCH OF LIONEL EITHER.
JOYCE WAS A HOUSEWIFE WHO WAS CHAFING IN THAT ROLE, LIKE MANY MOMS IN THE EARLY SEVENTIES.
SHE WAS ALWAYS PLEASANT TO ME, BUT SHE WAS ODD. VERY MOODY AND FRAGILE. IT WAS OBVIOUS SHE WAS LUGGING AROUND SOME HEAVY BAGGAGE.
BUT THERE WERE LOTS OF DAMAGED MOMS IN TOWN.
THE DAHMER HOUSE WAS SHOEHORNED ONTO A STEEP TWO-ACRE HILLSIDE COVERED IN THICK WOODS.

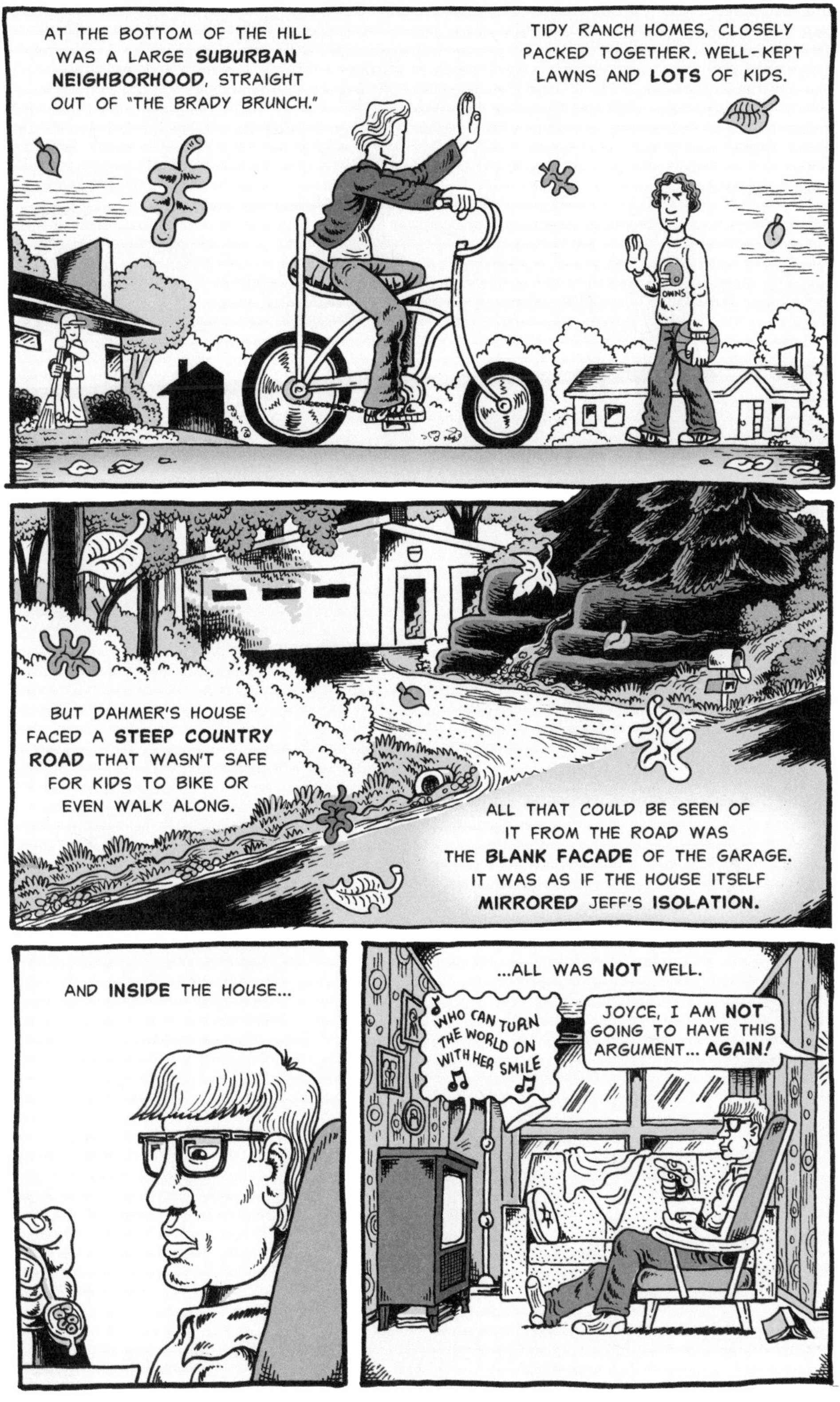
AT THE BOTTOM OF THE HILL WAS A LARGE SUBURBAN NEIGHBORHOOD, STRAIGHT OUT OF "THE BRADY BRUNCH."
TIDY RANCH HOMES, CLOSELY PACKED TOGETHER. WELL-KEPT LAWNS AND LOTS OF KIDS.
OWNS
BUT DAHMER'S HOUSE FACED A STEEP COUNTRY ROAD THAT WASN'T SAFE FOR KIDS TO BIKE OR EVEN WALK ALONG.
ALL THAT COULD BE SEEN OF IT FROM THE ROAD WAS THE BLANK FACADE OF THE GARAGE. IT WAS AS IF THE HOUSE ITSELF MIRRORED JEFF'S ISOLATION.
AND INSIDE THE HOUSE...
...ALL WAS NOT WELL.
WHO CAN TURN THE WORLD ON WITH HER SMILE
JOYCE, I AM NOT GOING TO HAVE THIS ARGUMENT... AGAIN!

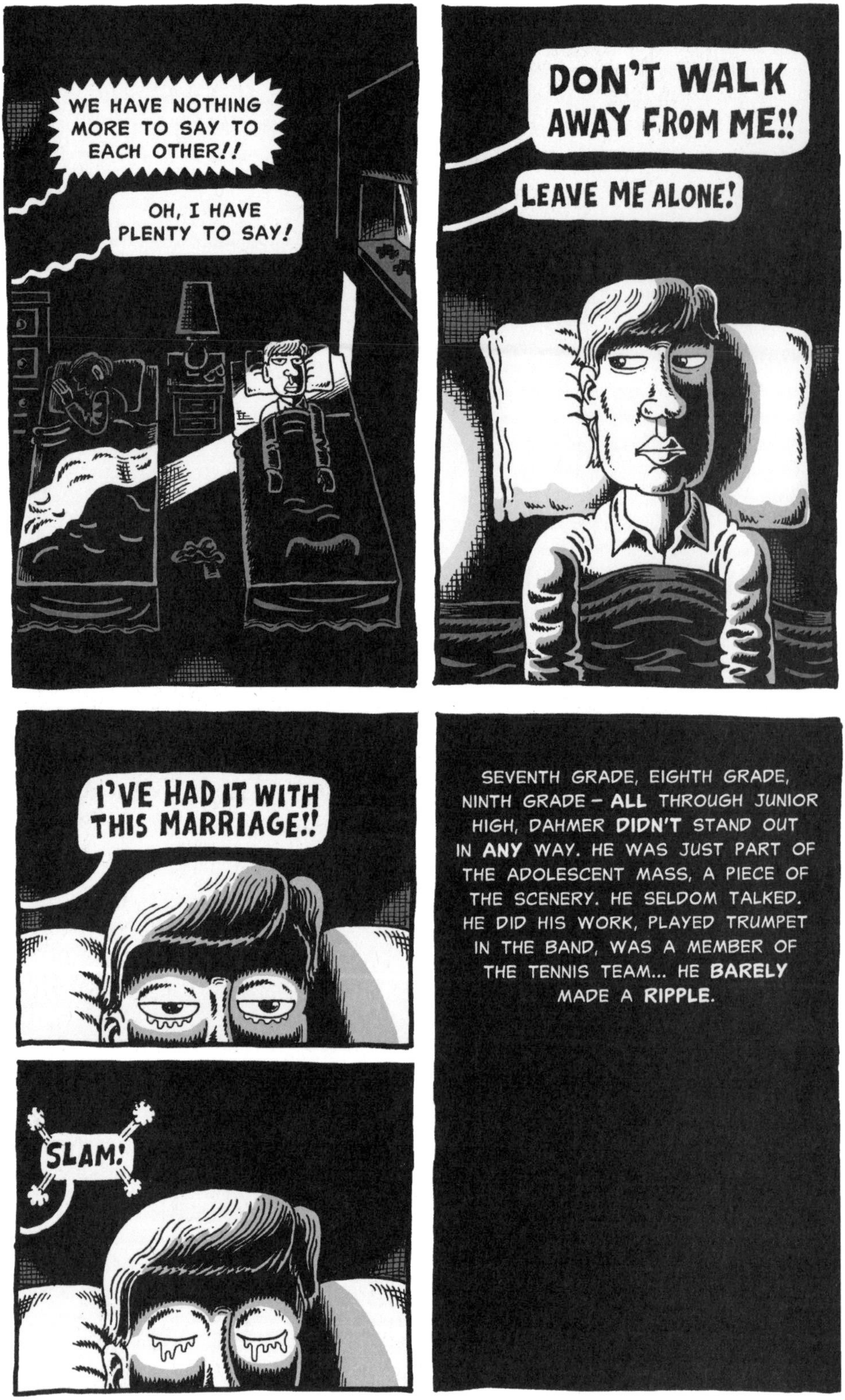
WE HAVE NOTHING MORE TO SAY TO EACH OTHER!!
OH, I HAVE PLENTY TO SAY!
DON'T WALK AWAY FROM ME!!
LEAVE ME ALONE!
I'VE HAD IT WITH THIS MARRIAGE!!
SLAM!
SEVENTH GRADE, EIGHTH GRADE, NINTH GRADE – ALL THROUGH JUNIOR HIGH, DAHMER DIDN'T STAND OUT IN ANY WAY. HE WAS JUST PART OF THE ADOLESCENT MASS, A PIECE OF THE SCENERY. HE SELDOM TALKED. HE DID HIS WORK, PLAYED TRUMPET IN THE BAND, WAS A MEMBER OF THE TENNIS TEAM... HE BARELY MADE A RIPPLE.

AND THEN... HE **CHANGED.**

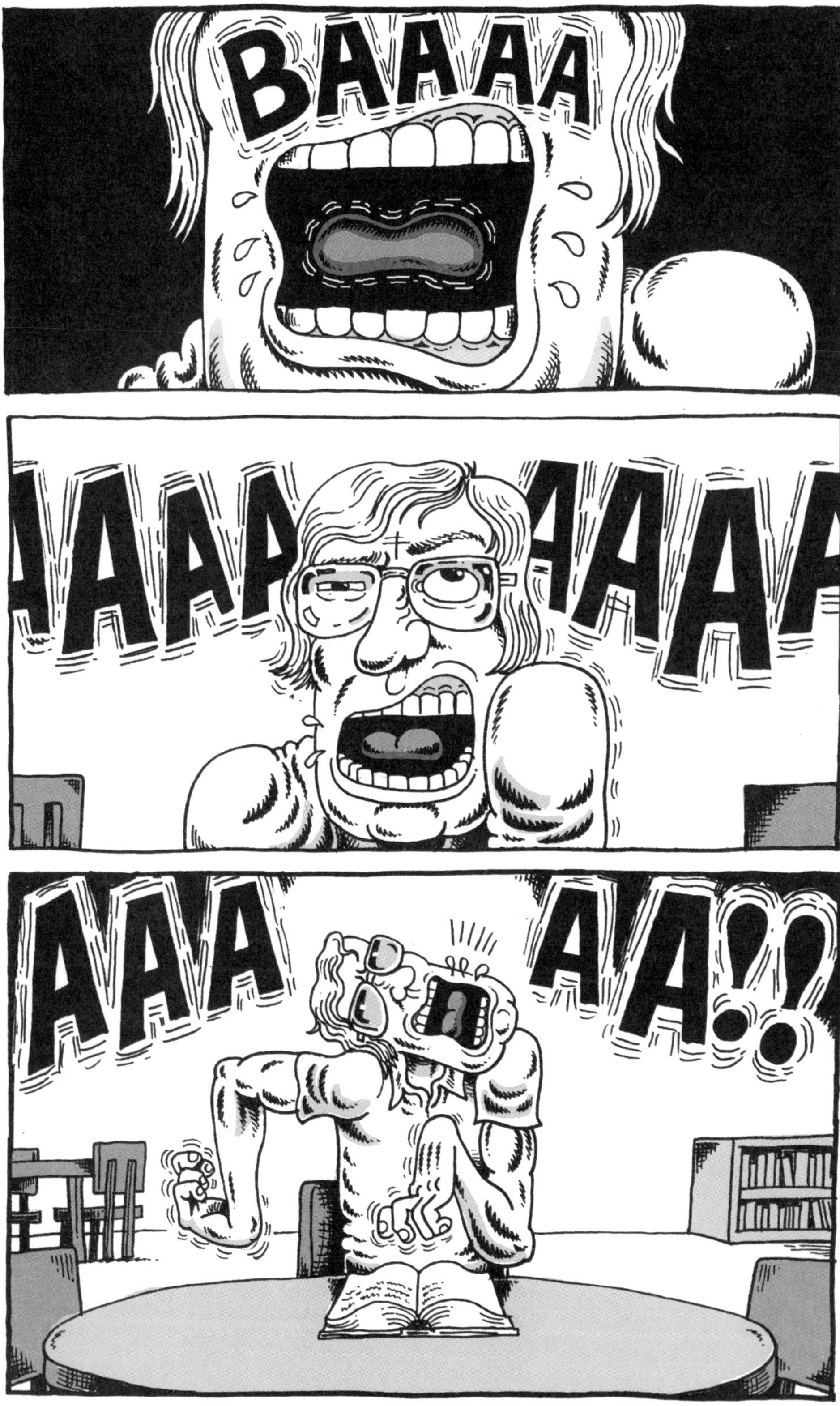
BAAAA
AAAA
AAAAA
AAA
AA!!

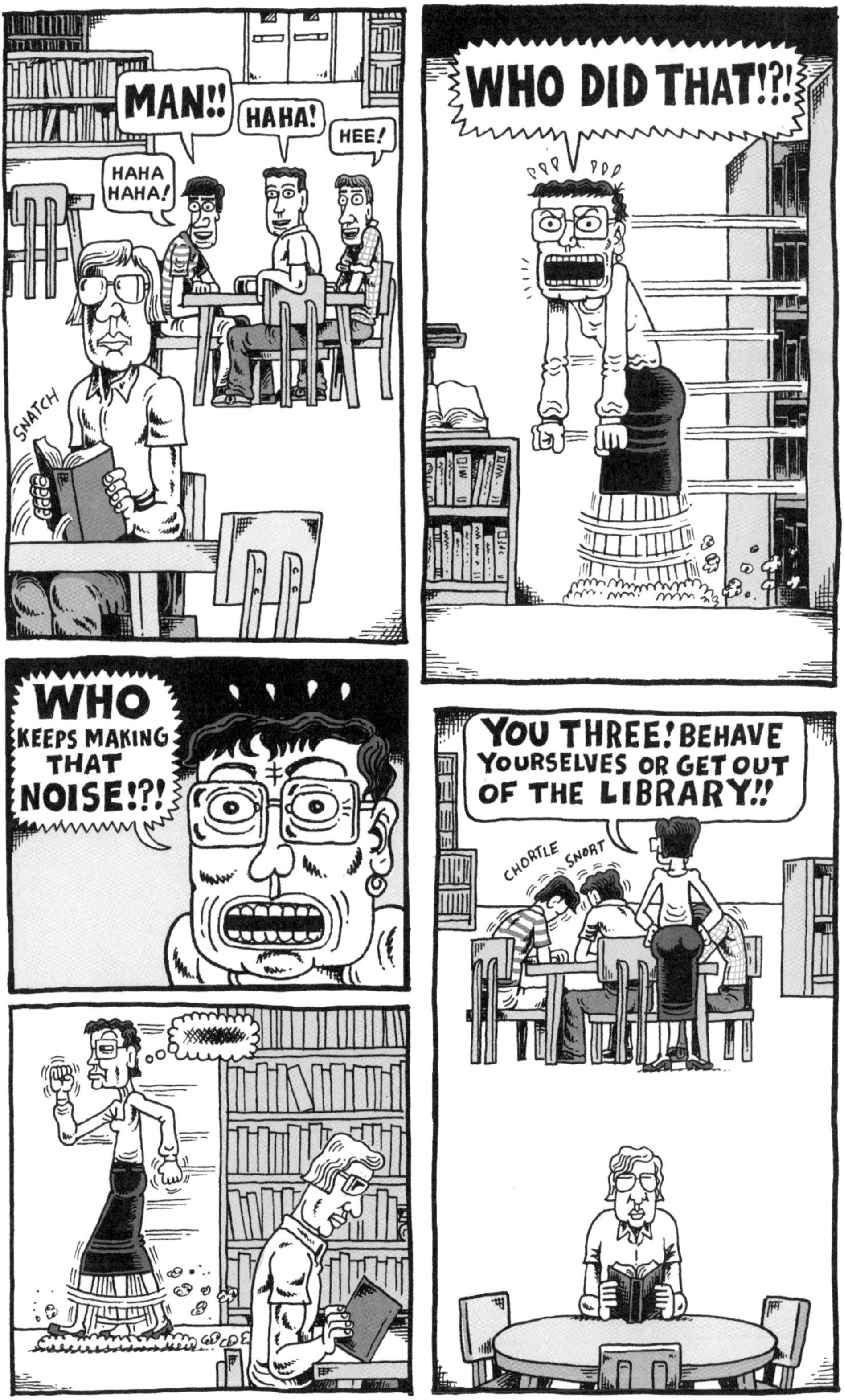
MAN!!
HAHA HAHA!
HAHA!
HEE!
SNATCH
WHO DID THAT!?!
WHO KEEPS MAKING THAT NOISE!?!
YOU THREE! BEHAVE YOURSELVES OR GET OUT OF THE LIBRARY!!
CHORTLE
SNORT

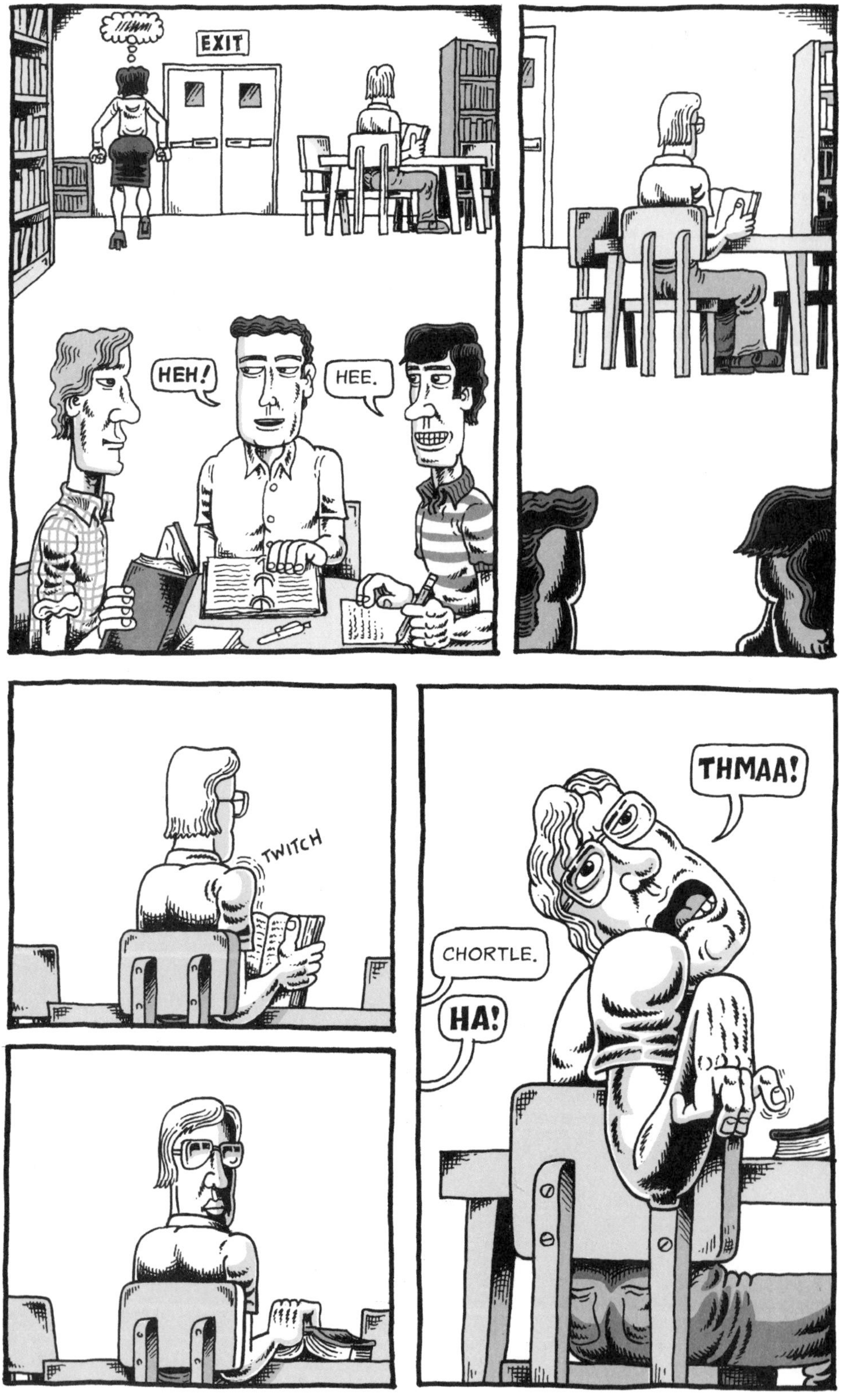

EXIT
HEH!
HEE.
TWITCH
THMAA!
CHORTLE.
HA!

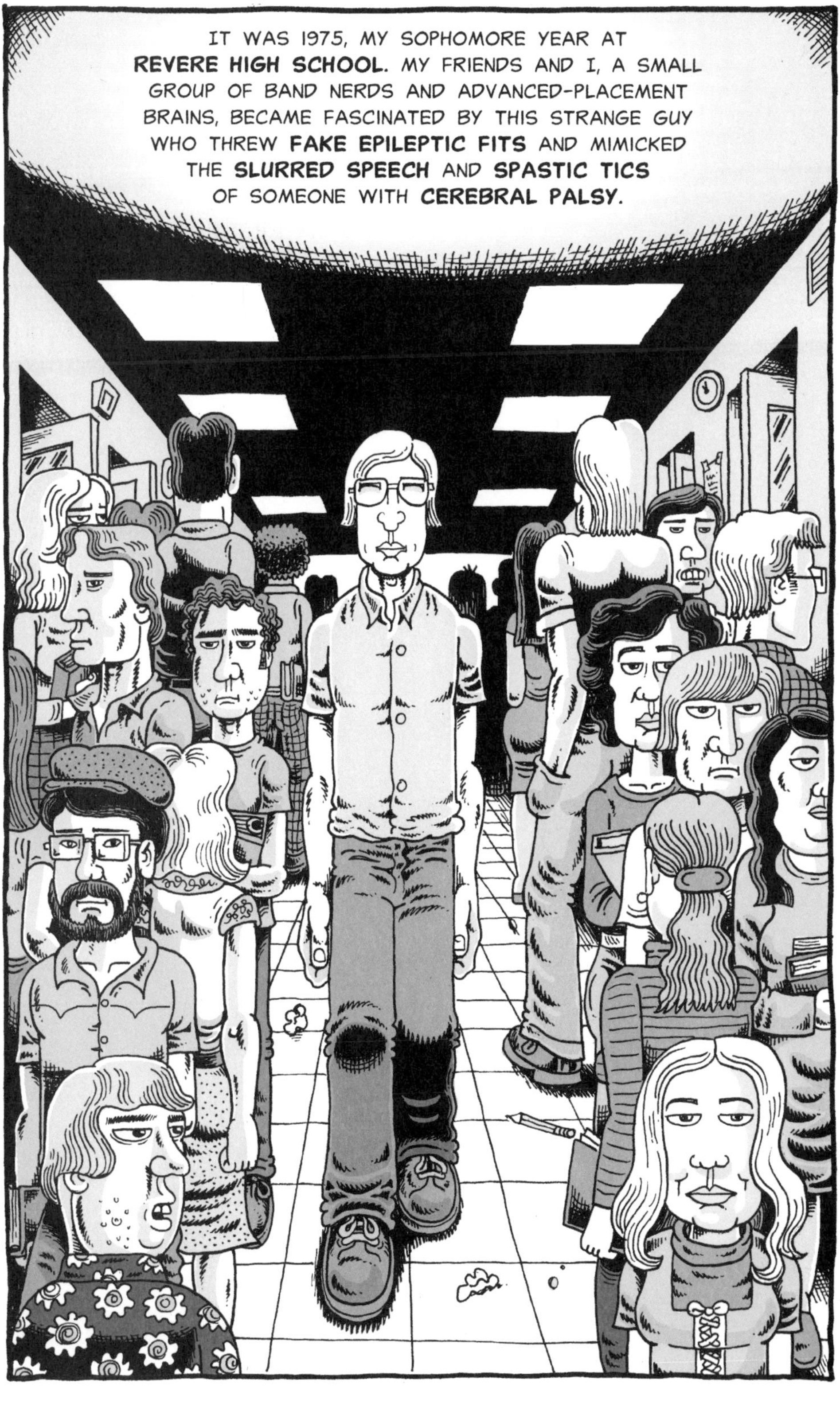
IT WAS 1975, MY SOPHOMORE YEAR AT REVERE HIGH SCHOOL. MY FRIENDS AND I, A SMALL GROUP OF BAND NERDS AND ADVANCED-PLACEMENT BRAINS, BECAME FASCINATED BY THIS STRANGE GUY WHO THREW FAKE EPILEPTIC FITS AND MIMICKED THE SLURRED SPEECH AND SPASTIC TICS OF SOMEONE WITH CEREBRAL PALSY.

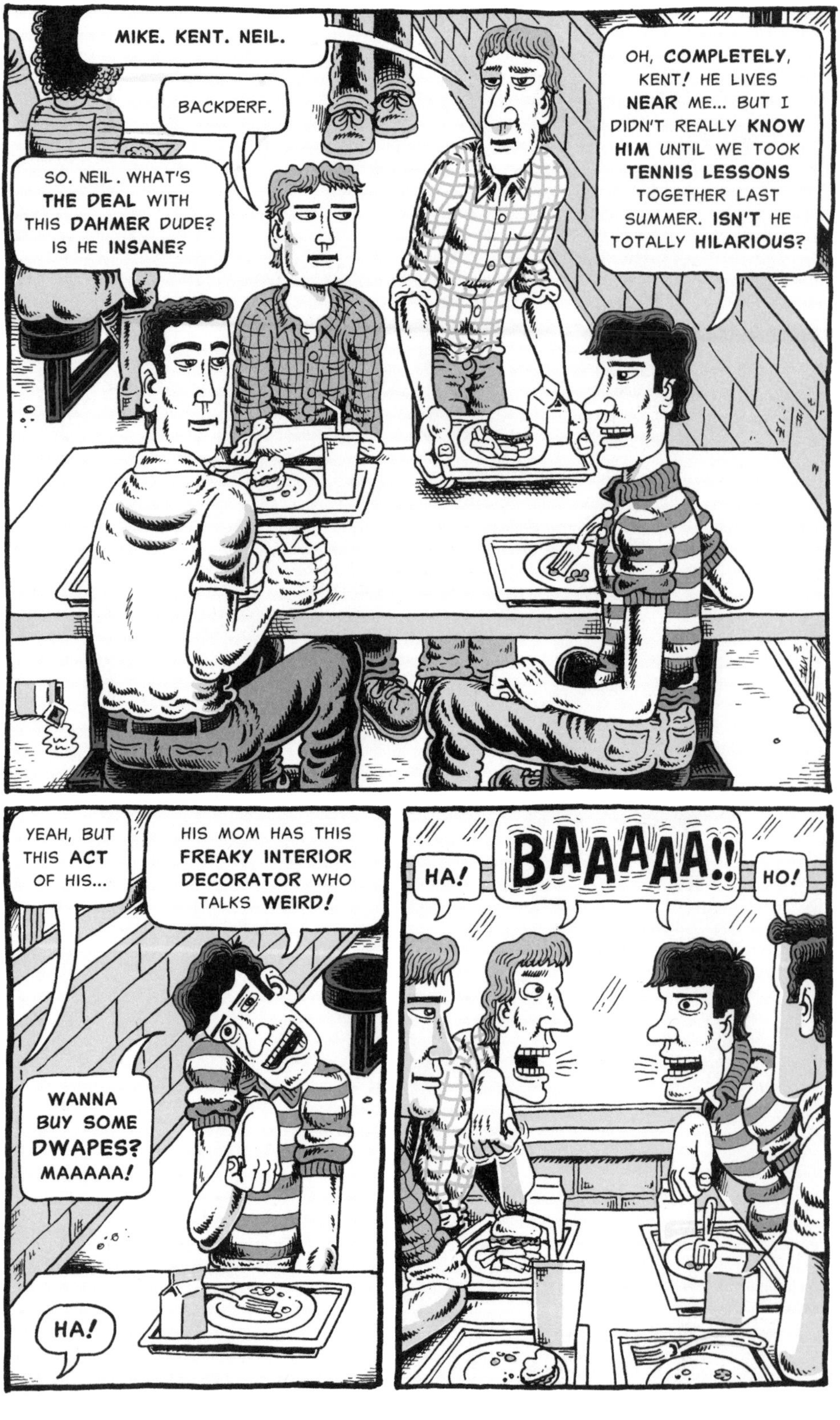
MIKE. KENT. NEIL.
BACKDERF.
SO. NEIL. WHAT'S THE DEAL WITH THIS DAHMER DUDE? IS HE INSANE?
OH, COMPLETELY, KENT! HE LIVES NEAR ME... BUT I DIDN'T REALLY KNOW HIM UNTIL WE TOOK TENNIS LESSONS TOGETHER LAST SUMMER. ISN'T HE TOTALLY HILARIOUS?
YEAH, BUT THIS ACT OF HIS...
HIS MOM HAS THIS FREAKY INTERIOR DECORATOR WHO TALKS WEIRD!
WANNA BUY SOME DWAPES? MAAAAA!
HA!
HA!
BAAAAA!!
HO!

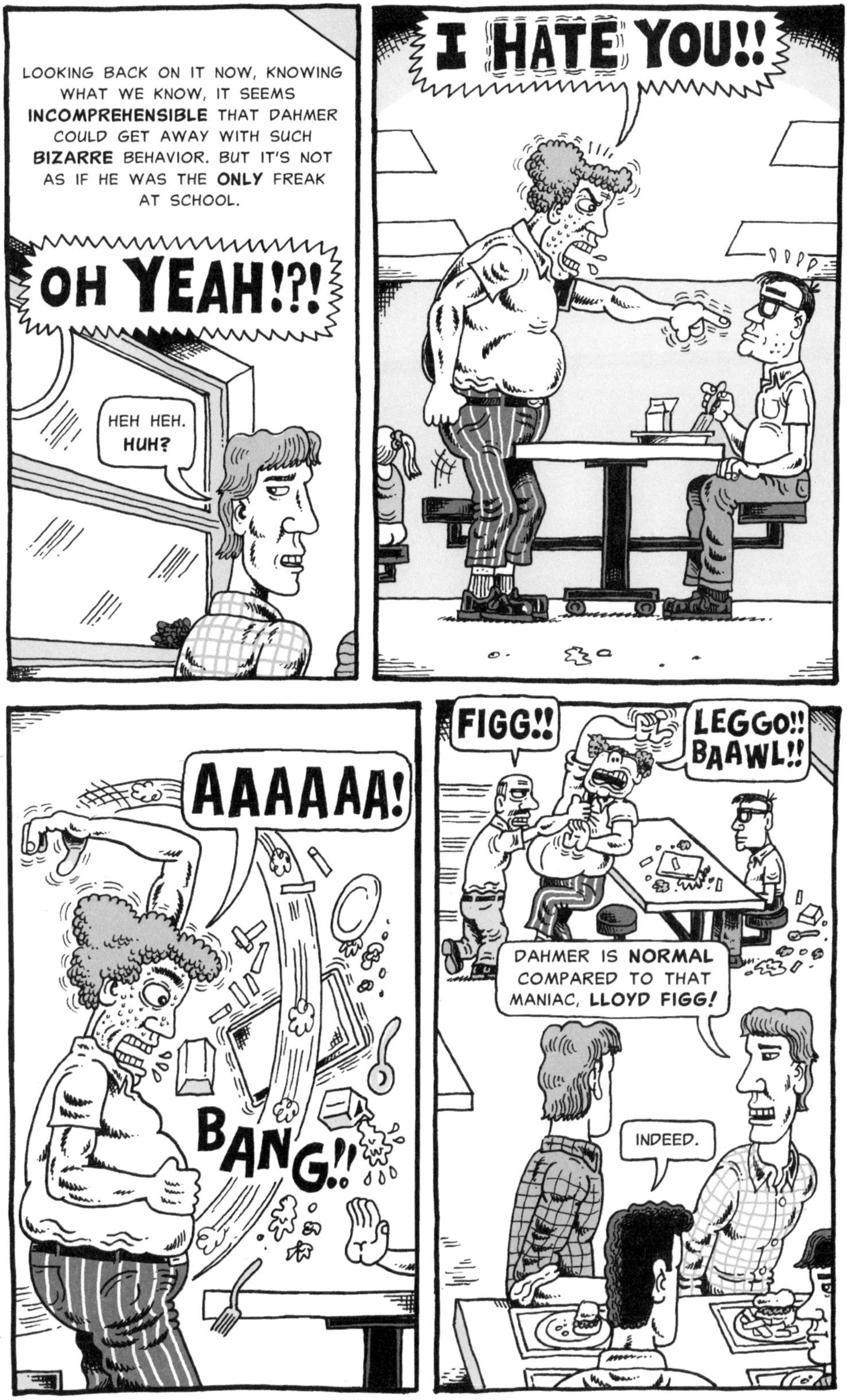
LOOKING BACK ON IT NOW, KNOWING WHAT WE KNOW, IT SEEMS INCOMPREHENSIBLE THAT DAHMER COULD GET AWAY WITH SUCH BIZARRE BEHAVIOR. BUT IT'S NOT AS IF HE WAS THE ONLY FREAK AT SCHOOL.
OH YEAH!?!
HEH HEH. HUH?
I HATE YOU!!
AAAAAA!
BANG!!
FIGG!!
LEGGO!! BAAWL!!
DAHMER IS NORMAL COMPARED TO THAT MANIAC, LLOYD FIGG!
INDEED.

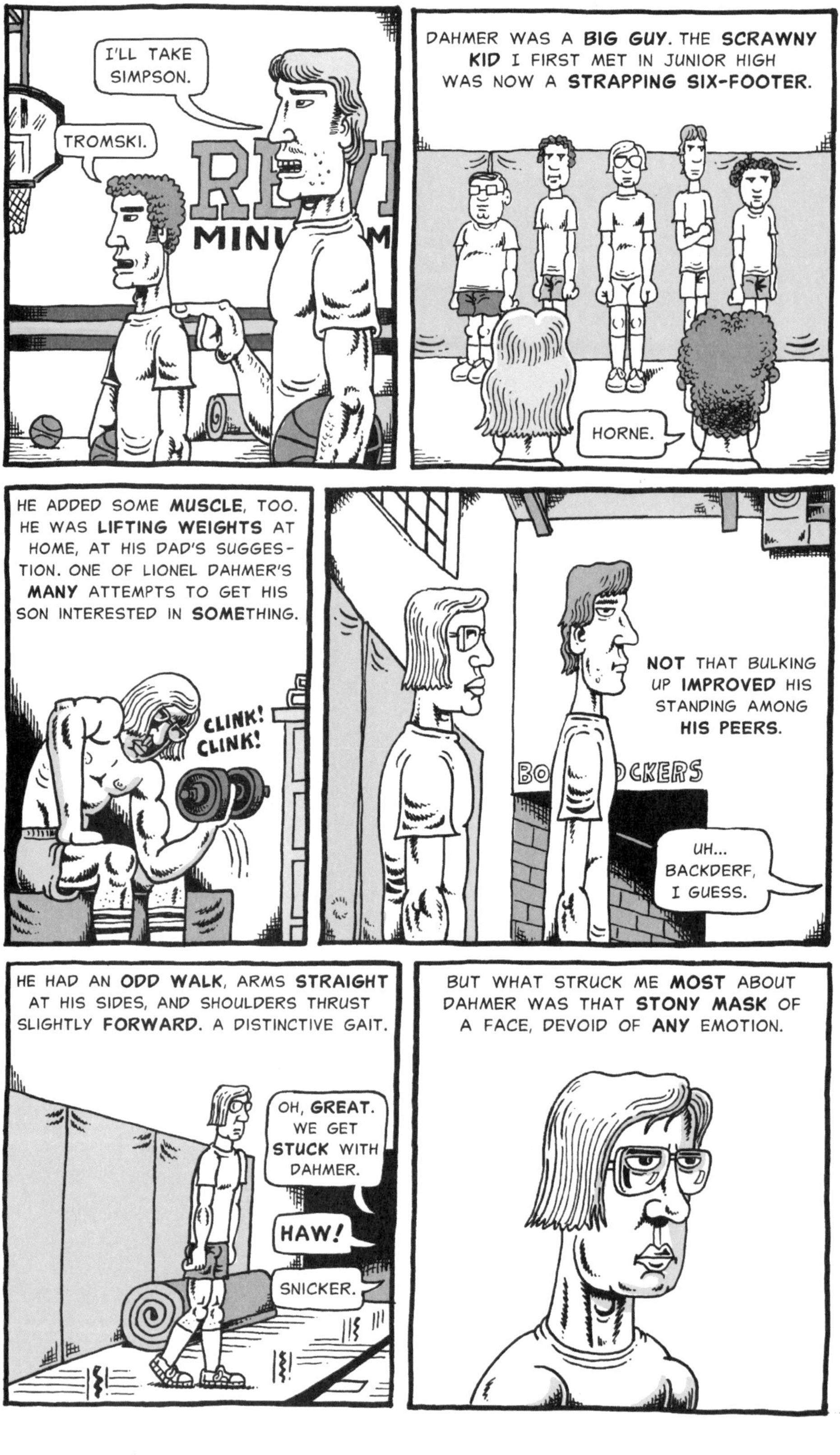
I'LL TAKE SIMPSON.
TROMSKI.
REV
MINU M
DAHMER WAS A BIG GUY. THE SCRAWNY KID I FIRST MET IN JUNIOR HIGH WAS NOW A STRAPPING SIX-FOOTER.
HORNE.
HE ADDED SOME MUSCLE, TOO. HE WAS LIFTING WEIGHTS AT HOME, AT HIS DAD'S SUGGESTION. ONE OF LIONEL DAHMER'S MANY ATTEMPTS TO GET HIS SON INTERESTED IN SOMETHING.
CLINK! CLINK!
NOT THAT BULKING UP IMPROVED HIS STANDING AMONG HIS PEERS.
BO CKERS
UH... BACKDERF, I GUESS.
HE HAD AN ODD WALK, ARMS STRAIGHT AT HIS SIDES, AND SHOULDERS THRUST SLIGHTLY FORWARD. A DISTINCTIVE GAIT.
OH, GREAT. WE GET STUCK WITH DAHMER.
HAW!
SNICKER.
BUT WHAT STRUCK ME MOST ABOUT DAHMER WAS THAT STONY MASK OF A FACE, DEVOID OF ANY EMOTION.

OUR INTEREST IN DAHMER MAY SOUND **MEAN-SPIRITED**, BUT IT REALLY WASN'T. WE **WEREN'T** PUTTING HIM DOWN. AFTER ALL, WE WEREN'T A WHOLE LOT HIGHER UP THE SOCIAL LADDER. HE GENUINELY **AMUSED US**, THAT'S ALL.

IT SEEMED HIS TRANSFORMATION FROM **SHY GEEK** TO **SPAZ FREAK** HAPPENED **OVERNIGHT**. IT PROBABLY DIDN'T. I SIMPLY HADN'T **NOTICED** DAHMER BEFORE. HE **WASN'T** ON **MY** RADAR SCREEN.

HEHWO, MR. BACKDUUUURF!

HE WAS **NOW**.

I WAS FIFTEEN. AND LIKE MOST FIFTEEN-YEAR-OLDS, THE **HORMONES** HAD KICKED IN **BIG-TIME**. I THOUGHT ABOUT **GIRLS** FROM DAWN TILL DUSK.

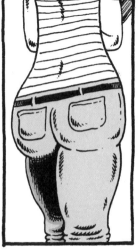

YOUR AVERAGE HORNY TEENAGE BOY, BUBBLING TO THE BRIM WITH **SEXUAL FRUSTRATION**.

SIGH.

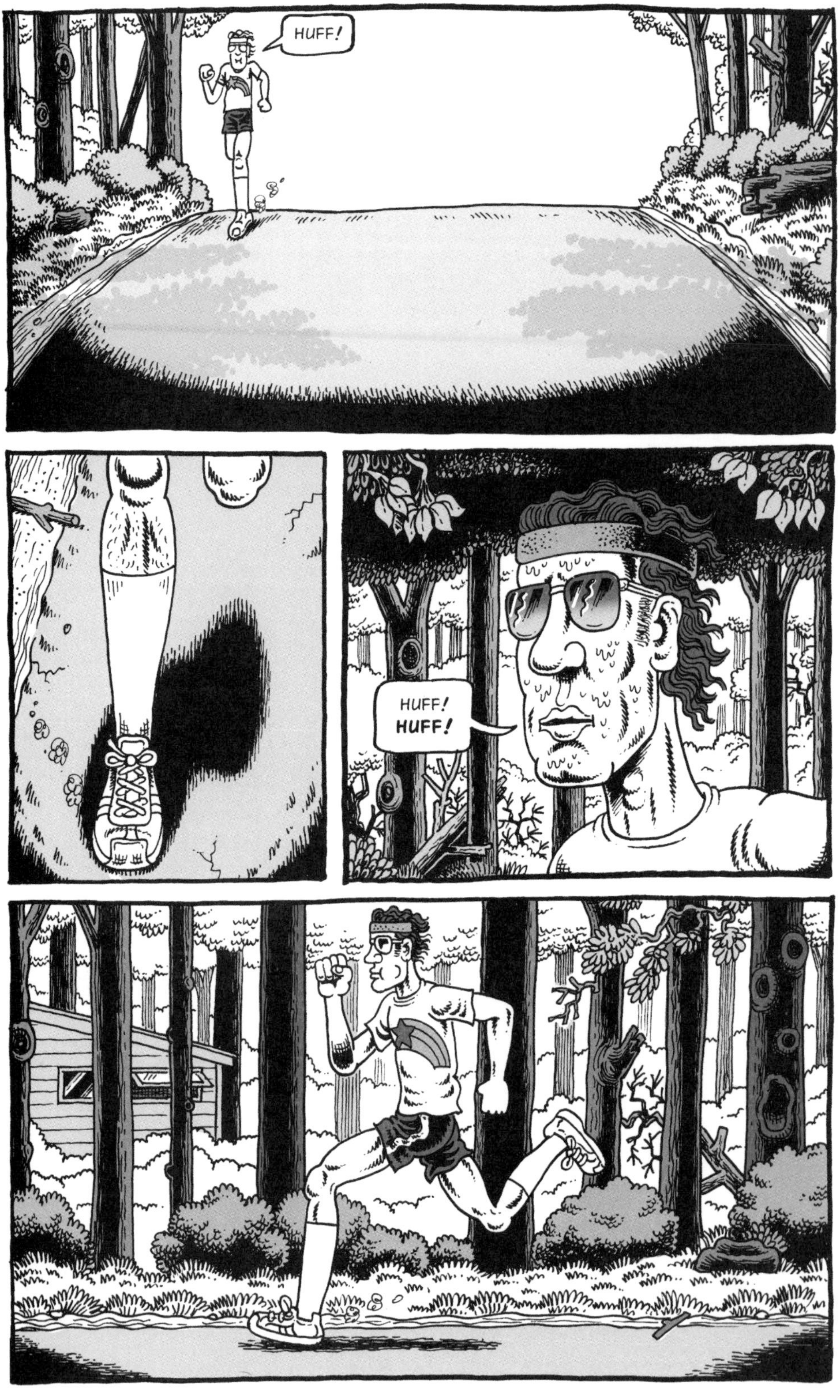

HUFF!
HUFF! HUFF!

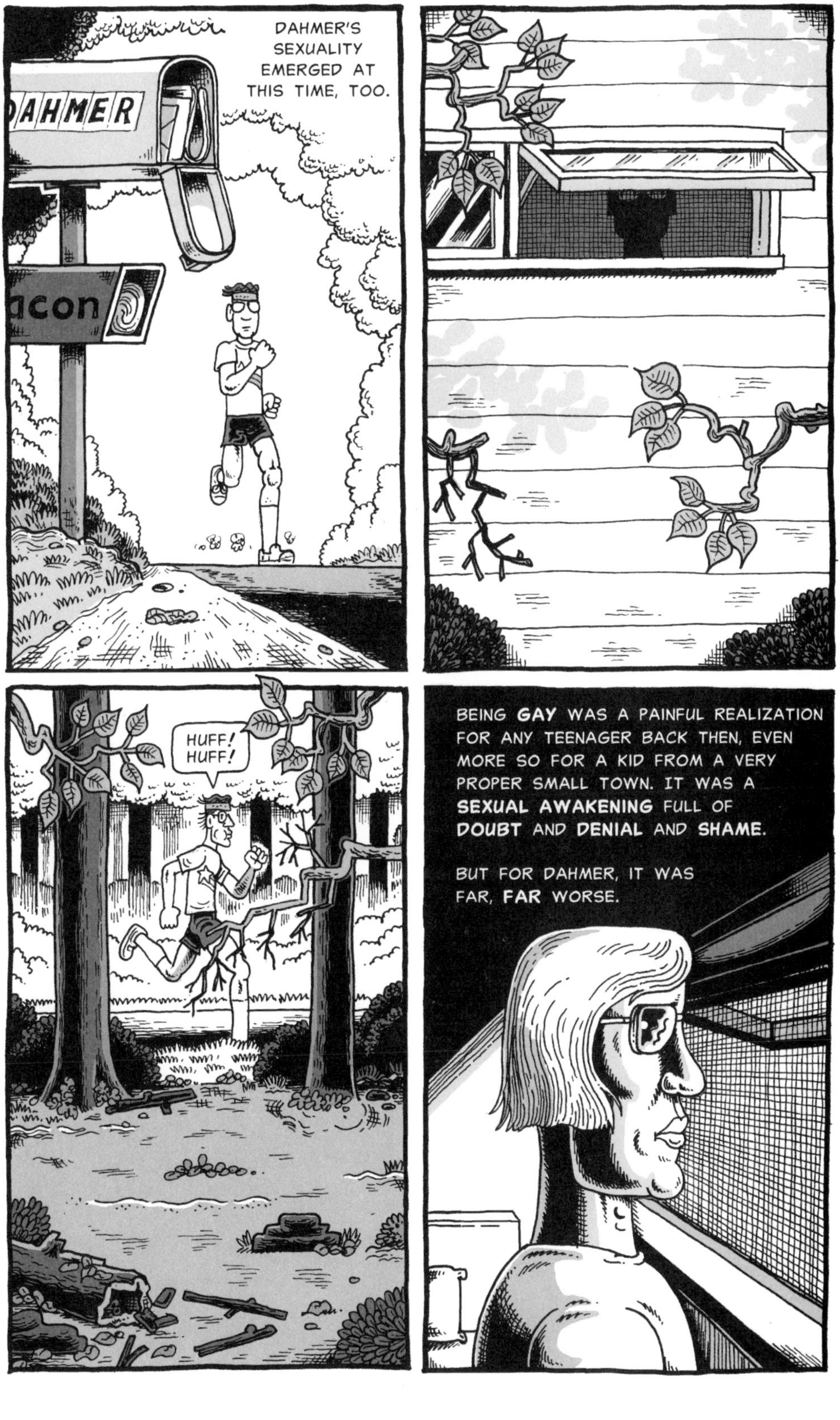
DAHMER
DAHMER'S SEXUALITY EMERGED AT THIS TIME, TOO.
acon
HUFF! HUFF!
BEING **GAY** WAS A PAINFUL REALIZATION FOR ANY TEENAGER BACK THEN, EVEN MORE SO FOR A KID FROM A VERY PROPER SMALL TOWN. IT WAS A **SEXUAL AWAKENING** FULL OF **DOUBT** AND **DENIAL** AND **SHAME.**
BUT FOR DAHMER, IT WAS FAR, **FAR** WORSE.

HE KEPT HIS HOMOSEXUALITY **HIDDEN** FROM EVERYONE. THAT WAS THE **NORM**.

MANY OF OUR CLASSMATES WERE GAY, AND NOT A SINGLE ONE CAME OUT IN HIGH SCHOOL.

BUT DAHMER HAD ANOTHER SECRET, A **TERRIBLE** SECRET.

IN DAHMER'S FANTASIES, **HIS** LOVERS...

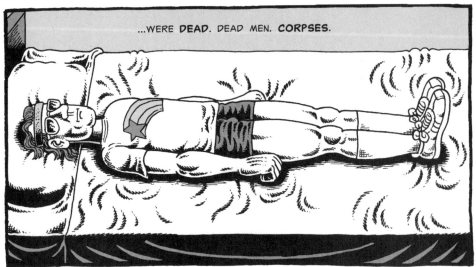

...WERE **DEAD**. DEAD MEN. **CORPSES**.

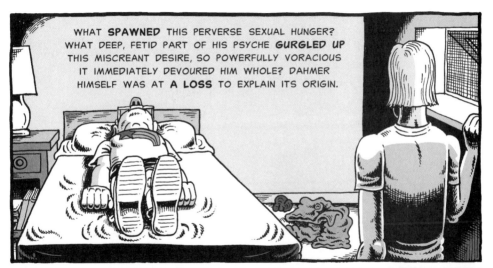

WHAT **SPAWNED** THIS PERVERSE SEXUAL HUNGER? WHAT DEEP, FETID PART OF HIS PSYCHE **GURGLED UP** THIS MISCREANT DESIRE, SO POWERFULLY VORACIOUS IT IMMEDIATELY DEVOURED HIM WHOLE? DAHMER HIMSELF WAS AT **A LOSS** TO EXPLAIN ITS ORIGIN.

"I **DON'T KNOW** WHERE IT CAME FROM," JEFF SAID, YEARS LATER. "I'LL PROBABLY **NEVER** KNOW."

AAAA ARG!!

"BUT I NEVER **DREAMED** IT WOULD BECOME **A REALITY.**"

SIGH.

BUT AT SCHOOL, JEFF, FOR THE **FIRST** TIME, HAD **FRIENDS.** OK, HE WAS MORE MASCOT THAN PAL. HE WAS, AFTER ALL, A PRETTY STRANGE KID. BUT HE'D ALWAYS BEEN A **NONENTITY.** NOW HE WAS THE **CENTER OF ATTENTION!**

TODAY'S MEETING OF THE **DAHMER FAN CLUB** IS HEREBY CALLED TO ORDER.

MAAAA!!

HA HA!!

HEE.

HA HA HO HA!

HA HA.

THIS, OUR SOPHOMORE YEAR, WAS, SAD TO SAY, VERY LIKELY THE **HAPPIEST PERIOD** OF DAHMER'S LIFE.

CHECK IT OUT.

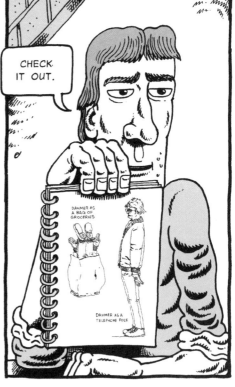

DAHMER AS A BAG OF GROCERIES

DAHMER AS A TELEPHONE POLE

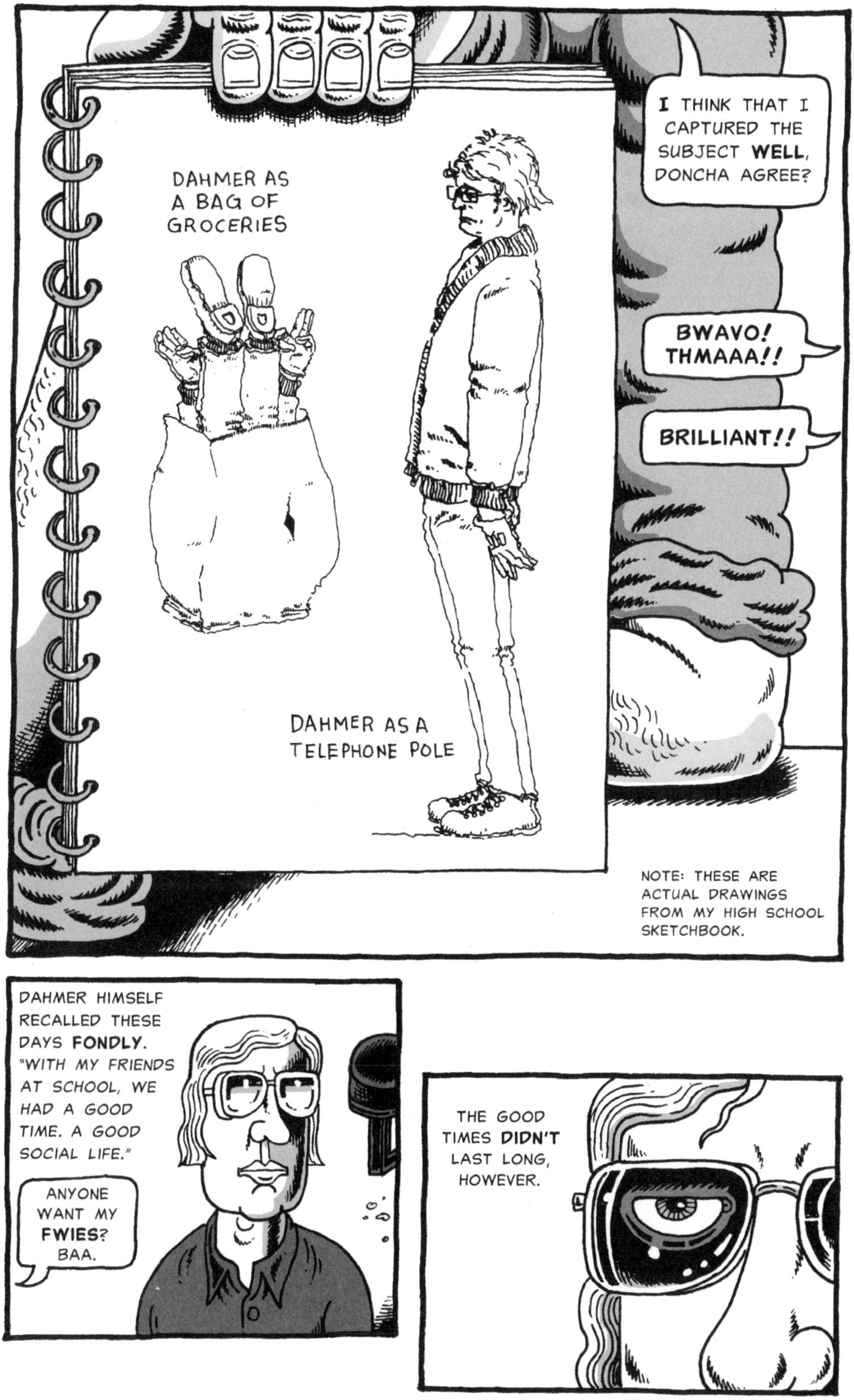

DAHMER AS A BAG OF GROCERIES
DAHMER AS A TELEPHONE POLE
I THINK THAT I CAPTURED THE SUBJECT WELL, DONCHA AGREE?
BWAVO! THMAAA!!
BRILLIANT!!
NOTE: THESE ARE ACTUAL DRAWINGS FROM MY HIGH SCHOOL SKETCHBOOK.
DAHMER HIMSELF RECALLED THESE DAYS FONDLY. "WITH MY FRIENDS AT SCHOOL, WE HAD A GOOD TIME. A GOOD SOCIAL LIFE."
ANYONE WANT MY FWIES? BAA.
THE GOOD TIMES DIDN'T LAST LONG, HOWEVER.

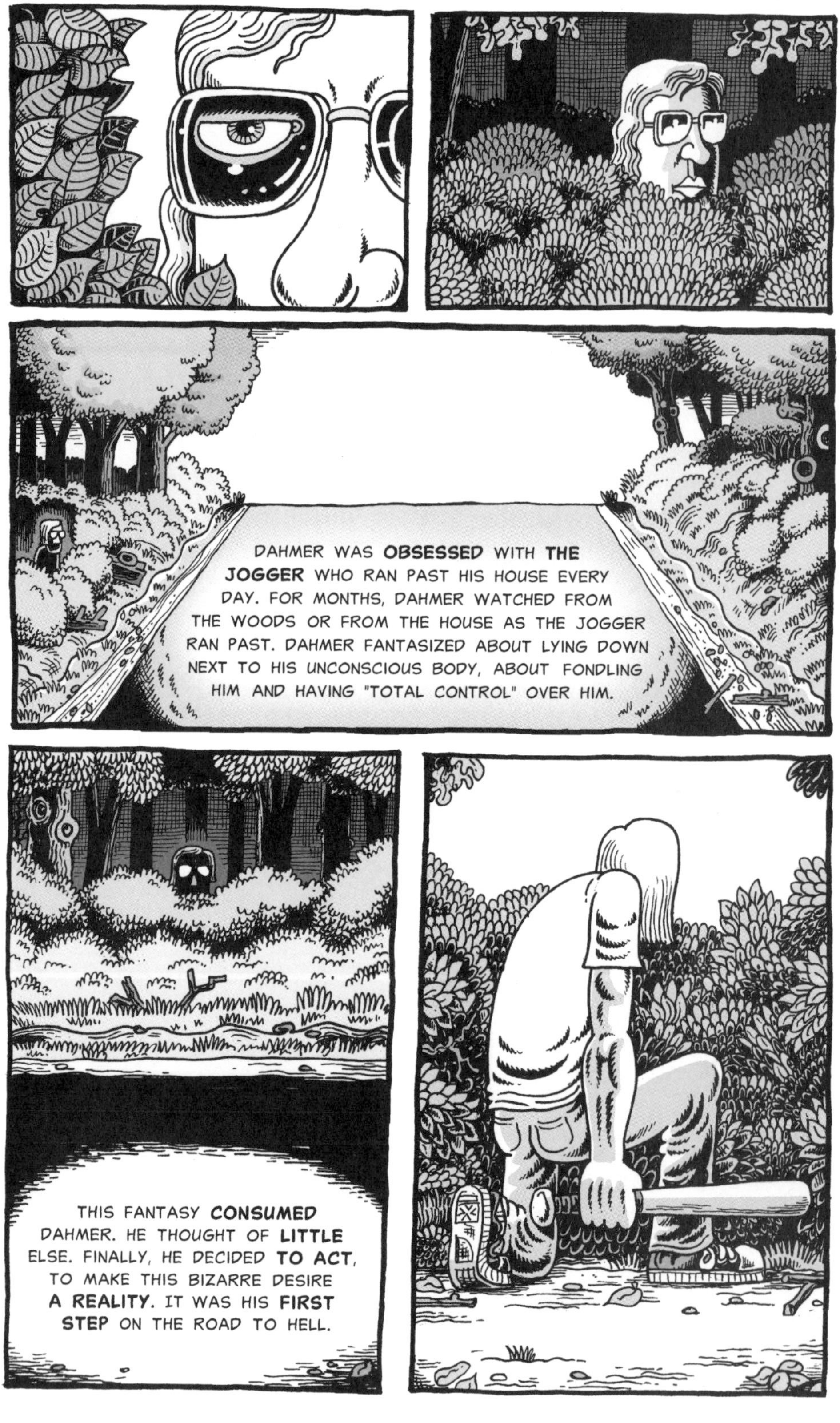
DAHMER WAS **OBSESSED** WITH **THE JOGGER** WHO RAN PAST HIS HOUSE EVERY DAY. FOR MONTHS, DAHMER WATCHED FROM THE WOODS OR FROM THE HOUSE AS THE JOGGER RAN PAST. DAHMER FANTASIZED ABOUT LYING DOWN NEXT TO HIS UNCONSCIOUS BODY, ABOUT FONDLING HIM AND HAVING "TOTAL CONTROL" OVER HIM.
THIS FANTASY **CONSUMED** DAHMER. HE THOUGHT OF **LITTLE** ELSE. FINALLY, HE DECIDED **TO ACT**, TO MAKE THIS BIZARRE DESIRE **A REALITY**. IT WAS HIS **FIRST STEP** ON THE ROAD TO HELL.

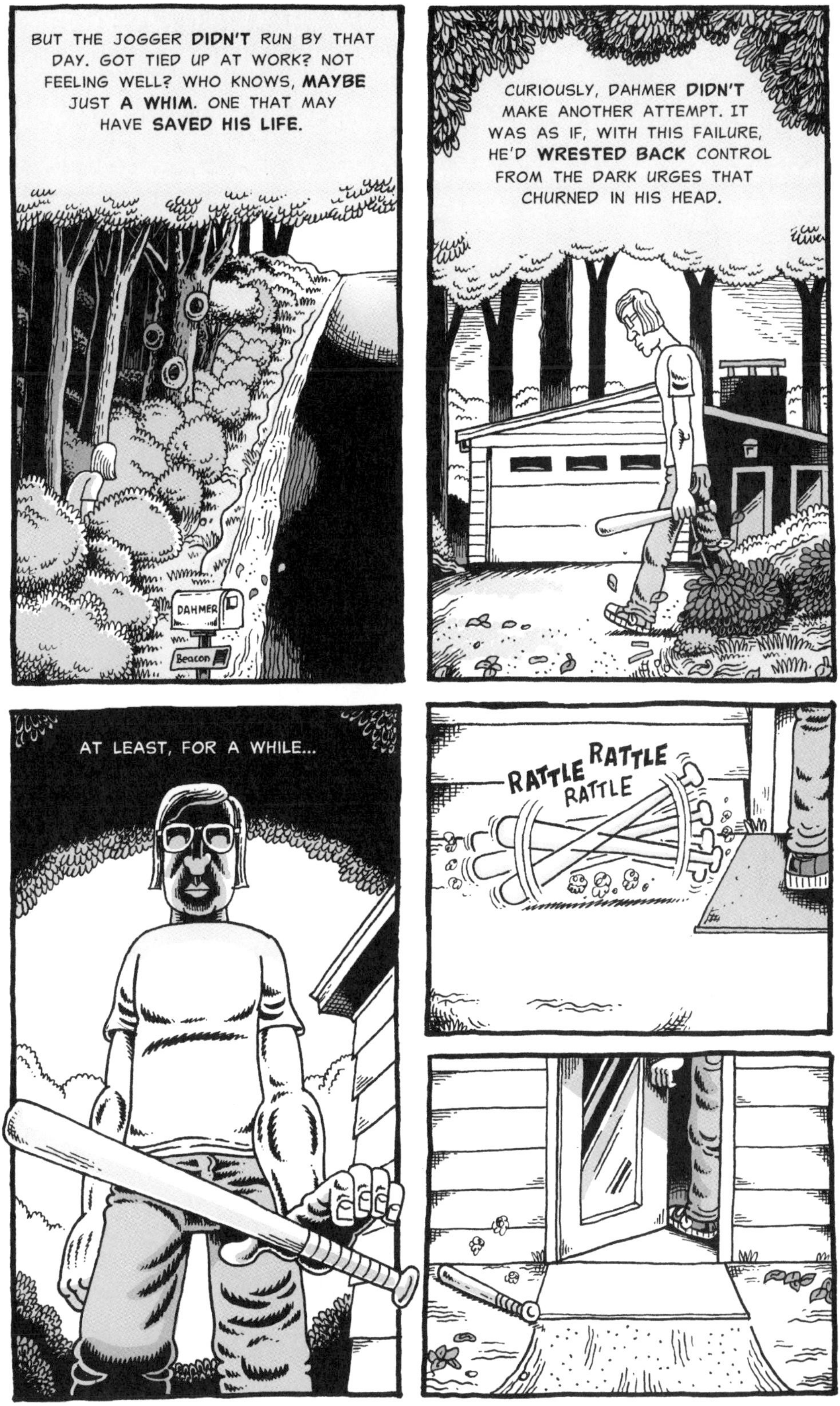
BUT THE JOGGER DIDN'T RUN BY THAT DAY. GOT TIED UP AT WORK? NOT FEELING WELL? WHO KNOWS, MAYBE JUST A WHIM. ONE THAT MAY HAVE SAVED HIS LIFE.
DAHMER
Beacon
CURIOUSLY, DAHMER DIDN'T MAKE ANOTHER ATTEMPT. IT WAS AS IF, WITH THIS FAILURE, HE'D WRESTED BACK CONTROL FROM THE DARK URGES THAT CHURNED IN HIS HEAD.
AT LEAST, FOR A WHILE...
RATTLE RATTLE RATTLE

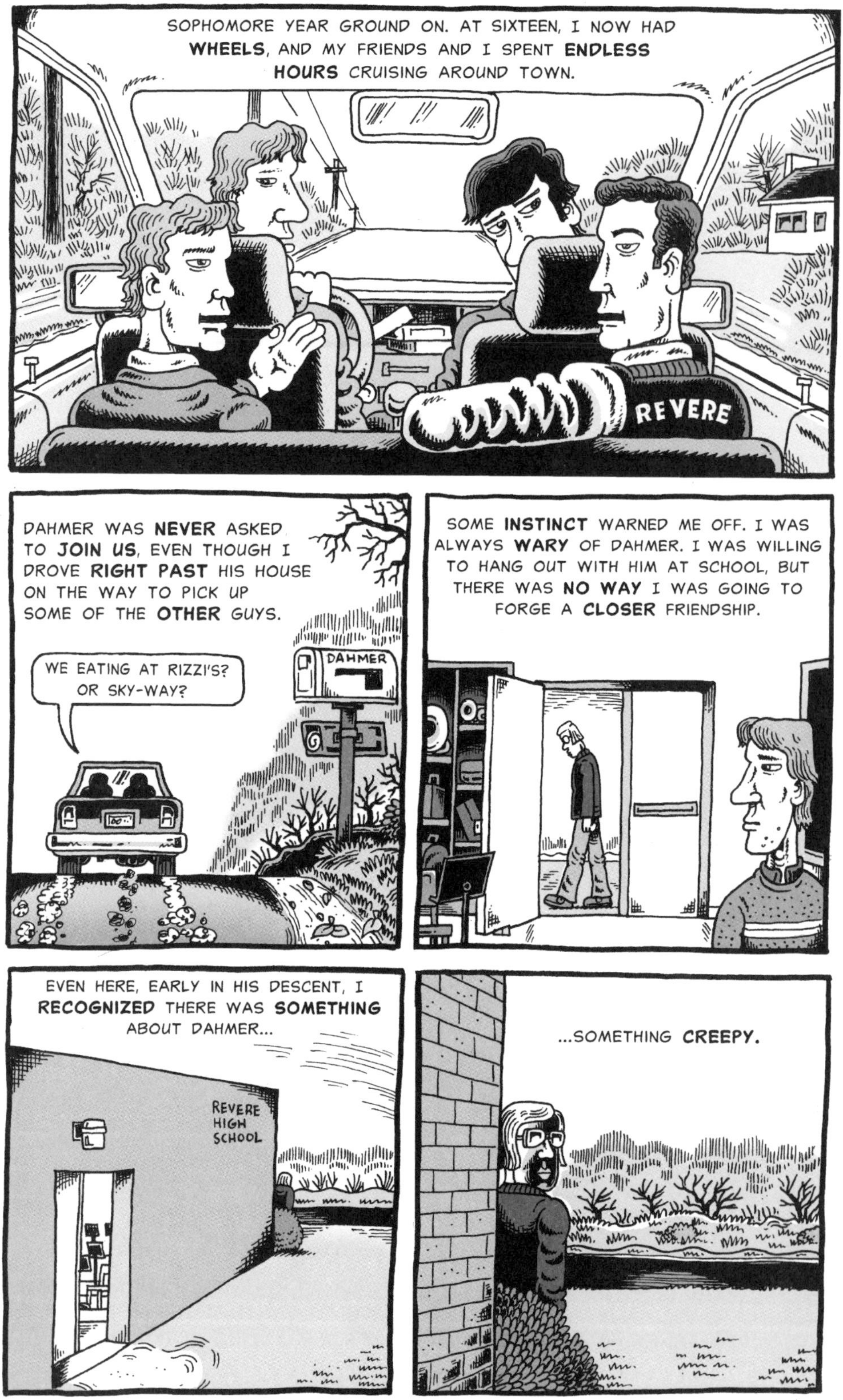
SOPHOMORE YEAR GROUND ON. AT SIXTEEN, I NOW HAD **WHEELS**, AND MY FRIENDS AND I SPENT **ENDLESS HOURS** CRUISING AROUND TOWN.
REVERE
DAHMER WAS **NEVER** ASKED TO **JOIN US**, EVEN THOUGH I DROVE **RIGHT PAST** HIS HOUSE ON THE WAY TO PICK UP SOME OF THE **OTHER** GUYS.
DAHMER
WE EATING AT RIZZI'S? OR SKY-WAY?
SOME **INSTINCT** WARNED ME OFF. I WAS ALWAYS **WARY** OF DAHMER. I WAS WILLING TO HANG OUT WITH HIM AT SCHOOL, BUT THERE WAS **NO WAY** I WAS GOING TO FORGE A **CLOSER** FRIENDSHIP.
EVEN HERE, EARLY IN HIS DESCENT, I **RECOGNIZED** THERE WAS **SOMETHING** ABOUT DAHMER...
REVERE HIGH SCHOOL
...SOMETHING **CREEPY**.

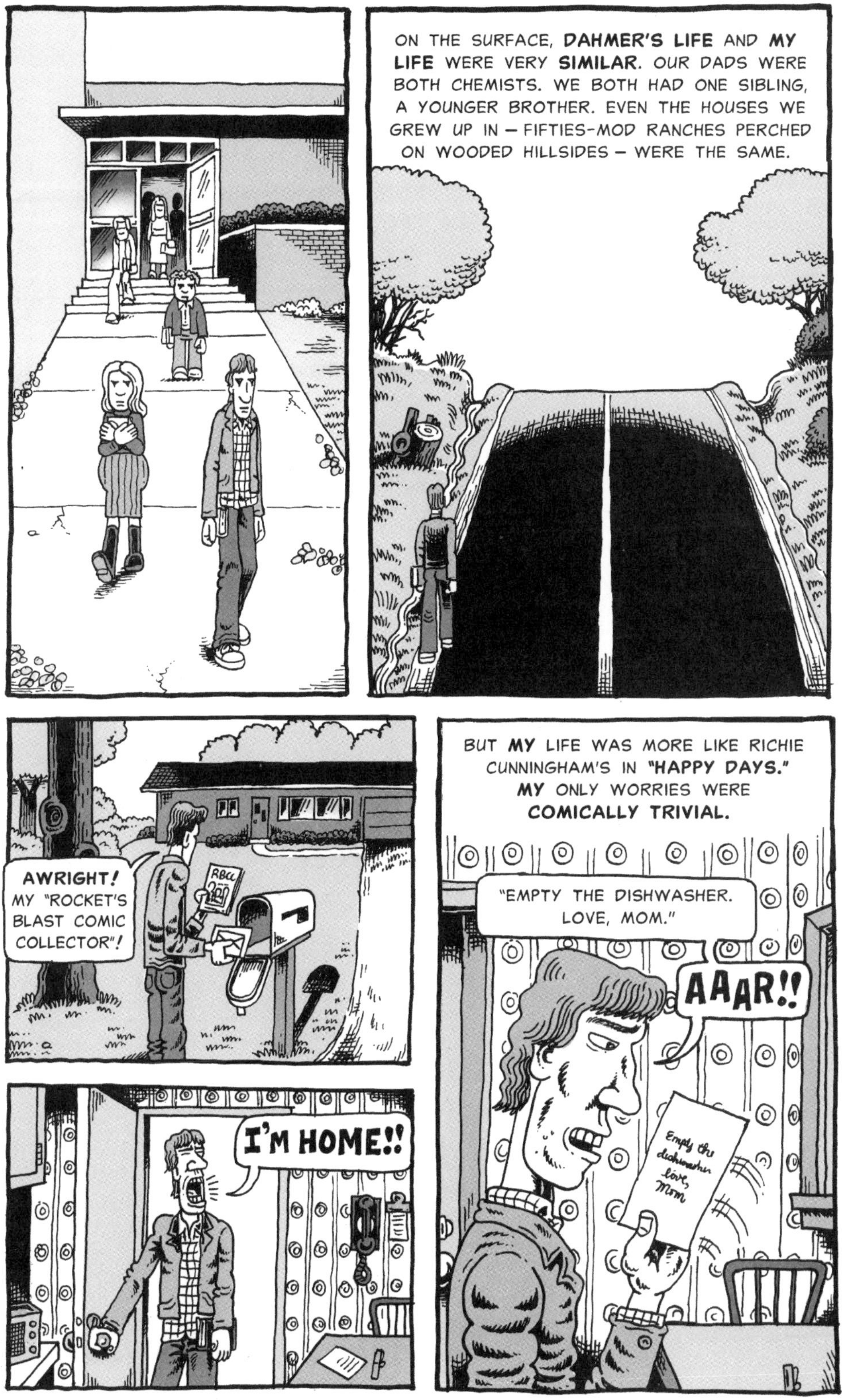
ON THE SURFACE, DAHMER'S LIFE AND MY LIFE WERE VERY SIMILAR. OUR DADS WERE BOTH CHEMISTS. WE BOTH HAD ONE SIBLING, A YOUNGER BROTHER. EVEN THE HOUSES WE GREW UP IN – FIFTIES-MOD RANCHES PERCHED ON WOODED HILLSIDES – WERE THE SAME.
AWRIGHT! MY "ROCKET'S BLAST COMIC COLLECTOR"!
RBCC
I'M HOME!!
BUT MY LIFE WAS MORE LIKE RICHIE CUNNINGHAM'S IN "HAPPY DAYS." MY ONLY WORRIES WERE COMICALLY TRIVIAL.
"EMPTY THE DISHWASHER. LOVE, MOM."
AAAR!!
Empty the dishwasher love, Mom

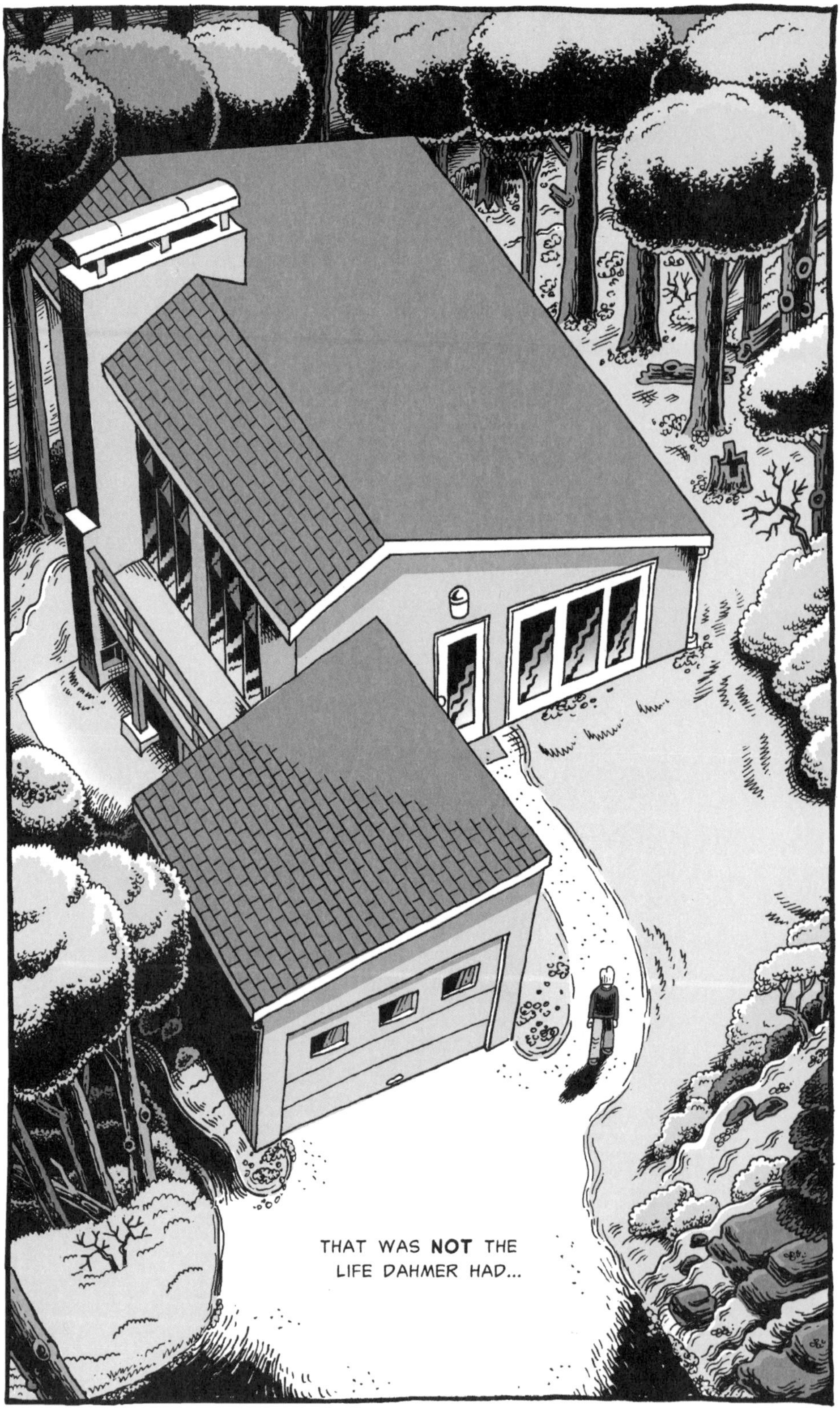
THAT WAS **NOT** THE
LIFE DAHMER HAD...

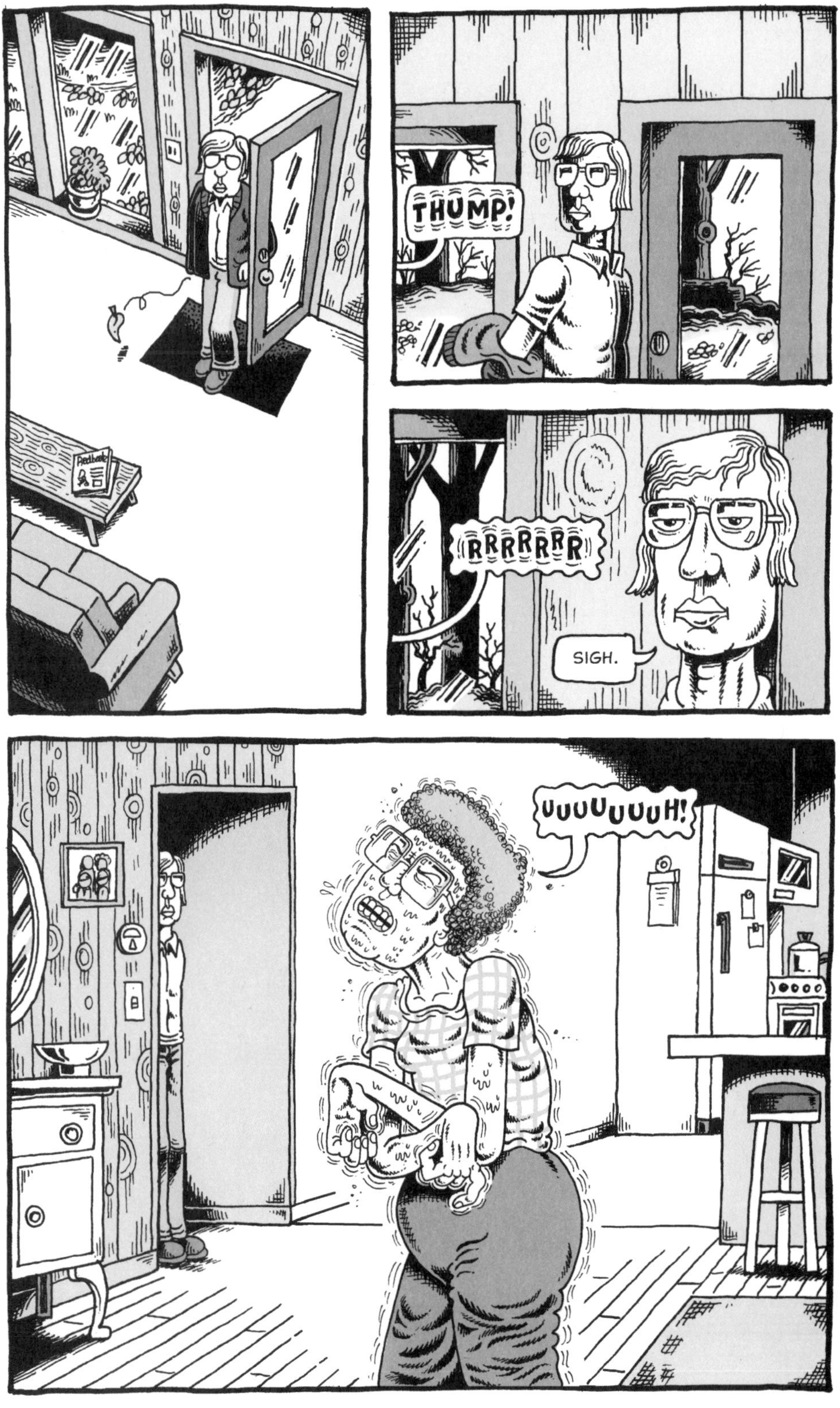
THUMP!
RRRRRRR
SIGH.
UUUUUUUH!

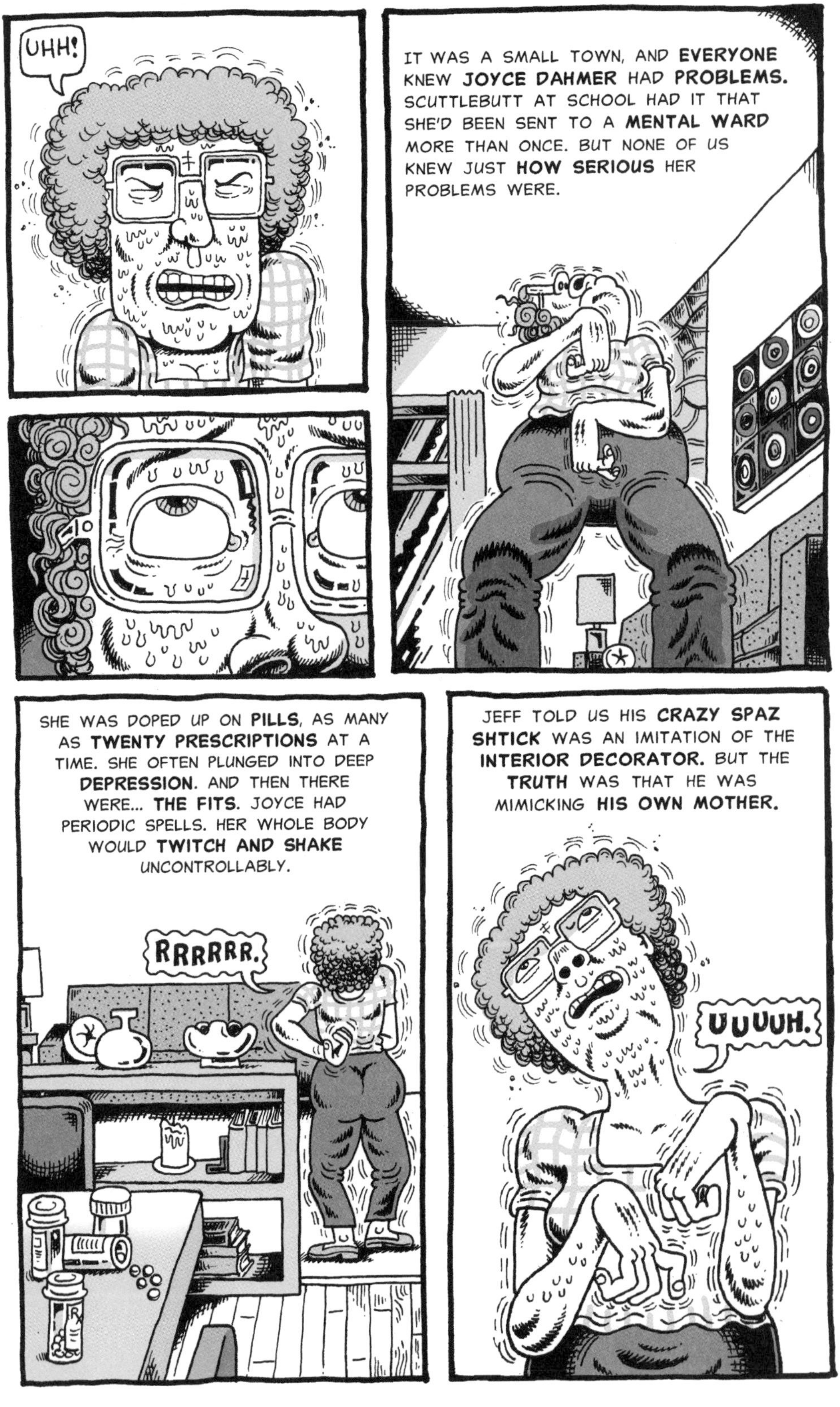
UHH!
IT WAS A SMALL TOWN, AND EVERYONE KNEW JOYCE DAHMER HAD PROBLEMS. SCUTTLEBUTT AT SCHOOL HAD IT THAT SHE'D BEEN SENT TO A MENTAL WARD MORE THAN ONCE. BUT NONE OF US KNEW JUST HOW SERIOUS HER PROBLEMS WERE.
SHE WAS DOPED UP ON PILLS, AS MANY AS TWENTY PRESCRIPTIONS AT A TIME. SHE OFTEN PLUNGED INTO DEEP DEPRESSION. AND THEN THERE WERE... THE FITS. JOYCE HAD PERIODIC SPELLS. HER WHOLE BODY WOULD TWITCH AND SHAKE UNCONTROLLABLY.
RRRRRR.
JEFF TOLD US HIS CRAZY SPAZ SHTICK WAS AN IMITATION OF THE INTERIOR DECORATOR. BUT THE TRUTH WAS THAT HE WAS MIMICKING HIS OWN MOTHER.
UUUUH.

WHUMP!

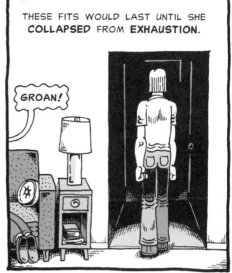

THESE FITS WOULD LAST UNTIL SHE **COLLAPSED** FROM **EXHAUSTION**.

GROAN!

THIS IS WHAT JEFF CAME HOME TO.

PANT!
PANT!

SIGH!

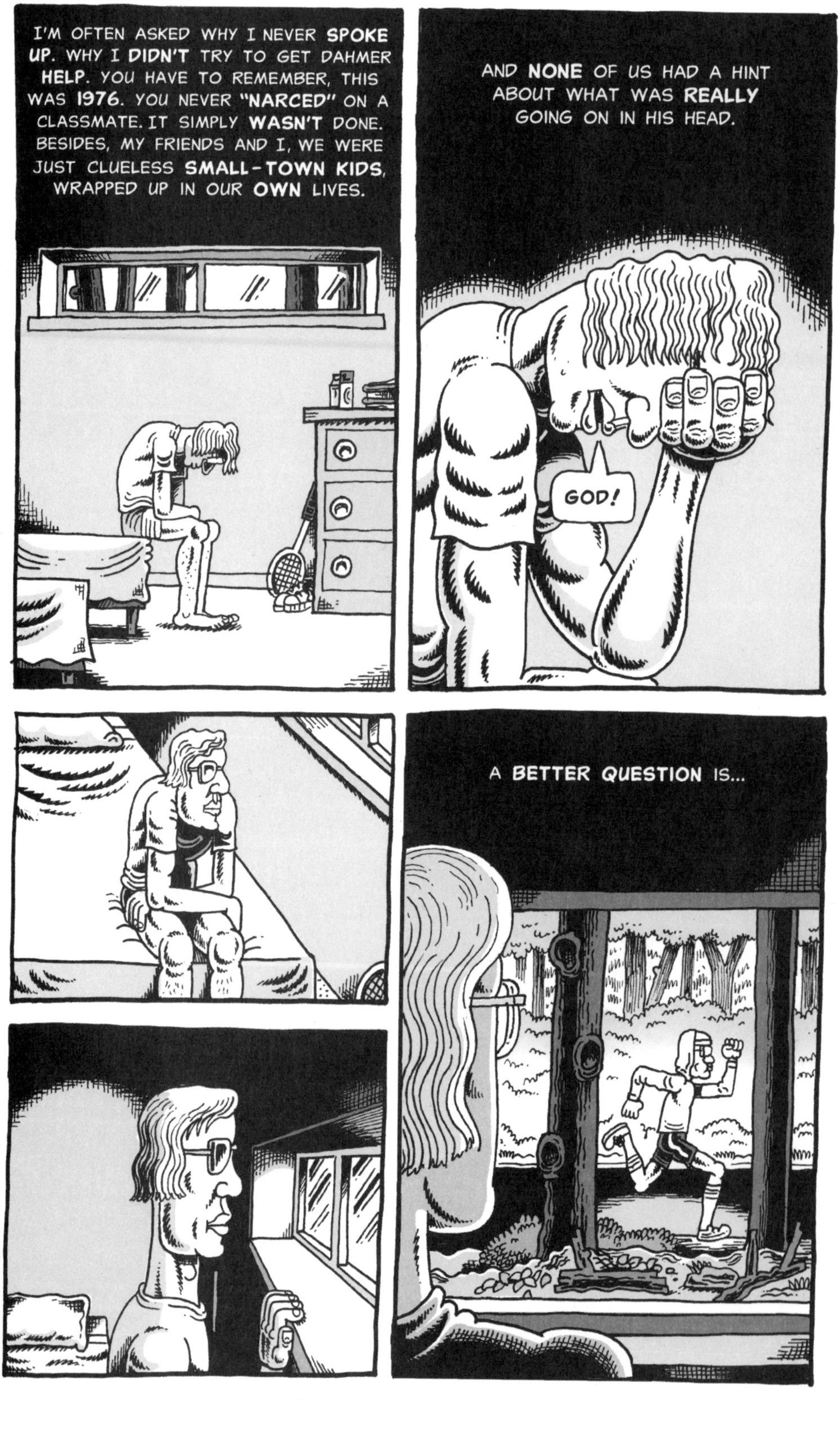

I'M OFTEN ASKED WHY I NEVER SPOKE UP. WHY I DIDN'T TRY TO GET DAHMER HELP. YOU HAVE TO REMEMBER, THIS WAS 1976. YOU NEVER "NARCED" ON A CLASSMATE. IT SIMPLY WASN'T DONE. BESIDES, MY FRIENDS AND I, WE WERE JUST CLUELESS SMALL-TOWN KIDS, WRAPPED UP IN OUR OWN LIVES.
AND NONE OF US HAD A HINT ABOUT WHAT WAS REALLY GOING ON IN HIS HEAD.
GOD!
A BETTER QUESTION IS...

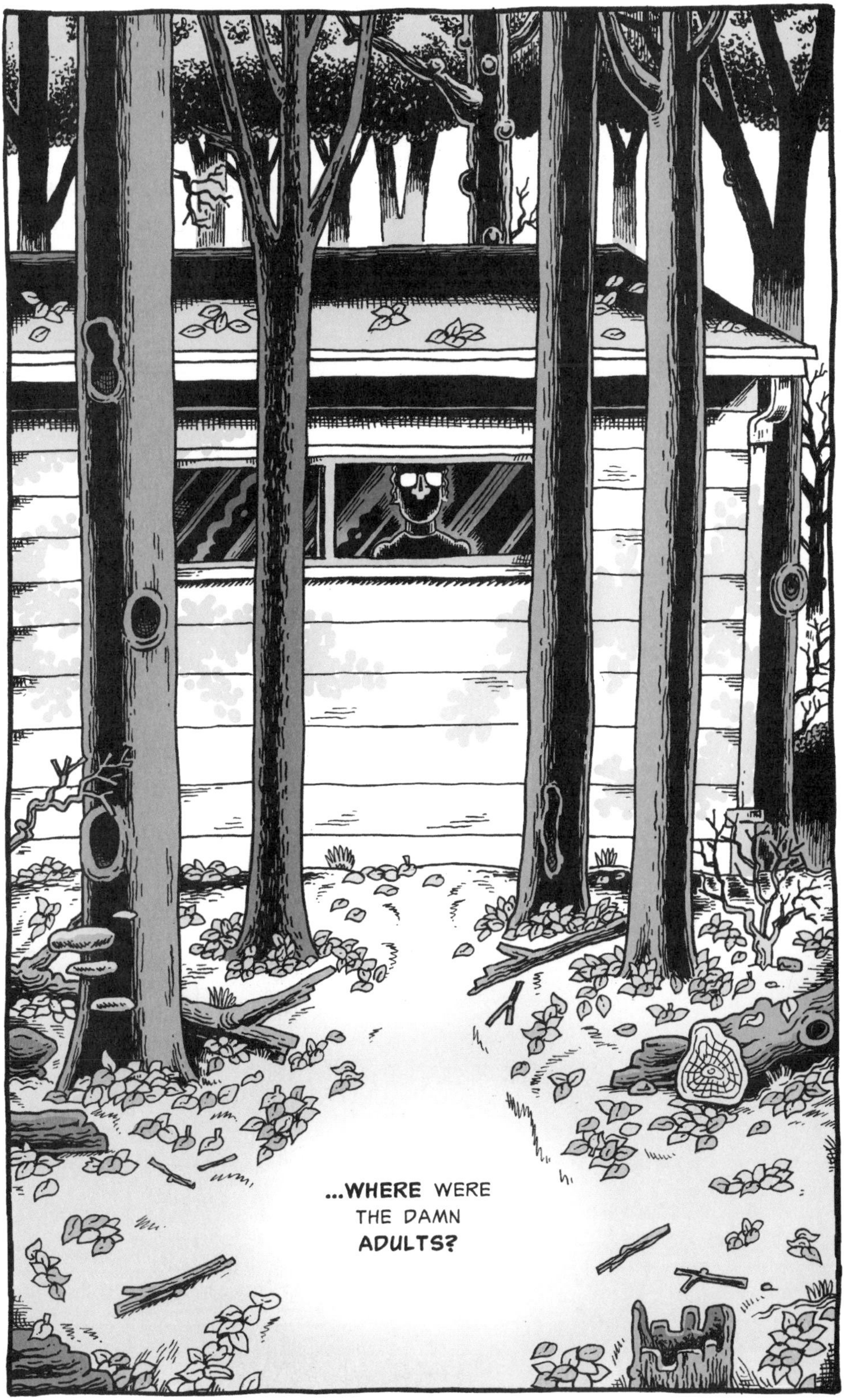
...WHERE WERE THE DAMN ADULTS?

PART 2

A Secret Life

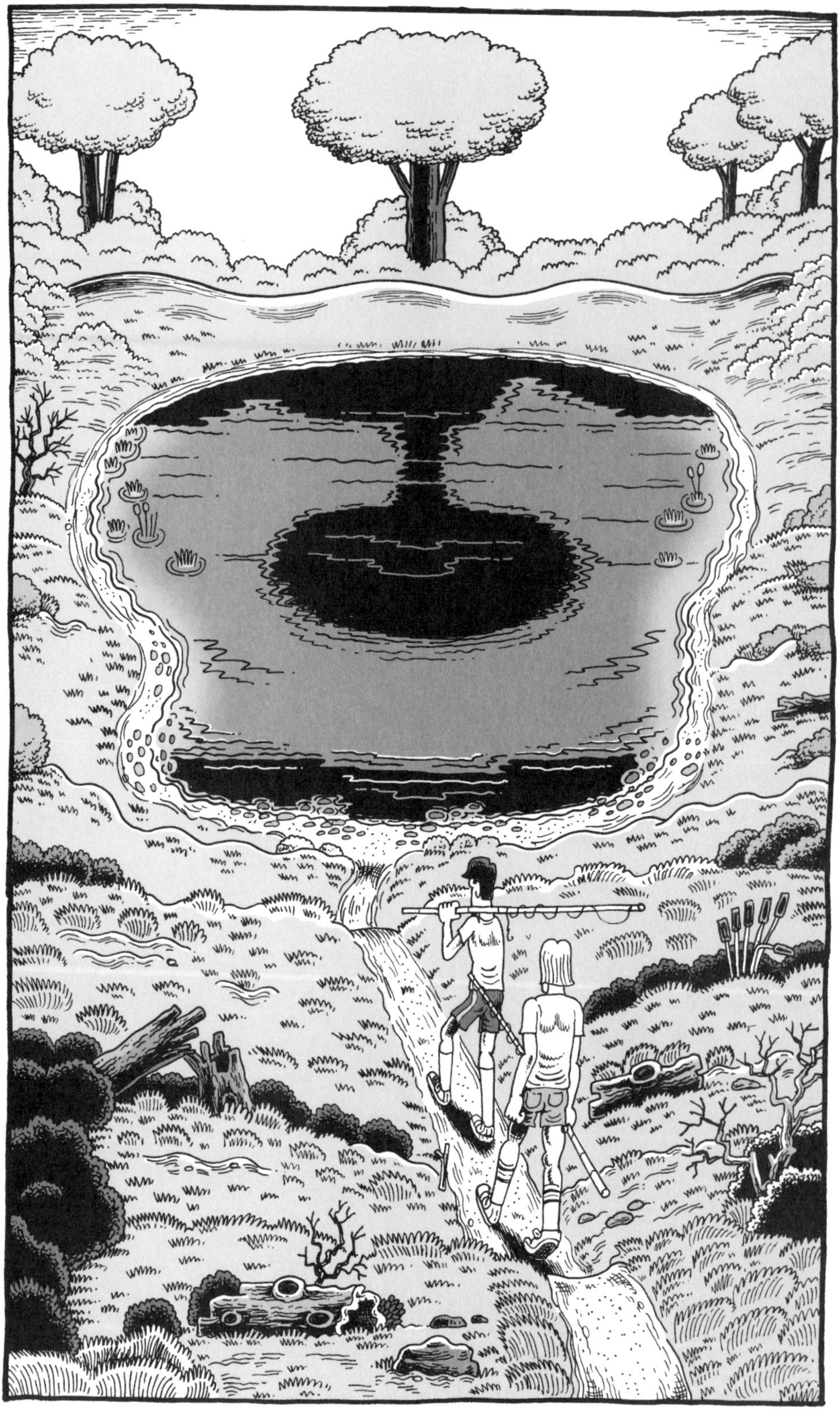

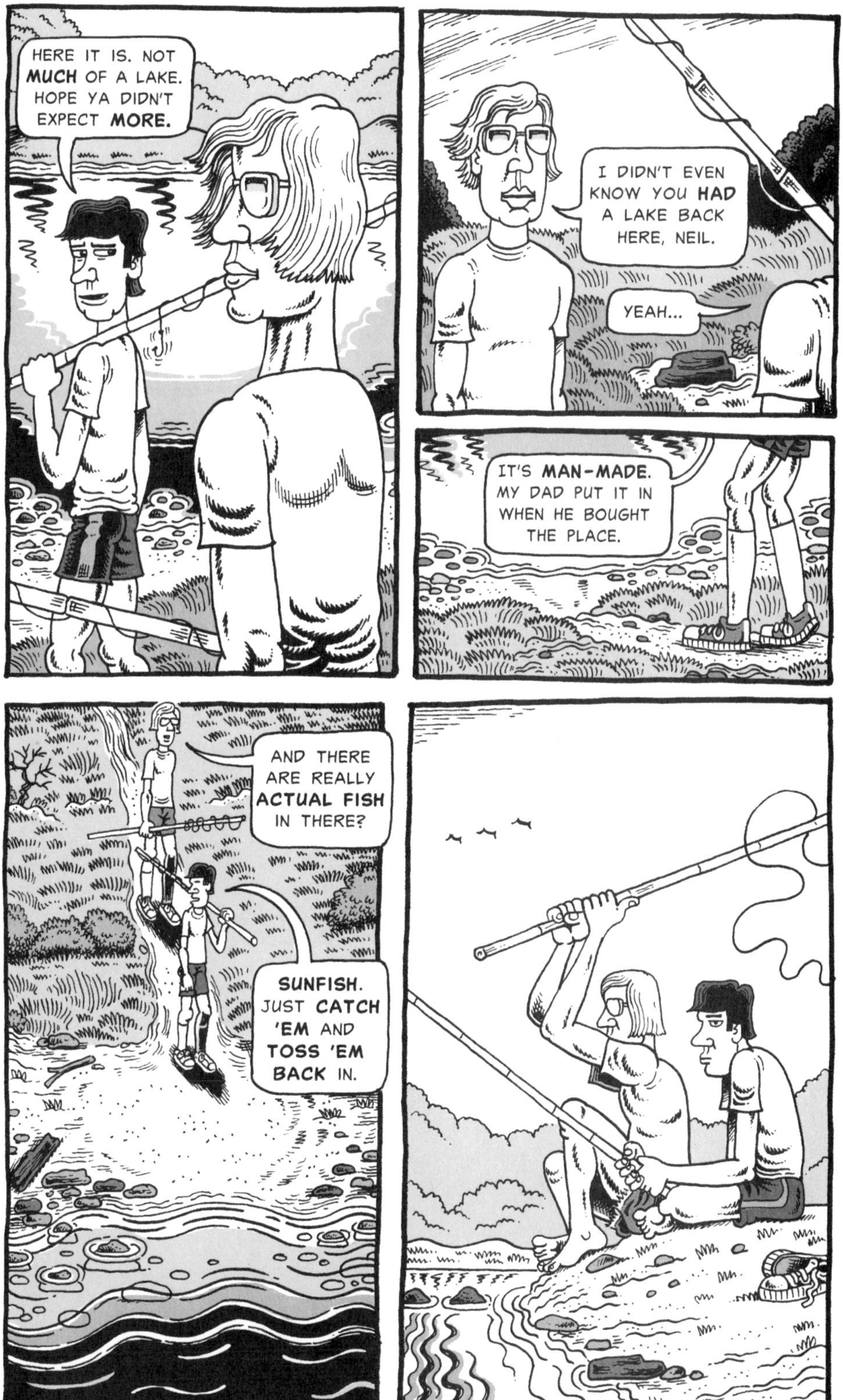
HERE IT IS. NOT **MUCH** OF A LAKE. HOPE YA DIDN'T EXPECT **MORE.**
I DIDN'T EVEN KNOW YOU **HAD** A LAKE BACK HERE, NEIL.
YEAH...
IT'S **MAN-MADE.** MY DAD PUT IT IN WHEN HE BOUGHT THE PLACE.
AND THERE ARE REALLY **ACTUAL FISH** IN THERE?
SUNFISH. JUST **CATCH 'EM** AND **TOSS 'EM BACK** IN.

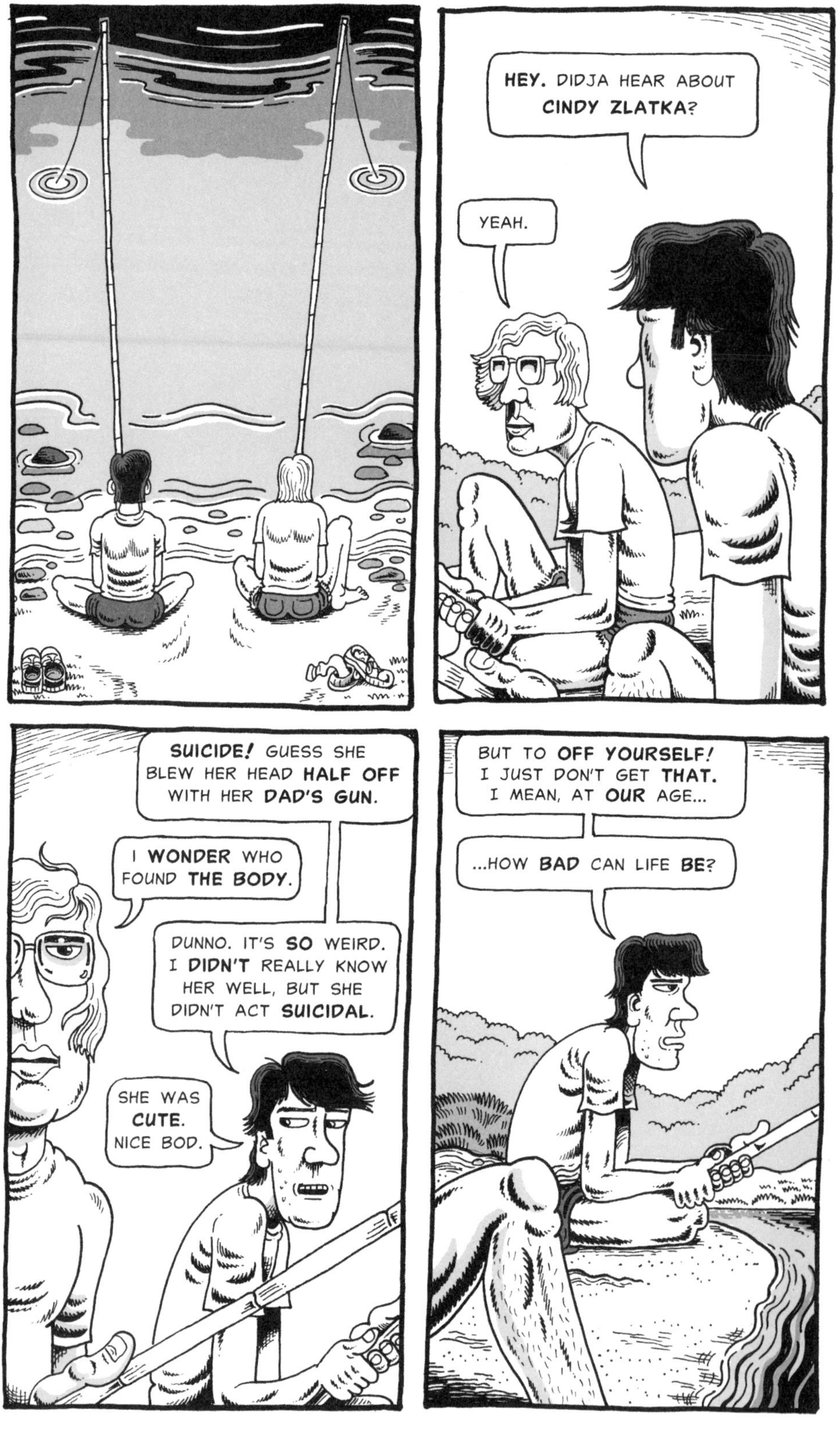
HEY. DIDJA HEAR ABOUT CINDY ZLATKA?
YEAH.
SUICIDE! GUESS SHE BLEW HER HEAD HALF OFF WITH HER DAD'S GUN.
I WONDER WHO FOUND THE BODY.
DUNNO. IT'S SO WEIRD. I DIDN'T REALLY KNOW HER WELL, BUT SHE DIDN'T ACT SUICIDAL.
SHE WAS CUTE. NICE BOD.
BUT TO OFF YOURSELF! I JUST DON'T GET THAT. I MEAN, AT OUR AGE...
...HOW BAD CAN LIFE BE?

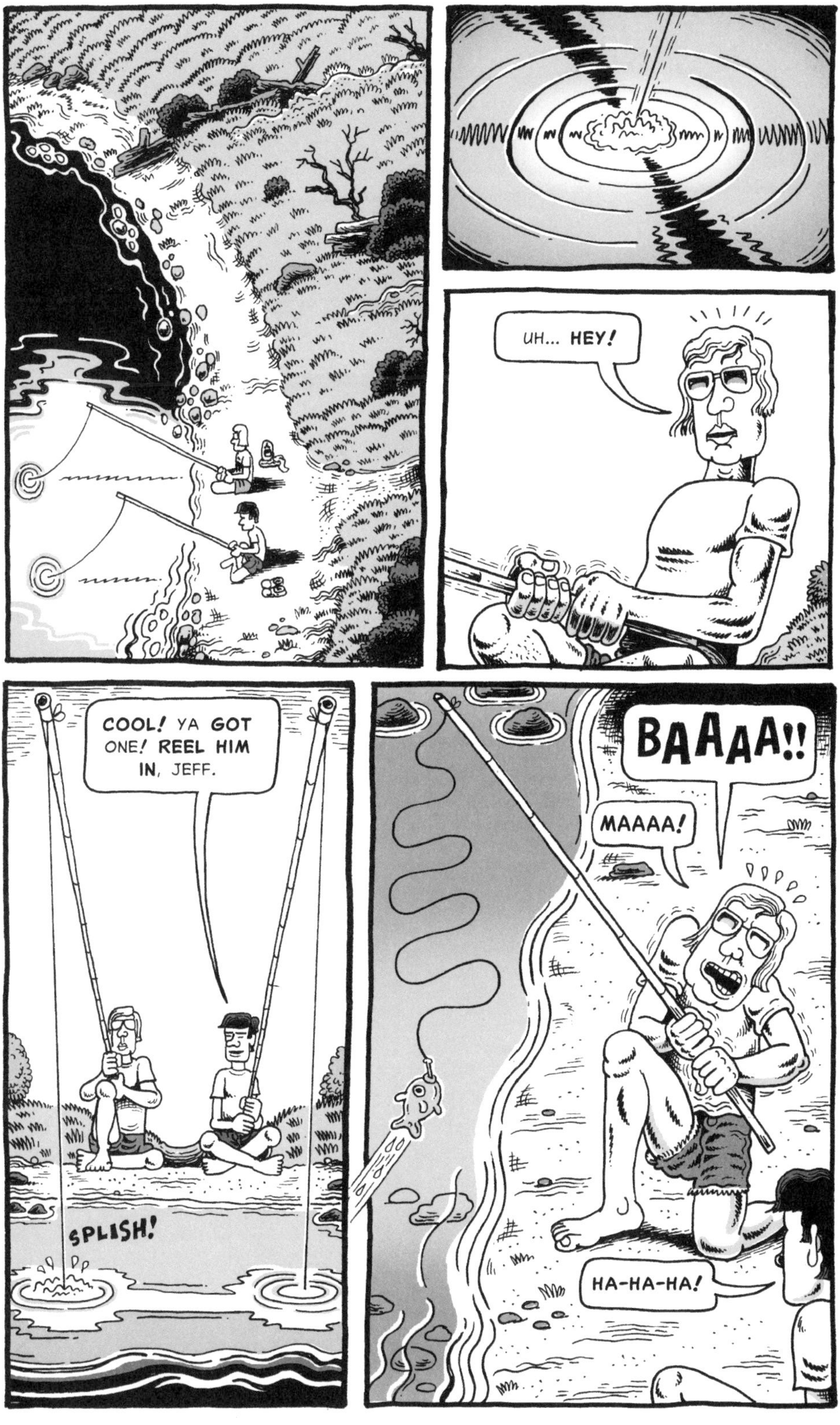
UH... HEY!
COOL! YA GOT ONE! REEL HIM IN, JEFF.
SPLISH!
BAAAA!!
MAAAA!
HA-HA-HA!

FLIP!

FLOP!

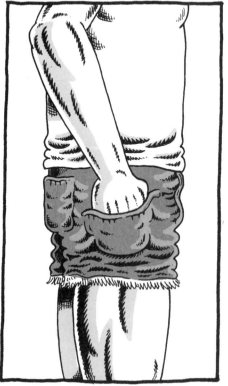

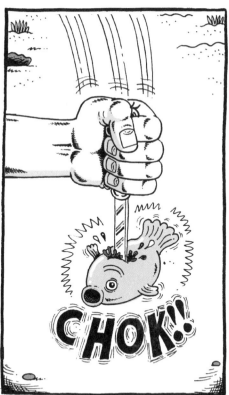

CHOK!!

SLICE!!

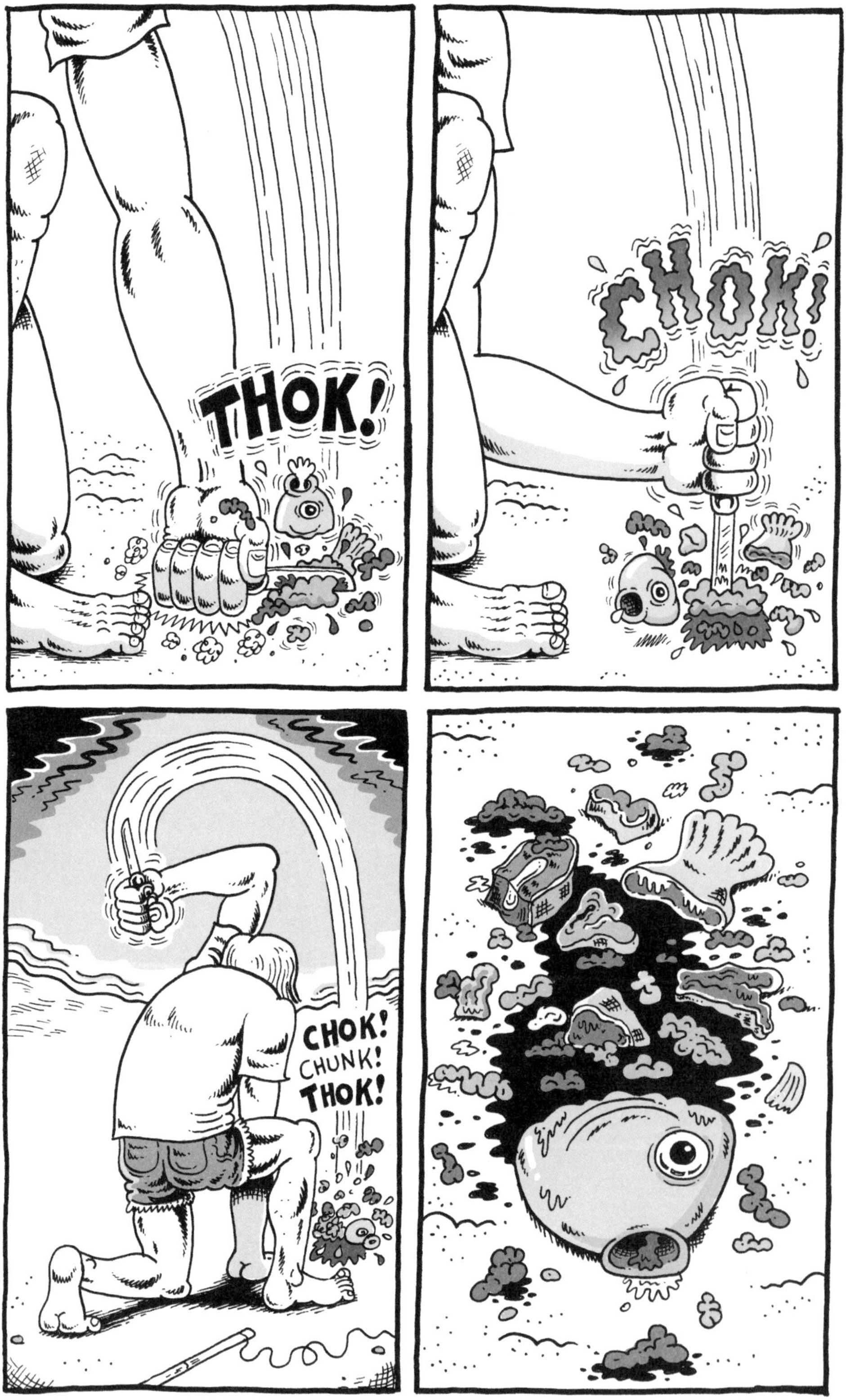
THOK!
CHOK!
CHOK!
CHUNK!
THOK!

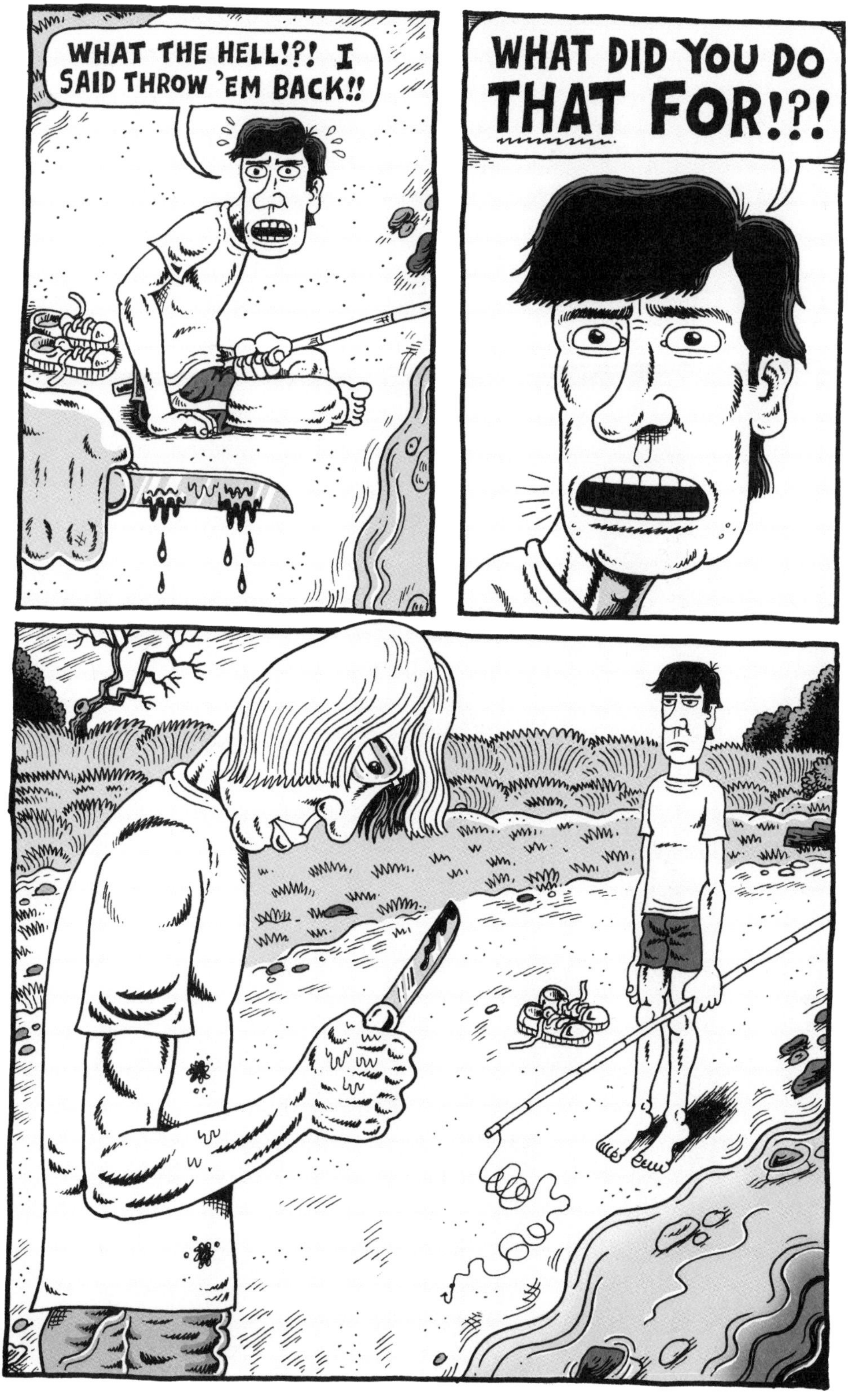
WHAT THE HELL!?! I SAID THROW 'EM BACK!!
WHAT DID YOU DO THAT FOR!?!

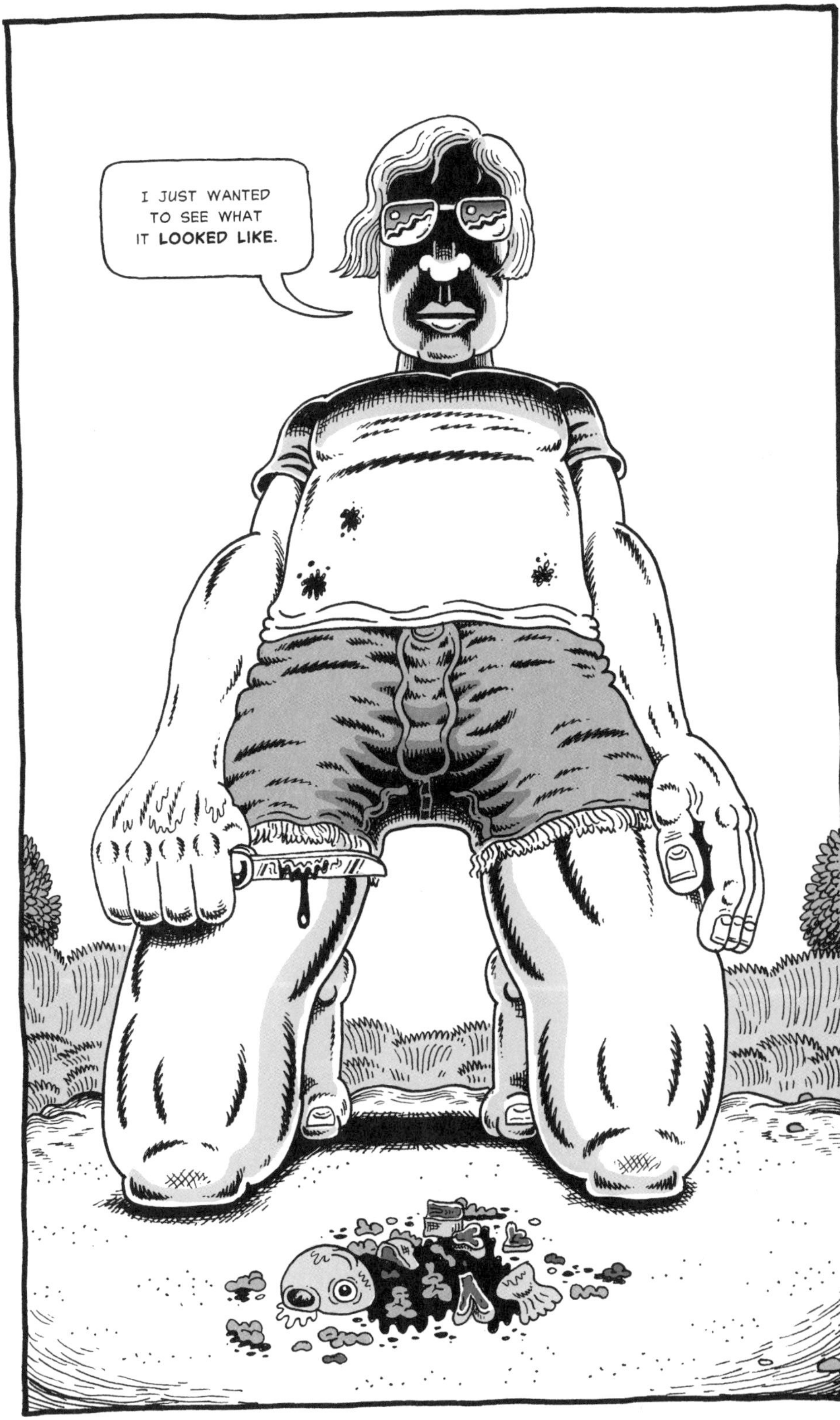
I JUST WANTED TO SEE WHAT IT **LOOKED LIKE**.

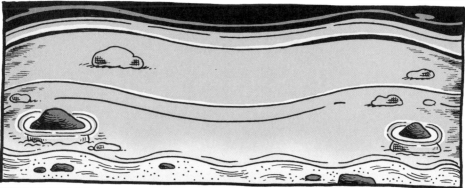

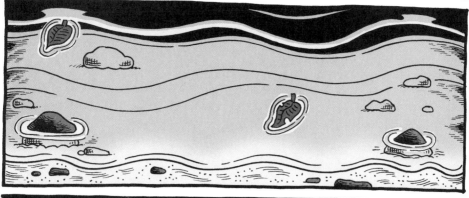

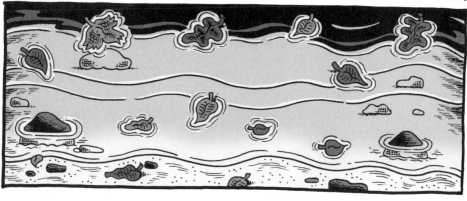

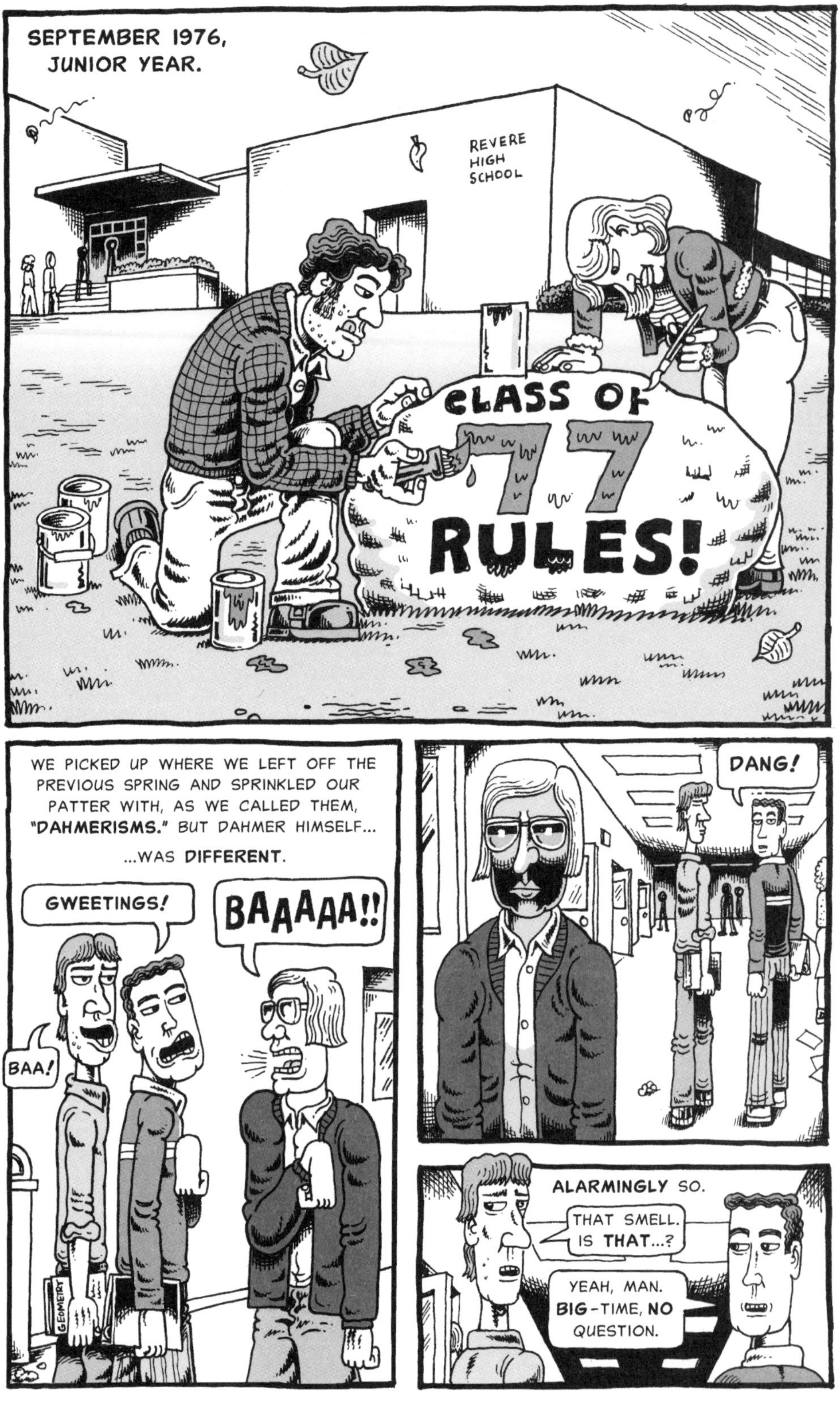
SEPTEMBER 1976,
JUNIOR YEAR.
REVERE
HIGH
SCHOOL
CLASS OF
77
RULES!
WE PICKED UP WHERE WE LEFT OFF THE PREVIOUS SPRING AND SPRINKLED OUR PATTER WITH, AS WE CALLED THEM, "DAHMERISMS." BUT DAHMER HIMSELF...
...WAS DIFFERENT.
GWEETINGS!
BAAAAA!!
BAA!
GEOMETRY
DANG!
ALARMINGLY SO.
THAT SMELL. IS THAT...?
YEAH, MAN. BIG-TIME, NO QUESTION.

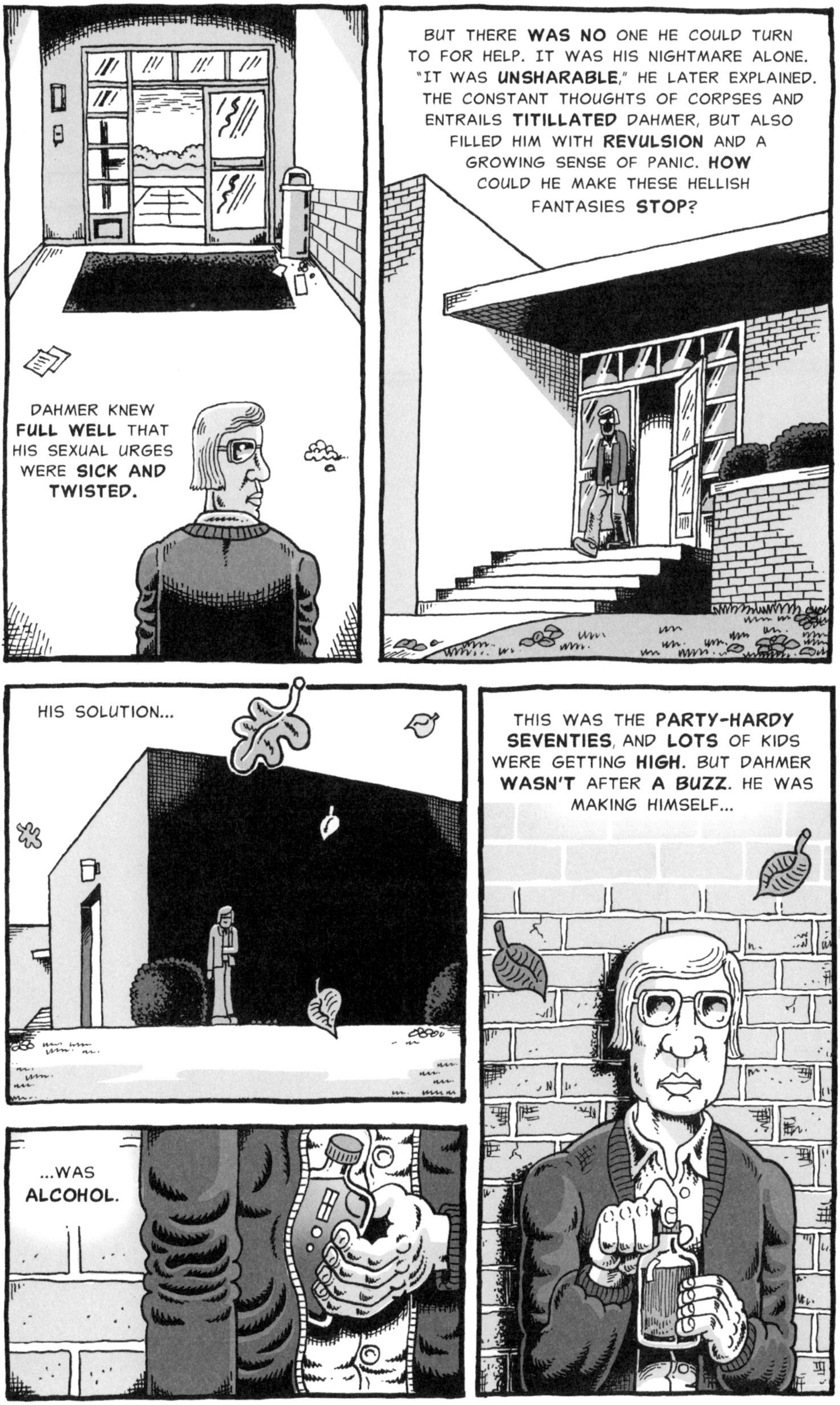

DAHMER KNEW FULL WELL THAT HIS SEXUAL URGES WERE SICK AND TWISTED.
BUT THERE WAS NO ONE HE COULD TURN TO FOR HELP. IT WAS HIS NIGHTMARE ALONE. "IT WAS UNSHARABLE," HE LATER EXPLAINED. THE CONSTANT THOUGHTS OF CORPSES AND ENTRAILS TITILLATED DAHMER, BUT ALSO FILLED HIM WITH REVULSION AND A GROWING SENSE OF PANIC. HOW COULD HE MAKE THESE HELLISH FANTASIES STOP?
HIS SOLUTION...
...WAS ALCOHOL.
THIS WAS THE PARTY-HARDY SEVENTIES, AND LOTS OF KIDS WERE GETTING HIGH. BUT DAHMER WASN'T AFTER A BUZZ. HE WAS MAKING HIMSELF...

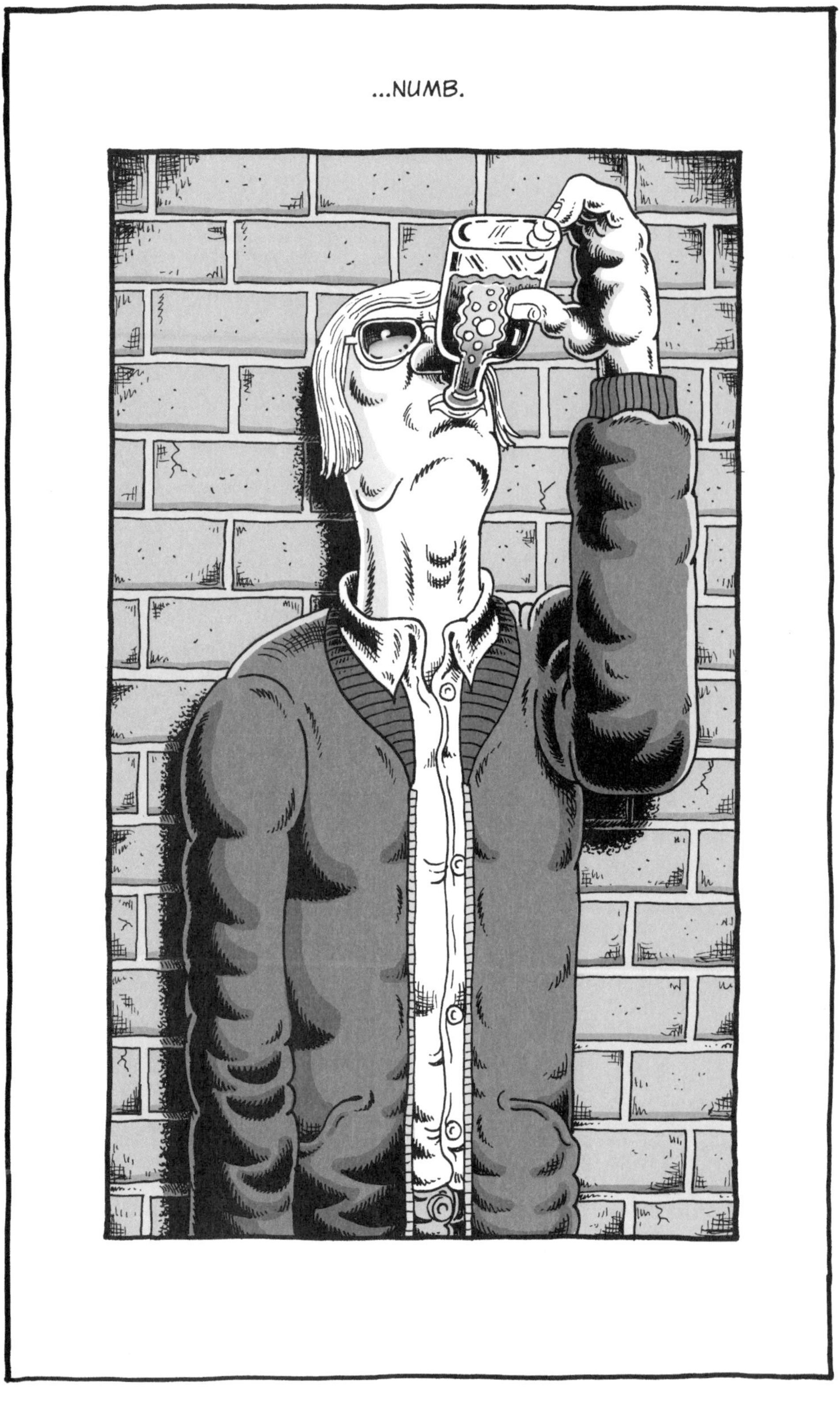
...NUMB.

HE WAS NOW TORTURED EVERY WAKING HOUR BY **GHASTLY SEXUAL FANTASIES.**

PANT.

URGES THAT WERE GROWING **STRONGER** AND **STRONGER.**

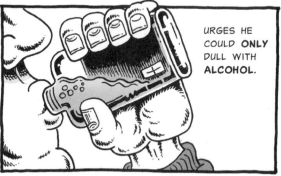

URGES HE COULD **ONLY** DULL WITH **ALCOHOL.**

I DIDN'T **DRINK** OR GET **HIGH.** BUT EVEN IN MY **NAÏVETÉ,** I RECOGNIZED THIS **WASN'T** FUN-LOVING PARTYING...

THIS WAS TWISTED.

PANT.

PANT.

SSSSSLURP!

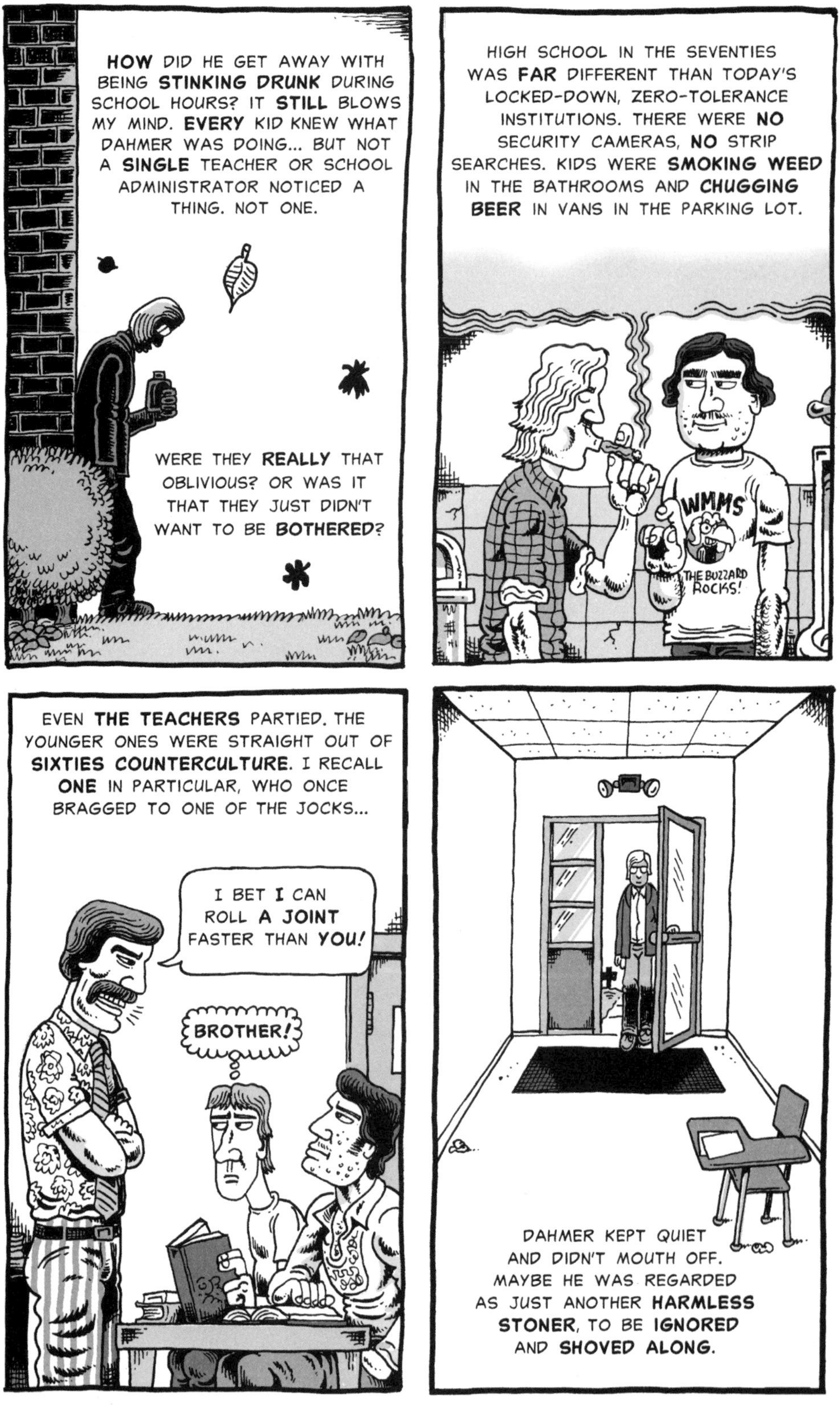
HOW DID HE GET AWAY WITH BEING STINKING DRUNK DURING SCHOOL HOURS? IT STILL BLOWS MY MIND. EVERY KID KNEW WHAT DAHMER WAS DOING... BUT NOT A SINGLE TEACHER OR SCHOOL ADMINISTRATOR NOTICED A THING. NOT ONE.
WERE THEY REALLY THAT OBLIVIOUS? OR WAS IT THAT THEY JUST DIDN'T WANT TO BE BOTHERED?
HIGH SCHOOL IN THE SEVENTIES WAS FAR DIFFERENT THAN TODAY'S LOCKED-DOWN, ZERO-TOLERANCE INSTITUTIONS. THERE WERE NO SECURITY CAMERAS, NO STRIP SEARCHES. KIDS WERE SMOKING WEED IN THE BATHROOMS AND CHUGGING BEER IN VANS IN THE PARKING LOT.
WMMS
THE BUZZARD ROCKS!
EVEN THE TEACHERS PARTIED. THE YOUNGER ONES WERE STRAIGHT OUT OF SIXTIES COUNTERCULTURE. I RECALL ONE IN PARTICULAR, WHO ONCE BRAGGED TO ONE OF THE JOCKS...
I BET I CAN ROLL A JOINT FASTER THAN YOU!
BROTHER!
DAHMER KEPT QUIET AND DIDN'T MOUTH OFF. MAYBE HE WAS REGARDED AS JUST ANOTHER HARMLESS STONER, TO BE IGNORED AND SHOVED ALONG.

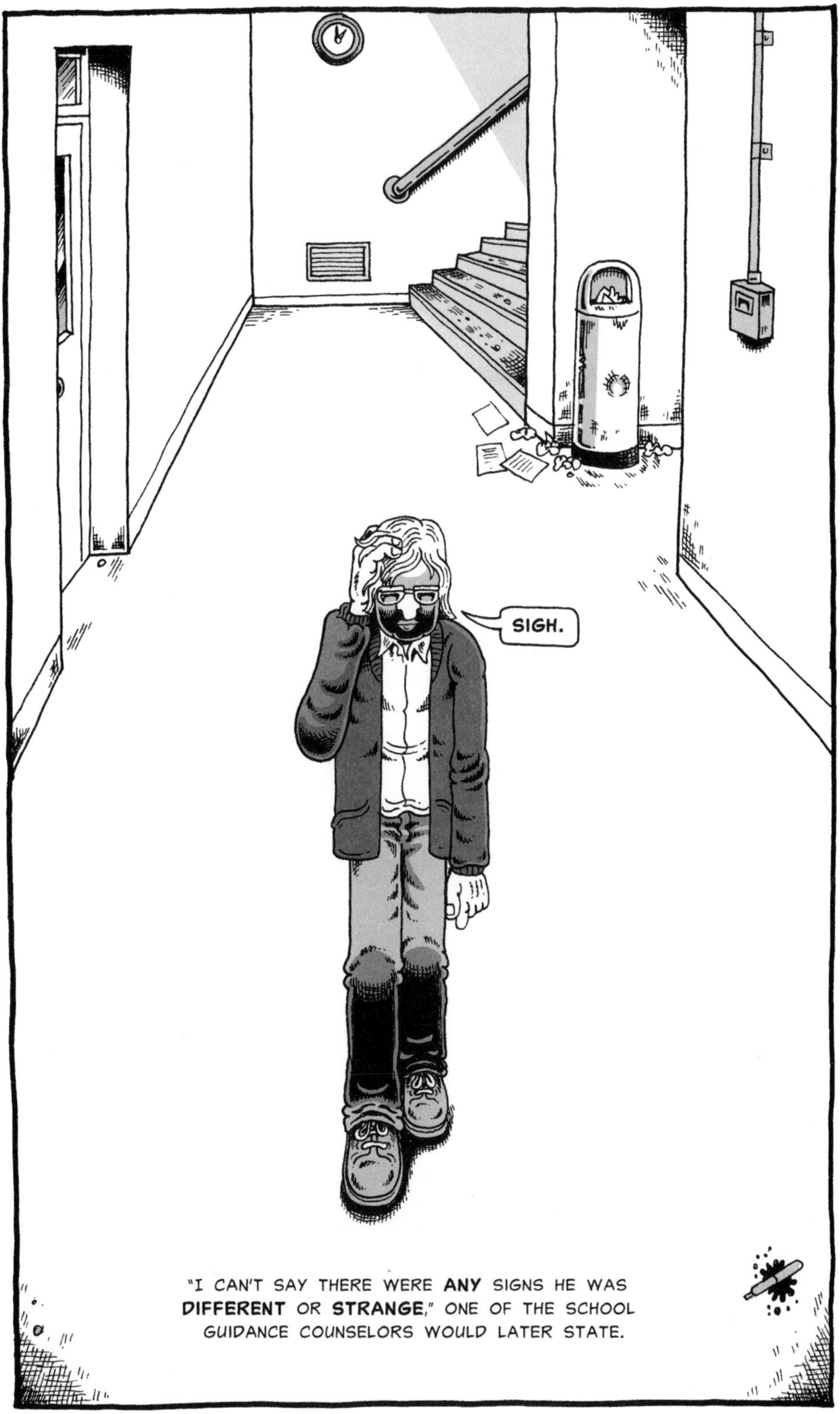
SIGH.
"I CAN'T SAY THERE WERE **ANY** SIGNS HE WAS **DIFFERENT** OR **STRANGE**," ONE OF THE SCHOOL GUIDANCE COUNSELORS WOULD LATER STATE.

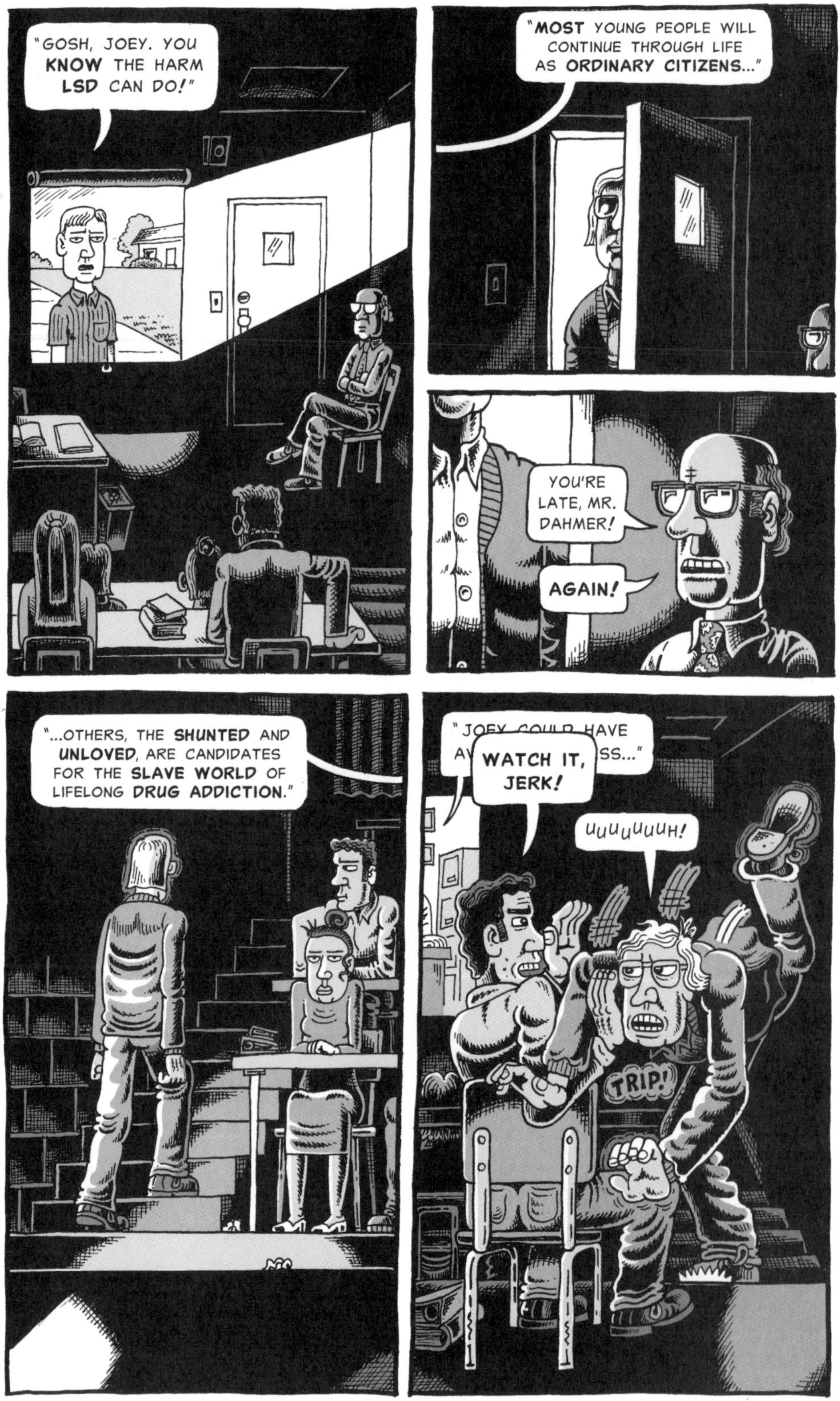
"GOSH, JOEY. YOU KNOW THE HARM LSD CAN DO!"
"MOST YOUNG PEOPLE WILL CONTINUE THROUGH LIFE AS ORDINARY CITIZENS..."
YOU'RE LATE, MR. DAHMER!
AGAIN!
"...OTHERS, THE SHUNTED AND UNLOVED, ARE CANDIDATES FOR THE SLAVE WORLD OF LIFELONG DRUG ADDICTION."
"JOEY COULD HAVE
SS..."
WATCH IT, JERK!
UUUUUUUH!
TRIP!

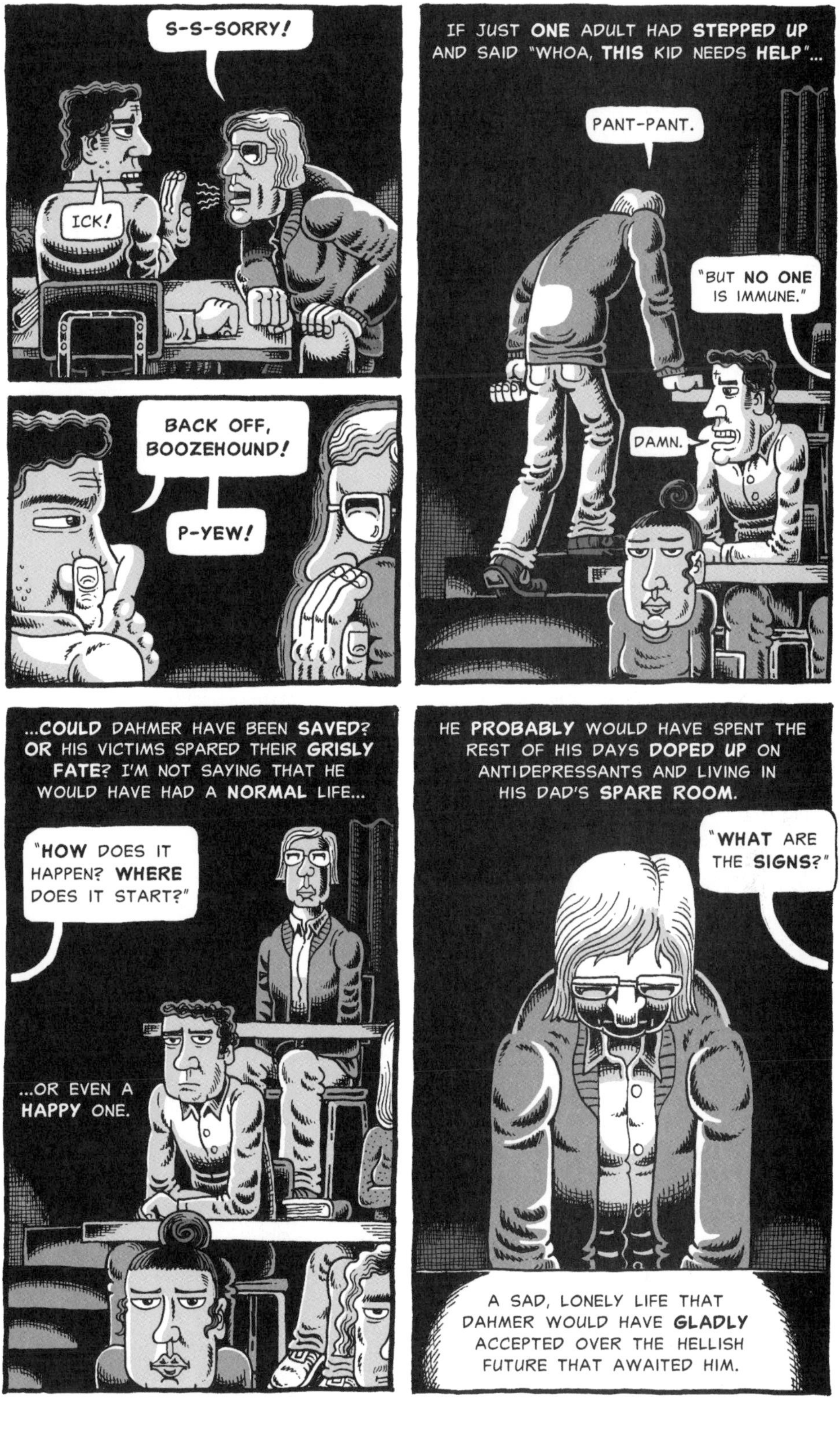
S-S-SORRY!
ICK!
BACK OFF, BOOZEHOUND!
P-YEW!
IF JUST ONE ADULT HAD STEPPED UP AND SAID "WHOA, THIS KID NEEDS HELP"...
PANT-PANT.
"BUT NO ONE IS IMMUNE."
DAMN.
...COULD DAHMER HAVE BEEN SAVED? OR HIS VICTIMS SPARED THEIR GRISLY FATE? I'M NOT SAYING THAT HE WOULD HAVE HAD A NORMAL LIFE...
"HOW DOES IT HAPPEN? WHERE DOES IT START?"
...OR EVEN A HAPPY ONE.
HE PROBABLY WOULD HAVE SPENT THE REST OF HIS DAYS DOPED UP ON ANTIDEPRESSANTS AND LIVING IN HIS DAD'S SPARE ROOM.
"WHAT ARE THE SIGNS?"
A SAD, LONELY LIFE THAT DAHMER WOULD HAVE GLADLY ACCEPTED OVER THE HELLISH FUTURE THAT AWAITED HIM.

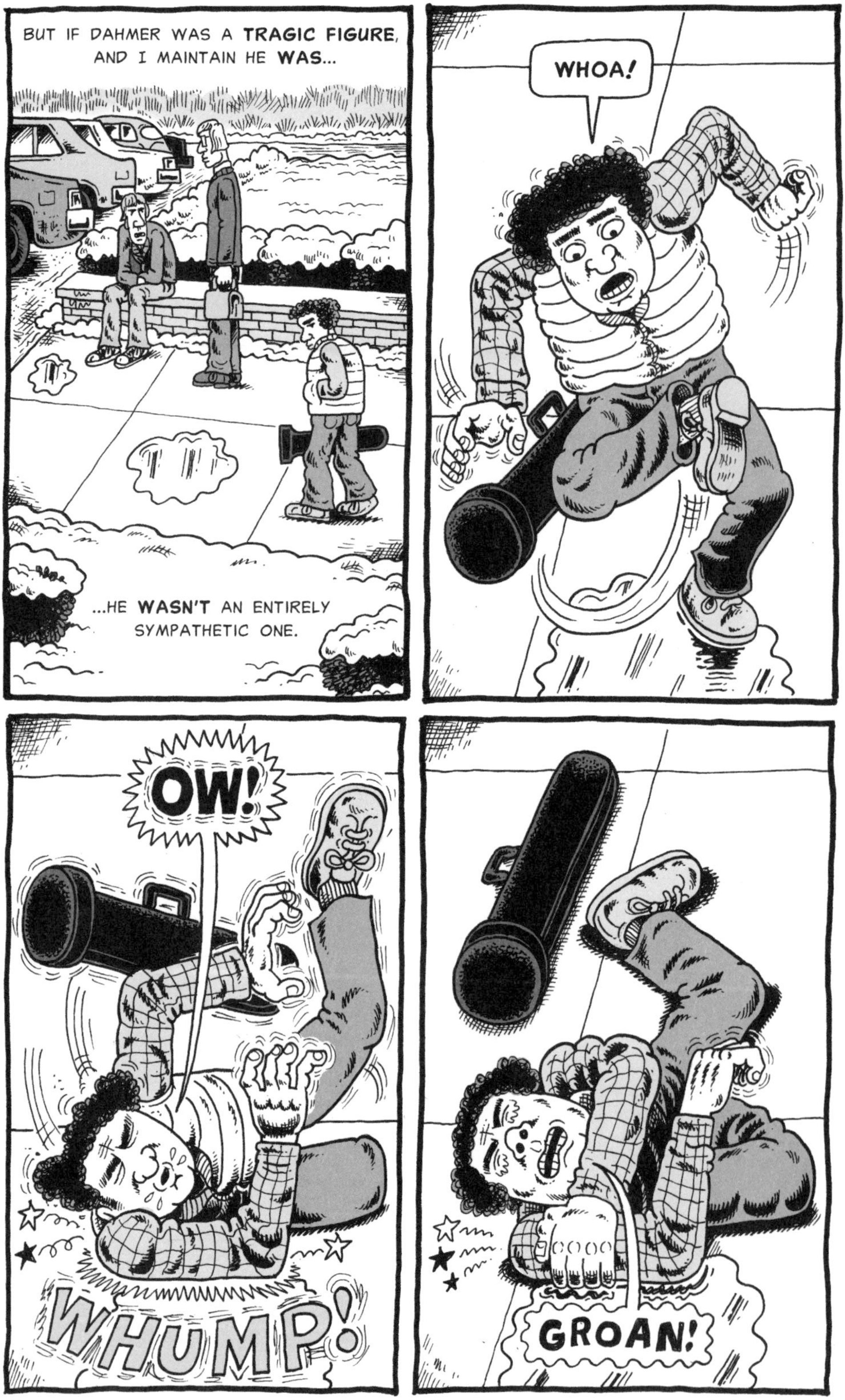

BUT IF DAHMER WAS A TRAGIC FIGURE, AND I MAINTAIN HE WAS...
...HE WASN'T AN ENTIRELY SYMPATHETIC ONE.
WHOA!
OW!
WHUMP!
GROAN!

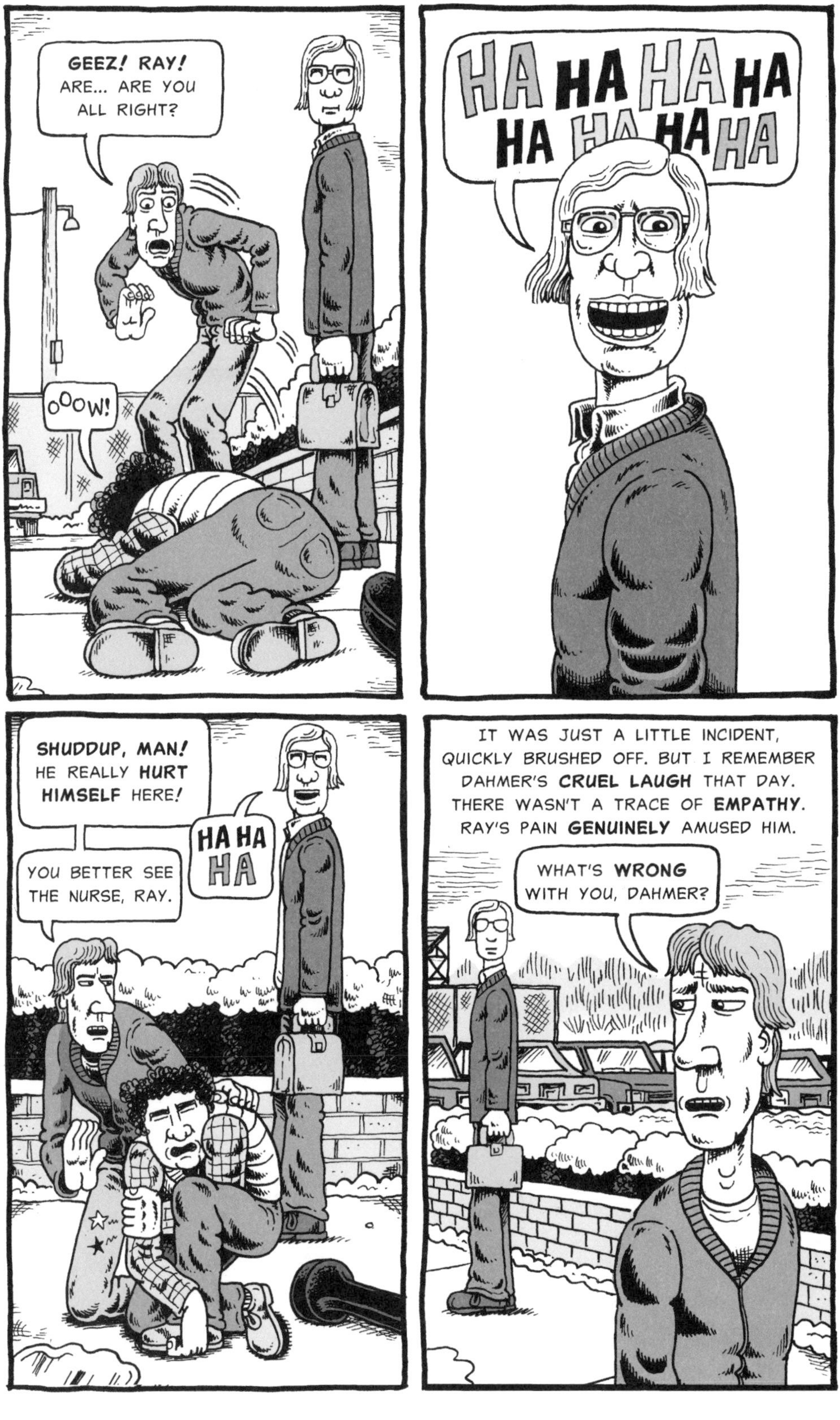

GEEZ! RAY! ARE... ARE YOU ALL RIGHT?
OOOW!
HA HA HA HA HA HA HA HA HA
SHUDDUP, MAN! HE REALLY HURT HIMSELF HERE!
YOU BETTER SEE THE NURSE, RAY.
HA HA HA
IT WAS JUST A LITTLE INCIDENT, QUICKLY BRUSHED OFF. BUT I REMEMBER DAHMER'S CRUEL LAUGH THAT DAY. THERE WASN'T A TRACE OF EMPATHY. RAY'S PAIN GENUINELY AMUSED HIM.
WHAT'S WRONG WITH YOU, DAHMER?

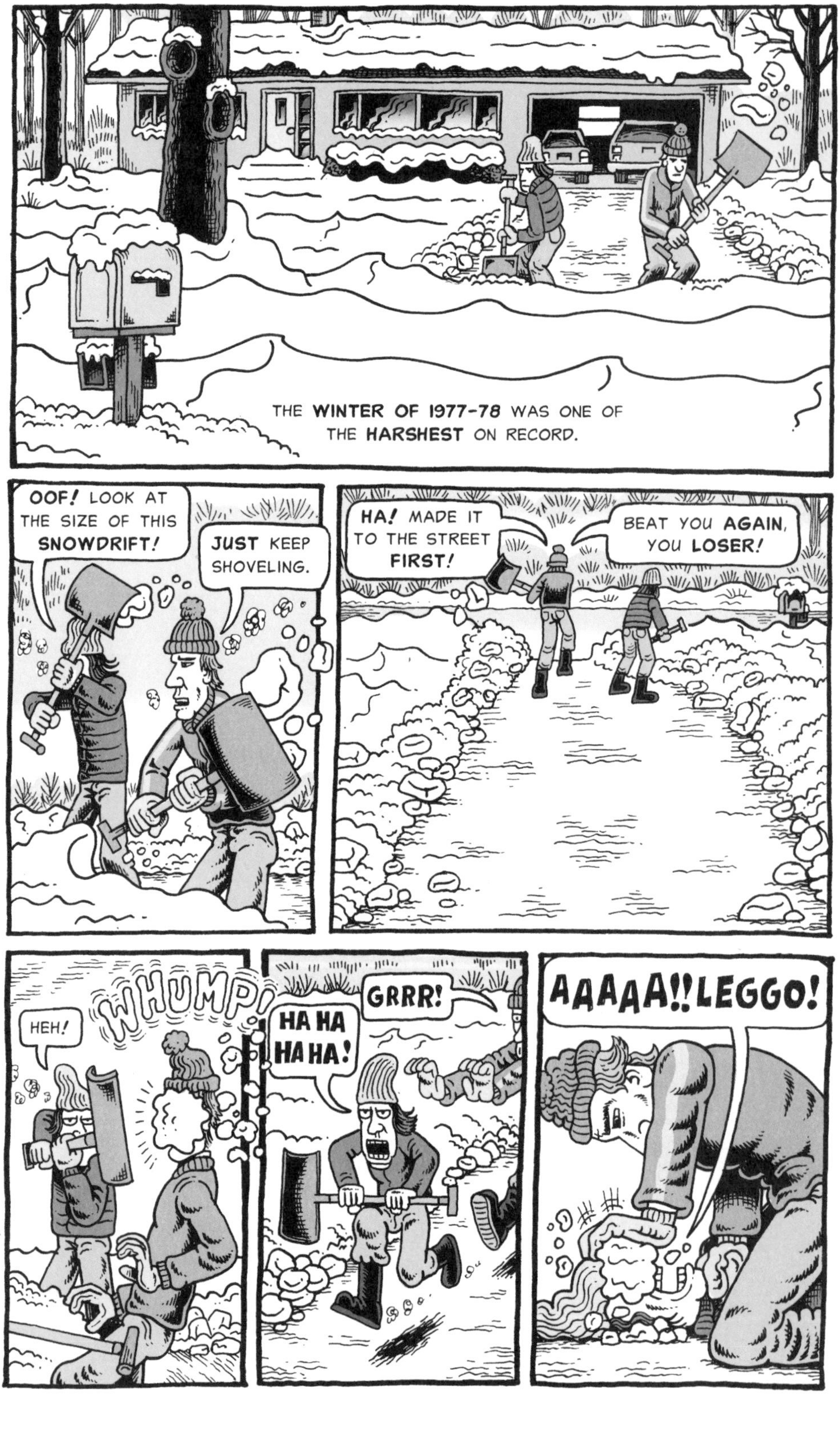
THE WINTER OF 1977-78 WAS ONE OF THE HARSHEST ON RECORD.
OOF! LOOK AT THE SIZE OF THIS SNOWDRIFT!
JUST KEEP SHOVELING.
HA! MADE IT TO THE STREET FIRST!
BEAT YOU AGAIN, YOU LOSER!
HEH!
WHUMP!
HA HA HA HA!
GRRR!
AAAAA!! LEGGO!

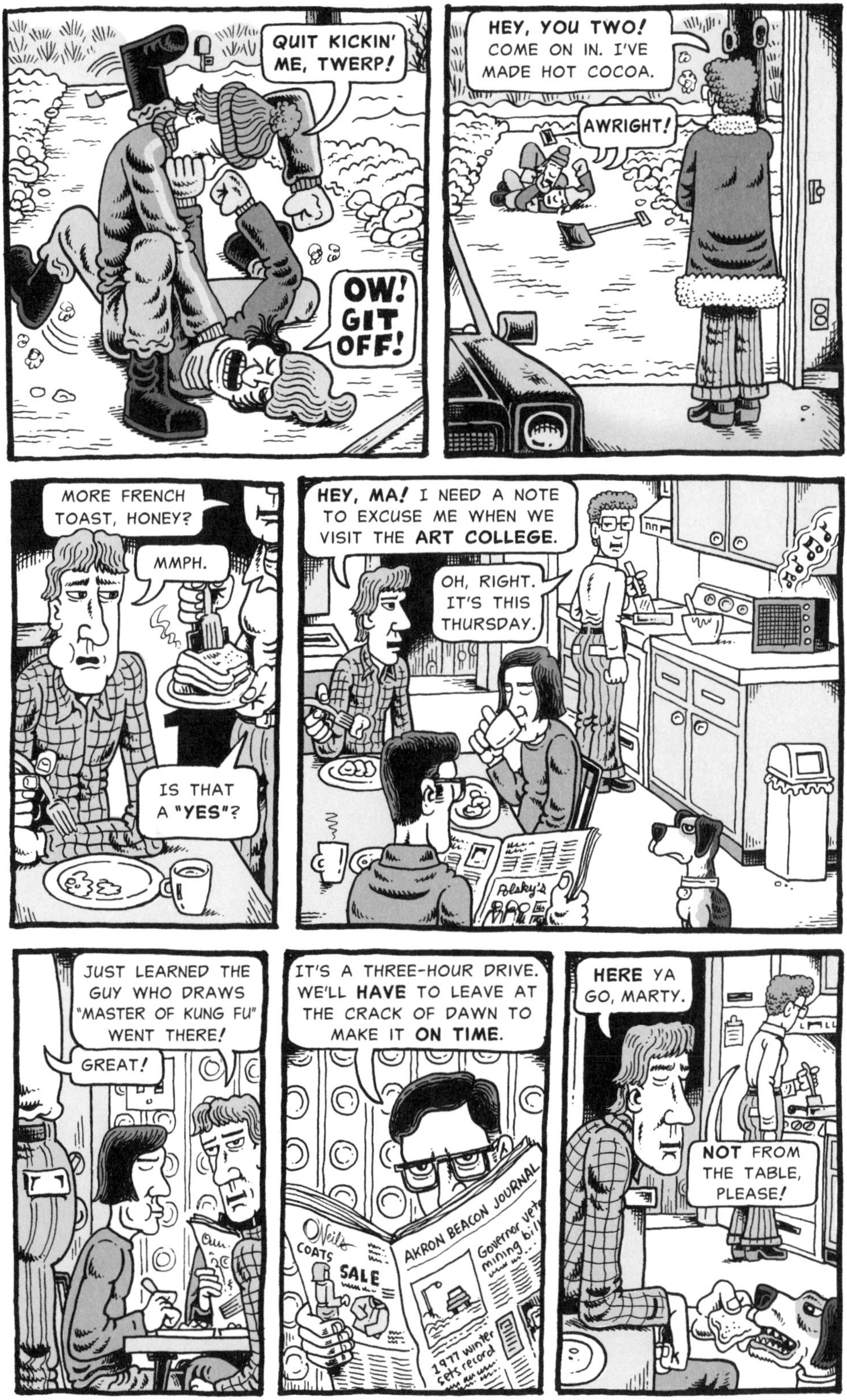
QUIT KICKIN' ME, TWERP!
OW! GIT OFF!
HEY, YOU TWO! COME ON IN. I'VE MADE HOT COCOA.
AWRIGHT!
MORE FRENCH TOAST, HONEY?
MMPH.
IS THAT A "YES"?
HEY, MA! I NEED A NOTE TO EXCUSE ME WHEN WE VISIT THE ART COLLEGE.
OH, RIGHT. IT'S THIS THURSDAY.
JUST LEARNED THE GUY WHO DRAWS "MASTER OF KUNG FU" WENT THERE!
GREAT!
IT'S A THREE-HOUR DRIVE. WE'LL HAVE TO LEAVE AT THE CRACK OF DAWN TO MAKE IT ON TIME.
AKRON BEACON JOURNAL
O'Neil's COATS SALE
1977 winter sets record
HERE YA GO, MARTY.
NOT FROM THE TABLE, PLEASE!

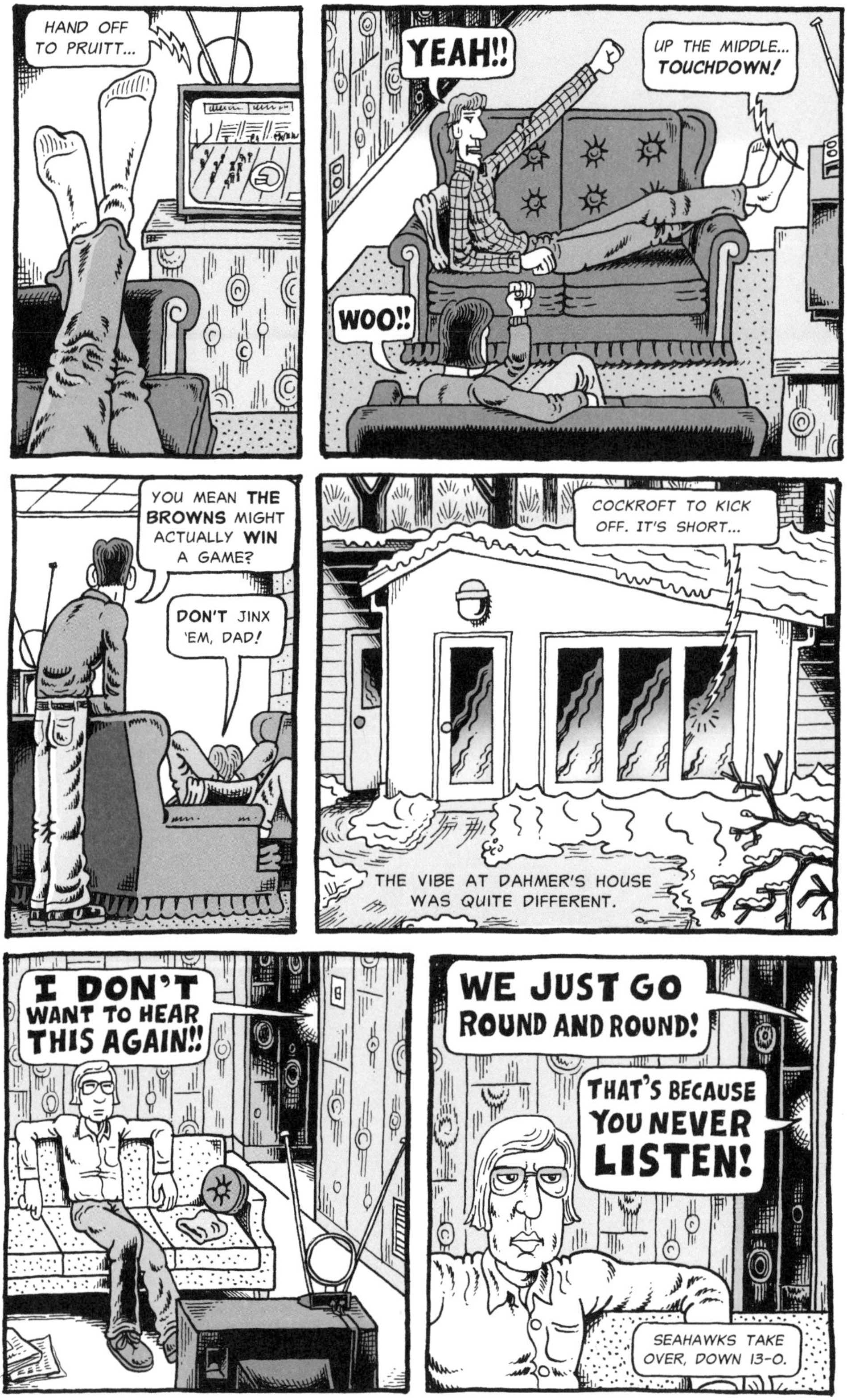
HAND OFF TO PRUITT...
YEAH!!
UP THE MIDDLE... TOUCHDOWN!
WOO!!
YOU MEAN THE BROWNS MIGHT ACTUALLY WIN A GAME?
DON'T JINX 'EM, DAD!
COCKROFT TO KICK OFF. IT'S SHORT...
THE VIBE AT DAHMER'S HOUSE WAS QUITE DIFFERENT.
I DON'T WANT TO HEAR THIS AGAIN!!
WE JUST GO ROUND AND ROUND!
THAT'S BECAUSE YOU NEVER LISTEN!
SEAHAWKS TAKE OVER, DOWN 13-0.

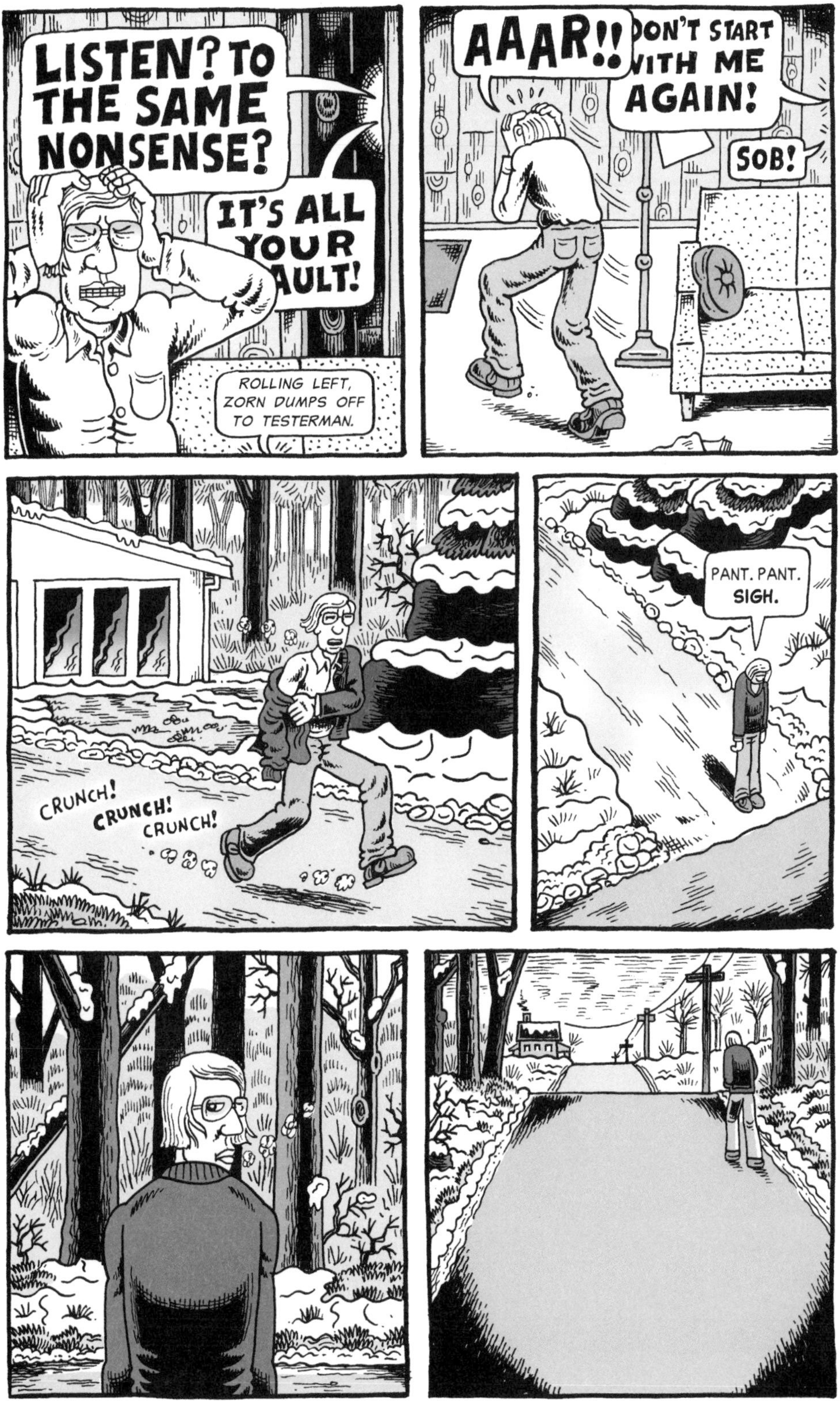
LISTEN? TO THE SAME NONSENSE?
IT'S ALL YOUR FAULT!
ROLLING LEFT, ZORN DUMPS OFF TO TESTERMAN.
AAAR!!
DON'T START WITH ME AGAIN!
SOB!
CRUNCH! CRUNCH! CRUNCH!
PANT. PANT. SIGH.

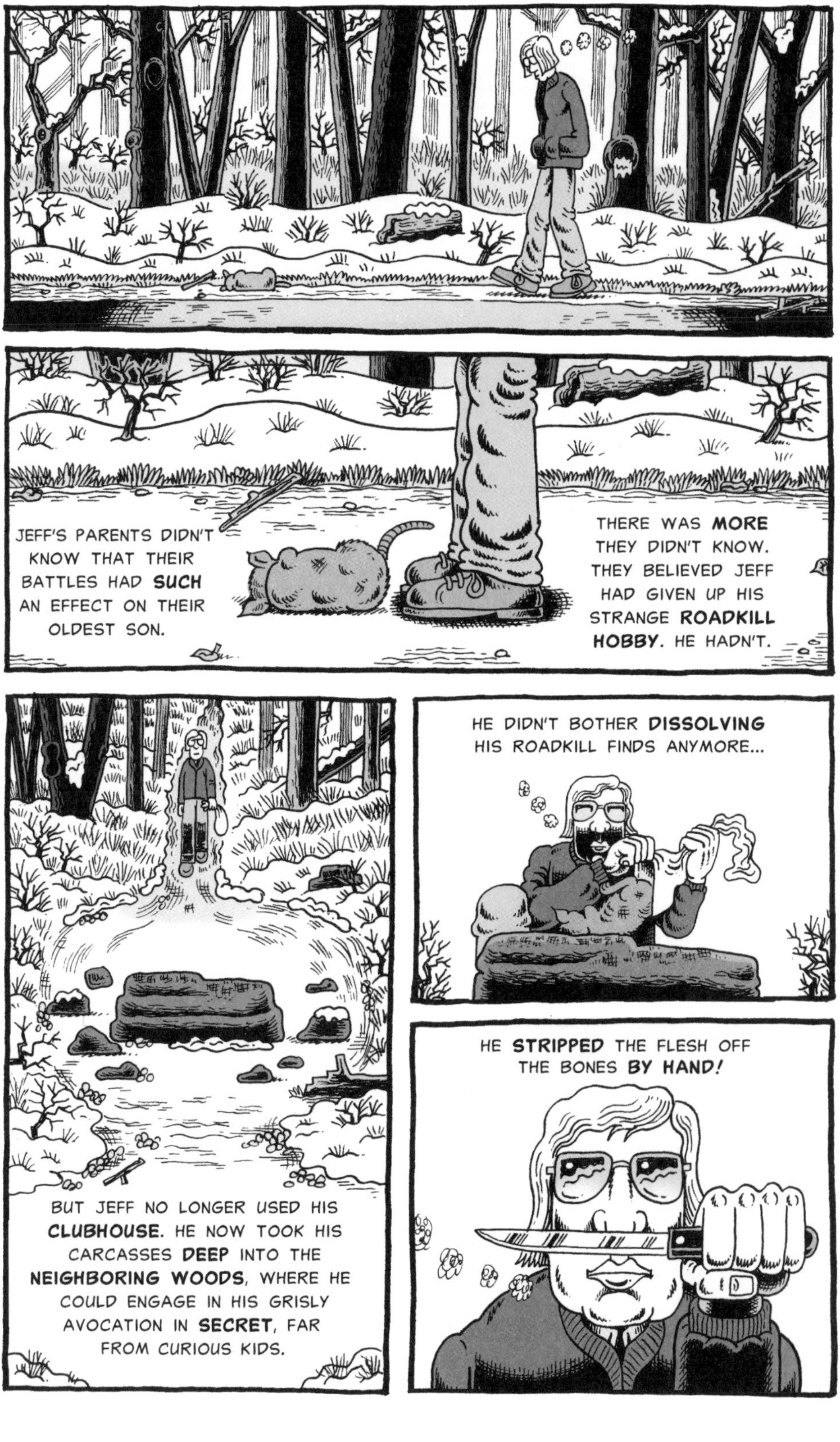
JEFF'S PARENTS DIDN'T KNOW THAT THEIR BATTLES HAD SUCH AN EFFECT ON THEIR OLDEST SON.
THERE WAS MORE THEY DIDN'T KNOW. THEY BELIEVED JEFF HAD GIVEN UP HIS STRANGE ROADKILL HOBBY. HE HADN'T.
BUT JEFF NO LONGER USED HIS CLUBHOUSE. HE NOW TOOK HIS CARCASSES DEEP INTO THE NEIGHBORING WOODS, WHERE HE COULD ENGAGE IN HIS GRISLY AVOCATION IN SECRET, FAR FROM CURIOUS KIDS.
HE DIDN'T BOTHER DISSOLVING HIS ROADKILL FINDS ANYMORE...
HE STRIPPED THE FLESH OFF THE BONES BY HAND!

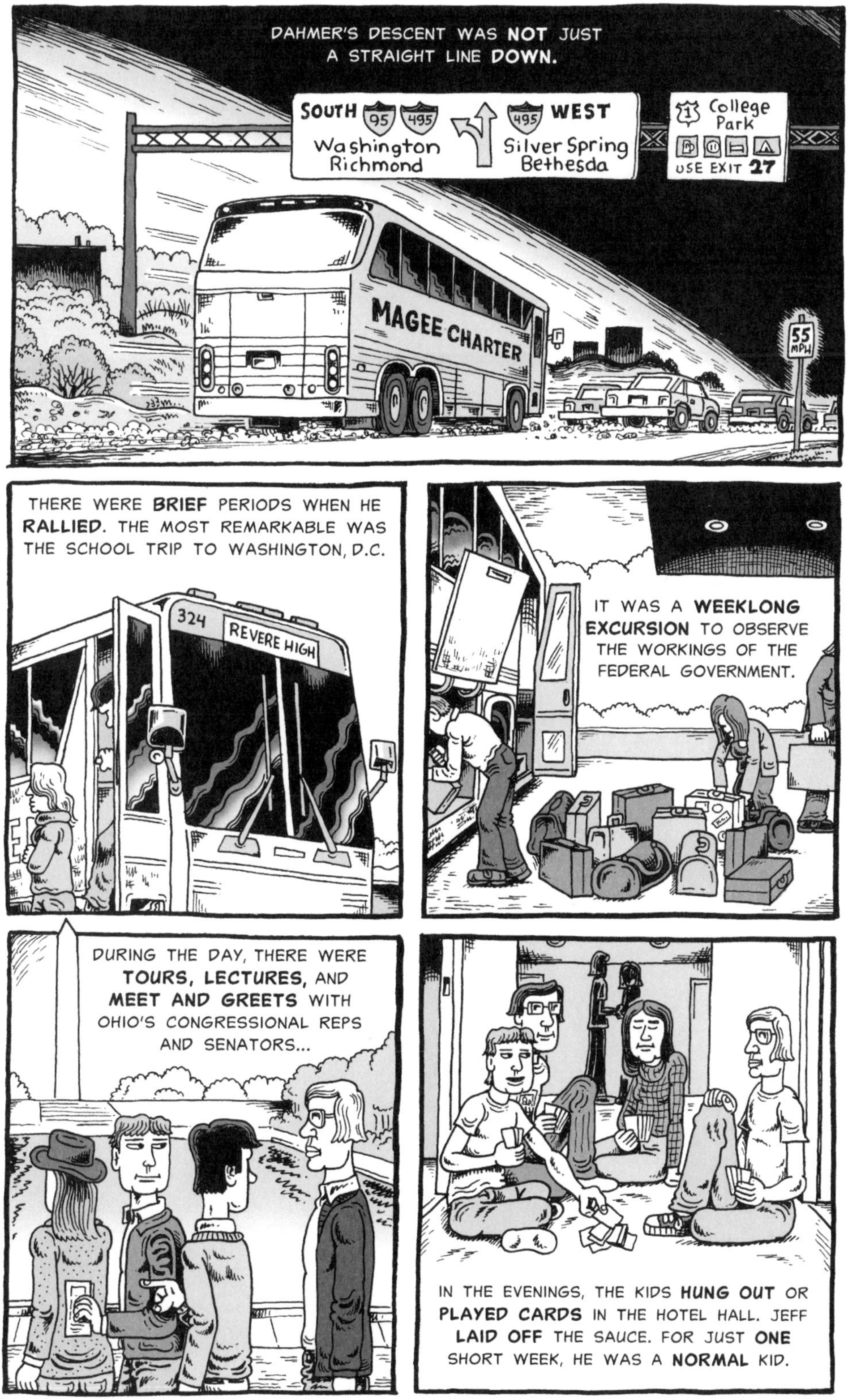
DAHMER'S DESCENT WAS NOT JUST A STRAIGHT LINE DOWN.
SOUTH 95 495 Washington Richmond
495 WEST Silver Spring Bethesda
1 College Park USE EXIT 27
MAGEE CHARTER
55 MPH
THERE WERE BRIEF PERIODS WHEN HE RALLIED. THE MOST REMARKABLE WAS THE SCHOOL TRIP TO WASHINGTON, D.C.
324 REVERE HIGH
IT WAS A WEEKLONG EXCURSION TO OBSERVE THE WORKINGS OF THE FEDERAL GOVERNMENT.
DURING THE DAY, THERE WERE TOURS, LECTURES, AND MEET AND GREETS WITH OHIO'S CONGRESSIONAL REPS AND SENATORS...
IN THE EVENINGS, THE KIDS HUNG OUT OR PLAYED CARDS IN THE HOTEL HALL. JEFF LAID OFF THE SAUCE. FOR JUST ONE SHORT WEEK, HE WAS A NORMAL KID.

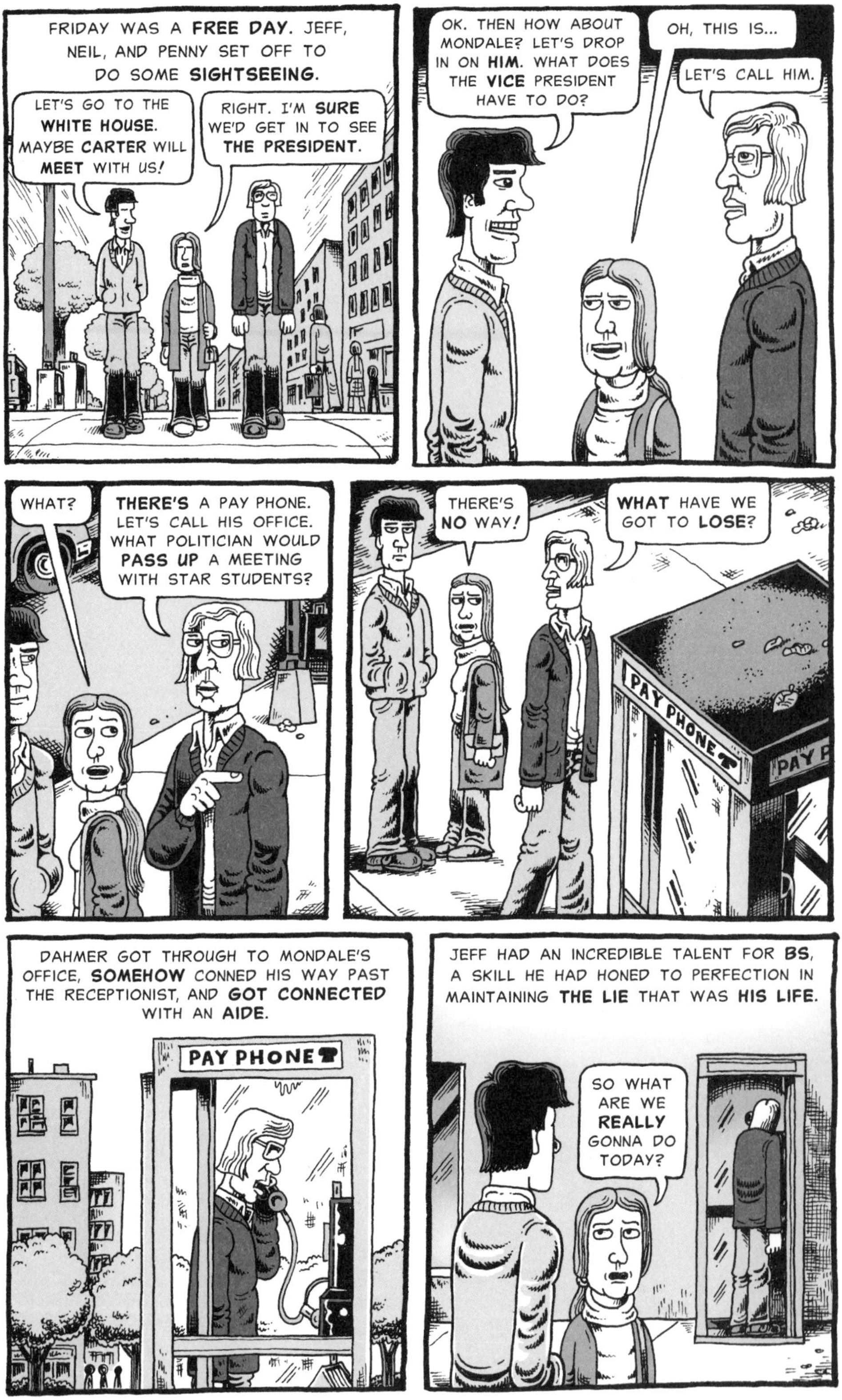

FRIDAY WAS A FREE DAY. JEFF, NEIL, AND PENNY SET OFF TO DO SOME SIGHTSEEING.
LET'S GO TO THE WHITE HOUSE. MAYBE CARTER WILL MEET WITH US!
RIGHT. I'M SURE WE'D GET IN TO SEE THE PRESIDENT.
OK. THEN HOW ABOUT MONDALE? LET'S DROP IN ON HIM. WHAT DOES THE VICE PRESIDENT HAVE TO DO?
OH, THIS IS...
LET'S CALL HIM.
WHAT?
THERE'S A PAY PHONE. LET'S CALL HIS OFFICE. WHAT POLITICIAN WOULD PASS UP A MEETING WITH STAR STUDENTS?
THERE'S NO WAY!
WHAT HAVE WE GOT TO LOSE?
PAY PHONE
PAY P
DAHMER GOT THROUGH TO MONDALE'S OFFICE, SOMEHOW CONNED HIS WAY PAST THE RECEPTIONIST, AND GOT CONNECTED WITH AN AIDE.
PAY PHONE
JEFF HAD AN INCREDIBLE TALENT FOR BS, A SKILL HE HAD HONED TO PERFECTION IN MAINTAINING THE LIE THAT WAS HIS LIFE.
SO WHAT ARE WE REALLY GONNA DO TODAY?

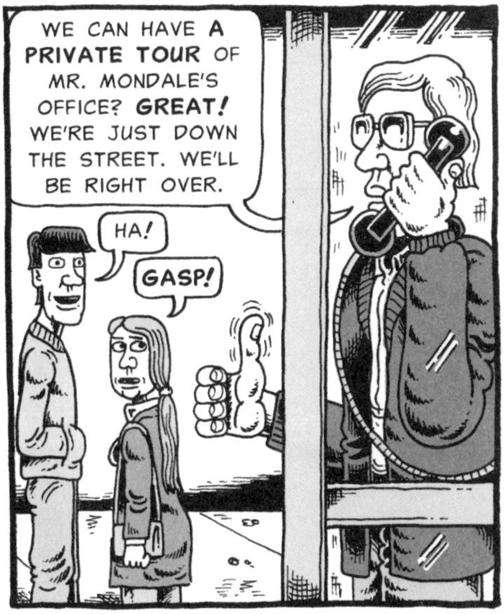
WE CAN HAVE **A PRIVATE TOUR** OF MR. MONDALE'S OFFICE? **GREAT!** WE'RE JUST DOWN THE STREET. WE'LL BE RIGHT OVER.
HA!
GASP!

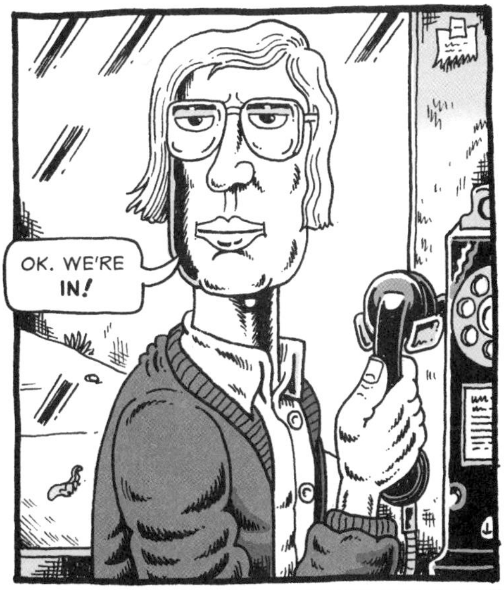
OK. WE'RE **IN!**

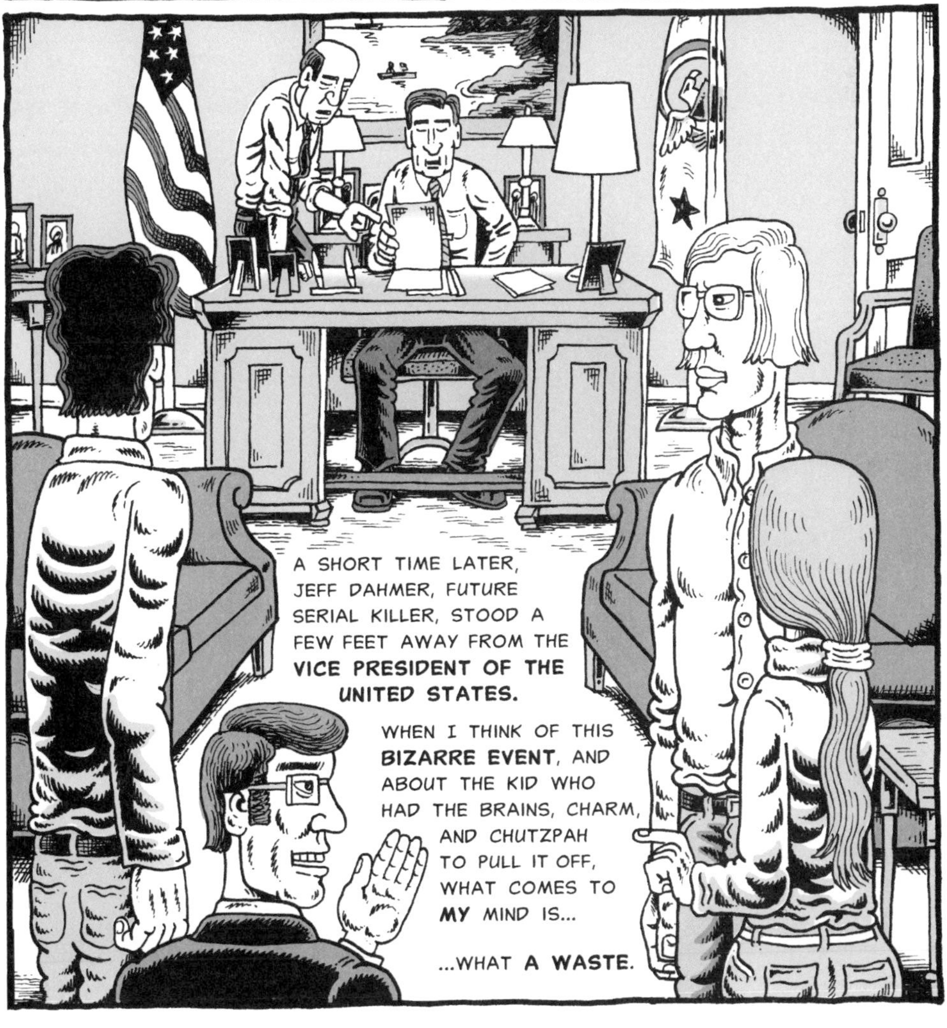
A SHORT TIME LATER, JEFF DAHMER, FUTURE SERIAL KILLER, STOOD A FEW FEET AWAY FROM THE **VICE PRESIDENT OF THE UNITED STATES.**
WHEN I THINK OF THIS **BIZARRE EVENT**, AND ABOUT THE KID WHO HAD THE BRAINS, CHARM, AND CHUTZPAH TO PULL IT OFF, WHAT COMES TO **MY** MIND IS...
...WHAT **A WASTE**.

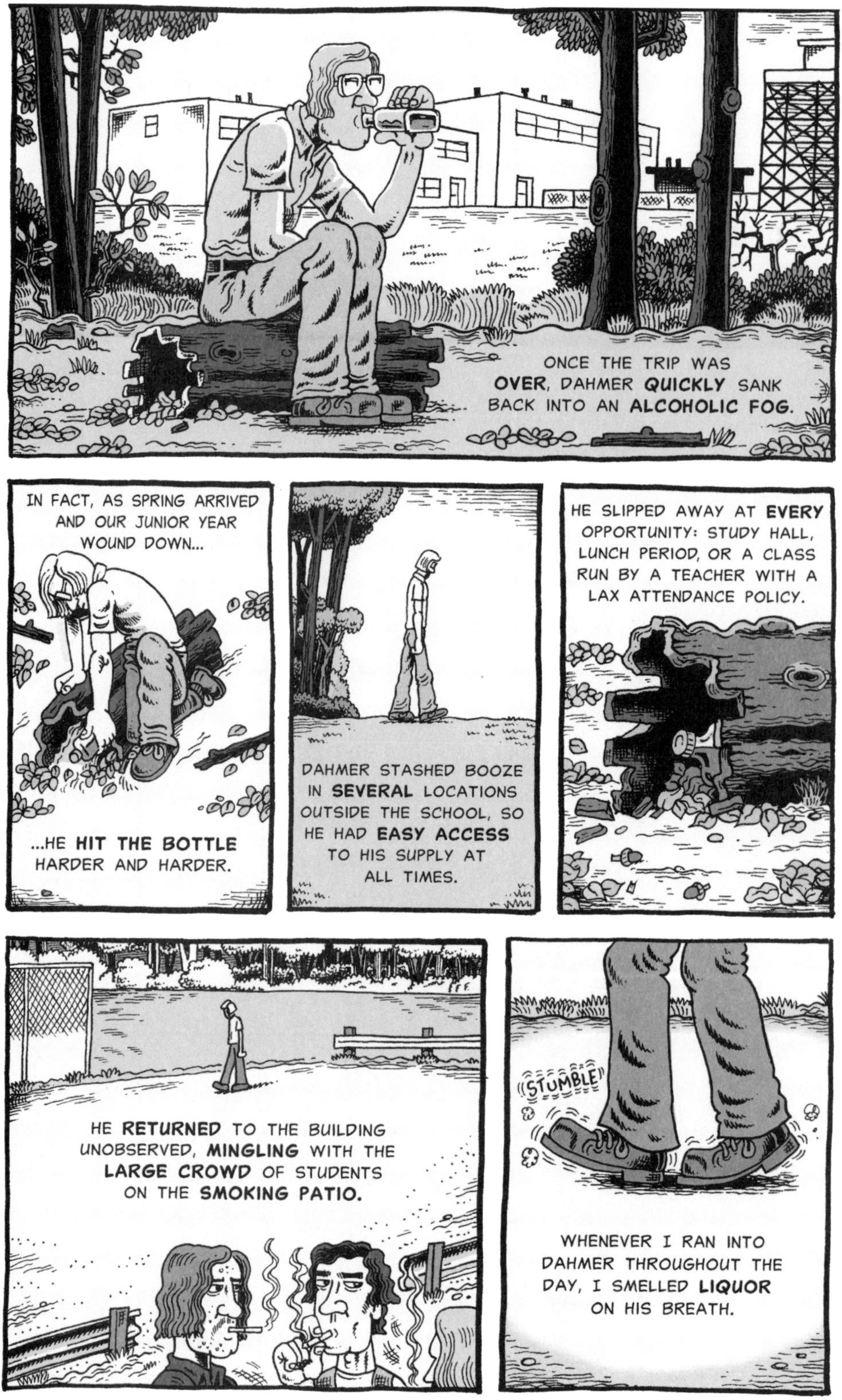

ONCE THE TRIP WAS OVER, DAHMER QUICKLY SANK BACK INTO AN ALCOHOLIC FOG.
IN FACT, AS SPRING ARRIVED AND OUR JUNIOR YEAR WOUND DOWN...
...HE HIT THE BOTTLE HARDER AND HARDER.
DAHMER STASHED BOOZE IN SEVERAL LOCATIONS OUTSIDE THE SCHOOL, SO HE HAD EASY ACCESS TO HIS SUPPLY AT ALL TIMES.
HE SLIPPED AWAY AT EVERY OPPORTUNITY: STUDY HALL, LUNCH PERIOD, OR A CLASS RUN BY A TEACHER WITH A LAX ATTENDANCE POLICY.
HE RETURNED TO THE BUILDING UNOBSERVED, MINGLING WITH THE LARGE CROWD OF STUDENTS ON THE SMOKING PATIO.
STUMBLE
WHENEVER I RAN INTO DAHMER THROUGHOUT THE DAY, I SMELLED LIQUOR ON HIS BREATH.

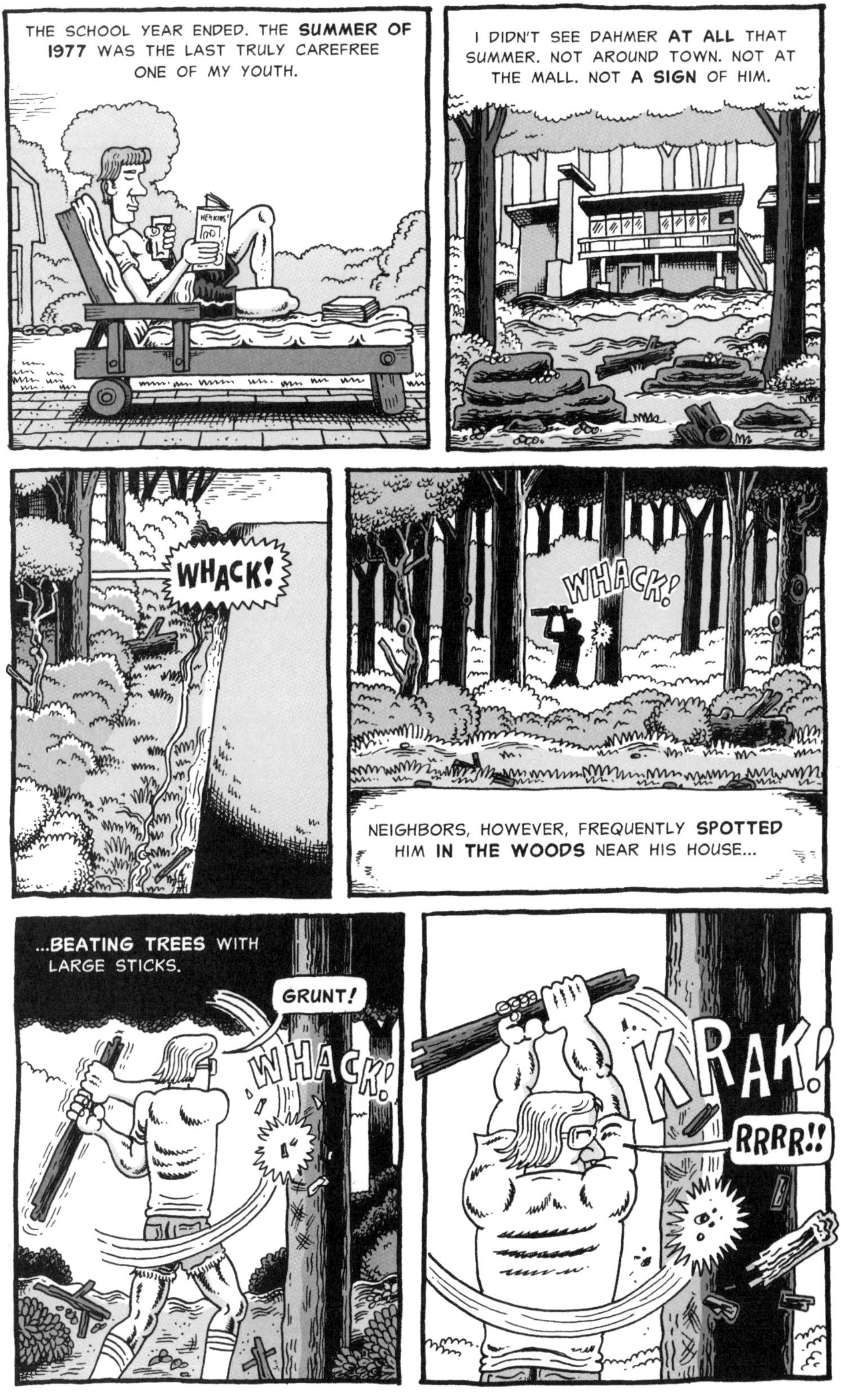
THE SCHOOL YEAR ENDED. THE SUMMER OF 1977 WAS THE LAST TRULY CAREFREE ONE OF MY YOUTH.
I DIDN'T SEE DAHMER AT ALL THAT SUMMER. NOT AROUND TOWN. NOT AT THE MALL. NOT A SIGN OF HIM.
WHACK!
WHACK!
NEIGHBORS, HOWEVER, FREQUENTLY SPOTTED HIM IN THE WOODS NEAR HIS HOUSE...
...BEATING TREES WITH LARGE STICKS.
GRUNT!
WHACK!
KRAK!
RRRR!!

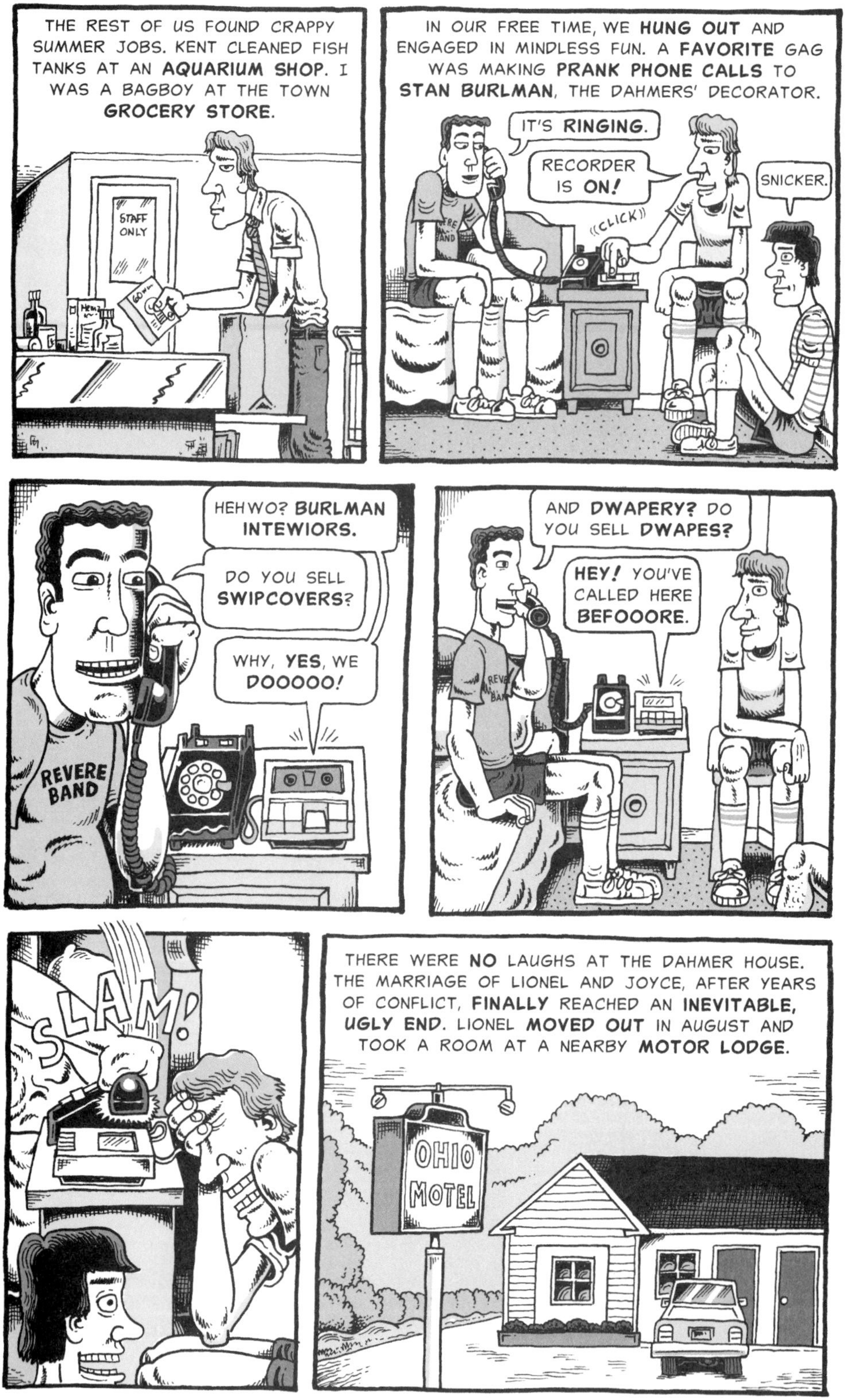
THE REST OF US FOUND CRAPPY SUMMER JOBS. KENT CLEANED FISH TANKS AT AN **AQUARIUM SHOP**. I WAS A BAGBOY AT THE TOWN **GROCERY STORE**.
STAFF ONLY
IN OUR FREE TIME, WE **HUNG OUT** AND ENGAGED IN MINDLESS FUN. A **FAVORITE** GAG WAS MAKING **PRANK PHONE CALLS** TO **STAN BURLMAN**, THE DAHMERS' DECORATOR.
IT'S **RINGING**.
RECORDER IS **ON!**
((CLICK))
SNICKER.
HEHWO? **BURLMAN INTEWIORS.**
DO YOU SELL **SWIPCOVERS?**
WHY, **YES**, WE **DOOOOO!**
REVERE BAND
AND **DWAPERY?** DO YOU SELL **DWAPES?**
HEY! YOU'VE CALLED HERE **BEFOOORE.**
SLAM!
THERE WERE **NO** LAUGHS AT THE DAHMER HOUSE. THE MARRIAGE OF LIONEL AND JOYCE, AFTER YEARS OF CONFLICT, **FINALLY** REACHED AN **INEVITABLE, UGLY END**. LIONEL **MOVED OUT** IN AUGUST AND TOOK A ROOM AT A NEARBY **MOTOR LODGE**.
OHIO MOTEL

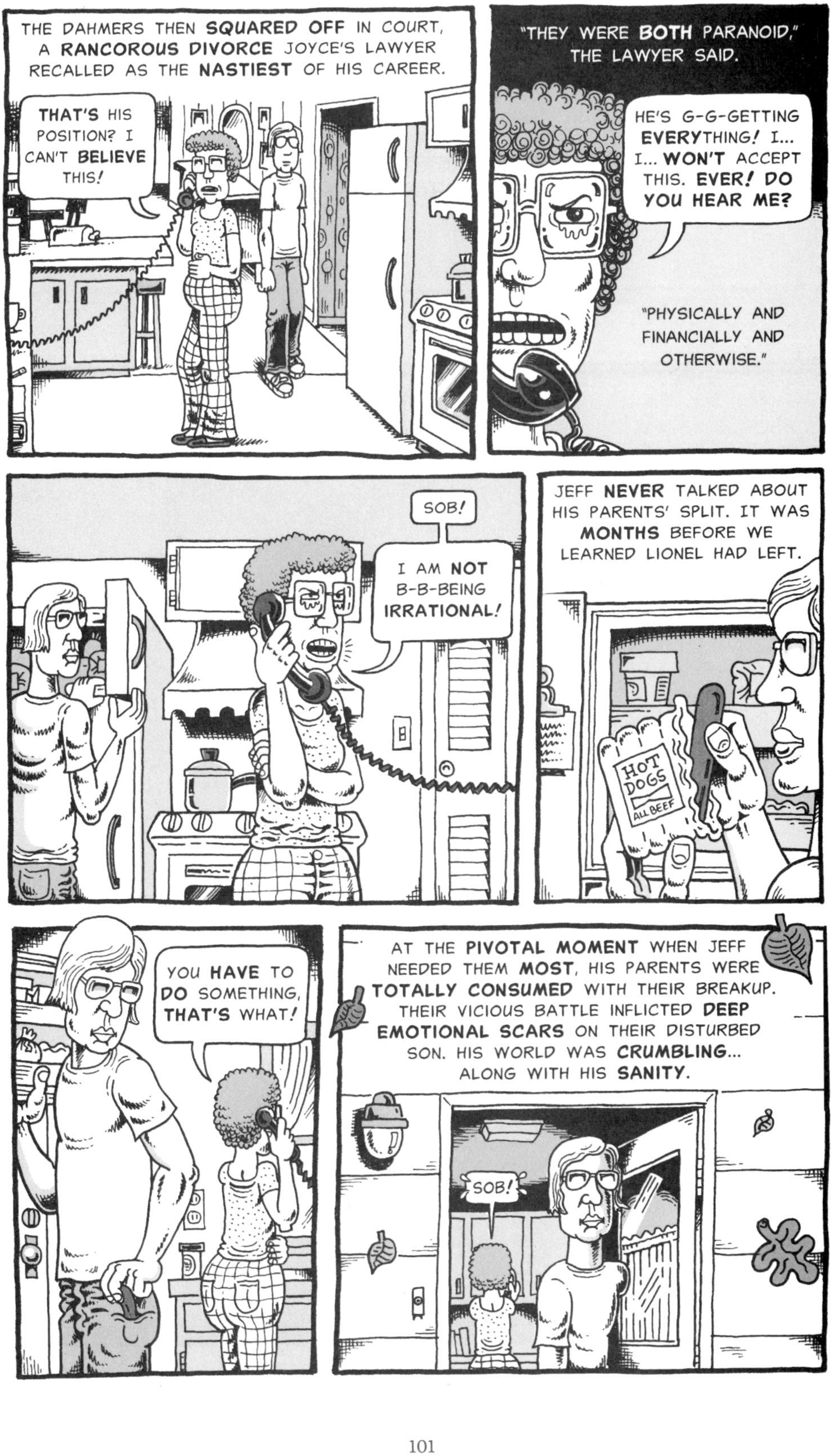
THE DAHMERS THEN SQUARED OFF IN COURT, A RANCOROUS DIVORCE JOYCE'S LAWYER RECALLED AS THE NASTIEST OF HIS CAREER.
THAT'S HIS POSITION? I CAN'T BELIEVE THIS!
"THEY WERE BOTH PARANOID," THE LAWYER SAID.
HE'S G-G-GETTING EVERYTHING! I... I... WON'T ACCEPT THIS. EVER! DO YOU HEAR ME?
"PHYSICALLY AND FINANCIALLY AND OTHERWISE."
SOB!
I AM NOT B-B-BEING IRRATIONAL!
JEFF NEVER TALKED ABOUT HIS PARENTS' SPLIT. IT WAS MONTHS BEFORE WE LEARNED LIONEL HAD LEFT.
HOT DOGS
ALL BEEF
YOU HAVE TO DO SOMETHING, THAT'S WHAT!
AT THE PIVOTAL MOMENT WHEN JEFF NEEDED THEM MOST, HIS PARENTS WERE TOTALLY CONSUMED WITH THEIR BREAKUP. THEIR VICIOUS BATTLE INFLICTED DEEP EMOTIONAL SCARS ON THEIR DISTURBED SON. HIS WORLD WAS CRUMBLING... ALONG WITH HIS SANITY.
SOB!

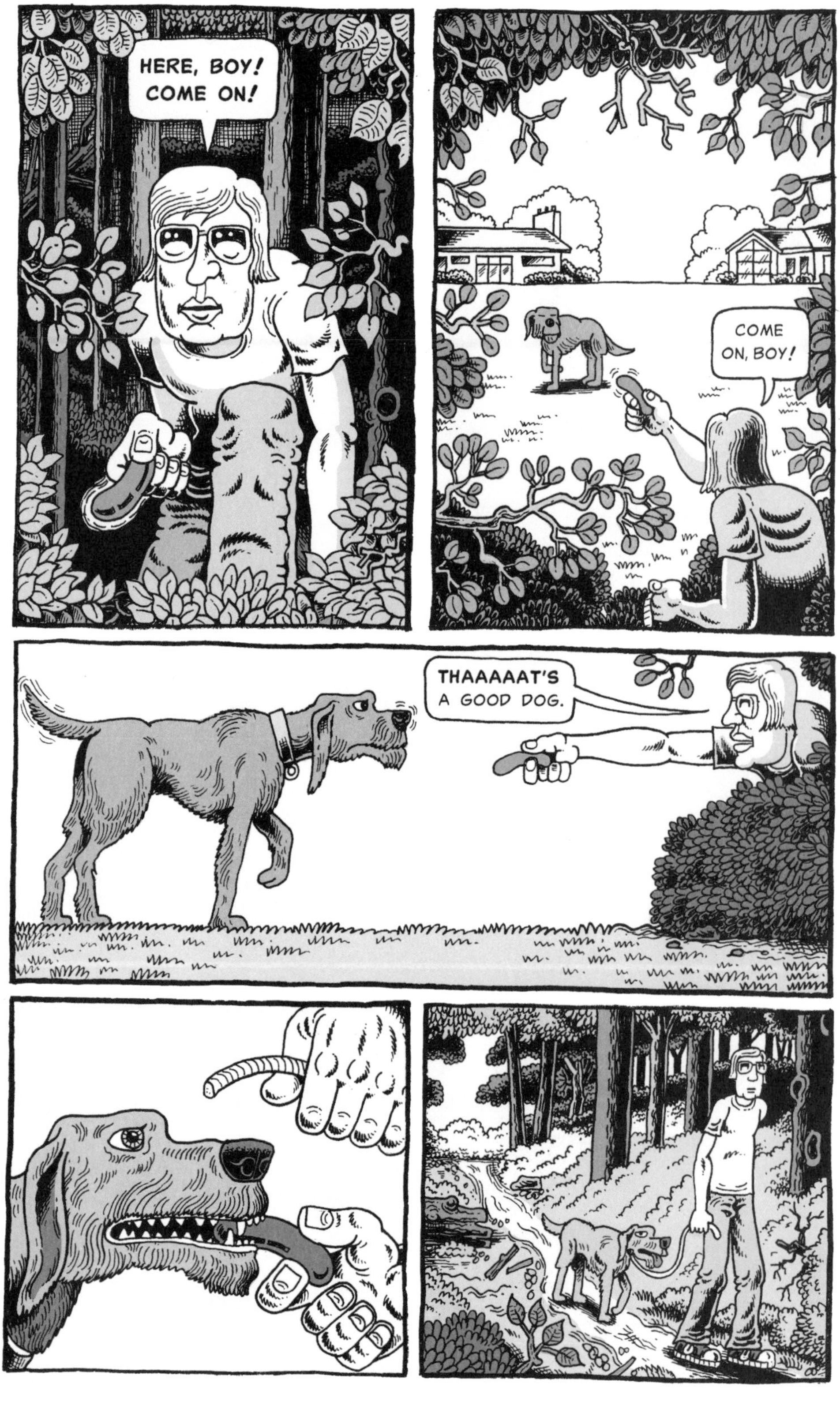
HERE, BOY! COME ON!
COME ON, BOY!
THAAAAAT'S A GOOD DOG.

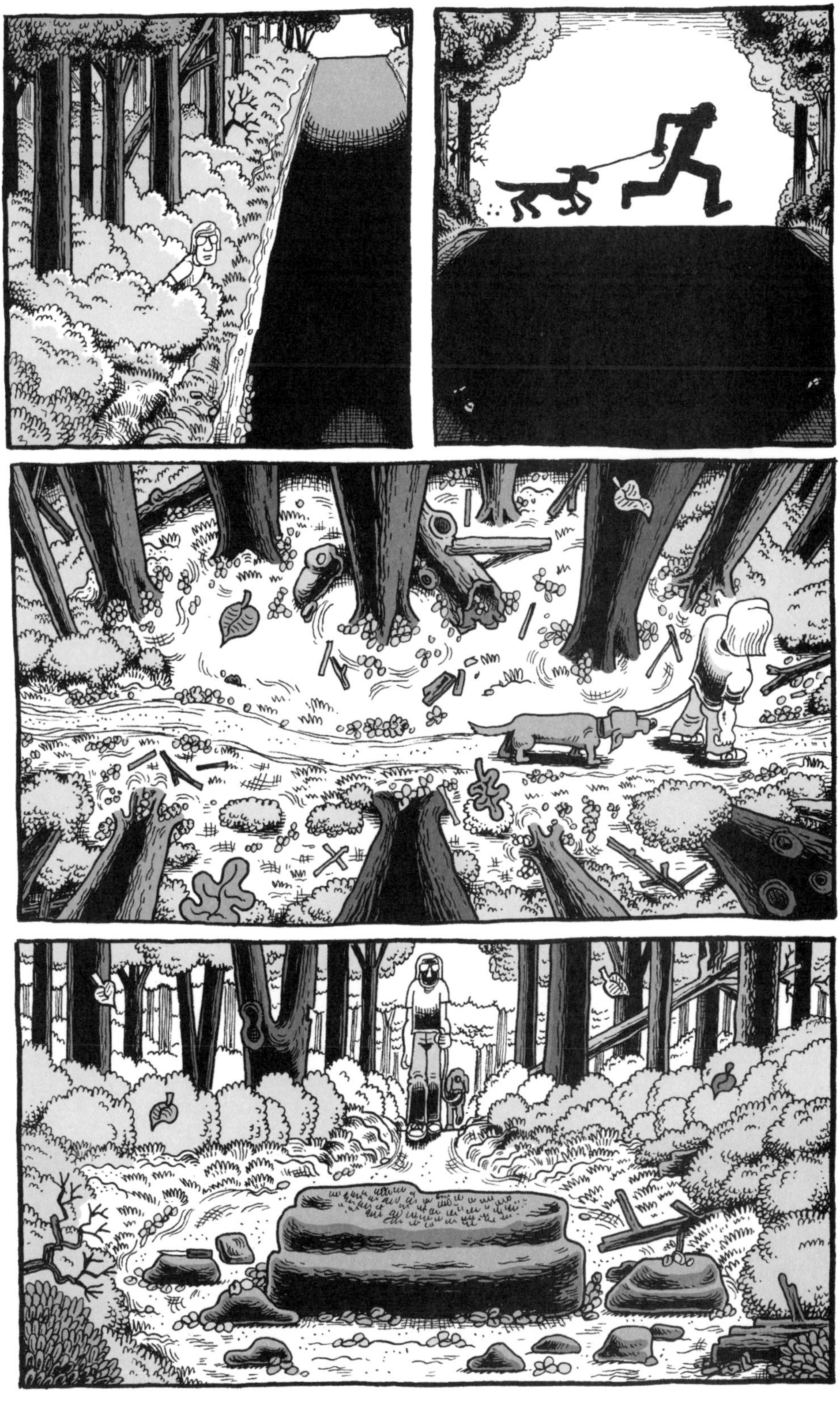

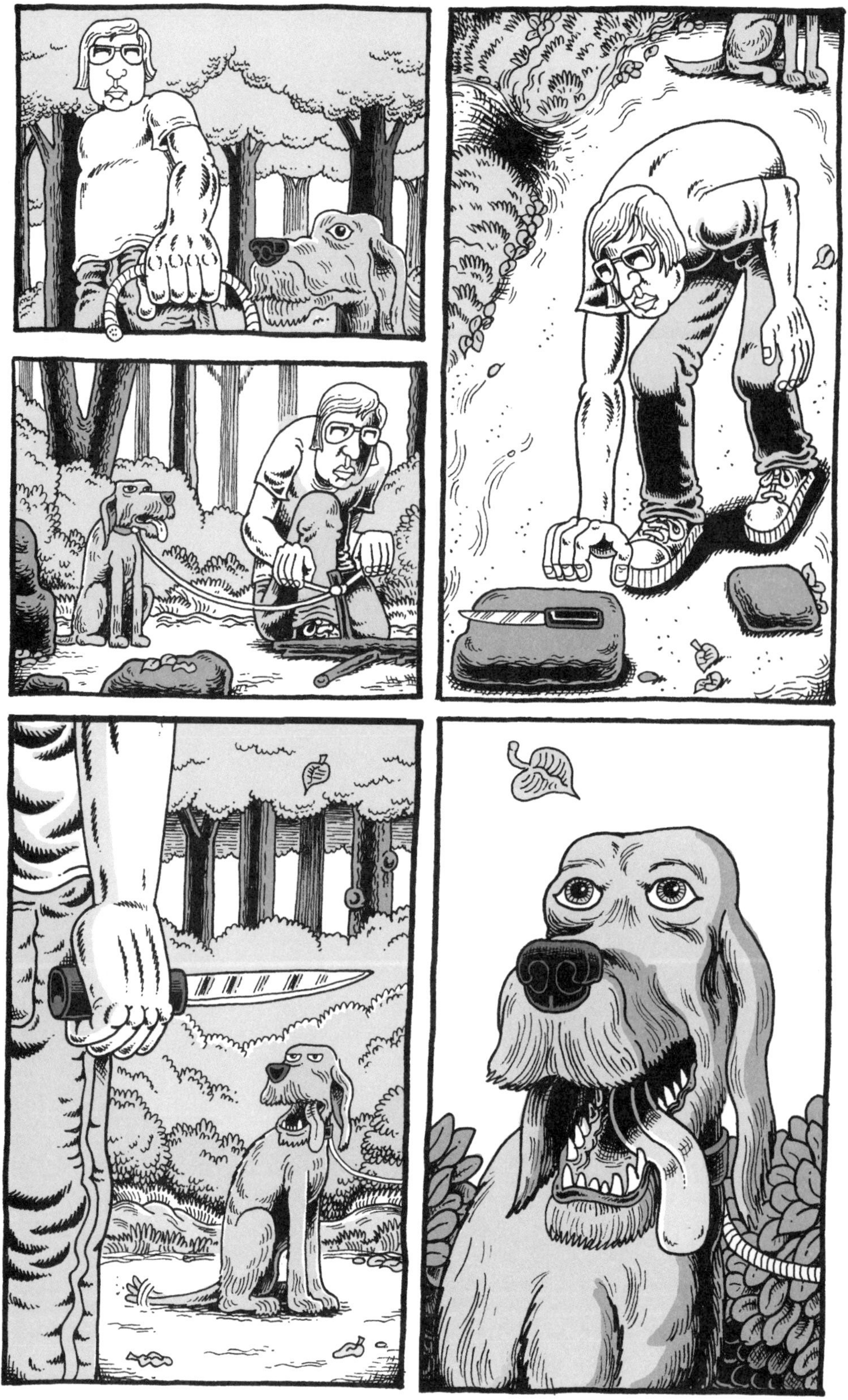

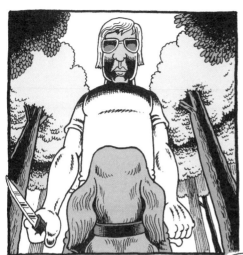

SIGH.

AAR!!

THOK!

GO ON!!
GO HOME!
GET!!

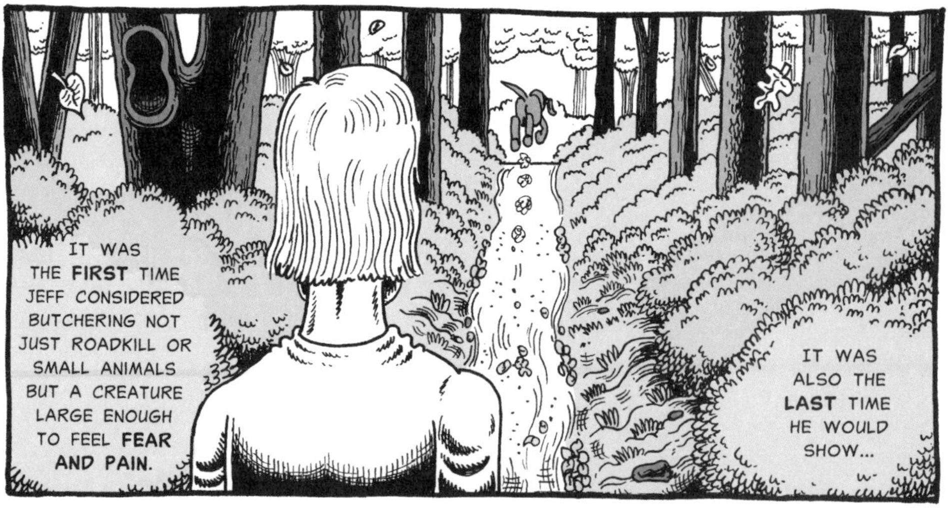
IT WAS THE **FIRST** TIME JEFF CONSIDERED BUTCHERING NOT JUST ROADKILL OR SMALL ANIMALS BUT A CREATURE LARGE ENOUGH TO FEEL **FEAR AND PAIN.**
IT WAS ALSO THE **LAST** TIME HE WOULD SHOW...

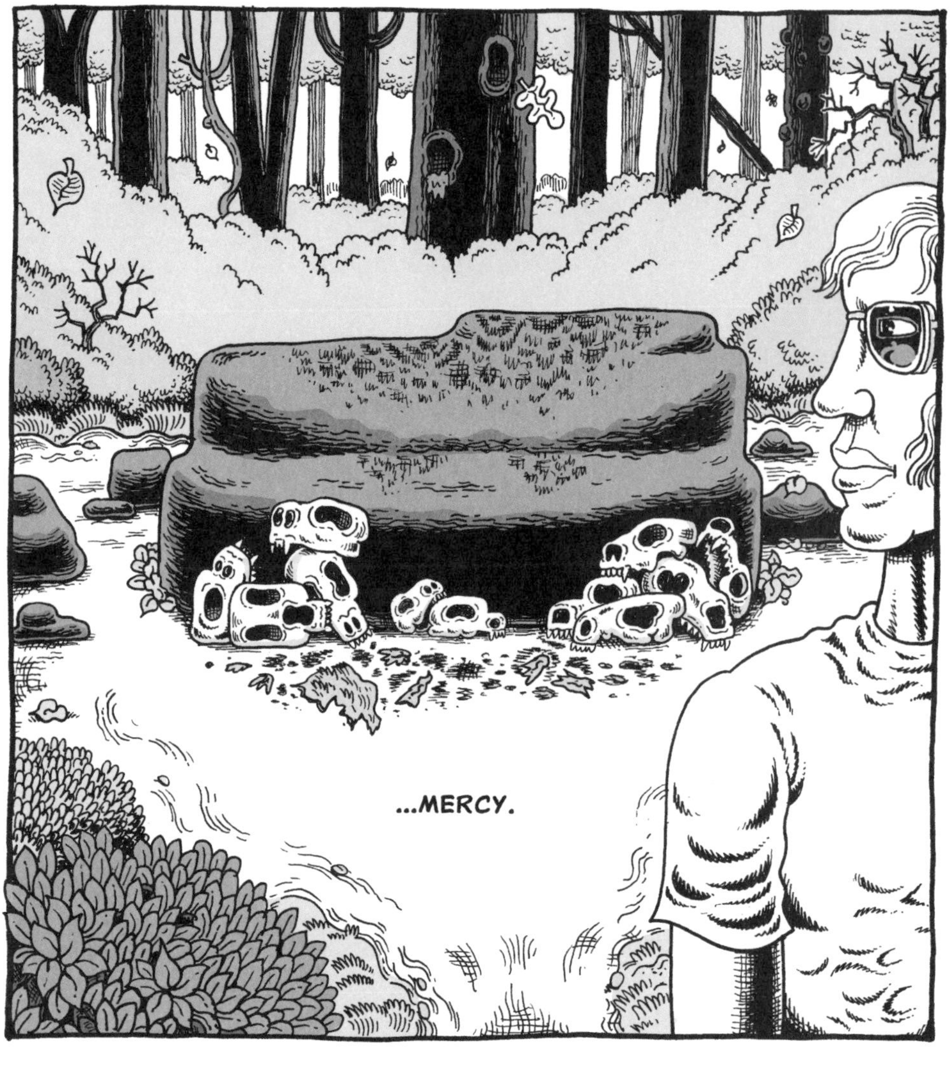
...MERCY.

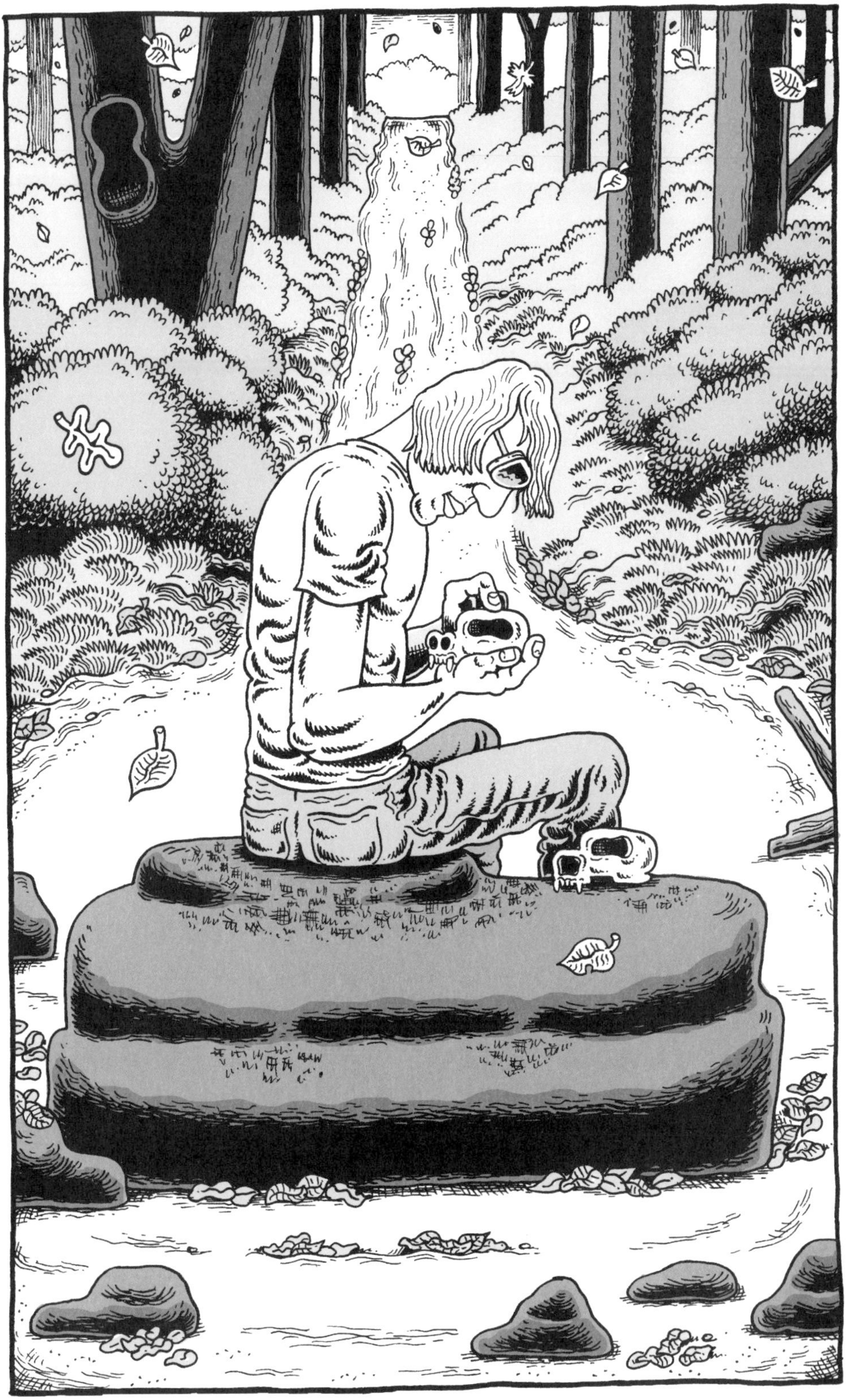

PART 3

The Dahmer Fan Club

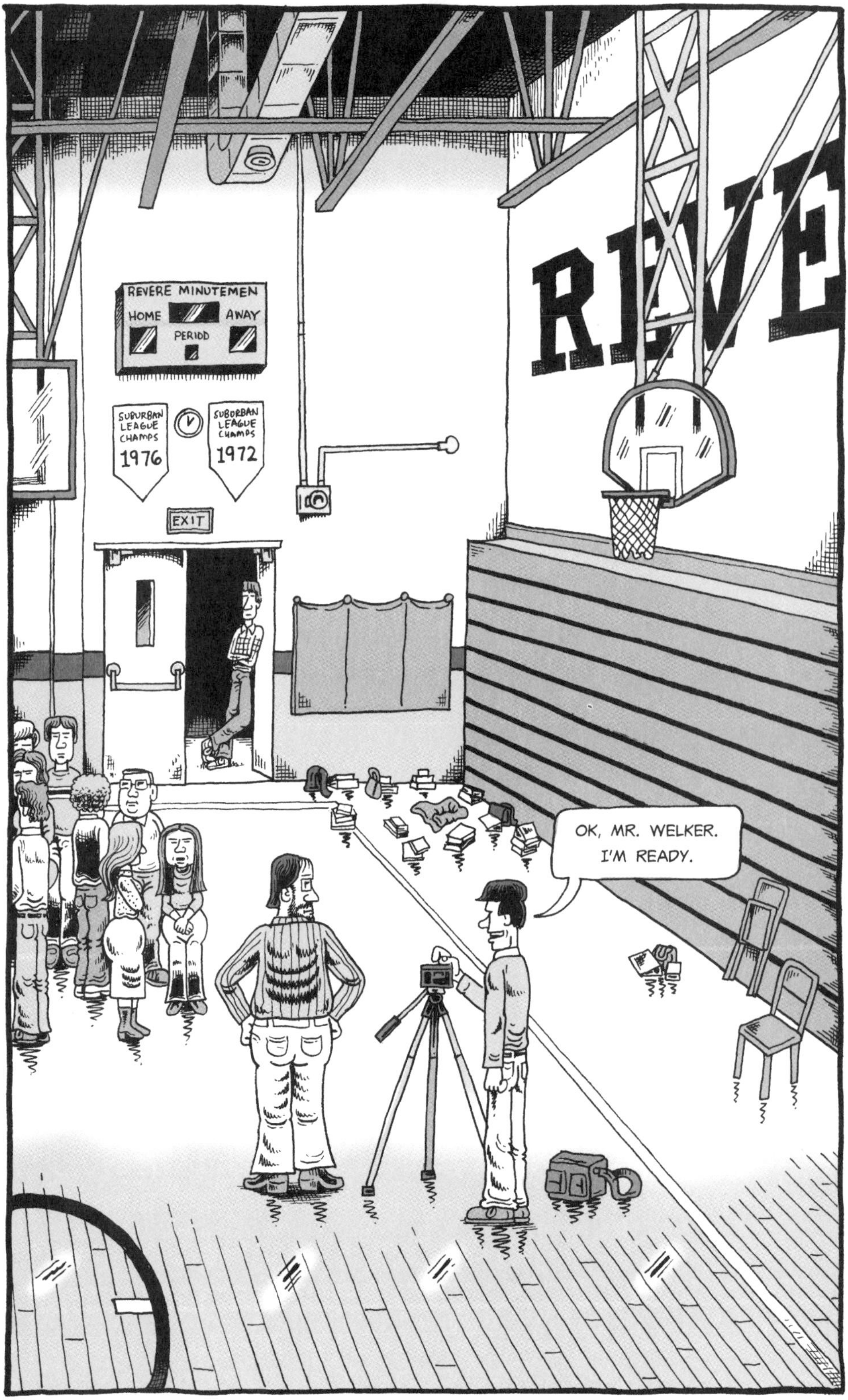
REVERE MINUTEMEN
HOME
AWAY
PERIOD
SUBURBAN LEAGUE CHAMPS 1976
SUBURBAN LEAGUE CHAMPS 1972
EXIT
REVE
OK, MR. WELKER. I'M READY.

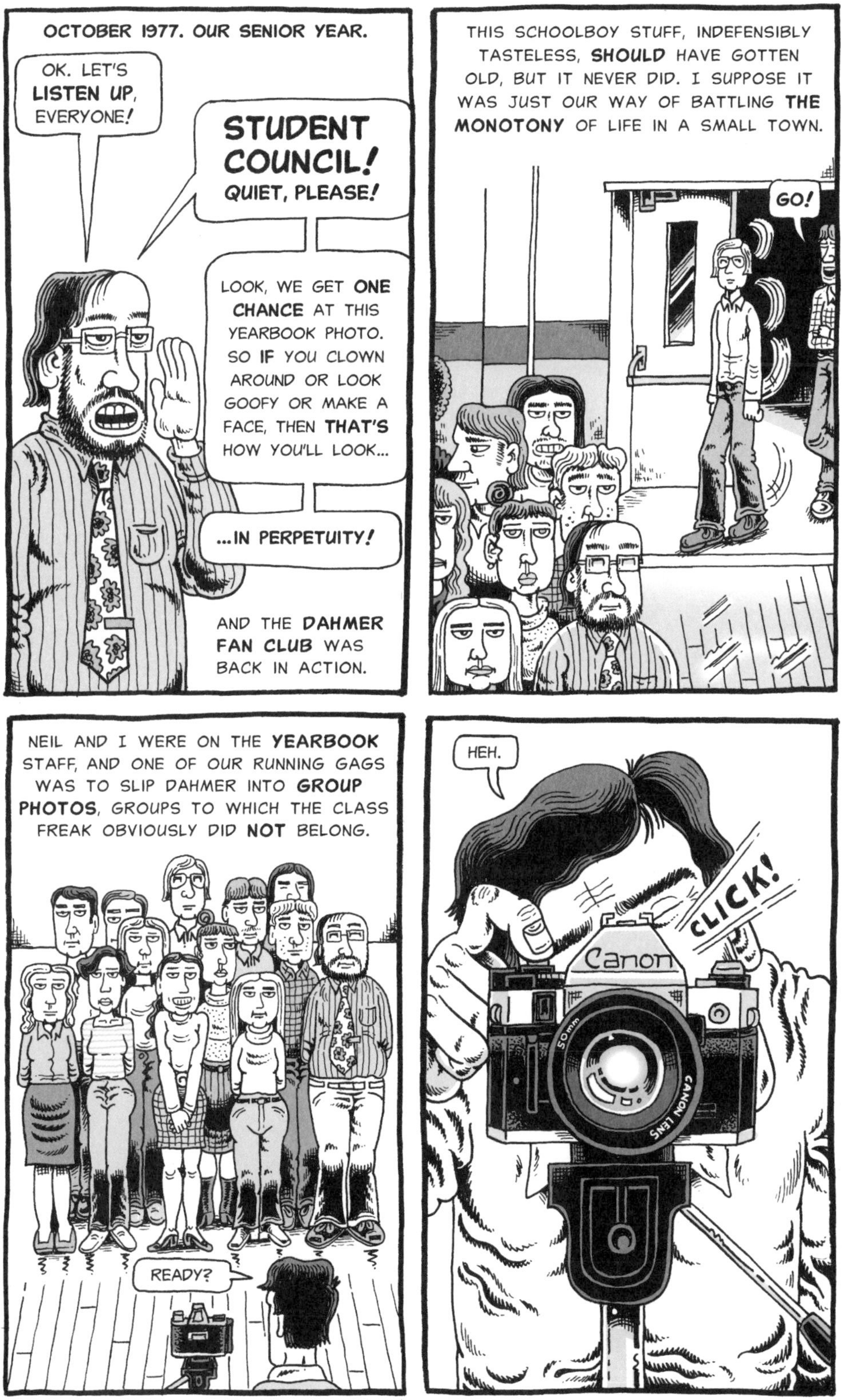

OCTOBER 1977. OUR SENIOR YEAR.
OK. LET'S LISTEN UP, EVERYONE!
STUDENT COUNCIL! QUIET, PLEASE!
LOOK, WE GET ONE CHANCE AT THIS YEARBOOK PHOTO. SO IF YOU CLOWN AROUND OR LOOK GOOFY OR MAKE A FACE, THEN THAT'S HOW YOU'LL LOOK...
...IN PERPETUITY!
AND THE DAHMER FAN CLUB WAS BACK IN ACTION.
THIS SCHOOLBOY STUFF, INDEFENSIBLY TASTELESS, SHOULD HAVE GOTTEN OLD, BUT IT NEVER DID. I SUPPOSE IT WAS JUST OUR WAY OF BATTLING THE MONOTONY OF LIFE IN A SMALL TOWN.
GO!
NEIL AND I WERE ON THE YEARBOOK STAFF, AND ONE OF OUR RUNNING GAGS WAS TO SLIP DAHMER INTO GROUP PHOTOS, GROUPS TO WHICH THE CLASS FREAK OBVIOUSLY DID NOT BELONG.
READY?
HEH.
CLICK!
Canon
50mm
CANON LENS

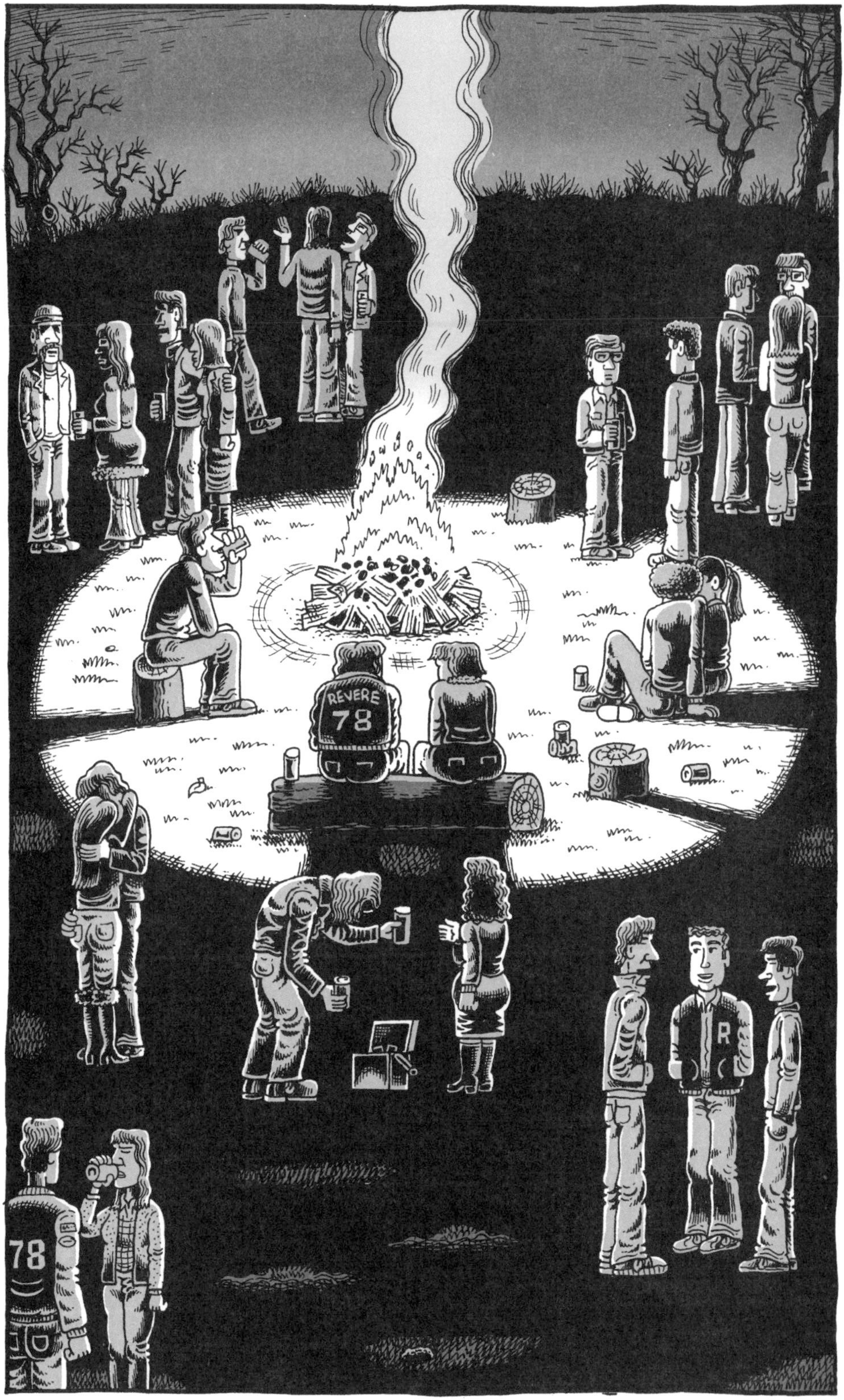
REVERE
78
R
78

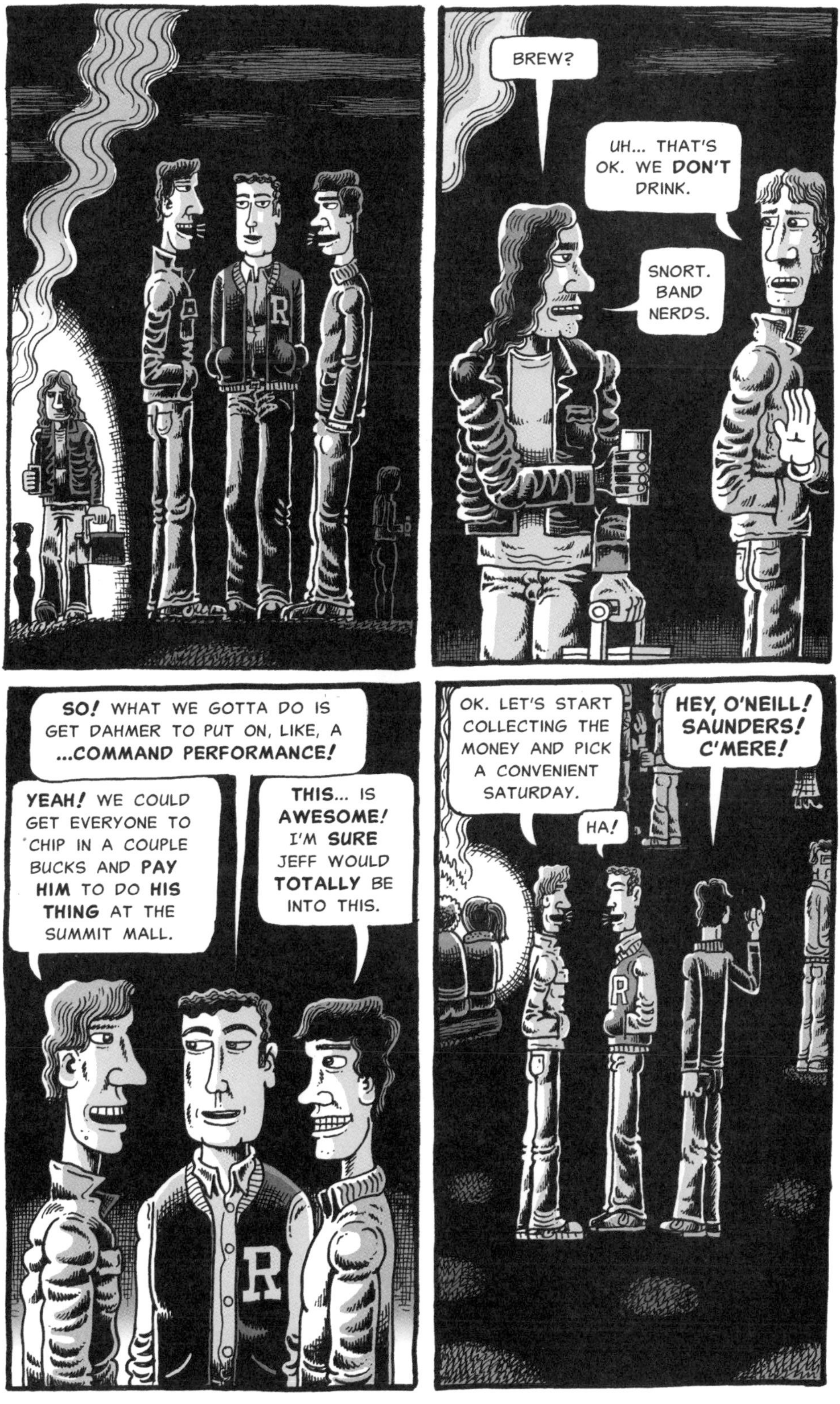
BREW?
UH... THAT'S OK. WE DON'T DRINK.
SNORT. BAND NERDS.
SO! WHAT WE GOTTA DO IS GET DAHMER TO PUT ON, LIKE, A ...COMMAND PERFORMANCE!
YEAH! WE COULD GET EVERYONE TO CHIP IN A COUPLE BUCKS AND PAY HIM TO DO HIS THING AT THE SUMMIT MALL.
THIS... IS AWESOME! I'M SURE JEFF WOULD TOTALLY BE INTO THIS.
OK. LET'S START COLLECTING THE MONEY AND PICK A CONVENIENT SATURDAY.
HA!
HEY, O'NEILL! SAUNDERS! C'MERE!

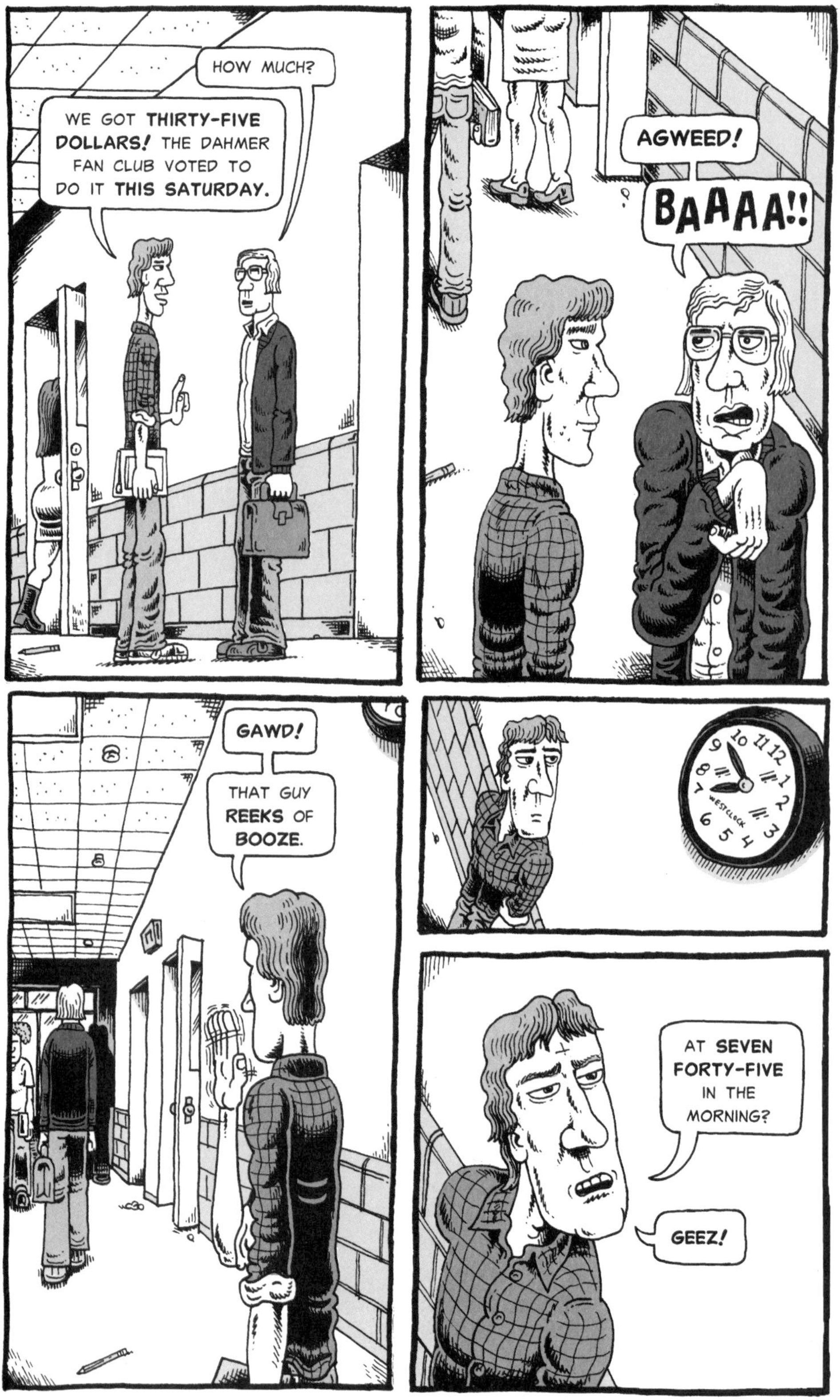
HOW MUCH?
WE GOT THIRTY-FIVE DOLLARS! THE DAHMER FAN CLUB VOTED TO DO IT THIS SATURDAY.
AGWEED!
BAAAA!!
GAWD!
THAT GUY REEKS OF BOOZE.
WESTCLOCK
AT SEVEN FORTY-FIVE IN THE MORNING?
GEEZ!

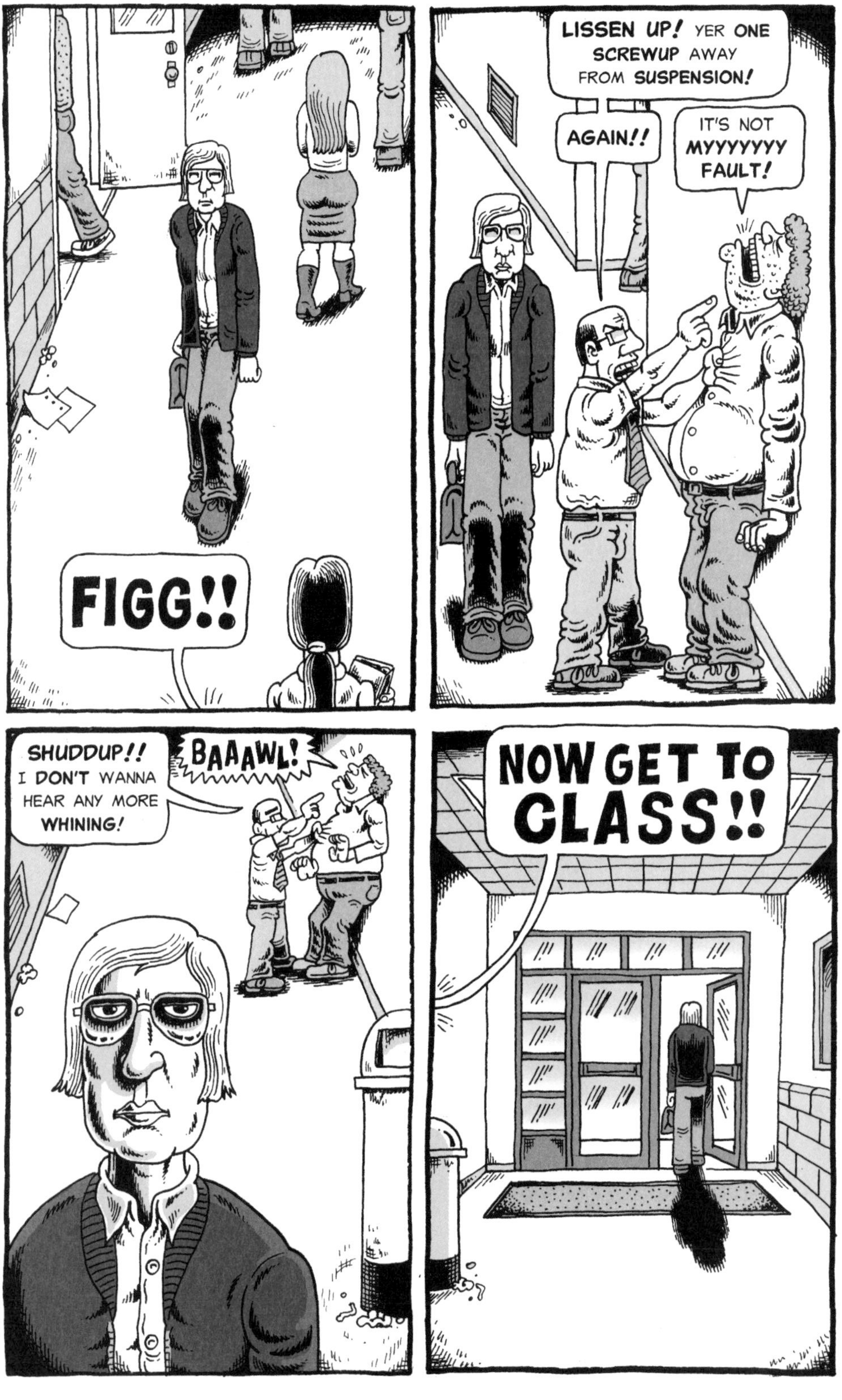
FIGG!!
LISSEN UP! YER ONE SCREWUP AWAY FROM SUSPENSION!
AGAIN!!
IT'S NOT MYYYYYYY FAULT!
SHUDDUP!! I DON'T WANNA HEAR ANY MORE WHINING!
BAAAWL!
NOW GET TO CLASS!!

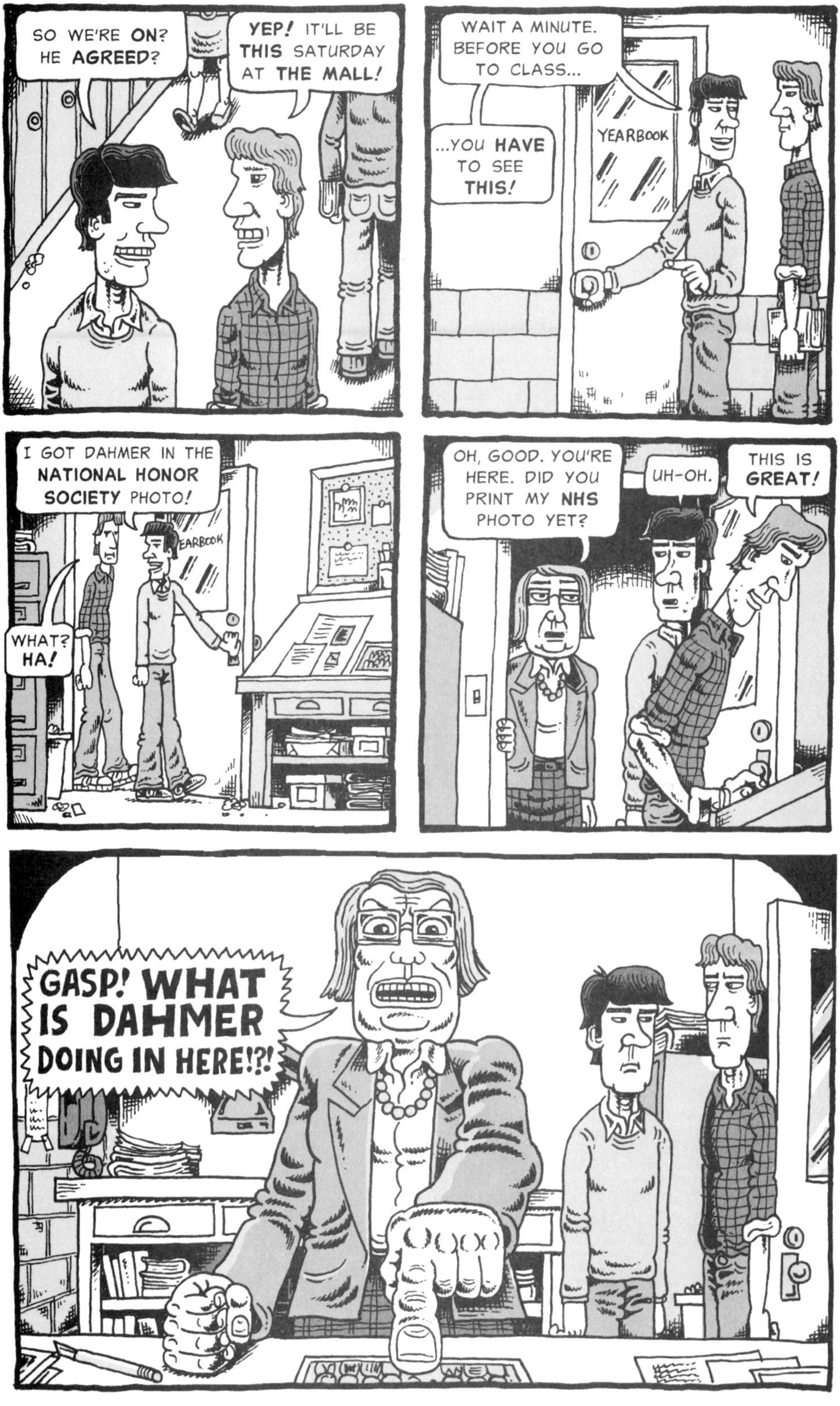
SO WE'RE **ON**? HE **AGREED**?
YEP! IT'LL BE **THIS** SATURDAY AT **THE MALL!**
WAIT A MINUTE. BEFORE YOU GO TO CLASS...
...YOU **HAVE** TO SEE **THIS!**
YEARBOOK
I GOT DAHMER IN THE **NATIONAL HONOR SOCIETY** PHOTO!
WHAT? **HA!**
OH, GOOD. YOU'RE HERE. DID YOU PRINT MY **NHS** PHOTO YET?
UH-OH.
THIS IS **GREAT!**
GASP! WHAT IS DAHMER DOING IN HERE!?!

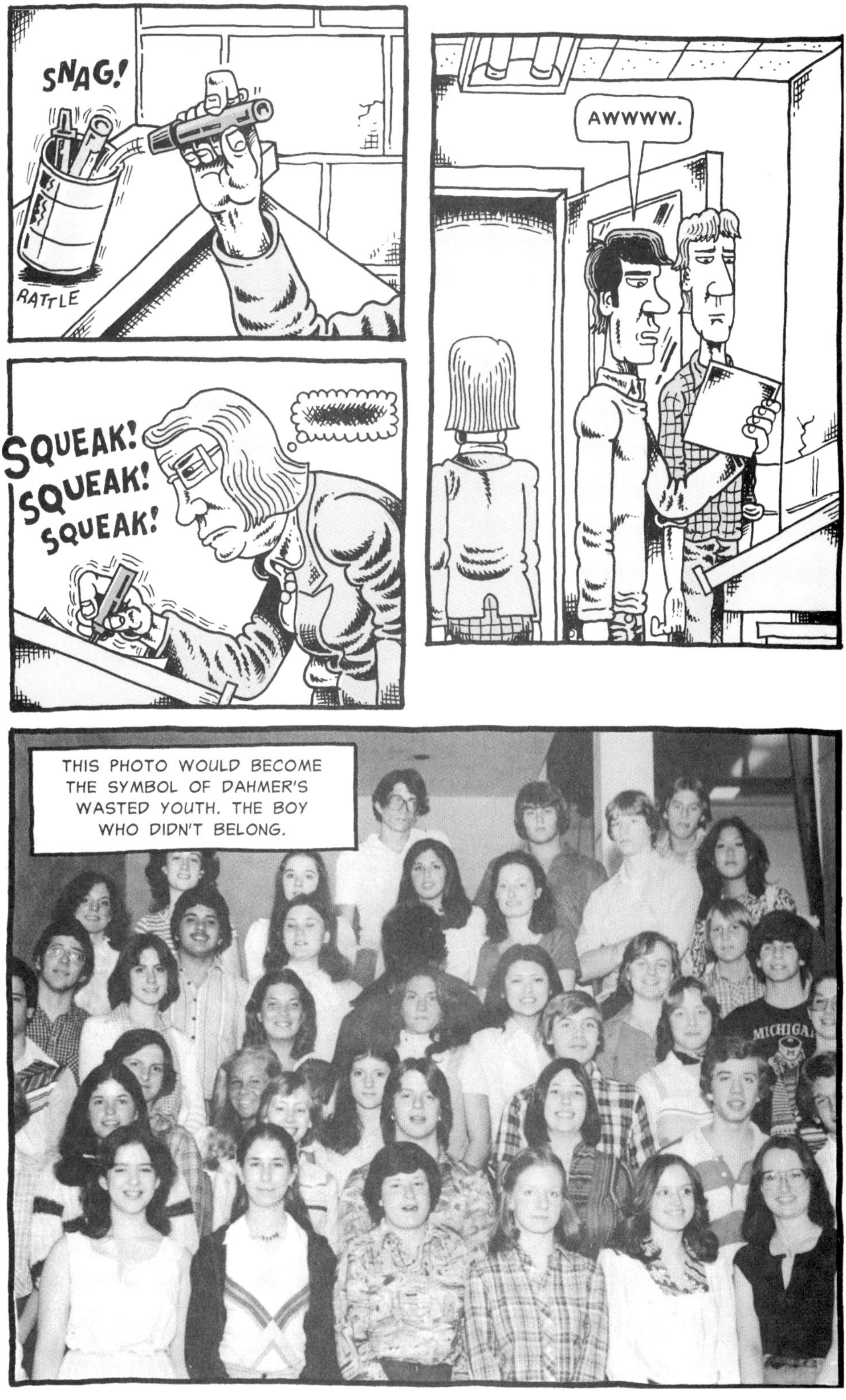
SNAG!
RATTLE
SQUEAK! SQUEAK! SQUEAK!
AWWWW.
THIS PHOTO WOULD BECOME THE SYMBOL OF DAHMER'S WASTED YOUTH. THE BOY WHO DIDN'T BELONG.
MICHIGAN

AS THE OFFICIAL **MINISTER OF PROPAGANDA** FOR THE **DAHMER FAN CLUB**, I DID **MY** PART. I PUT A **CARTOON DAHMER** INTO EVERYTHING I DREW – COMICS FOR THE SCHOOL PAPER AND THE YEARBOOK, POSTERS FOR STUDENT COUNCIL AND SPORTS PEP RALLIES. HE EVEN POPPED UP IN ART CLASS ASSIGNMENTS.

IN FACT, THE ART TEACHERS GOT SO **FED UP**, THEY GAVE ME A "D" IN ART AS **PUNISHMENT** FOR DRAWING TOO MANY INCOMPREHENSIBLE (TO THEM) CARTOONS AND NOT ENOUGH, AS THEY PUT IT, "REAL ART."

MY **CARTOON DAHMER** WAS **SO** UBIQUITOUS, HE BECAME SOMETHING OF A **BIZARRO SCHOOL MASCOT!**

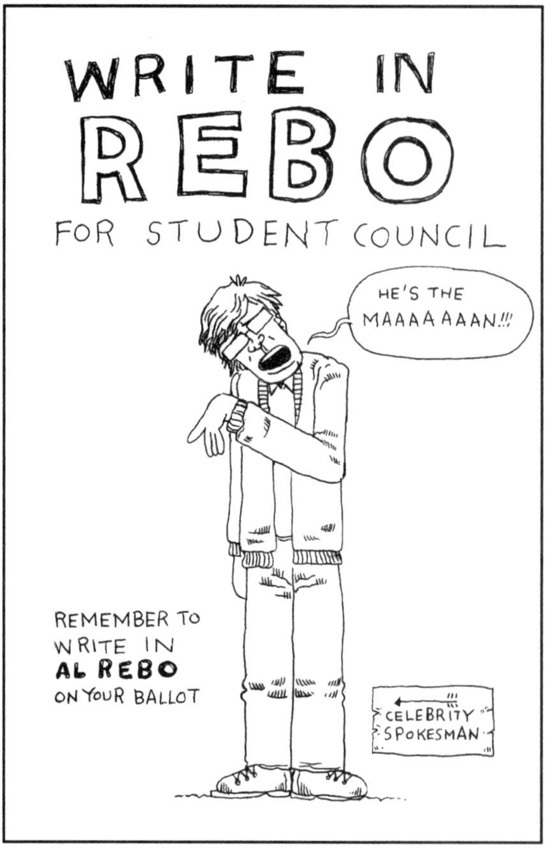

WRITE IN
REBO
FOR STUDENT COUNCIL
HE'S THE MAAAAAAAN!!!
REMEMBER TO WRITE IN AL REBO ON YOUR BALLOT
CELEBRITY SPOKESMAN

RIGHT: A FLYER FOR STUDENT COUNCIL ELECTIONS, 1977.

BELOW: DRAWING FOR THE 1978 YEARBOOK. DAHMER IS THE LARGE FIGURE IN THE CROWD ON THE RIGHT (IN FRONT OF THE GUY WITH THE TUBA). ALMOST EVERYTHING IN THE WORD BALLOONS ARE "DAHMERISMS."

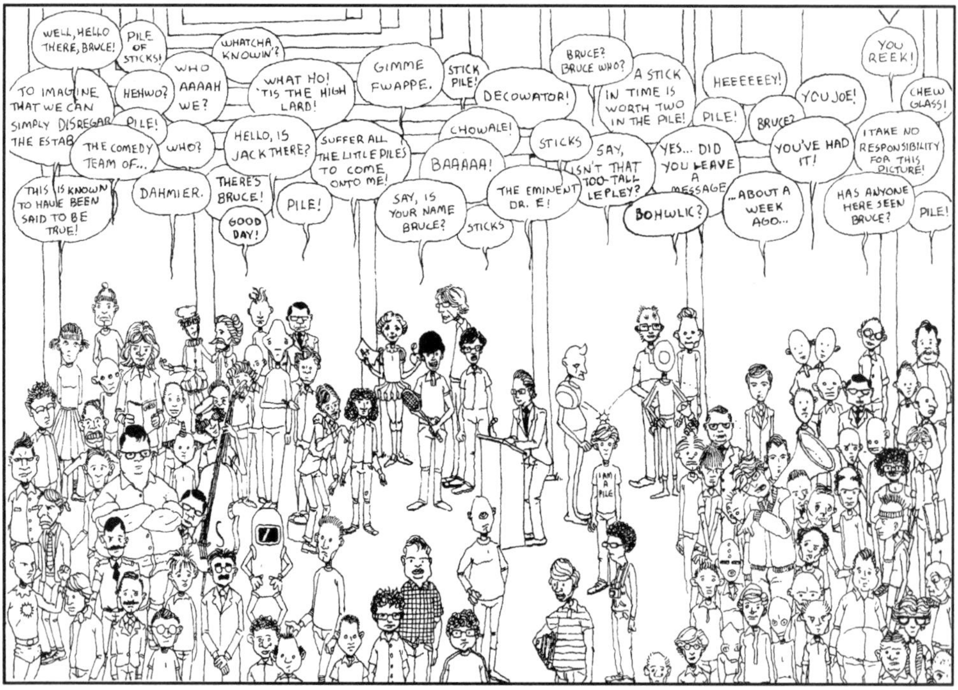

WELL, HELLO THERE, BRUCE!
PILE OF STICKS!
WHATCHA KNOWIN'?
TO IMAGINE THAT WE CAN SIMPLY DISREGAR THE ESTAB
HEHWO?
WHO AAAAH WE?
WHAT HO! 'TIS THE HIGH LARD!
GIMME FWAPPE.
STICK PILE!
PILE!
THE COMEDY TEAM OF...
WHO?
HELLO, IS JACK THERE?
SUFFER ALL THE LITTLE PILES TO COME ONTO ME!
THIS IS KNOWN TO HAVE BEEN SAID TO BE TRUE!
DAHMIER.
THERE'S BRUCE!
GOOD DAY!
PILE!
SAY, IS YOUR NAME BRUCE?
BRUCE? BRUCE WHO?
DECOWATOR!
A STICK IN TIME IS WORTH TWO IN THE PILE!
HEEEEEEY!
YOU REEK!
CHOWALE!
BAAAAA!
STICKS
PILE!
BRUCE?
YOU JOE!
CHEW GLASS!
THE EMINENT DR. E!
STICKS
SAY, ISN'T THAT TOO-TALL LEPLEY?
YES... DID YOU LEAVE A MESSAGE
BOHWLIC?
...ABOUT A WEEK AGO...
YOU'VE HAD IT!
I TAKE NO RESPONSIBILITY FOR THIS PICTURE!
HAS ANYONE HERE SEEN BRUCE?
PILE!

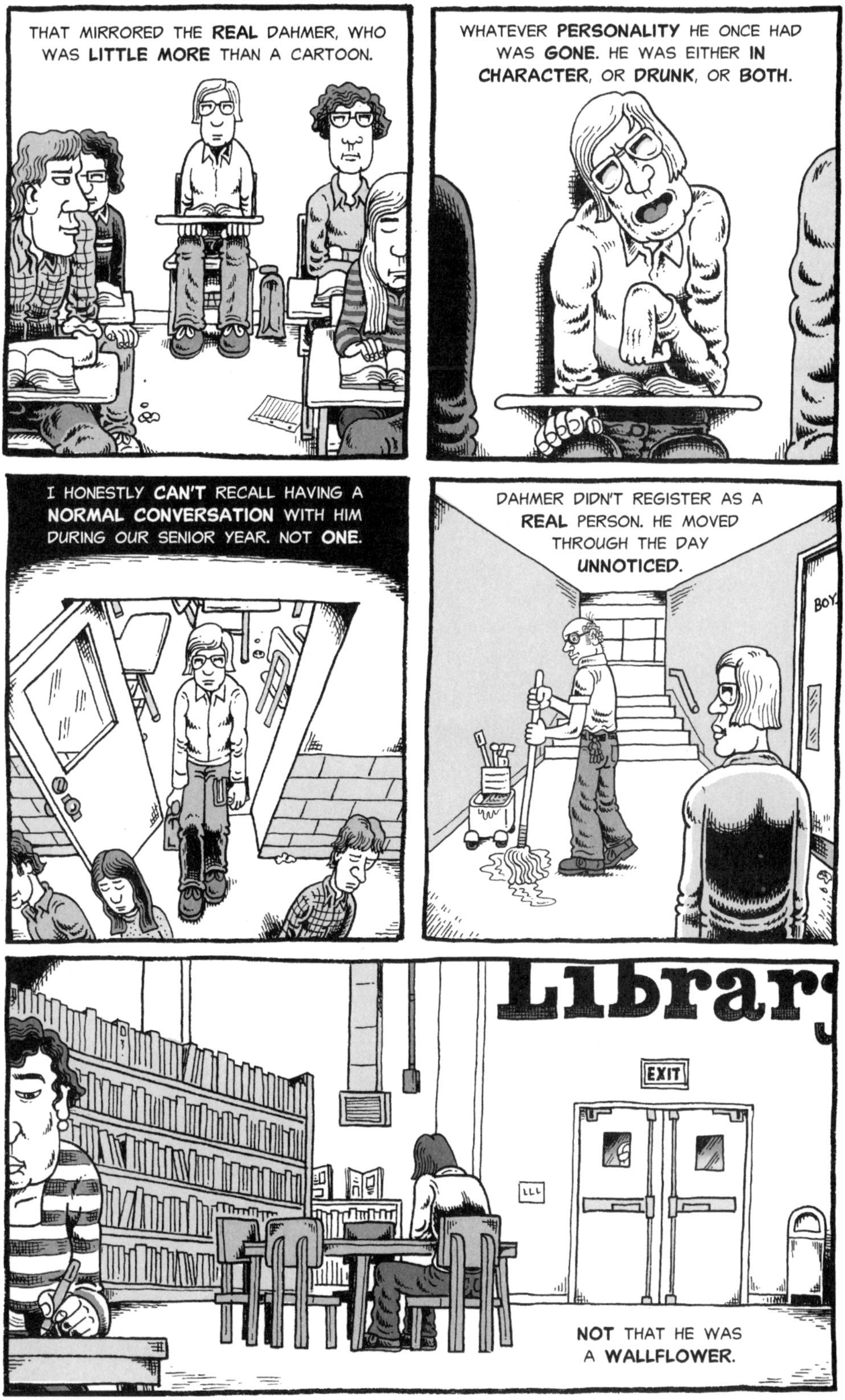
THAT MIRRORED THE REAL DAHMER, WHO WAS LITTLE MORE THAN A CARTOON.
WHATEVER PERSONALITY HE ONCE HAD WAS GONE. HE WAS EITHER IN CHARACTER, OR DRUNK, OR BOTH.
I HONESTLY CAN'T RECALL HAVING A NORMAL CONVERSATION WITH HIM DURING OUR SENIOR YEAR. NOT ONE.
DAHMER DIDN'T REGISTER AS A REAL PERSON. HE MOVED THROUGH THE DAY UNNOTICED.
EXIT
NOT THAT HE WAS A WALLFLOWER.

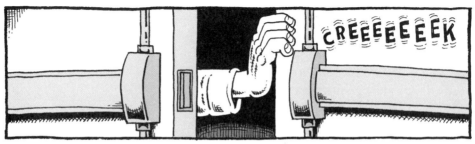

MISSUS WOOD-AAAARD!!

WHO WAS THAT!?! DID ANYONE SEE!?!

AAARGH! WHO KEEPS DOING THAT?

MRS. WOODARD **NEVER DID** CATCH HER TORMENTOR. DAHMER THE SERIAL KILLER BELIEVED HE WOULD **NEVER** BE CAUGHT, THAT HE POSSESSED SOME **SPECIAL TALENT** THAT ALLOWED HIM TO ESCAPE DETECTION.

WHY **WOULDN'T** HE THINK THAT? HE HAD THIS ABILITY MOST OF HIS LIFE.

CREEEEEEEK

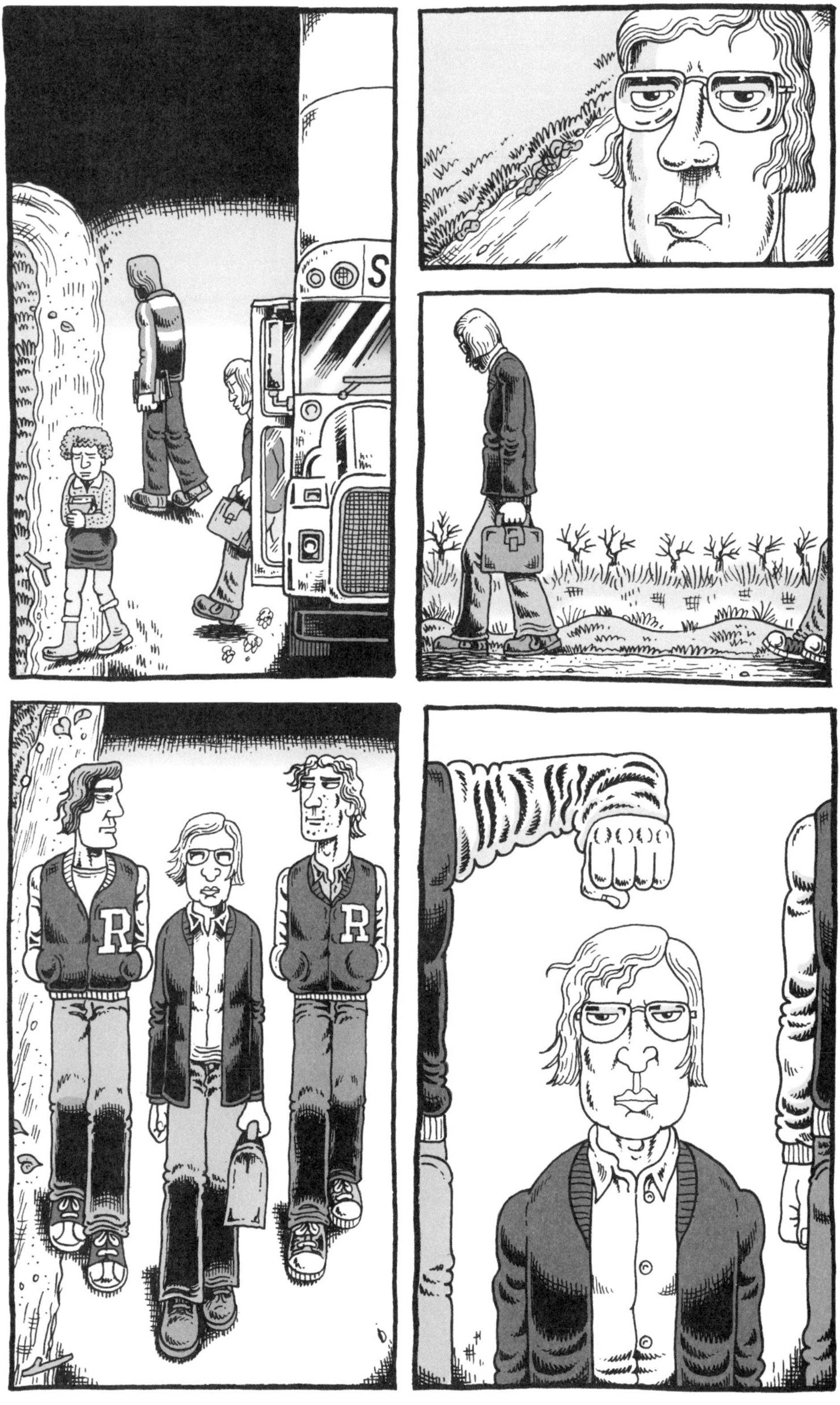

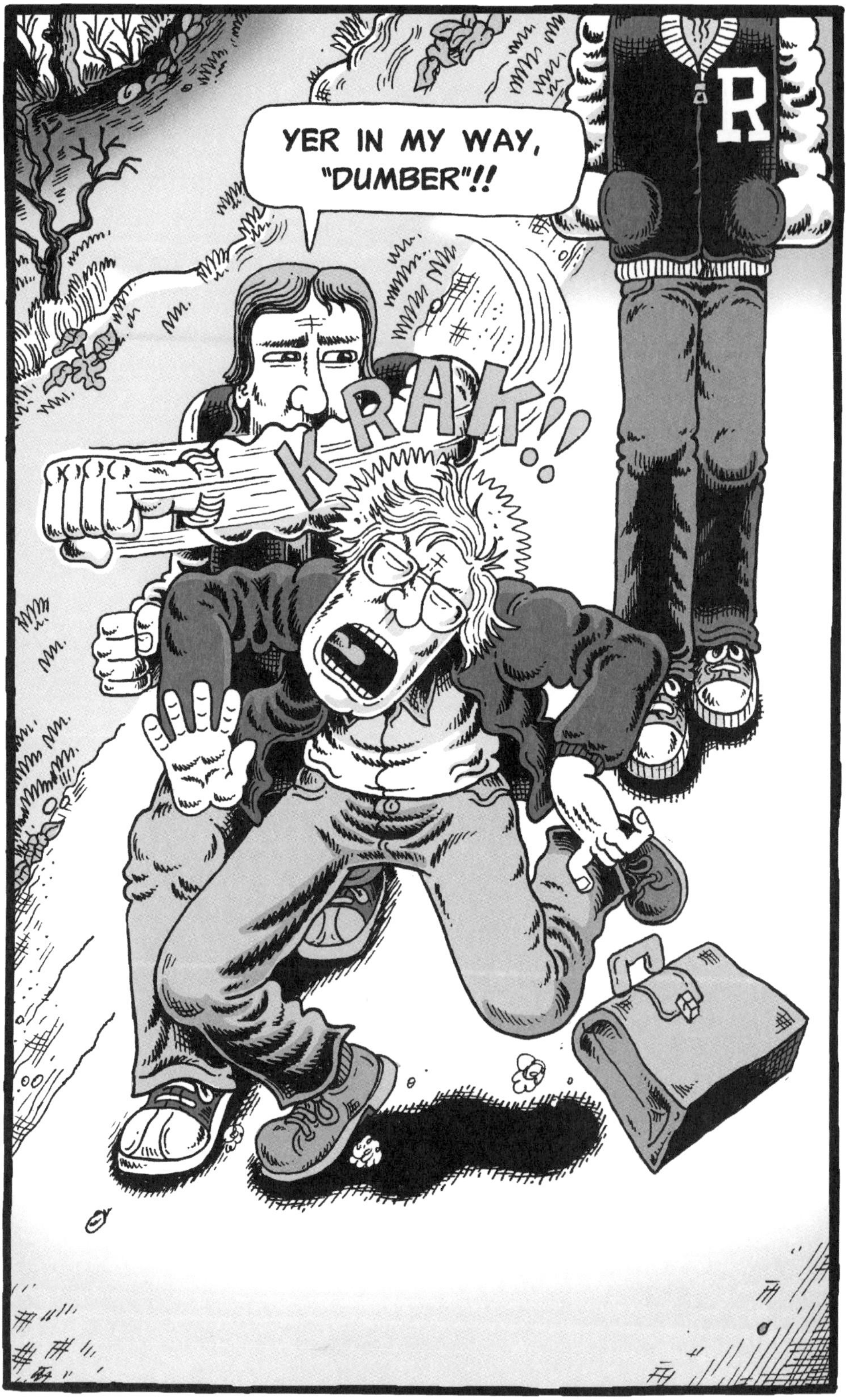
YER IN MY WAY, "DUMBER"!!
KRAK!!

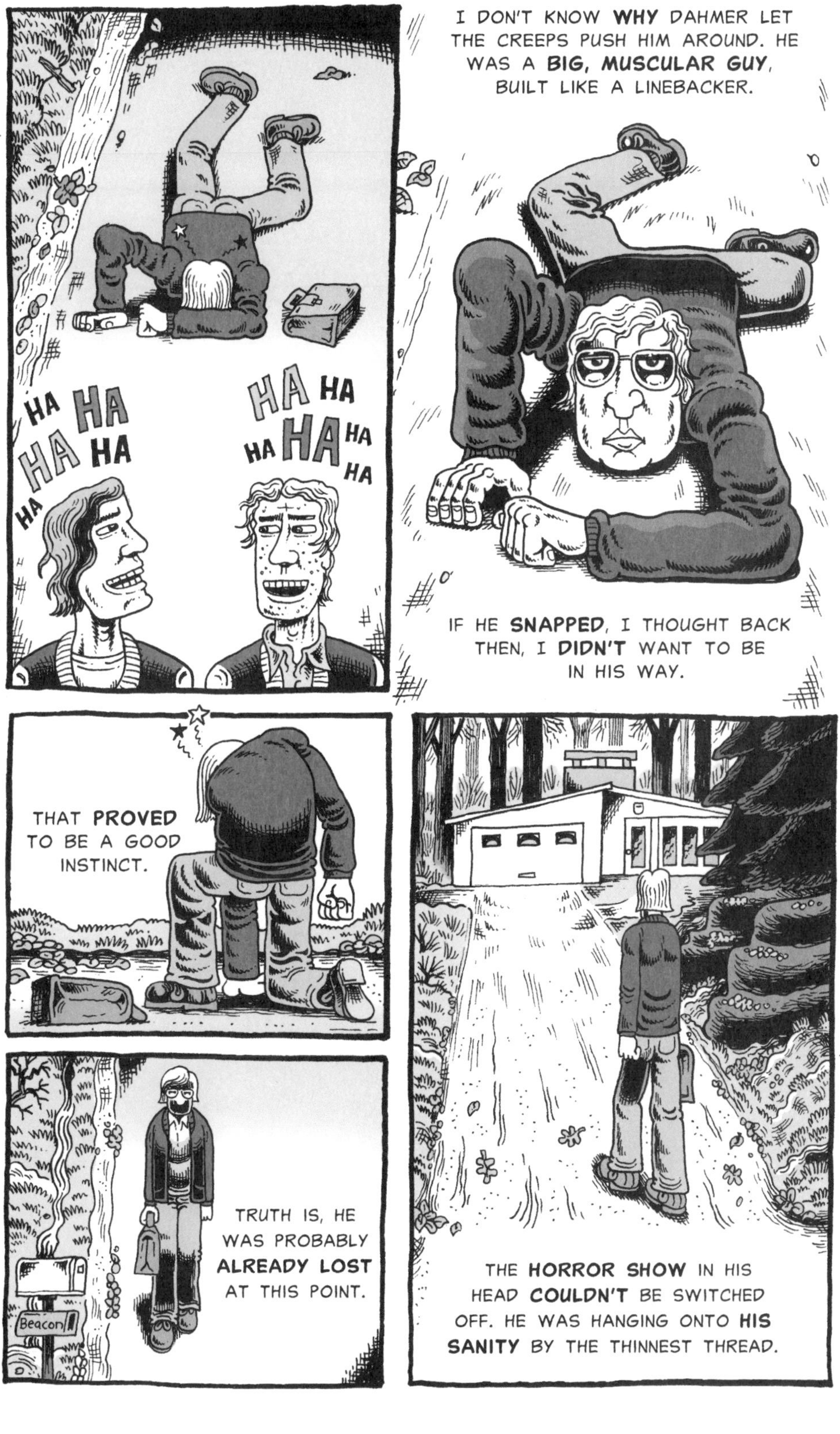

HA HA HA HA HA HA
HA HA HA HA HA HA HA
I DON'T KNOW **WHY** DAHMER LET THE CREEPS PUSH HIM AROUND. HE WAS A **BIG, MUSCULAR GUY**, BUILT LIKE A LINEBACKER.
IF HE **SNAPPED**, I THOUGHT BACK THEN, I **DIDN'T** WANT TO BE IN HIS WAY.
THAT **PROVED** TO BE A GOOD INSTINCT.
Beacon
TRUTH IS, HE WAS PROBABLY **ALREADY LOST** AT THIS POINT.
THE **HORROR SHOW** IN HIS HEAD **COULDN'T** BE SWITCHED OFF. HE WAS HANGING ONTO **HIS SANITY** BY THE THINNEST THREAD.

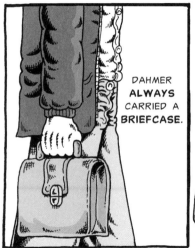

DAHMER **ALWAYS** CARRIED A **BRIEFCASE.**

HEY, NICE **PURSE,** DAHMER**!**

HEE HEE.

A BRIEFCASE WAS **NOT** PART OF THE **TEENAGE UNIFORM** IN THE SEVENTIES. **NOT** EVEN THE **NERDIEST** OF KIDS WOULD **DARE** LUG ONE AROUND.

IT WAS, OF COURSE, **HOW** HE SNUCK HIS **BOOZE** INTO SCHOOL.

DAHMER'S NEED FOR LIQUOR WAS NOW **SO** GREAT, HE **ALWAYS** KEPT A BOTTLE ON HIM. THE BRIEFCASE WAS AN **INGENIOUS COVER.** A GUY WITH A BRIEFCASE DIDN'T FIT THE **STONER PROFILE.** A GUY WITH A BRIEFCASE DIDN'T HAVE TO WORRY ABOUT A **PAT DOWN.**

HEY.

WHAZZUP.

YOU GOT MY **STUFF?**

YEP. **YOU** GOT MY **BREAD?**

124

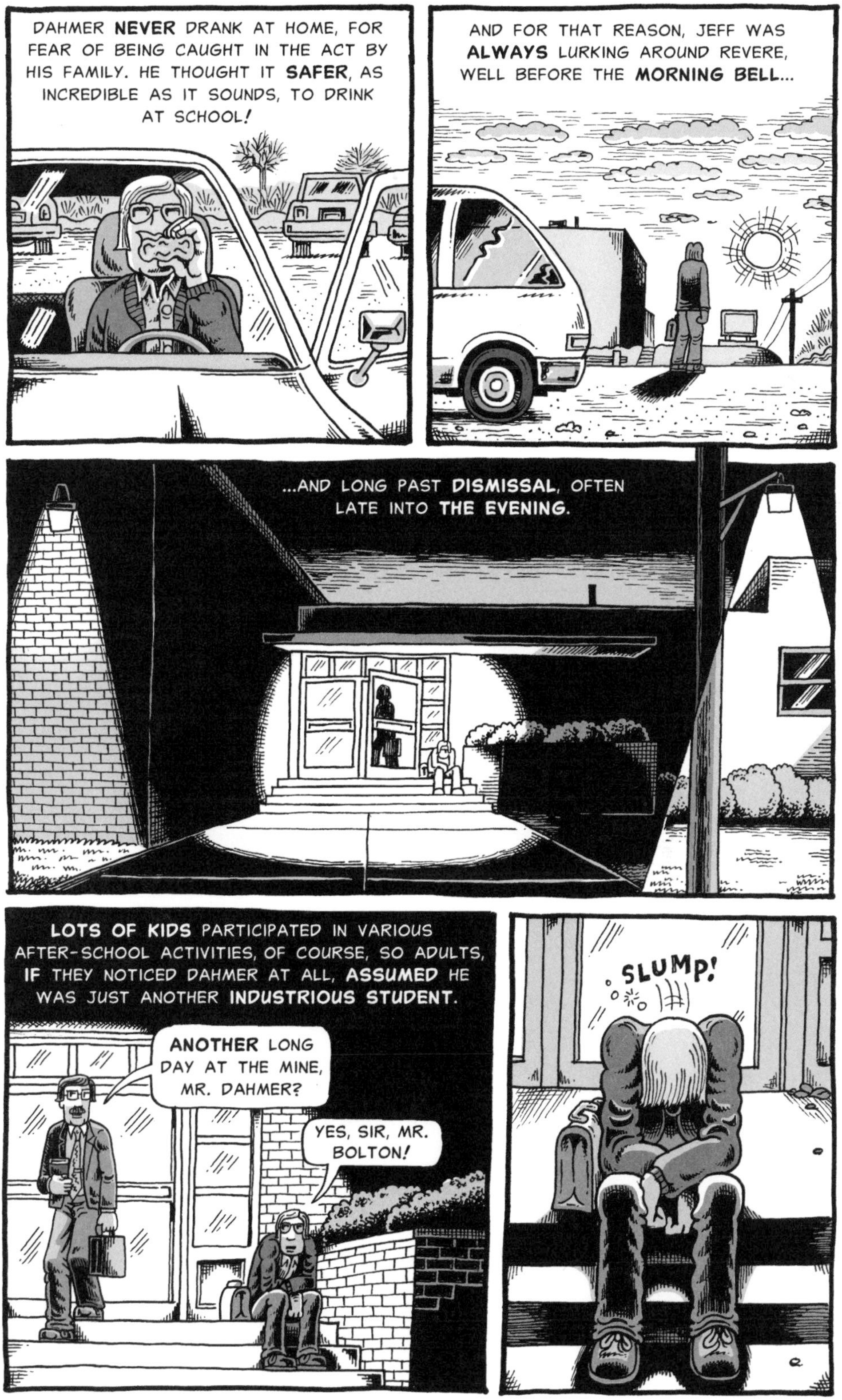
DAHMER NEVER DRANK AT HOME, FOR FEAR OF BEING CAUGHT IN THE ACT BY HIS FAMILY. HE THOUGHT IT SAFER, AS INCREDIBLE AS IT SOUNDS, TO DRINK AT SCHOOL!
AND FOR THAT REASON, JEFF WAS ALWAYS LURKING AROUND REVERE, WELL BEFORE THE MORNING BELL...
...AND LONG PAST DISMISSAL, OFTEN LATE INTO THE EVENING.
LOTS OF KIDS PARTICIPATED IN VARIOUS AFTER-SCHOOL ACTIVITIES, OF COURSE, SO ADULTS, IF THEY NOTICED DAHMER AT ALL, ASSUMED HE WAS JUST ANOTHER INDUSTRIOUS STUDENT.
ANOTHER LONG DAY AT THE MINE, MR. DAHMER?
YES, SIR, MR. BOLTON!
SLUMP!

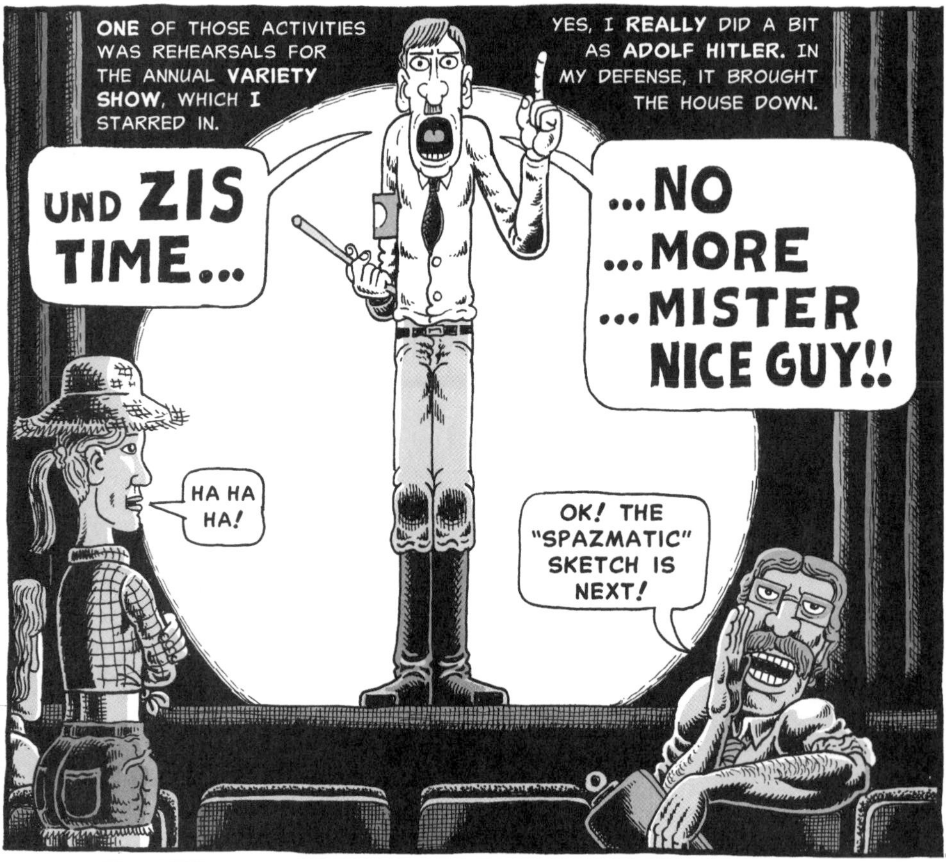
ONE OF THOSE ACTIVITIES WAS REHEARSALS FOR THE ANNUAL VARIETY SHOW, WHICH I STARRED IN.
YES, I REALLY DID A BIT AS ADOLF HITLER. IN MY DEFENSE, IT BROUGHT THE HOUSE DOWN.
UND ZIS TIME...
...NO ...MORE ...MISTER NICE GUY!!
HA HA HA!
OK! THE "SPAZMATIC" SKETCH IS NEXT!

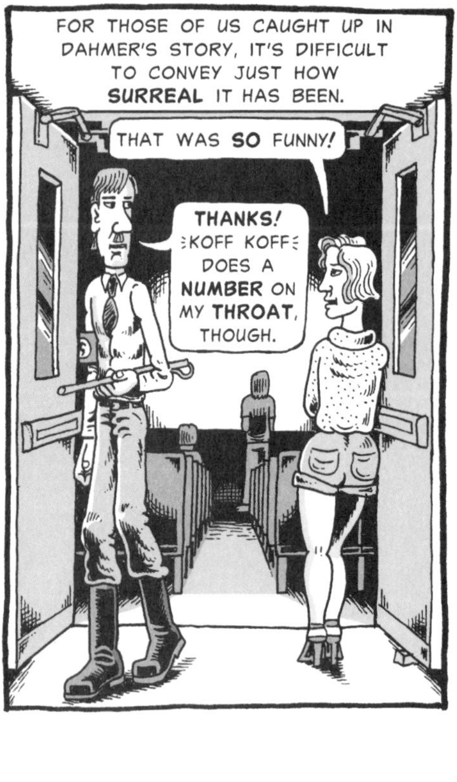
FOR THOSE OF US CAUGHT UP IN DAHMER'S STORY, IT'S DIFFICULT TO CONVEY JUST HOW SURREAL IT HAS BEEN.
THAT WAS SO FUNNY!
THANKS! KOFF KOFF DOES A NUMBER ON MY THROAT, THOUGH.

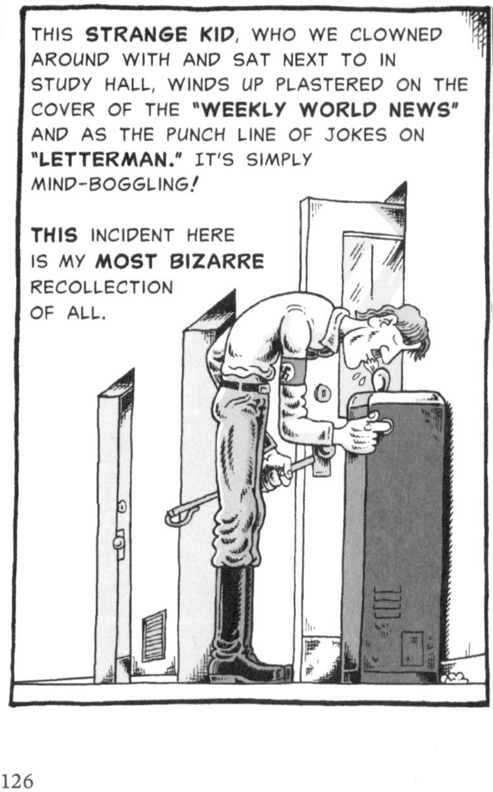
THIS STRANGE KID, WHO WE CLOWNED AROUND WITH AND SAT NEXT TO IN STUDY HALL, WINDS UP PLASTERED ON THE COVER OF THE "WEEKLY WORLD NEWS" AND AS THE PUNCH LINE OF JOKES ON "LETTERMAN." IT'S SIMPLY MIND-BOGGLING!
THIS INCIDENT HERE IS MY MOST BIZARRE RECOLLECTION OF ALL.

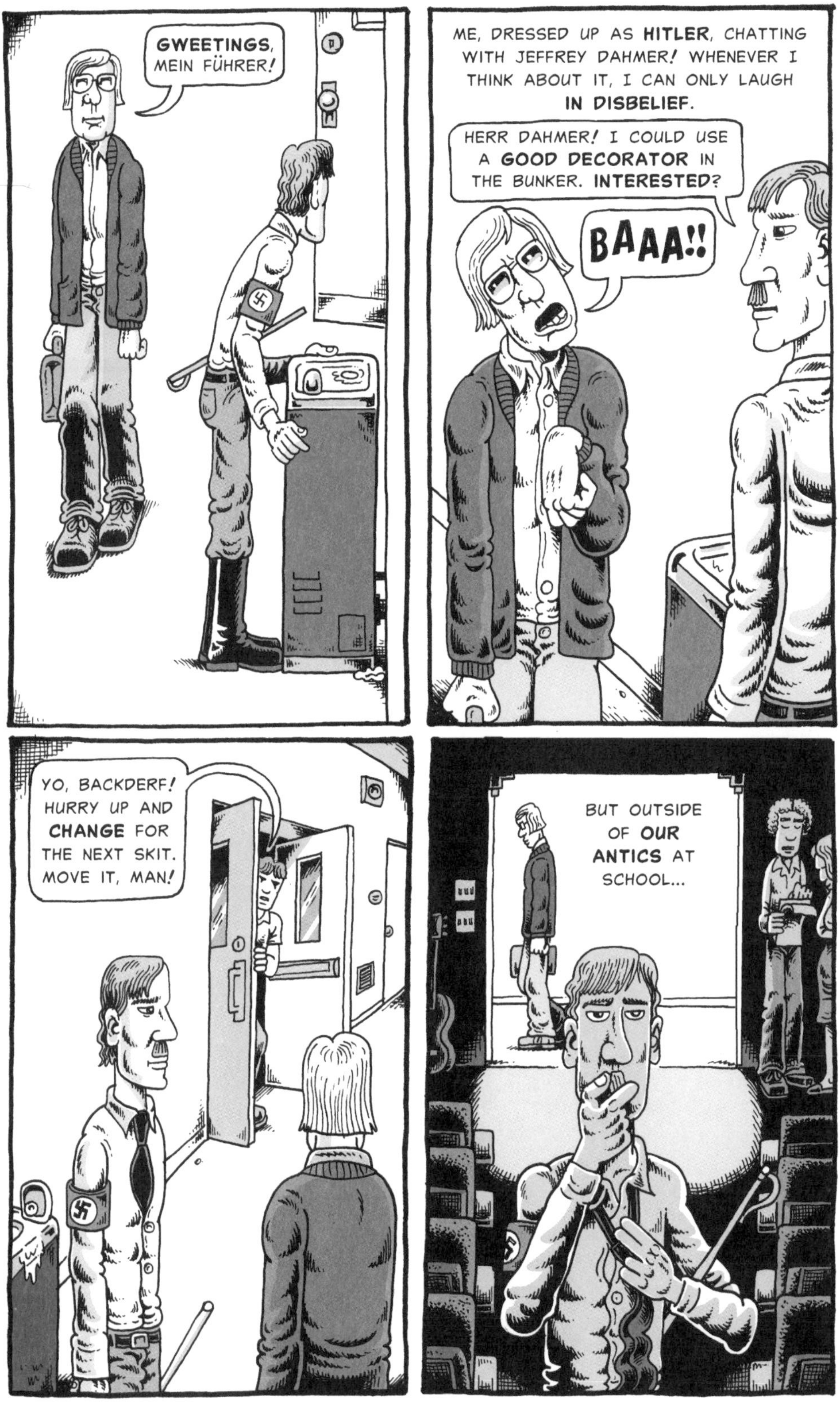
GWEETINGS, MEIN FÜHRER!
ME, DRESSED UP AS HITLER, CHATTING WITH JEFFREY DAHMER! WHENEVER I THINK ABOUT IT, I CAN ONLY LAUGH IN DISBELIEF.
HERR DAHMER! I COULD USE A GOOD DECORATOR IN THE BUNKER. INTERESTED?
BAAA!!
YO, BACKDERF! HURRY UP AND CHANGE FOR THE NEXT SKIT. MOVE IT, MAN!
BUT OUTSIDE OF OUR ANTICS AT SCHOOL...

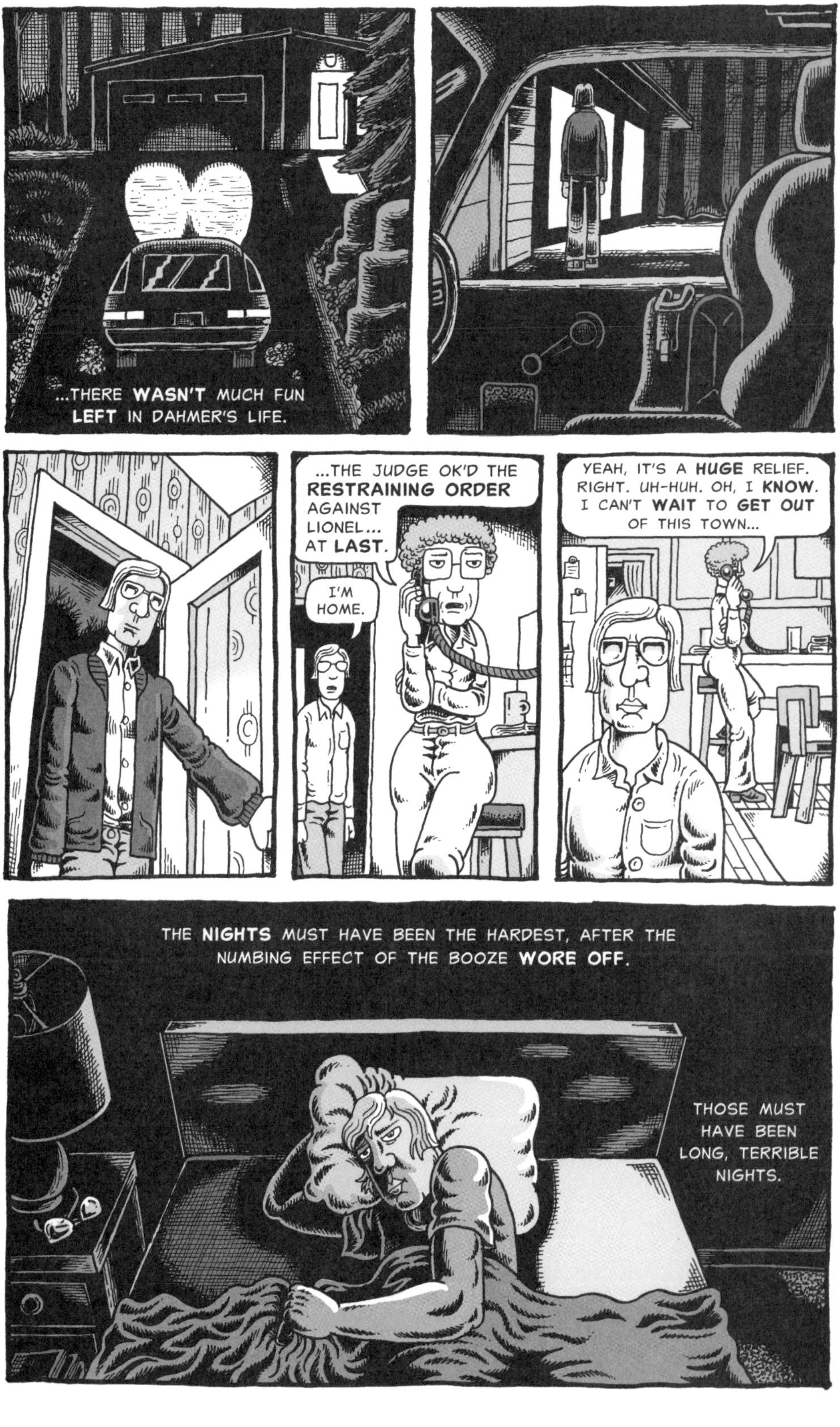
...THERE **WASN'T** MUCH FUN **LEFT** IN DAHMER'S LIFE.
...THE JUDGE OK'D THE **RESTRAINING ORDER** AGAINST LIONEL... AT **LAST**.
I'M HOME.
YEAH, IT'S A **HUGE** RELIEF. RIGHT. UH-HUH. OH, I **KNOW**. I CAN'T **WAIT** TO **GET OUT** OF THIS TOWN...
THE **NIGHTS** MUST HAVE BEEN THE HARDEST, AFTER THE NUMBING EFFECT OF THE BOOZE **WORE OFF**.
THOSE MUST HAVE BEEN LONG, TERRIBLE NIGHTS.

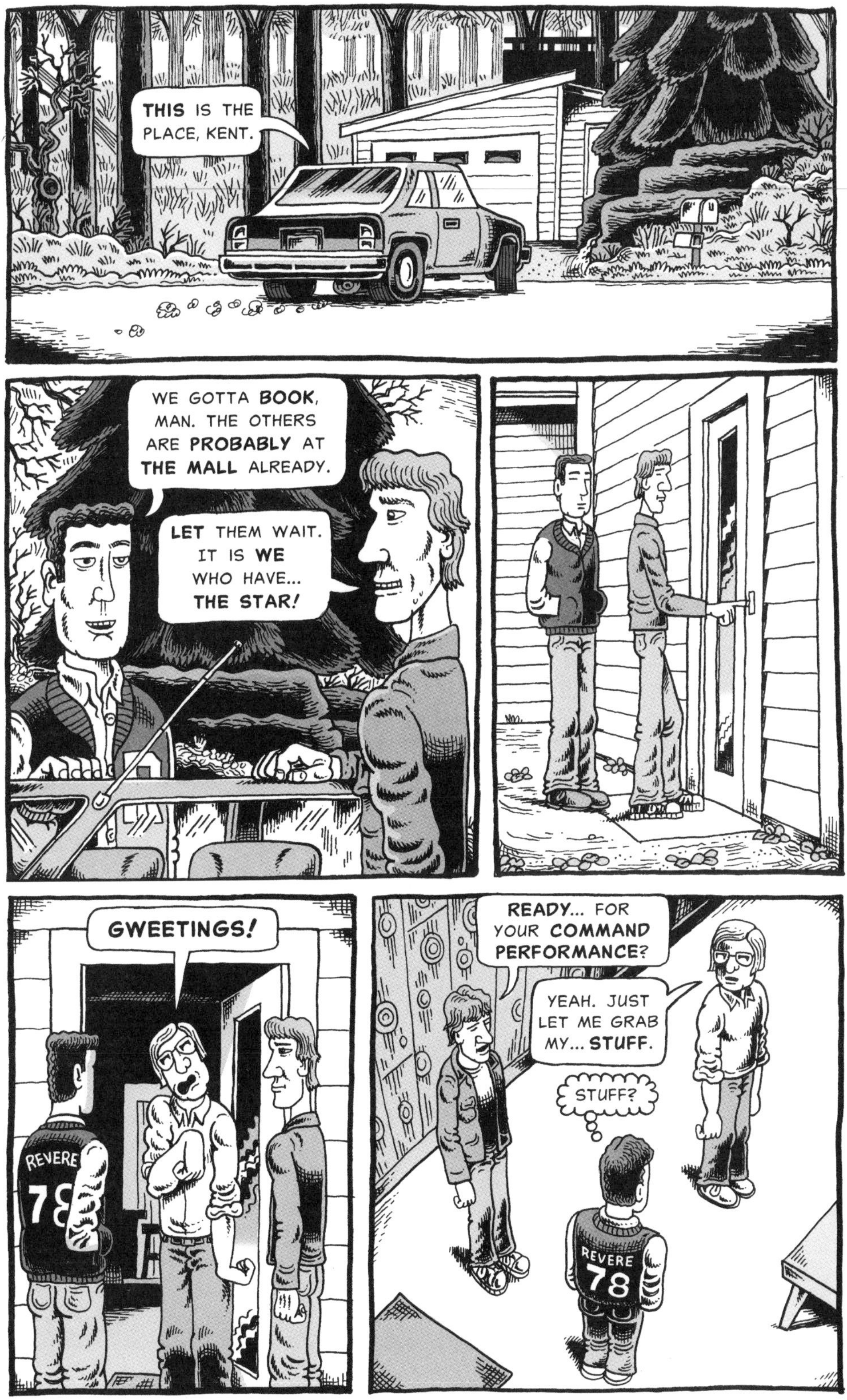
THIS IS THE PLACE, KENT.
WE GOTTA BOOK, MAN. THE OTHERS ARE PROBABLY AT THE MALL ALREADY.
LET THEM WAIT. IT IS WE WHO HAVE... THE STAR!
GWEETINGS!
REVERE 78
READY... FOR YOUR COMMAND PERFORMANCE?
YEAH. JUST LET ME GRAB MY... STUFF.
STUFF?
REVERE 78

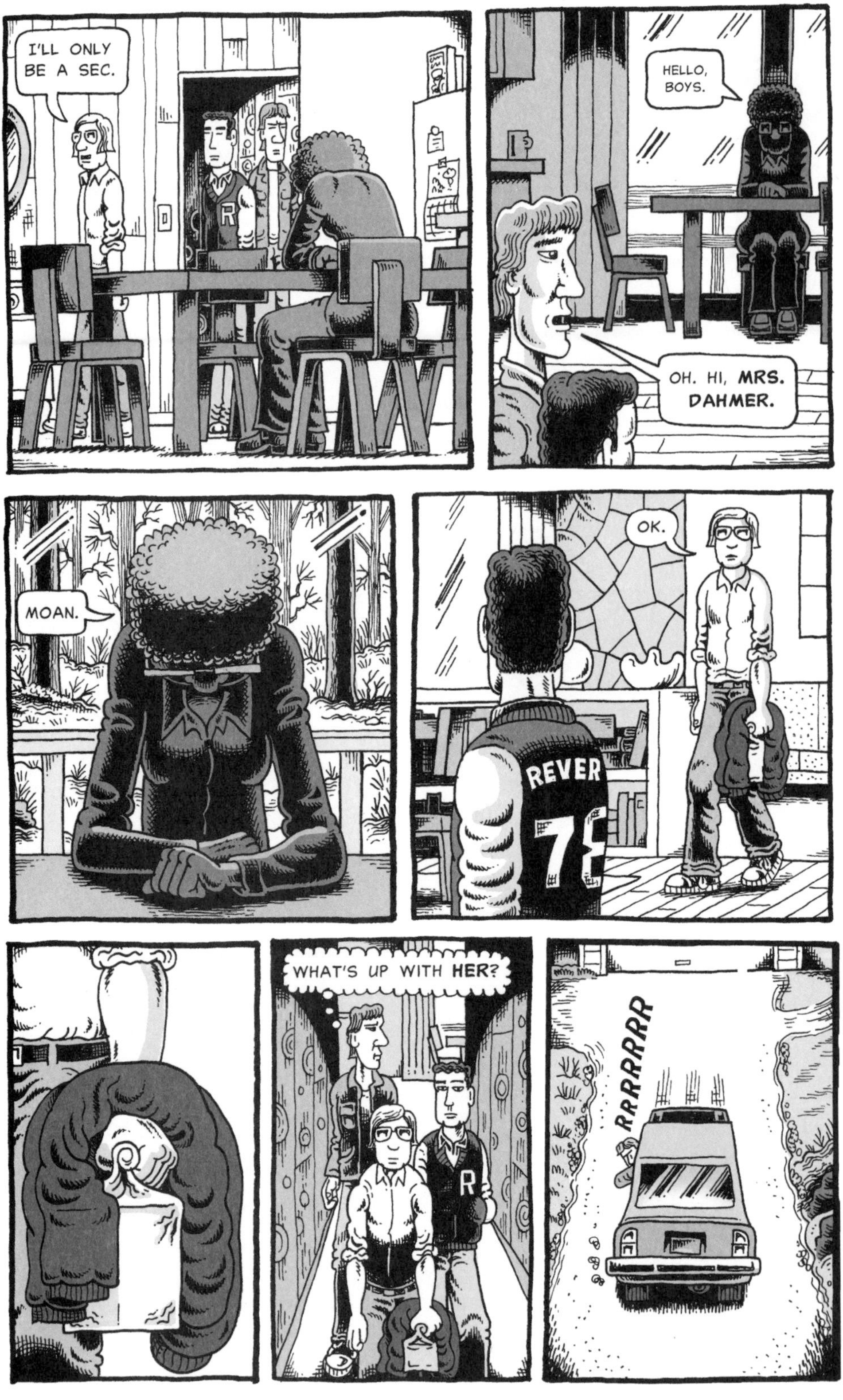
I'LL ONLY BE A SEC.
HELLO, BOYS.
OH. HI, MRS. DAHMER.
MOAN.
OK.
REVER
78
WHAT'S UP WITH HER?
RRRRRRR

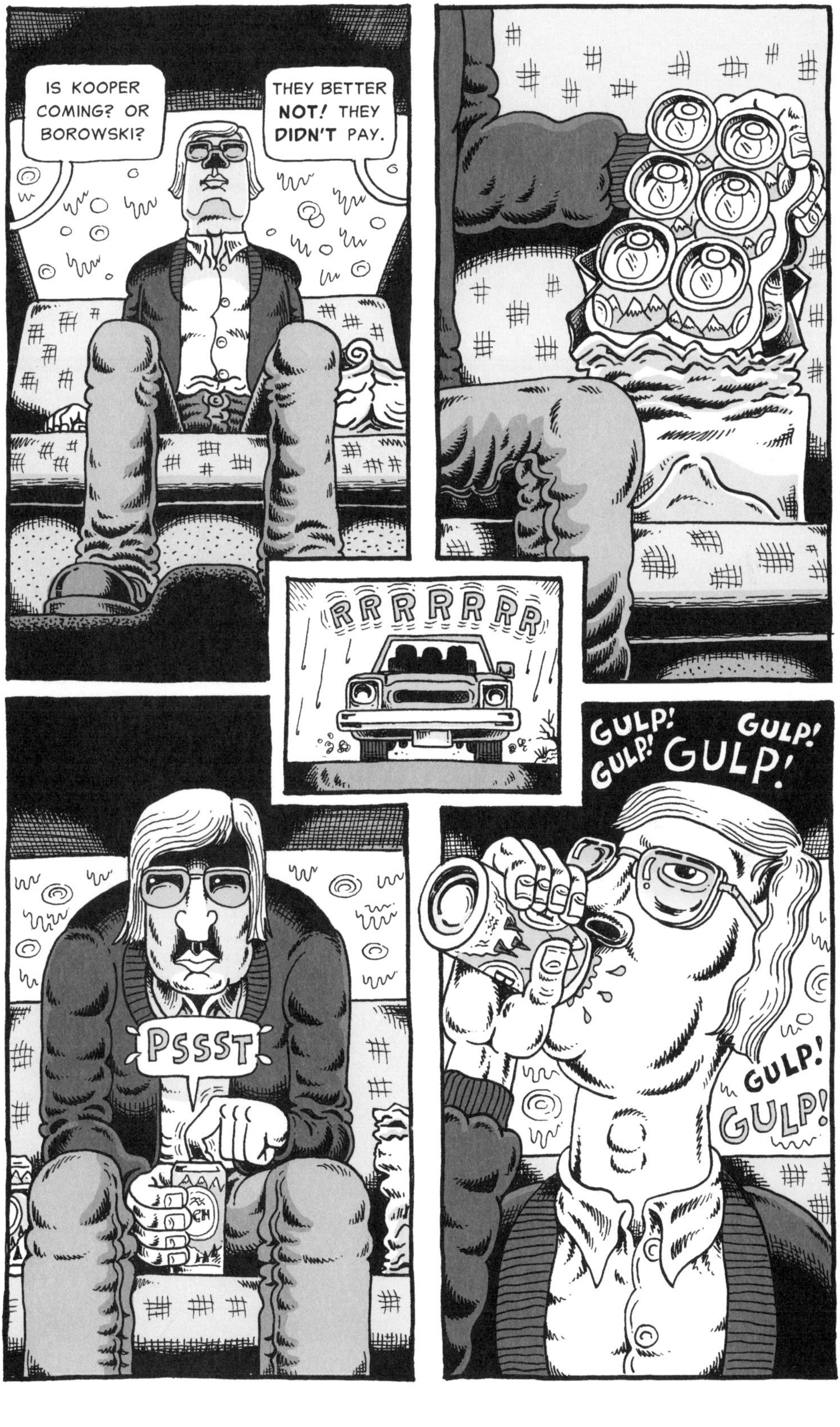

IS KOOPER COMING? OR BOROWSKI?
THEY BETTER **NOT!** THEY **DIDN'T** PAY.
RRRRRRR
PSSST
GULP! GULP! GULP! GULP!
GULP! GULP!

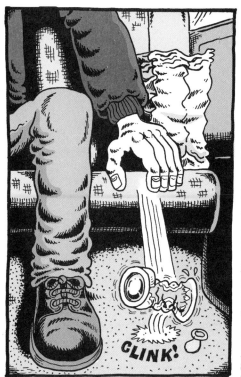

EACH OF US IN THE DAHMER FAN CLUB HAD **A MOMENT** WHEN THE REALIZATION HIT THAT DAHMER WAS NOT JUST ODD, BUT **TRULY SCARY.**

CLINK!

THIS WAS **MY** MOMENT.

GLUB! GLUB!

DANG!

132

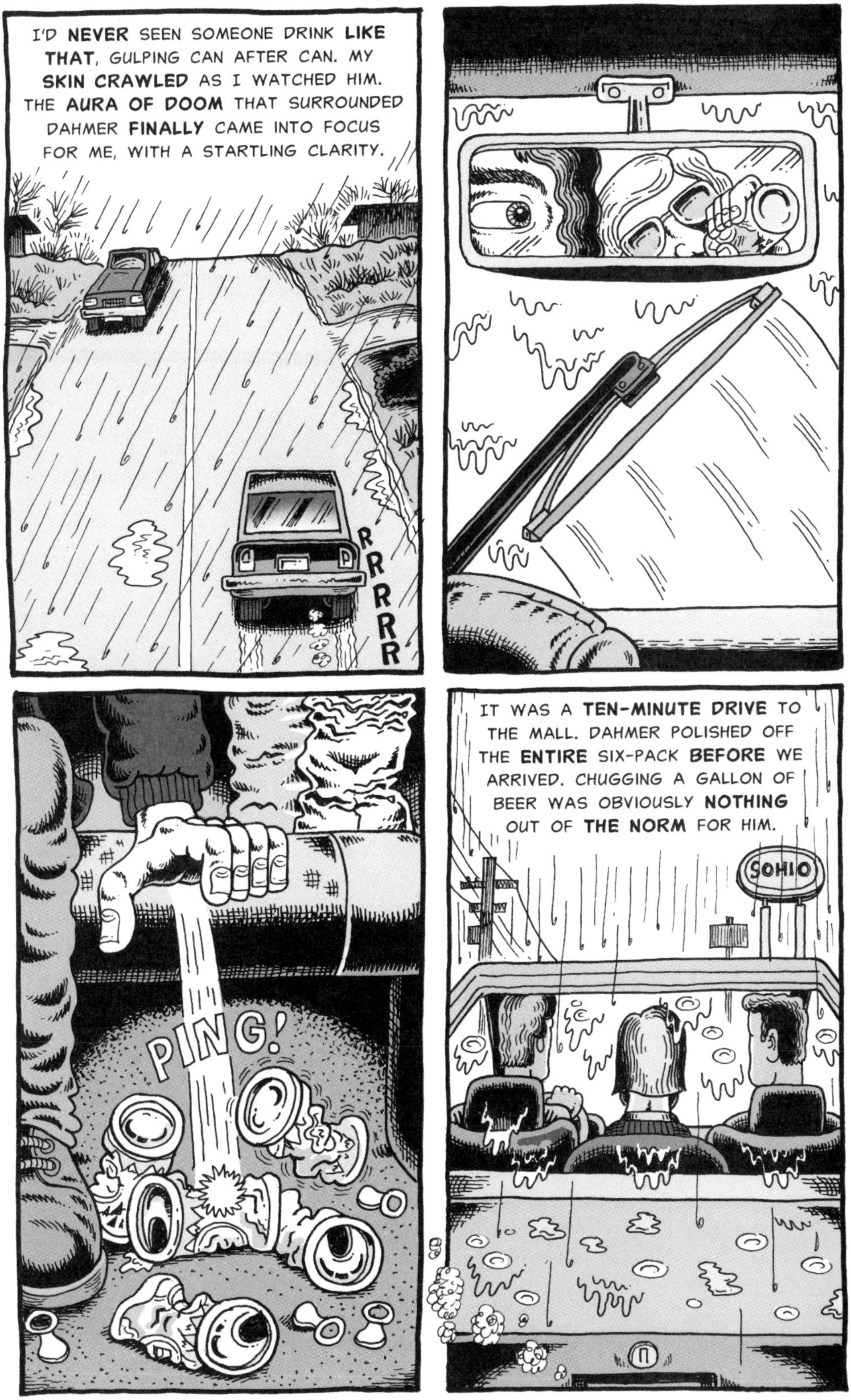
I'D NEVER SEEN SOMEONE DRINK LIKE THAT, GULPING CAN AFTER CAN. MY SKIN CRAWLED AS I WATCHED HIM. THE AURA OF DOOM THAT SURROUNDED DAHMER FINALLY CAME INTO FOCUS FOR ME, WITH A STARTLING CLARITY.
RRRRR
PING!
IT WAS A TEN-MINUTE DRIVE TO THE MALL. DAHMER POLISHED OFF THE ENTIRE SIX-PACK BEFORE WE ARRIVED. CHUGGING A GALLON OF BEER WAS OBVIOUSLY NOTHING OUT OF THE NORM FOR HIM.
SOHIO

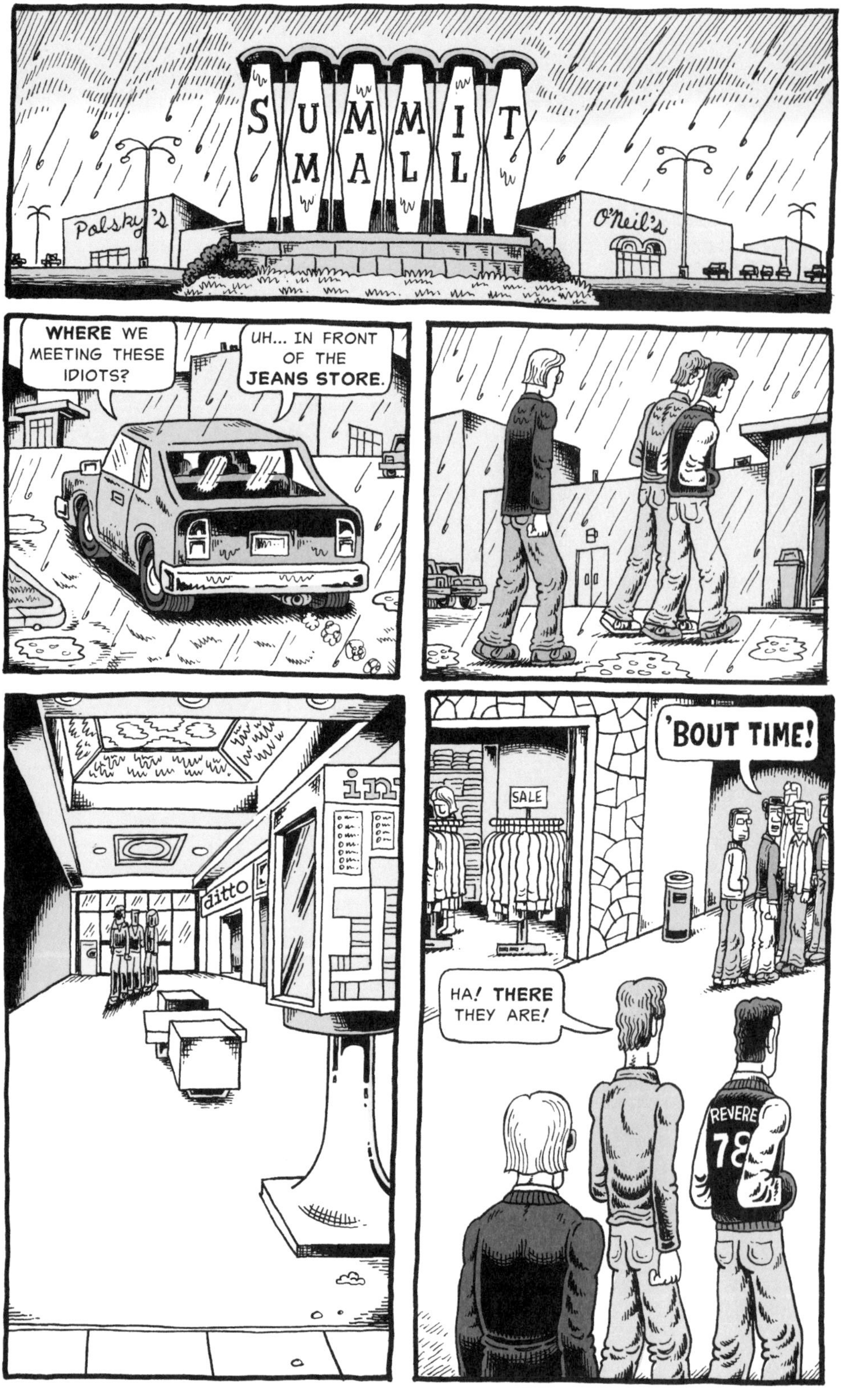
SUMMIT MALL
Polsky's
O'Neil's
WHERE WE MEETING THESE IDIOTS?
UH... IN FRONT OF THE JEANS STORE.
ditto
SALE
'BOUT TIME!
HA! THERE THEY ARE!
REVERE
78

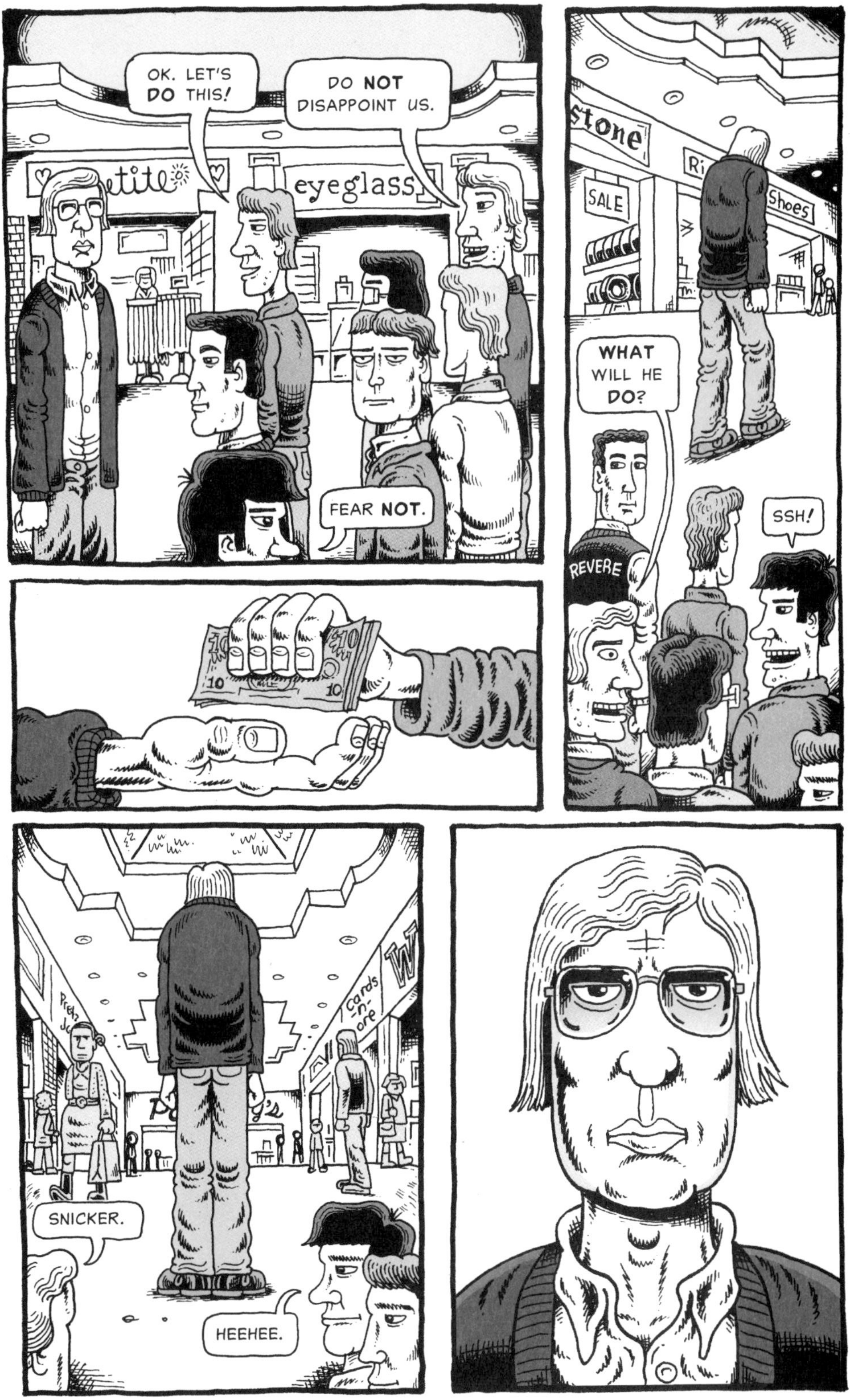
OK. LET'S DO THIS!
DO NOT DISAPPOINT US.
etite
eyeglass
FEAR NOT.
stone
SALE
Shoes
WHAT WILL HE DO?
SSH!
REVERE
10
SNICKER.
HEEHEE.

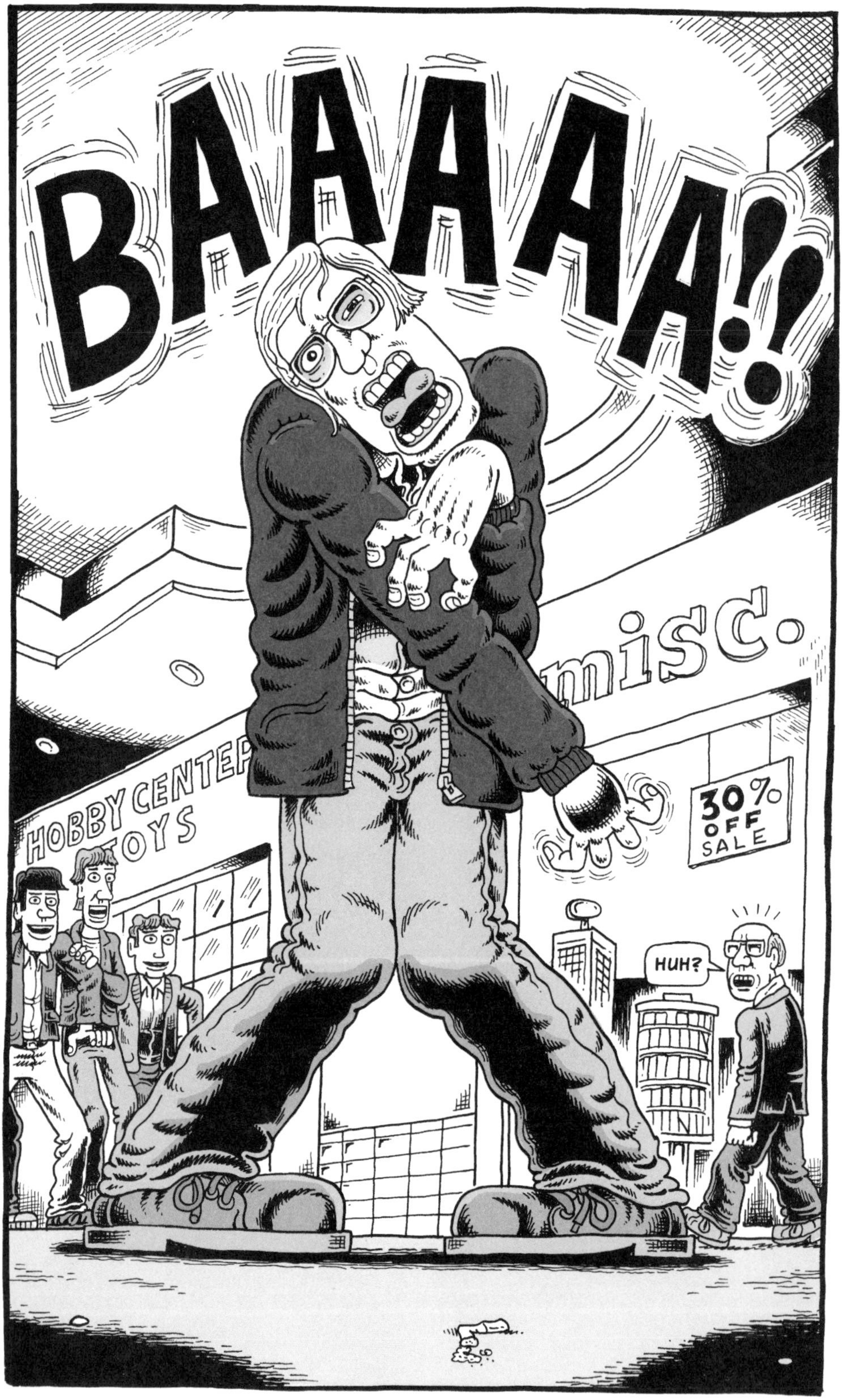
BAAAAA!?
misc.
HOBBY CENTER
TOYS
30% OFF SALE
HUH?

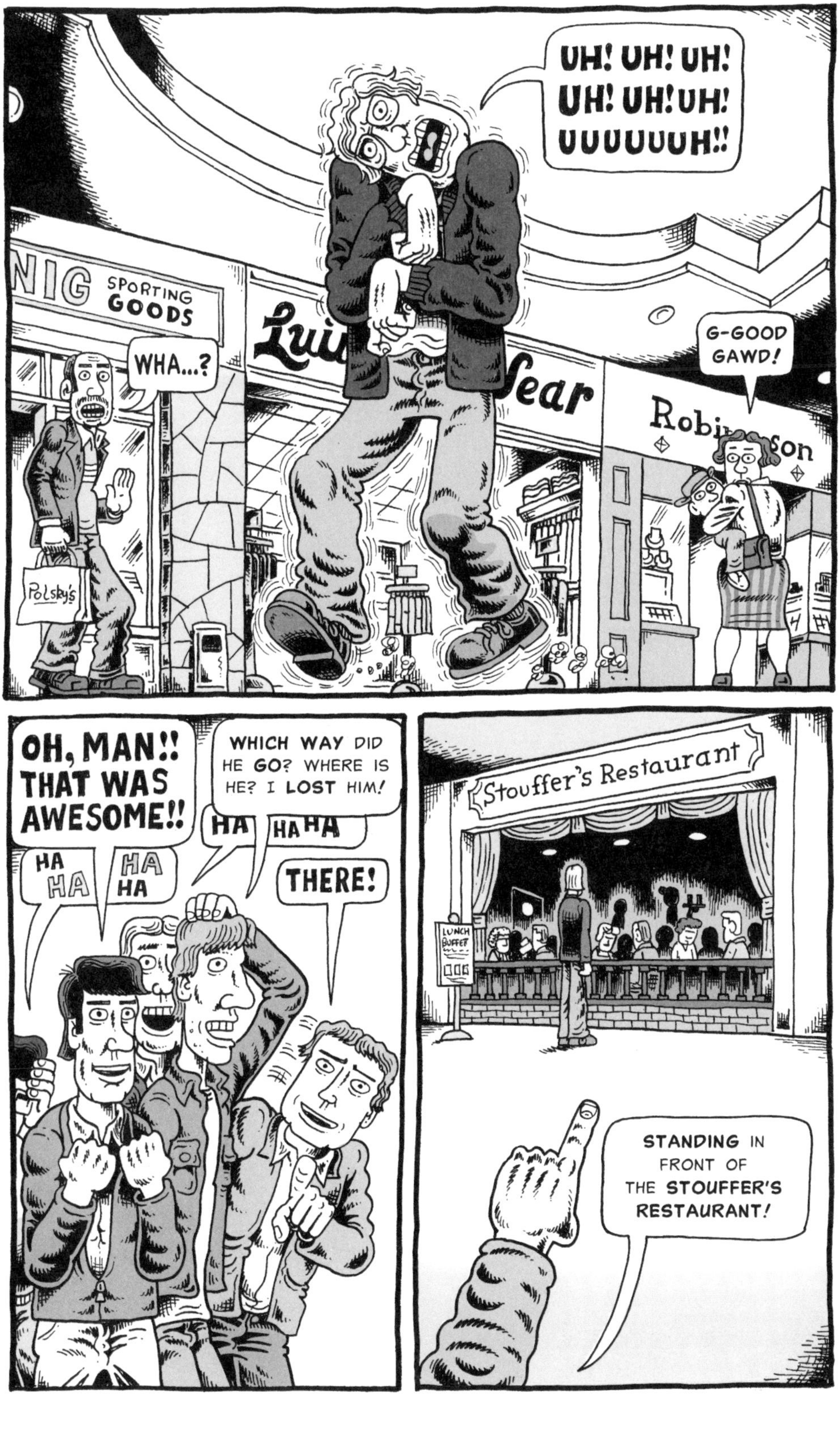
UH! UH! UH!
UH! UH! UH!
UUUUUUH!!
NIG SPORTING GOODS
WHA...?
Polsky's
G-GOOD GAWD!
Robinson
OH, MAN!! THAT WAS AWESOME!!
HA HA
HA HA
WHICH WAY DID HE GO? WHERE IS HE? I LOST HIM!
HA
HA HA
THERE!
Stouffer's Restaurant
LUNCH BUFFET
STANDING IN FRONT OF THE STOUFFER'S RESTAURANT!

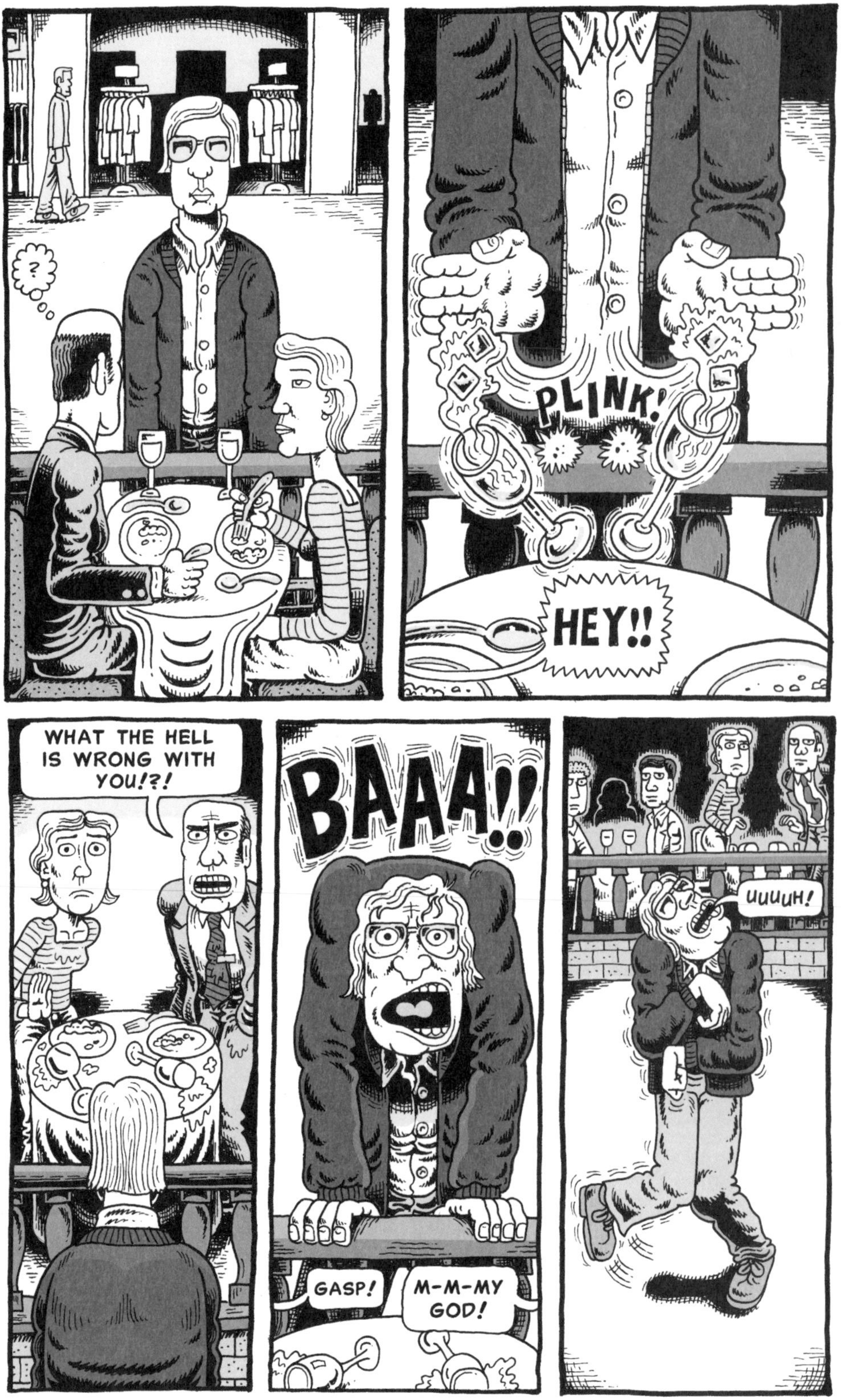
?
PLINK!
HEY!!
WHAT THE HELL IS WRONG WITH YOU!?!
BAAA!!
GASP!
M-M-MY GOD!
UUUUH!

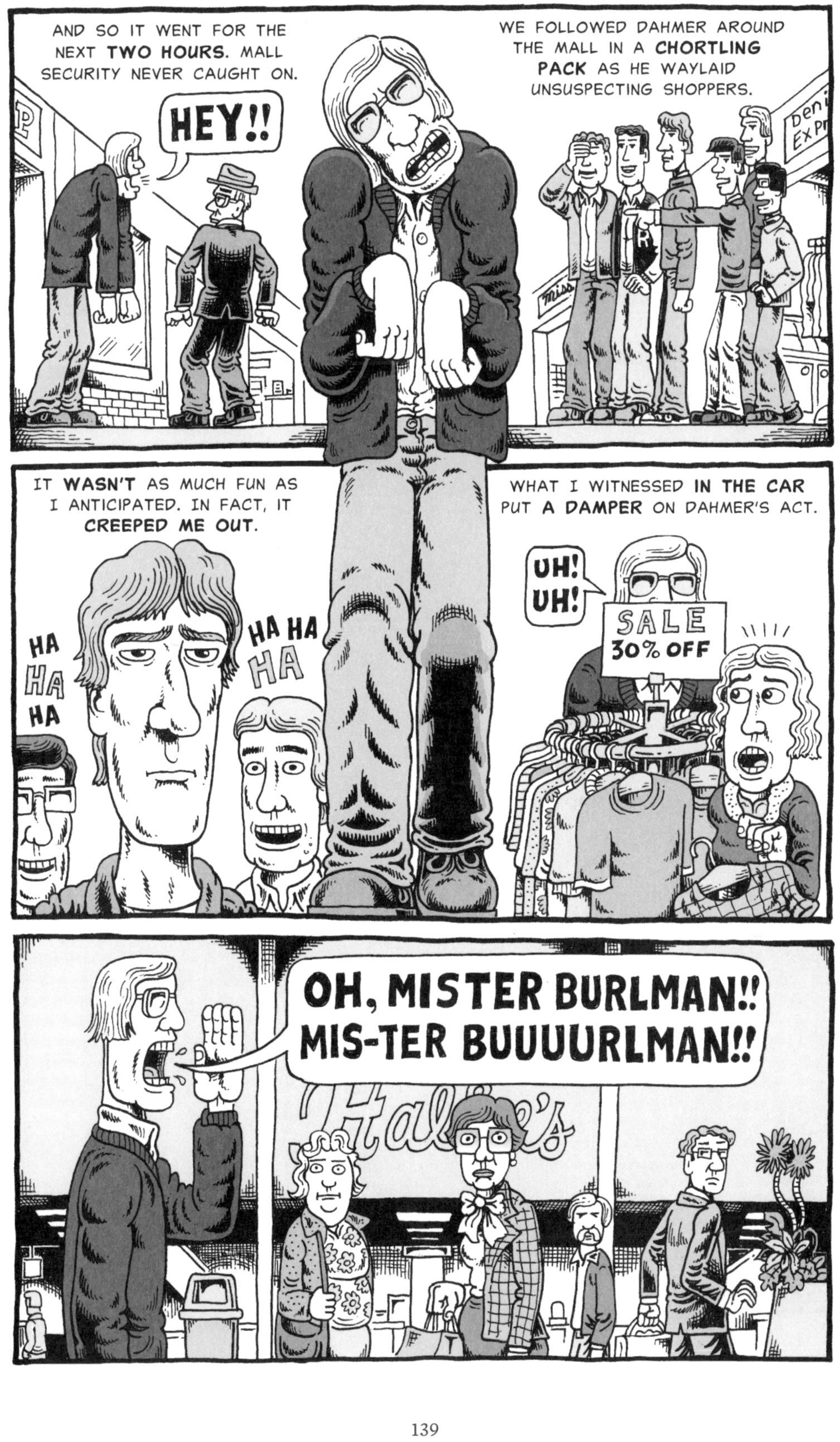
AND SO IT WENT FOR THE NEXT TWO HOURS. MALL SECURITY NEVER CAUGHT ON.
HEY!!
WE FOLLOWED DAHMER AROUND THE MALL IN A CHORTLING PACK AS HE WAYLAID UNSUSPECTING SHOPPERS.
IT WASN'T AS MUCH FUN AS I ANTICIPATED. IN FACT, IT CREEPED ME OUT.
HA HA HA
HA HA HA
WHAT I WITNESSED IN THE CAR PUT A DAMPER ON DAHMER'S ACT.
UH! UH!
SALE 30% OFF
OH, MISTER BURLMAN!! MIS-TER BUUUURLMAN!!

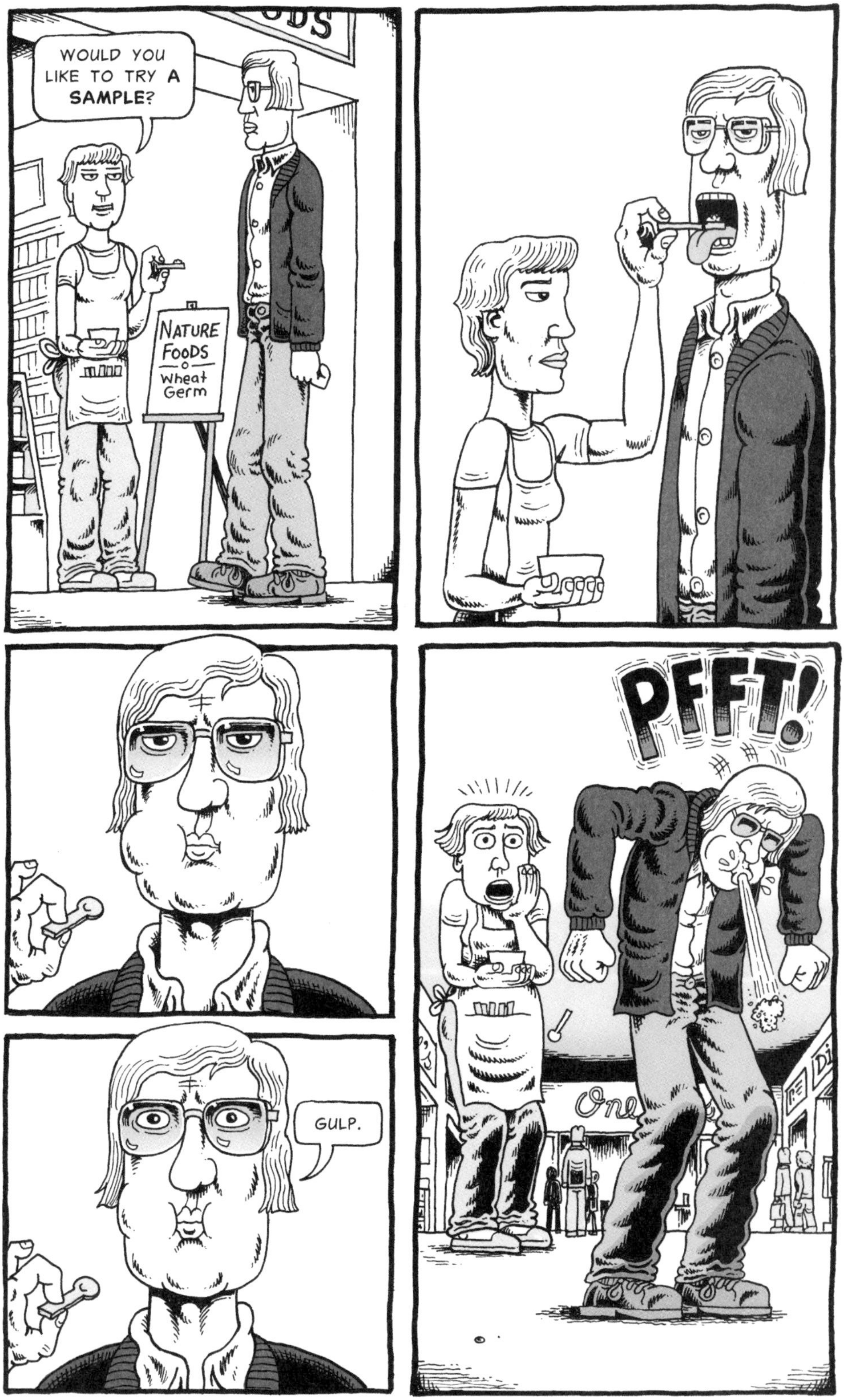
WOULD YOU LIKE TO TRY A SAMPLE?
NATURE FOODS
Wheat Germ
GULP.
PFFT!

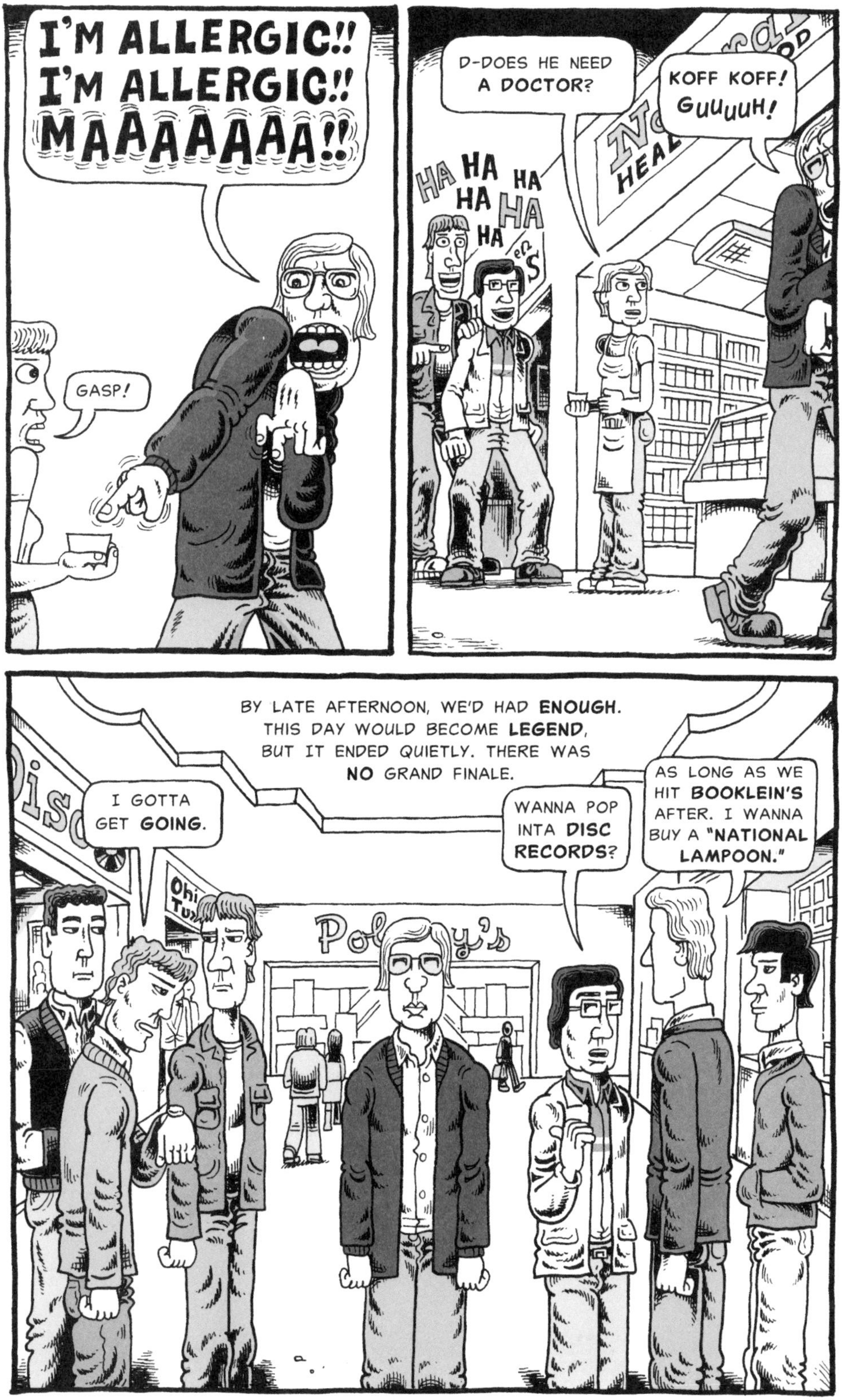
I'M ALLERGIC!! I'M ALLERGIC!! MAAAAAAA!!
GASP!
HA HA HA HA HA HA
D-DOES HE NEED A DOCTOR?
KOFF KOFF! GUUUUH!
BY LATE AFTERNOON, WE'D HAD ENOUGH. THIS DAY WOULD BECOME LEGEND, BUT IT ENDED QUIETLY. THERE WAS NO GRAND FINALE.
I GOTTA GET GOING.
WANNA POP INTA DISC RECORDS?
AS LONG AS WE HIT BOOKLEIN'S AFTER. I WANNA BUY A "NATIONAL LAMPOON."

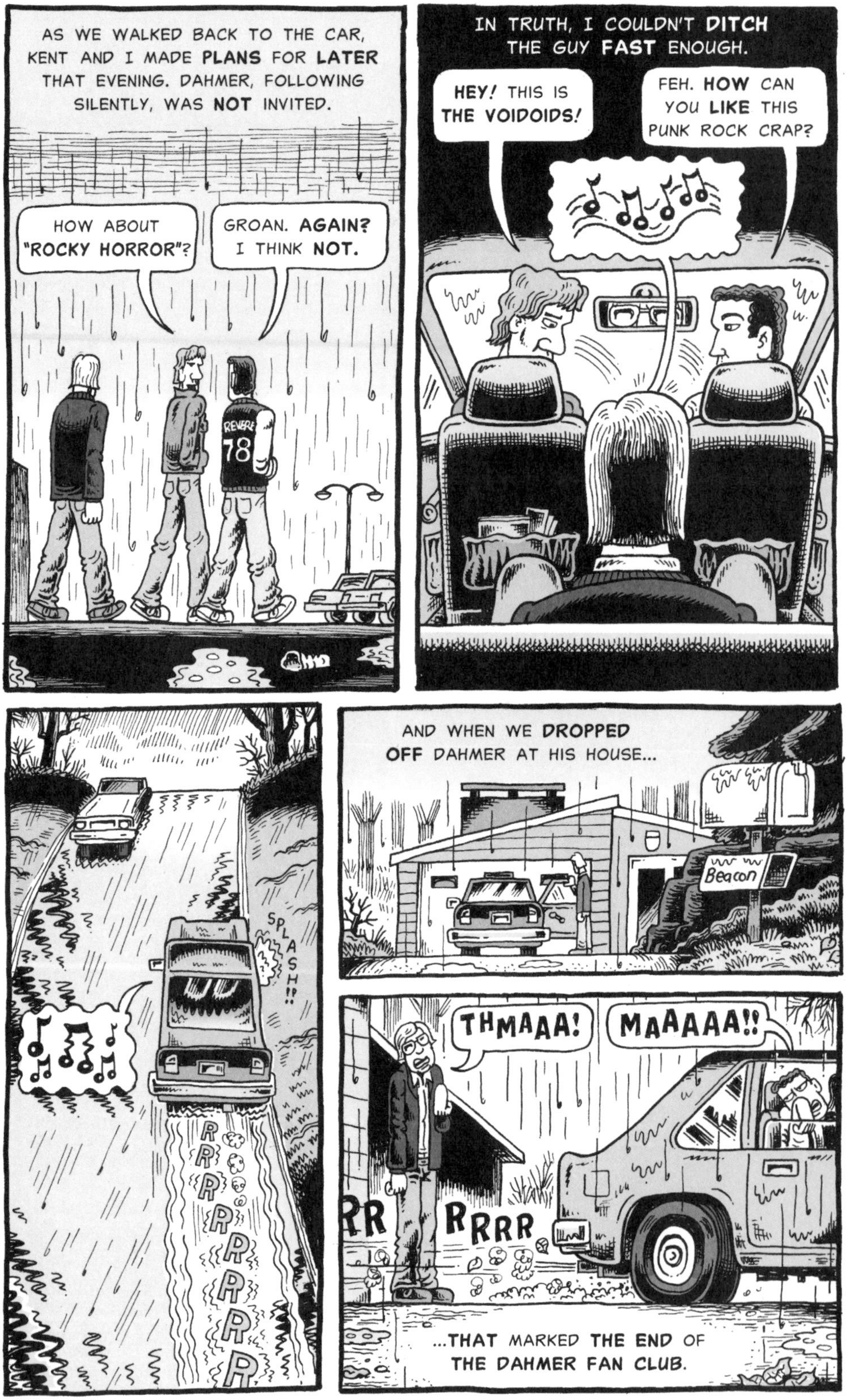
AS WE WALKED BACK TO THE CAR, KENT AND I MADE PLANS FOR LATER THAT EVENING. DAHMER, FOLLOWING SILENTLY, WAS NOT INVITED.
HOW ABOUT "ROCKY HORROR"?
GROAN. AGAIN? I THINK NOT.
REVERE
78
IN TRUTH, I COULDN'T DITCH THE GUY FAST ENOUGH.
HEY! THIS IS THE VOIDOIDS!
FEH. HOW CAN YOU LIKE THIS PUNK ROCK CRAP?
SPLASH!!
RRRRRRRR
AND WHEN WE DROPPED OFF DAHMER AT HIS HOUSE...
Beacon
THMAAA!
MAAAAA!!
RR
RRRR
...THAT MARKED THE END OF THE DAHMER FAN CLUB.

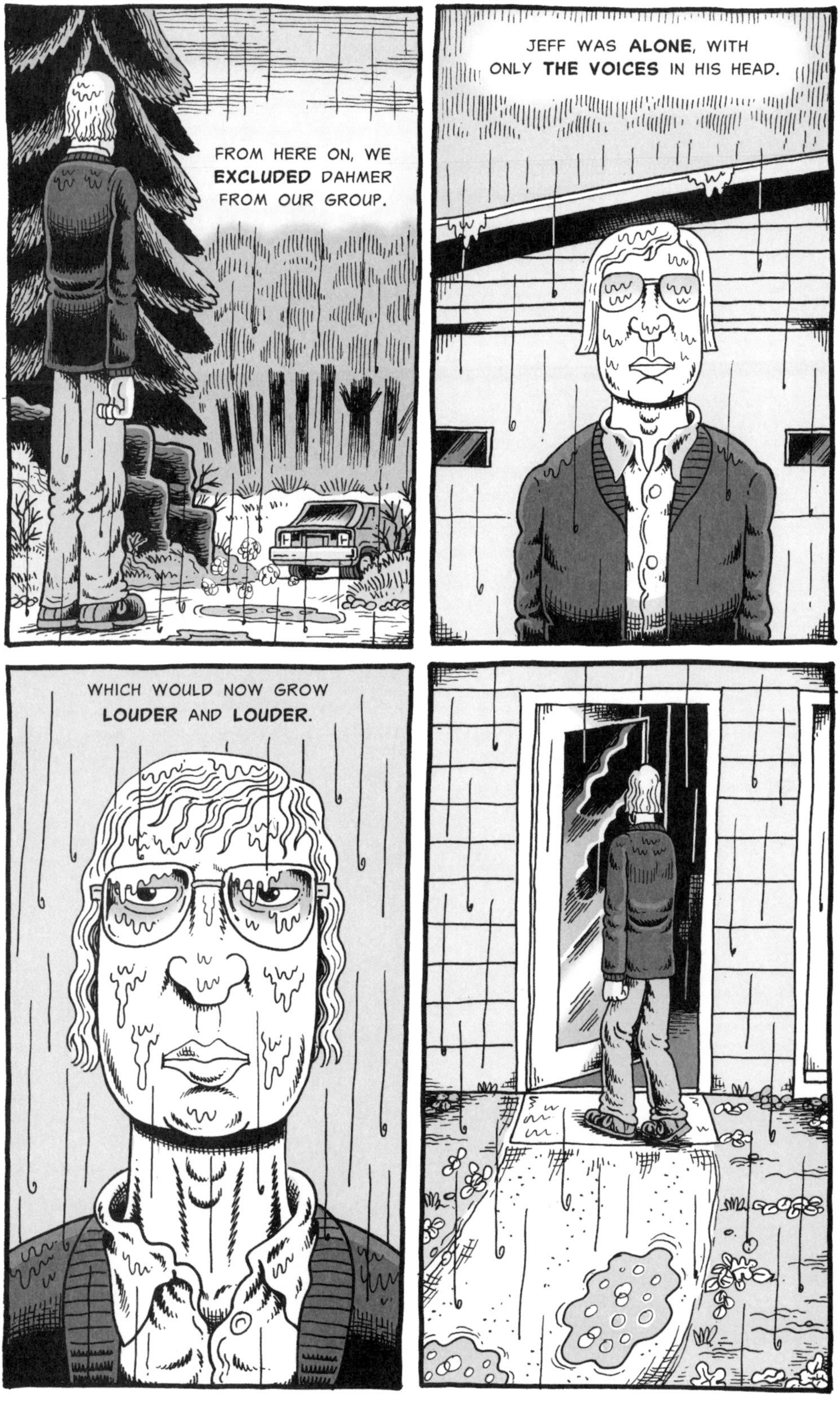
FROM HERE ON, WE EXCLUDED DAHMER FROM OUR GROUP.
JEFF WAS ALONE, WITH ONLY THE VOICES IN HIS HEAD.
WHICH WOULD NOW GROW LOUDER AND LOUDER.

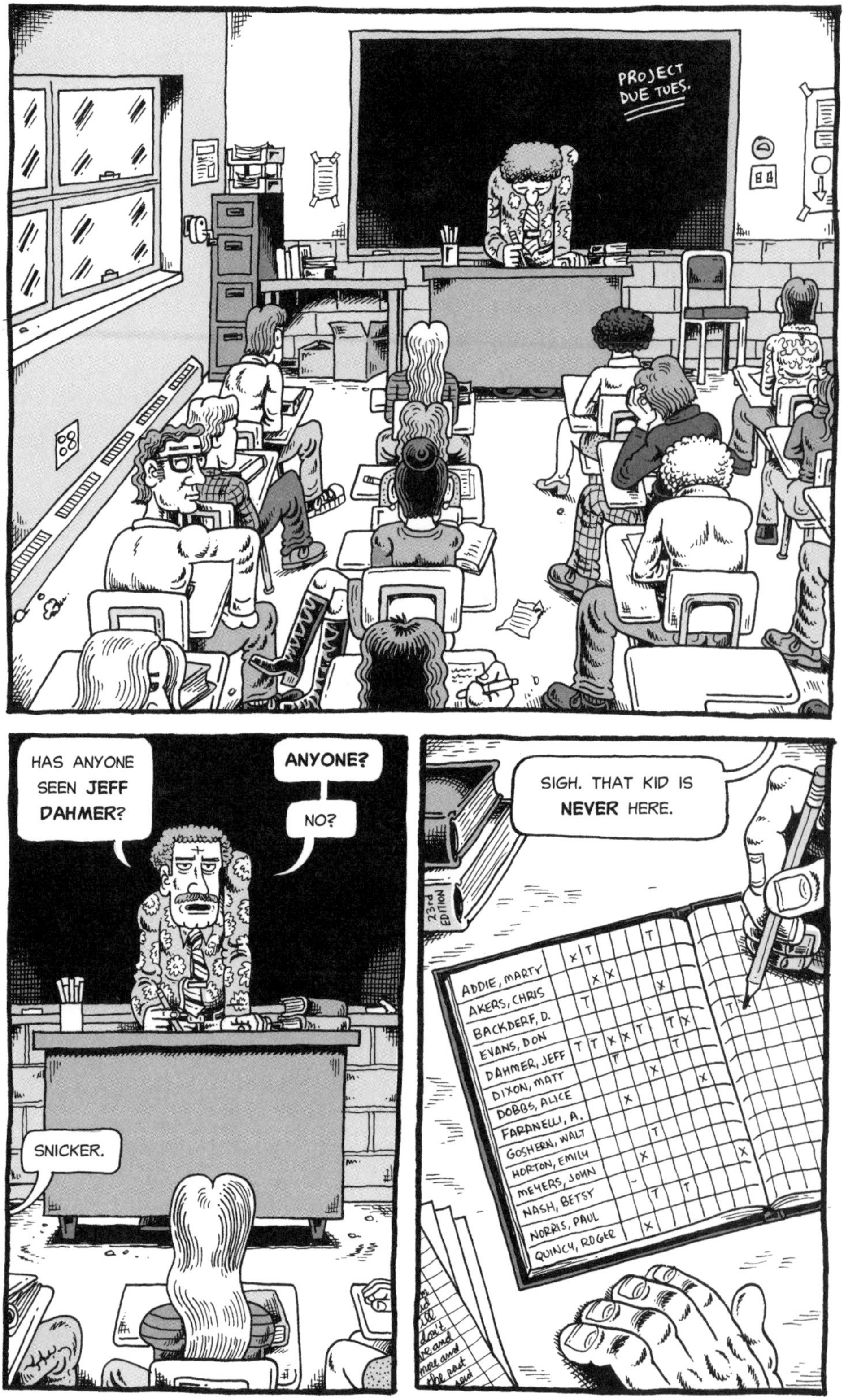
PROJECT DUE TUES.
HAS ANYONE SEEN JEFF DAHMER?
ANYONE?
NO?
SNICKER.
SIGH. THAT KID IS NEVER HERE.
23rd EDITION
ADDIE, MARTY
AKERS, CHRIS
BACKDERF, D.
EVANS, DON
DAHMER, JEFF
DIXON, MATT
DOBBS, ALICE
FARANELLI, A.
GOSHERN, WALT
HORTON, EMILY
MEYERS, JOHN
NASH, BETSY
NORRIS, PAUL
QUINCY, ROGER

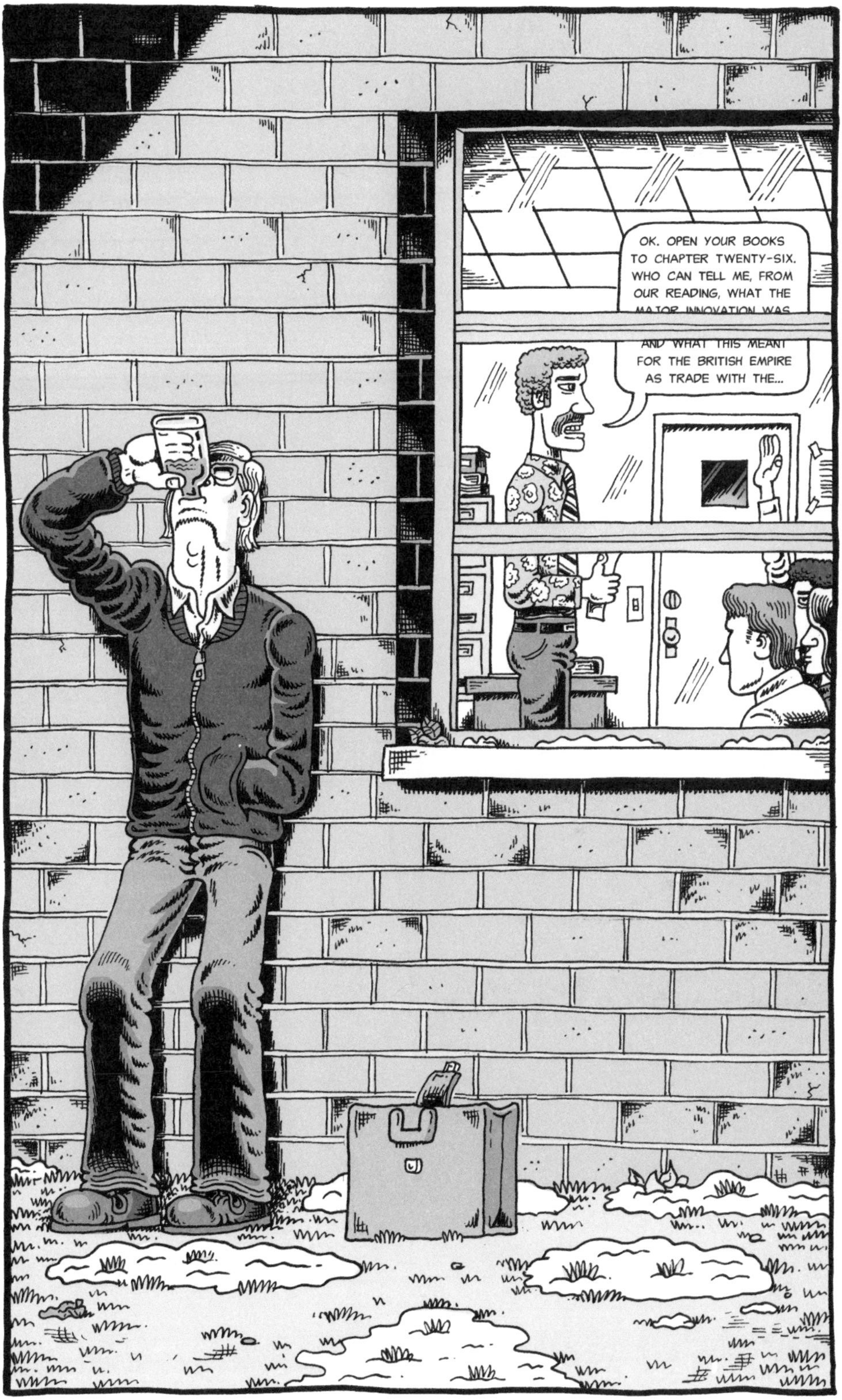
OK. OPEN YOUR BOOKS TO CHAPTER TWENTY-SIX. WHO CAN TELL ME, FROM OUR READING, WHAT THE MAJOR INNOVATION WAS
AND WHAT THIS MEANT FOR THE BRITISH EMPIRE AS TRADE WITH THE...

PART 4

Becoming the Monster

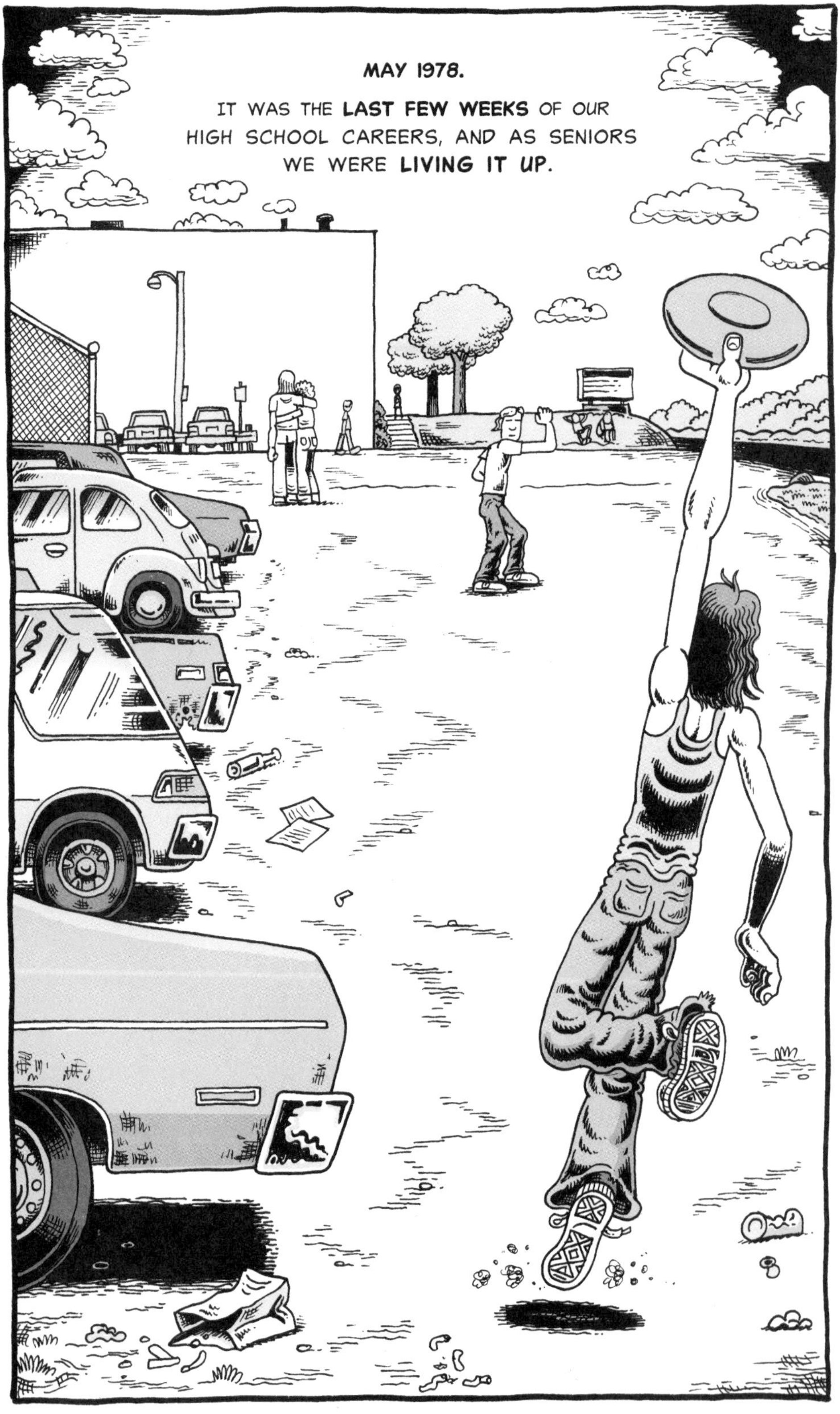
MAY 1978.
IT WAS THE LAST FEW WEEKS OF OUR HIGH SCHOOL CAREERS, AND AS SENIORS WE WERE LIVING IT UP.

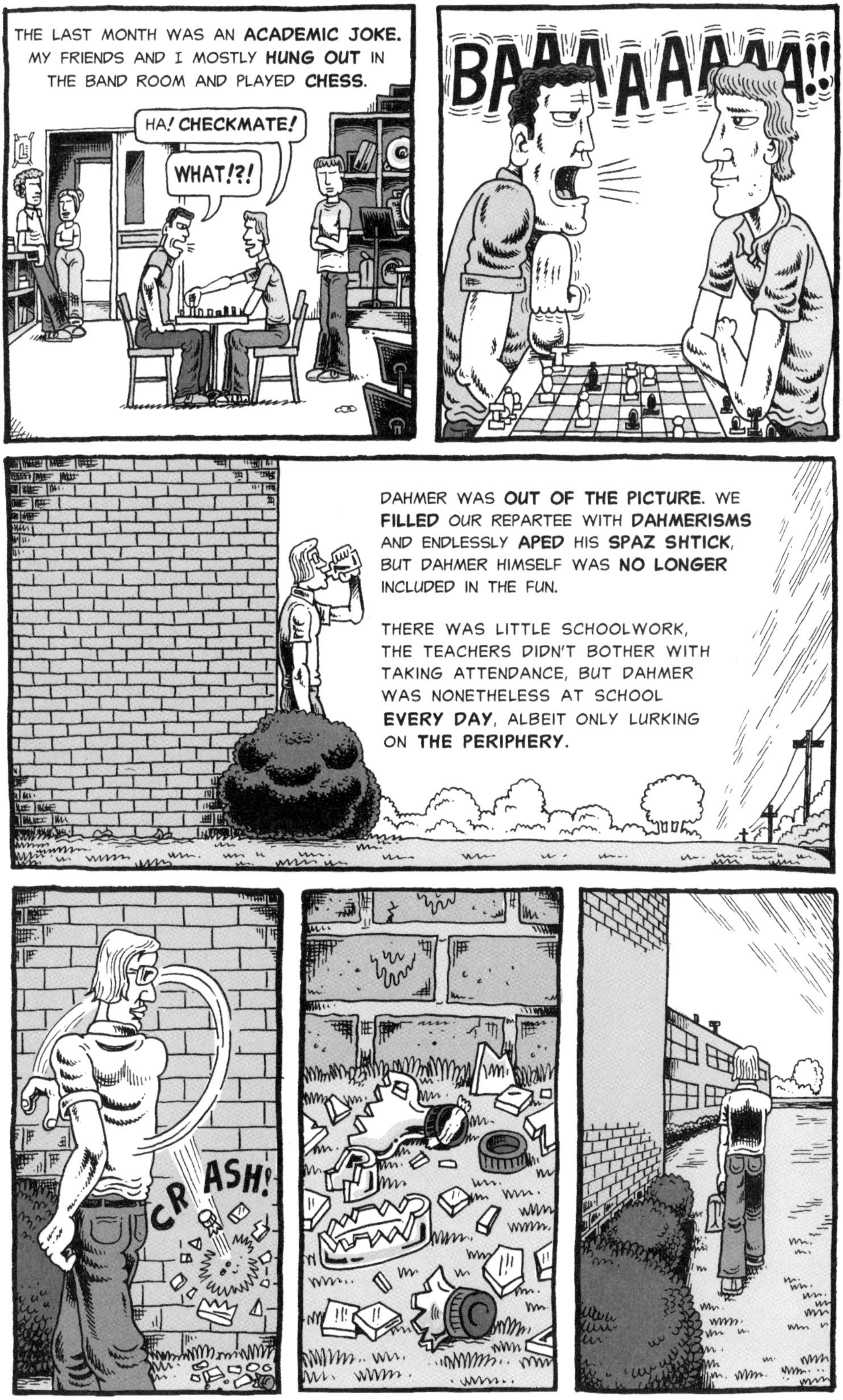
THE LAST MONTH WAS AN ACADEMIC JOKE. MY FRIENDS AND I MOSTLY HUNG OUT IN THE BAND ROOM AND PLAYED CHESS.
HA! CHECKMATE!
WHAT!?!
BAAAAAAAA!!
DAHMER WAS OUT OF THE PICTURE. WE FILLED OUR REPARTEE WITH DAHMERISMS AND ENDLESSLY APED HIS SPAZ SHTICK, BUT DAHMER HIMSELF WAS NO LONGER INCLUDED IN THE FUN.
THERE WAS LITTLE SCHOOLWORK, THE TEACHERS DIDN'T BOTHER WITH TAKING ATTENDANCE, BUT DAHMER WAS NONETHELESS AT SCHOOL EVERY DAY, ALBEIT ONLY LURKING ON THE PERIPHERY.
CRASH!

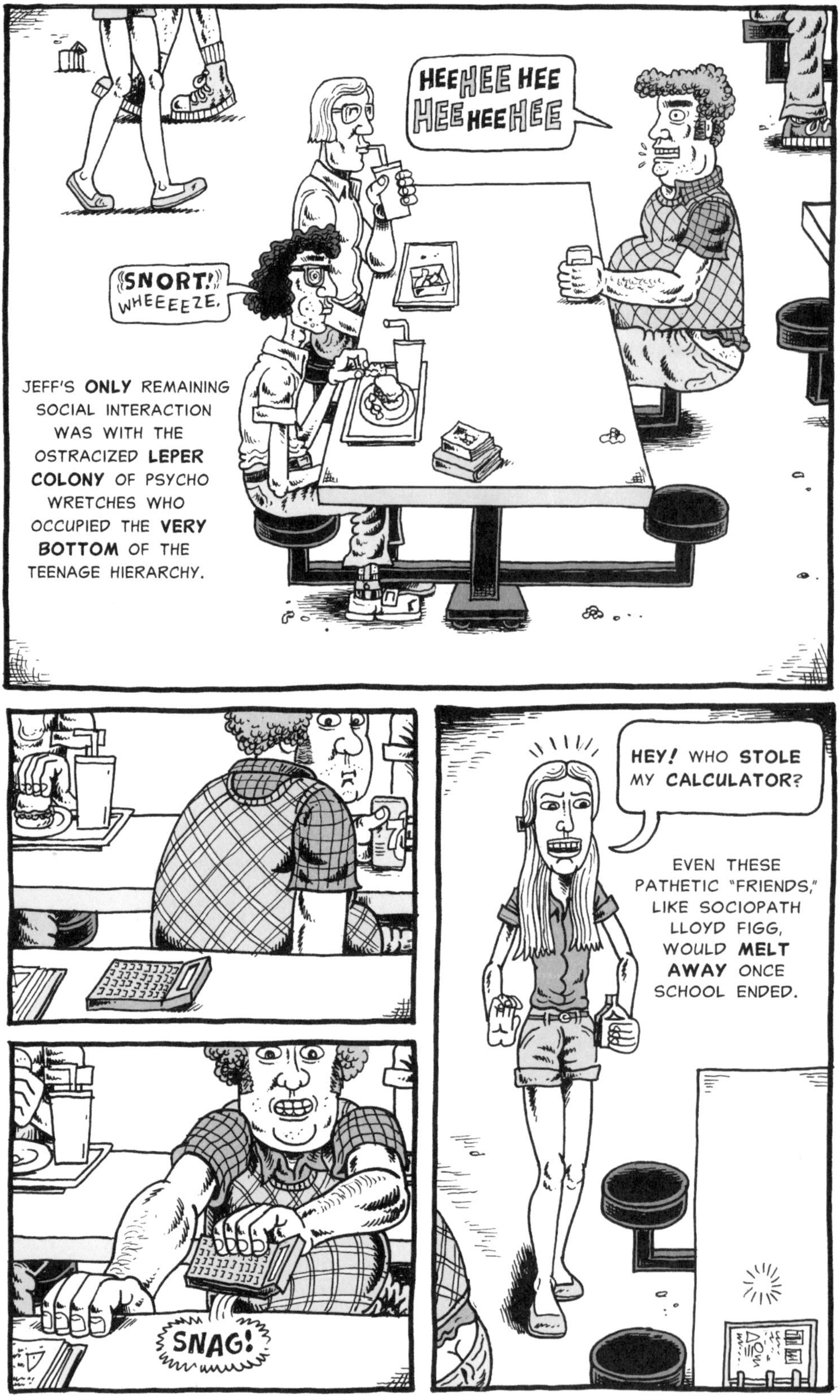
HEE HEE HEE HEE HEE HEE
SNORT! WHEEEEZE.
JEFF'S ONLY REMAINING SOCIAL INTERACTION WAS WITH THE OSTRACIZED LEPER COLONY OF PSYCHO WRETCHES WHO OCCUPIED THE VERY BOTTOM OF THE TEENAGE HIERARCHY.
SNAG!
HEY! WHO STOLE MY CALCULATOR?
EVEN THESE PATHETIC "FRIENDS," LIKE SOCIOPATH LLOYD FIGG, WOULD MELT AWAY ONCE SCHOOL ENDED.

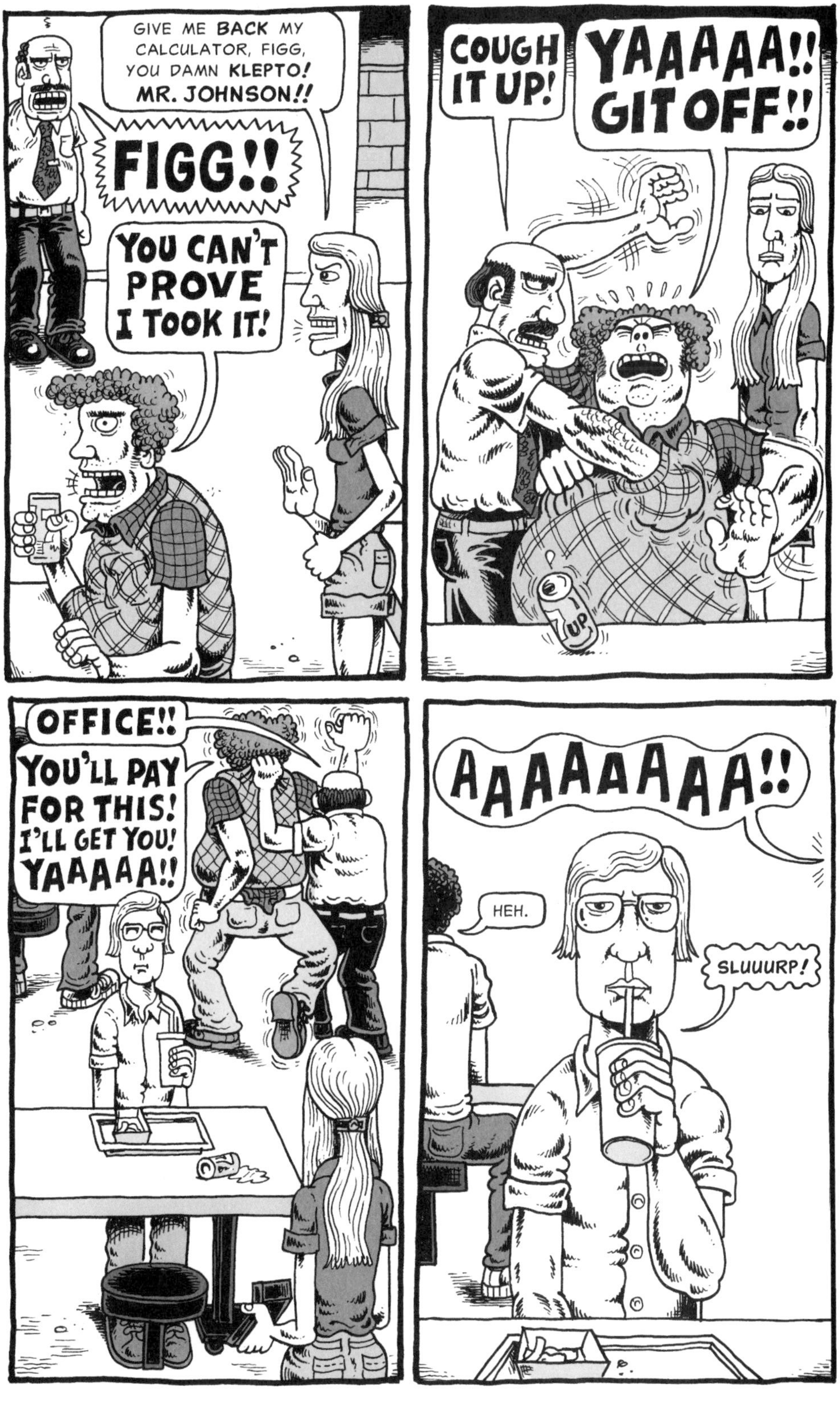
GIVE ME BACK MY CALCULATOR, FIGG, YOU DAMN KLEPTO! MR. JOHNSON!!
FIGG!!
YOU CAN'T PROVE I TOOK IT!
COUGH IT UP!
YAAAAA!! GIT OFF!!
UP
OFFICE!!
YOU'LL PAY FOR THIS! I'LL GET YOU! YAAAAA!!
AAAAAAAA!!
HEH.
SLUUURP!

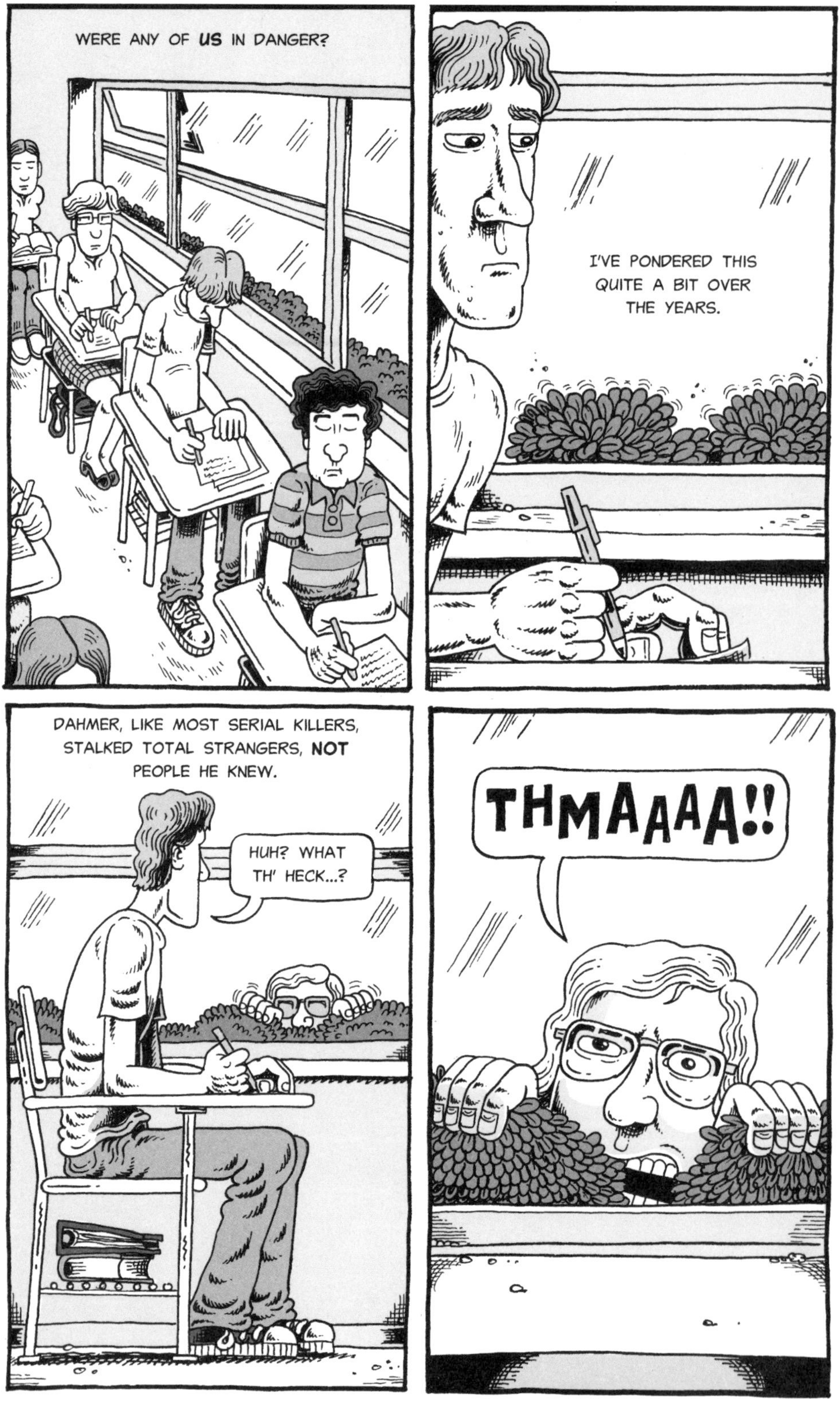
WERE ANY OF **US** IN DANGER?
I'VE PONDERED THIS QUITE A BIT OVER THE YEARS.
DAHMER, LIKE MOST SERIAL KILLERS, STALKED TOTAL STRANGERS, **NOT** PEOPLE HE KNEW.
HUH? WHAT TH' HECK...?
THMAAAA!!

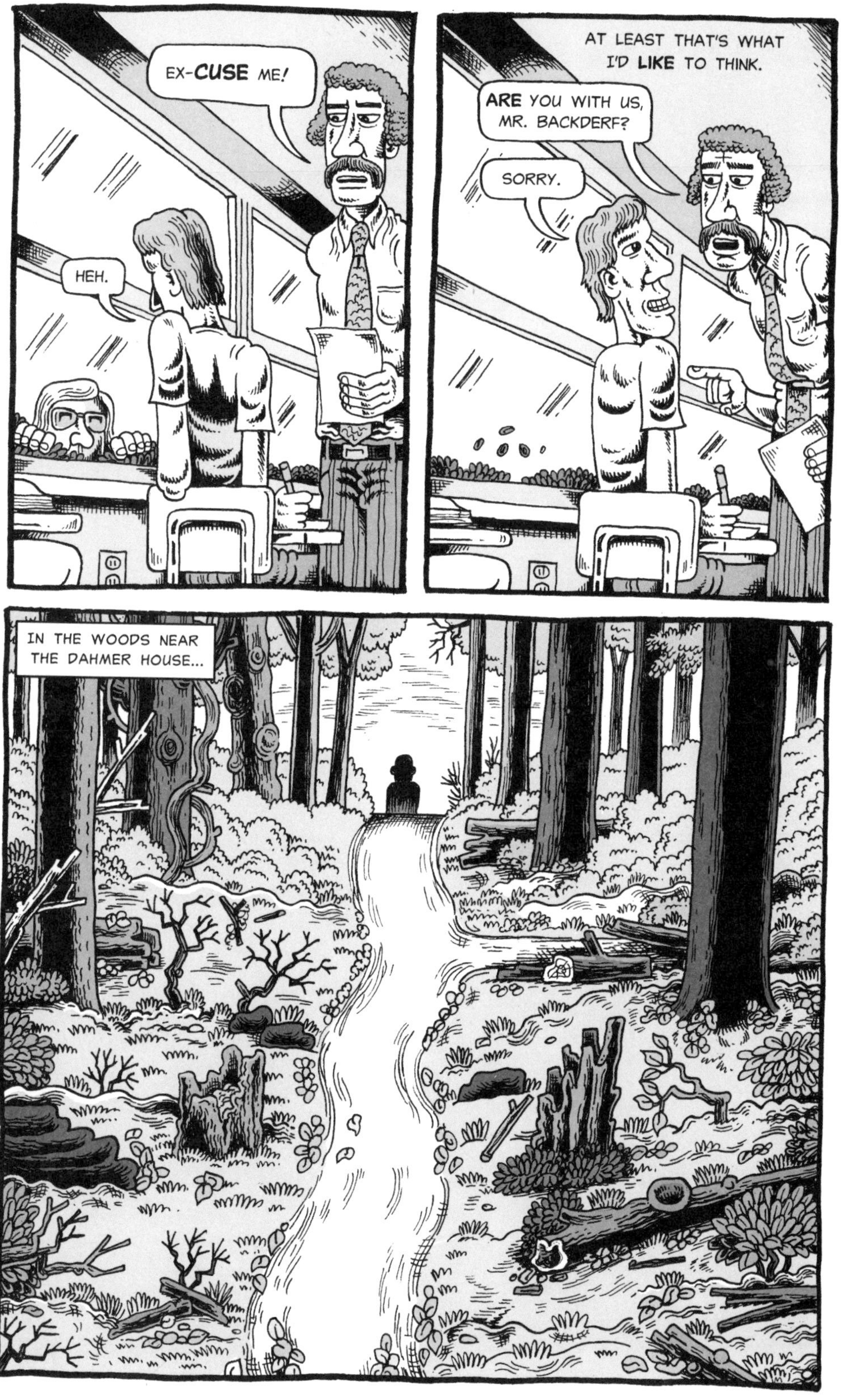
EX-CUSE ME!
HEH.
AT LEAST THAT'S WHAT I'D LIKE TO THINK.
ARE YOU WITH US, MR. BACKDERF?
SORRY.
IN THE WOODS NEAR THE DAHMER HOUSE...

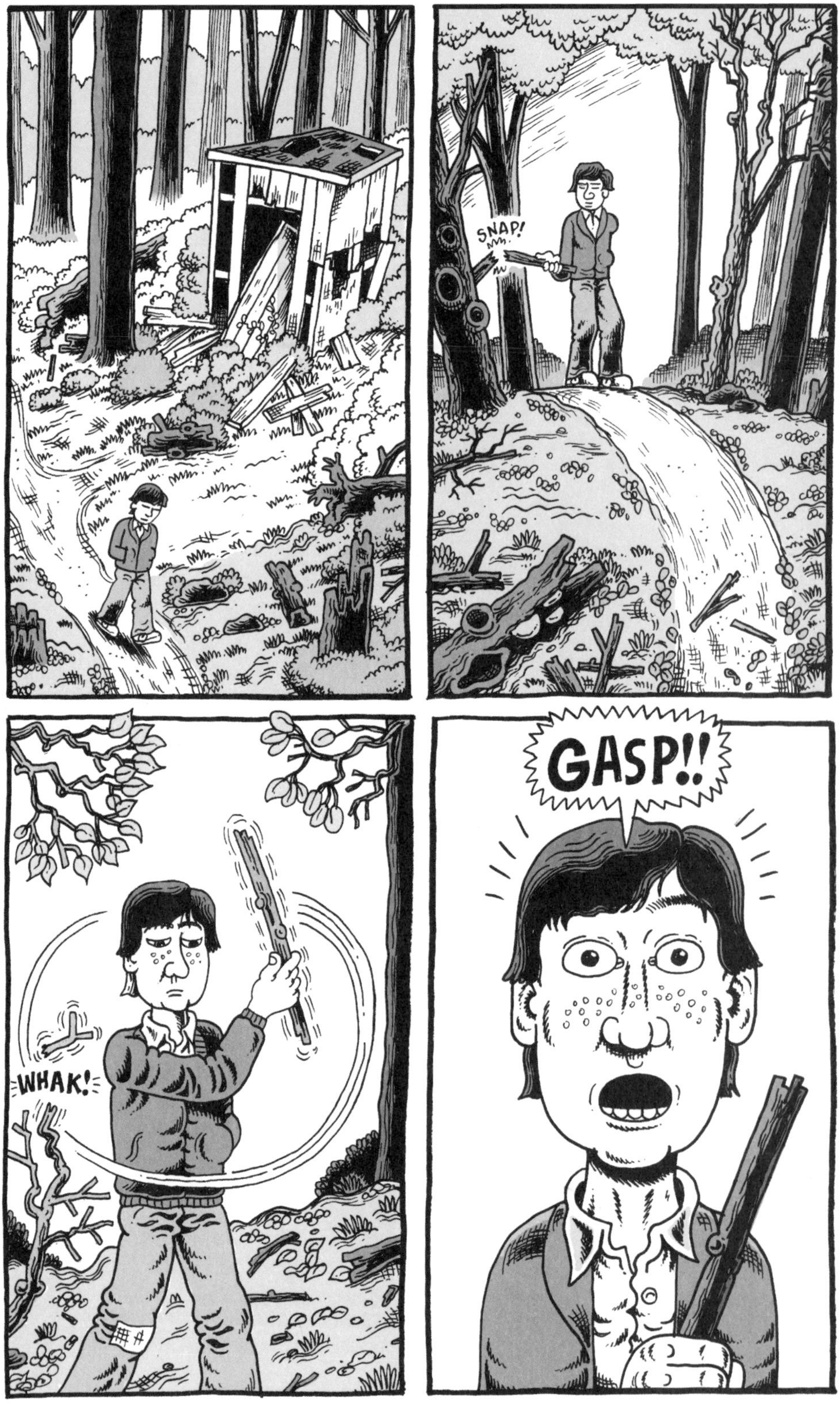
SNAP!
WHAK!
GASP!!

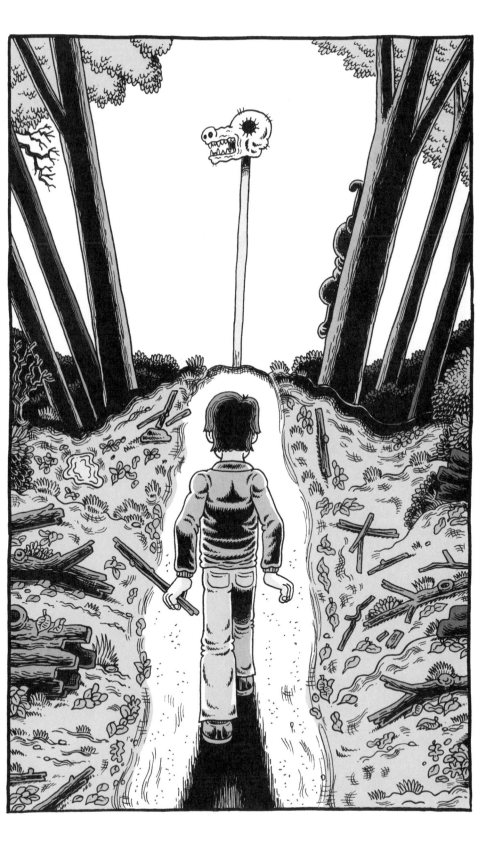

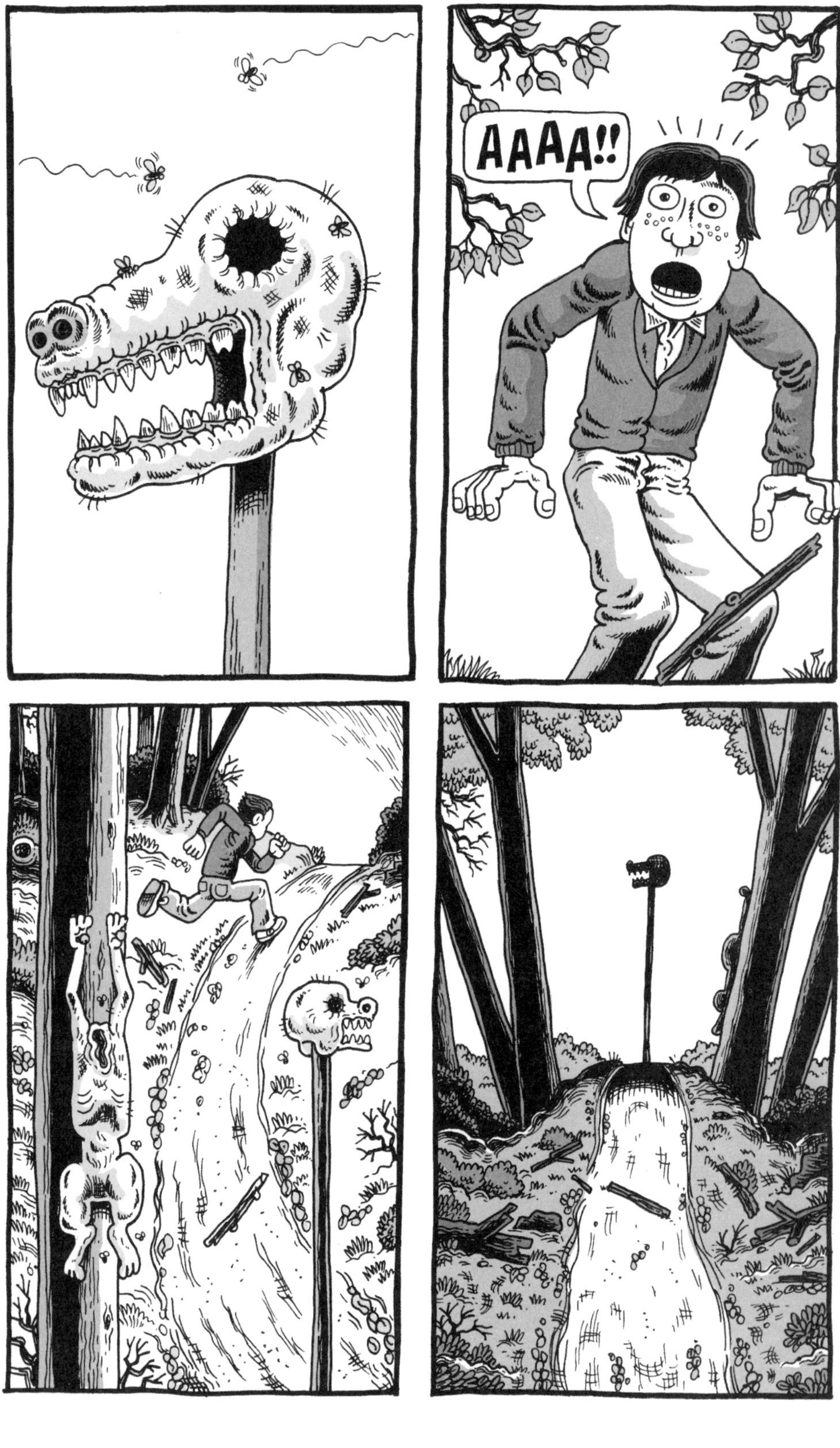
AAAA!!

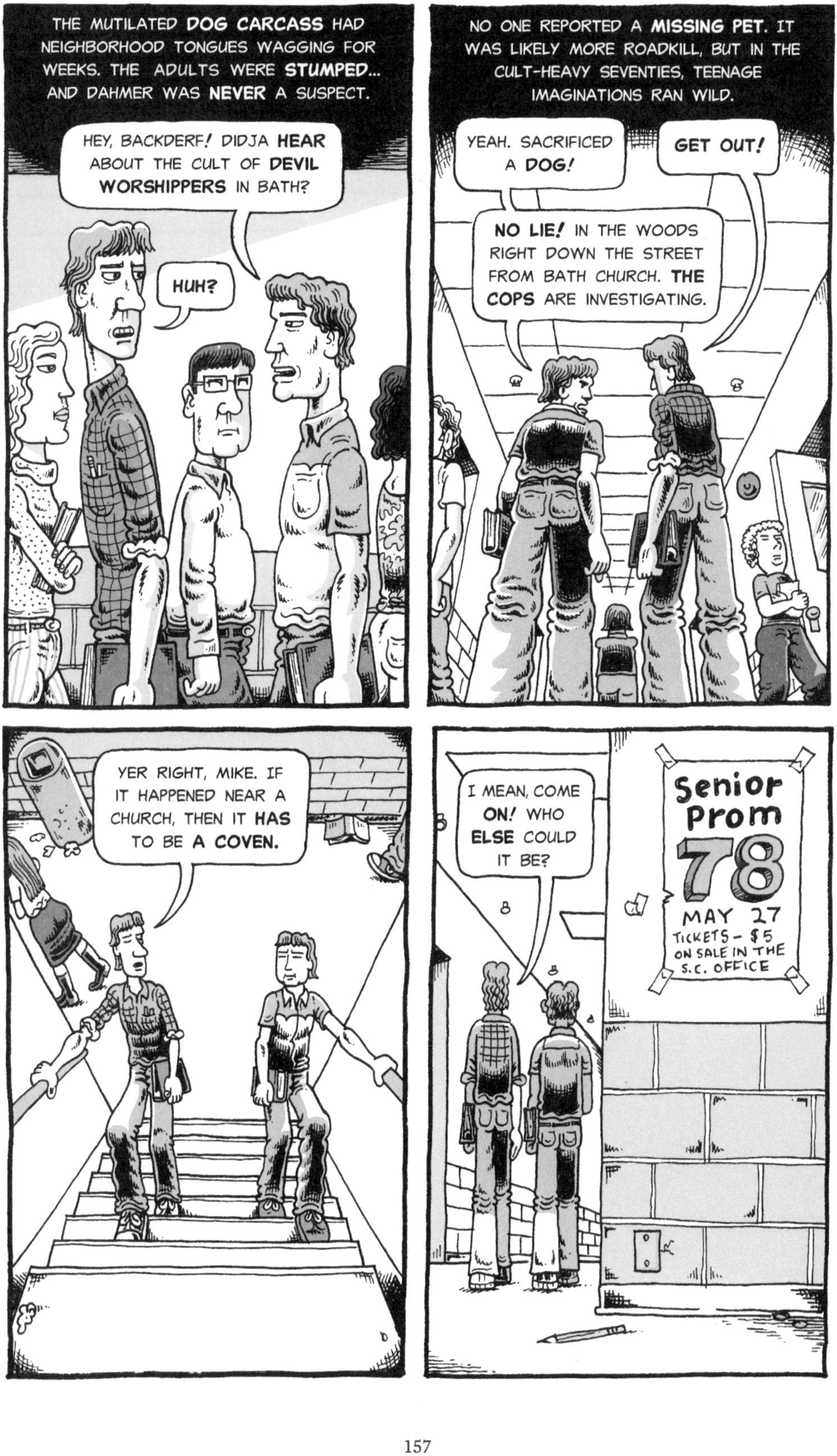
THE MUTILATED DOG CARCASS HAD NEIGHBORHOOD TONGUES WAGGING FOR WEEKS. THE ADULTS WERE STUMPED... AND DAHMER WAS NEVER A SUSPECT.
HEY, BACKDERF! DIDJA HEAR ABOUT THE CULT OF DEVIL WORSHIPPERS IN BATH?
HUH?
NO ONE REPORTED A MISSING PET. IT WAS LIKELY MORE ROADKILL, BUT IN THE CULT-HEAVY SEVENTIES, TEENAGE IMAGINATIONS RAN WILD.
YEAH. SACRIFICED A DOG!
GET OUT!
NO LIE! IN THE WOODS RIGHT DOWN THE STREET FROM BATH CHURCH. THE COPS ARE INVESTIGATING.
YER RIGHT, MIKE. IF IT HAPPENED NEAR A CHURCH, THEN IT HAS TO BE A COVEN.
I MEAN, COME ON! WHO ELSE COULD IT BE?
Senior Prom 78
MAY 27
TICKETS - $5 ON SALE IN THE S.C. OFFICE

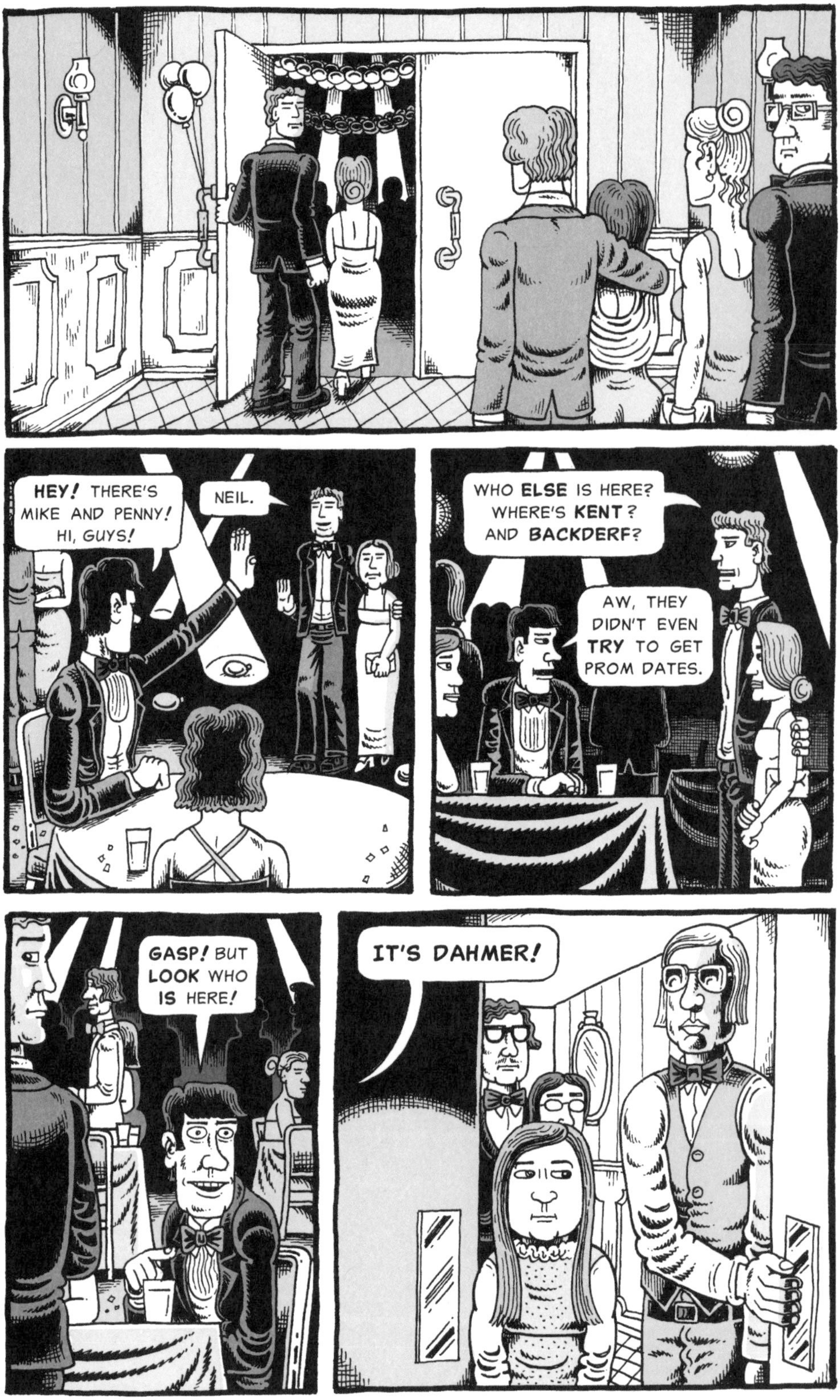
HEY! THERE'S MIKE AND PENNY! HI, GUYS!
NEIL.
WHO ELSE IS HERE? WHERE'S KENT? AND BACKDERF?
AW, THEY DIDN'T EVEN TRY TO GET PROM DATES.
GASP! BUT LOOK WHO IS HERE!
IT'S DAHMER!

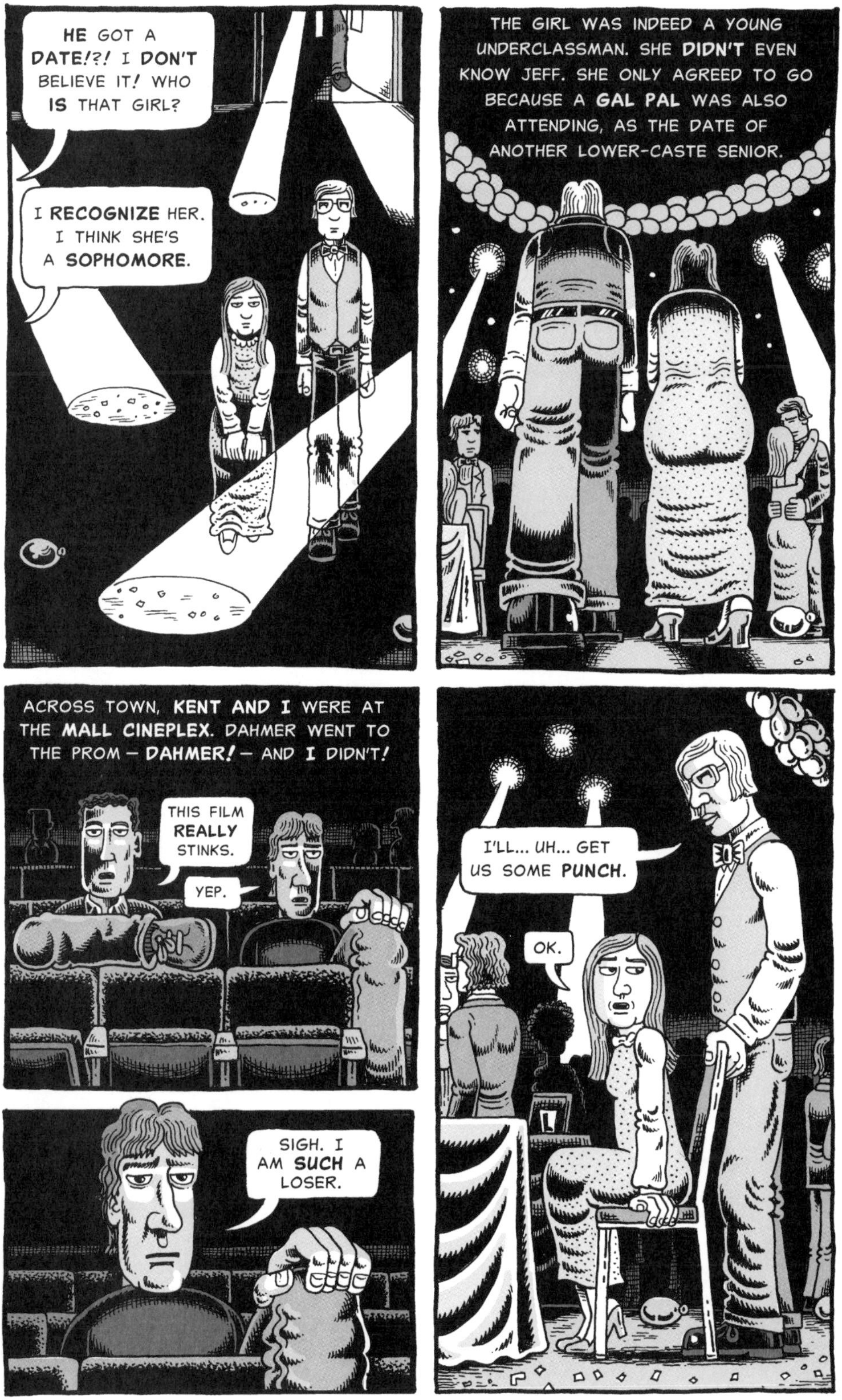
HE GOT A DATE!?! I DON'T BELIEVE IT! WHO IS THAT GIRL?
I RECOGNIZE HER. I THINK SHE'S A SOPHOMORE.
THE GIRL WAS INDEED A YOUNG UNDERCLASSMAN. SHE DIDN'T EVEN KNOW JEFF. SHE ONLY AGREED TO GO BECAUSE A GAL PAL WAS ALSO ATTENDING, AS THE DATE OF ANOTHER LOWER-CASTE SENIOR.
ACROSS TOWN, KENT AND I WERE AT THE MALL CINEPLEX. DAHMER WENT TO THE PROM — DAHMER! — AND I DIDN'T!
THIS FILM REALLY STINKS.
YEP.
SIGH. I AM SUCH A LOSER.
I'LL... UH... GET US SOME PUNCH.
OK.

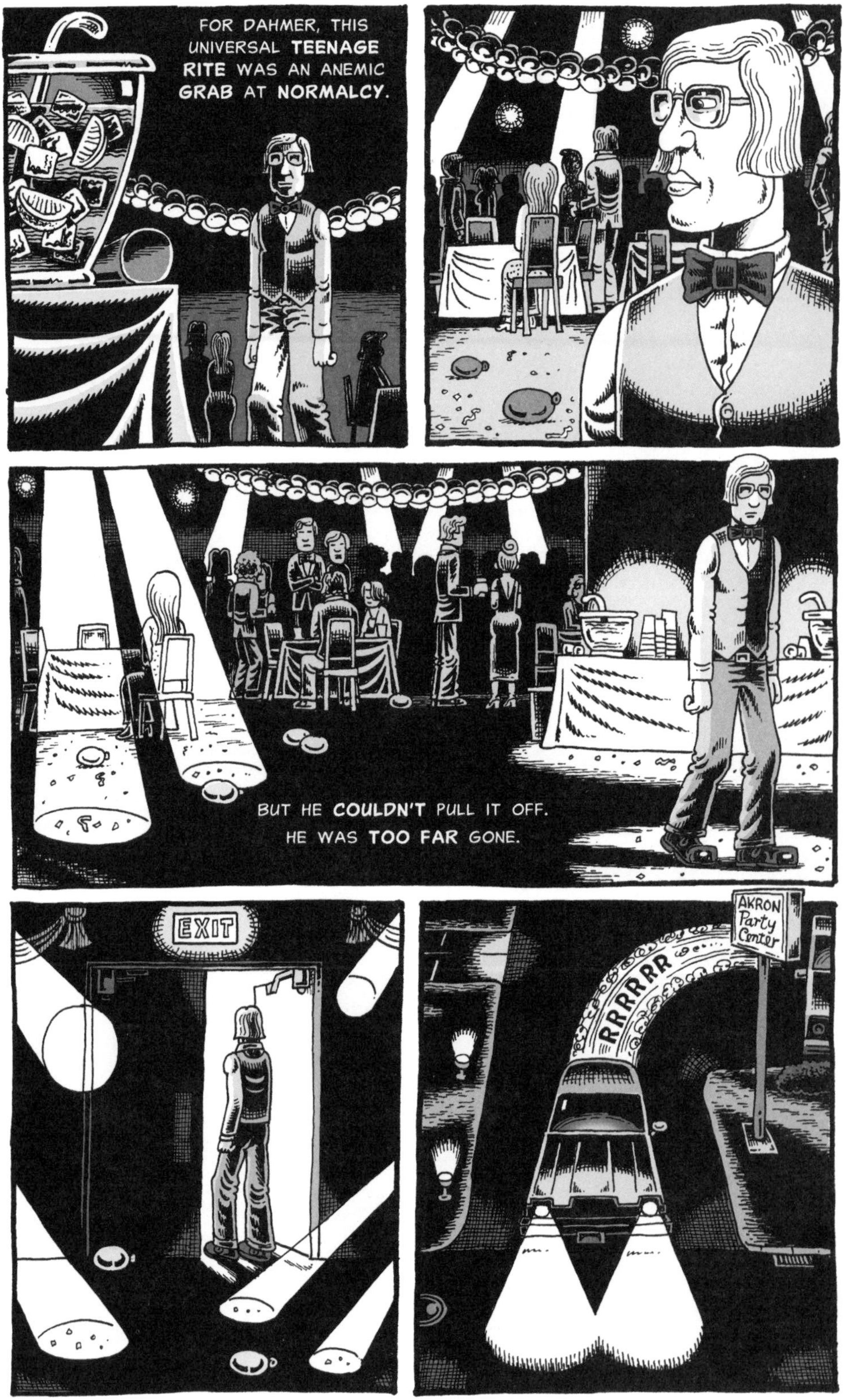
FOR DAHMER, THIS UNIVERSAL TEENAGE RITE WAS AN ANEMIC GRAB AT NORMALCY.
BUT HE COULDN'T PULL IT OFF. HE WAS TOO FAR GONE.
EXIT
AKRON Party Center
RRRRRR

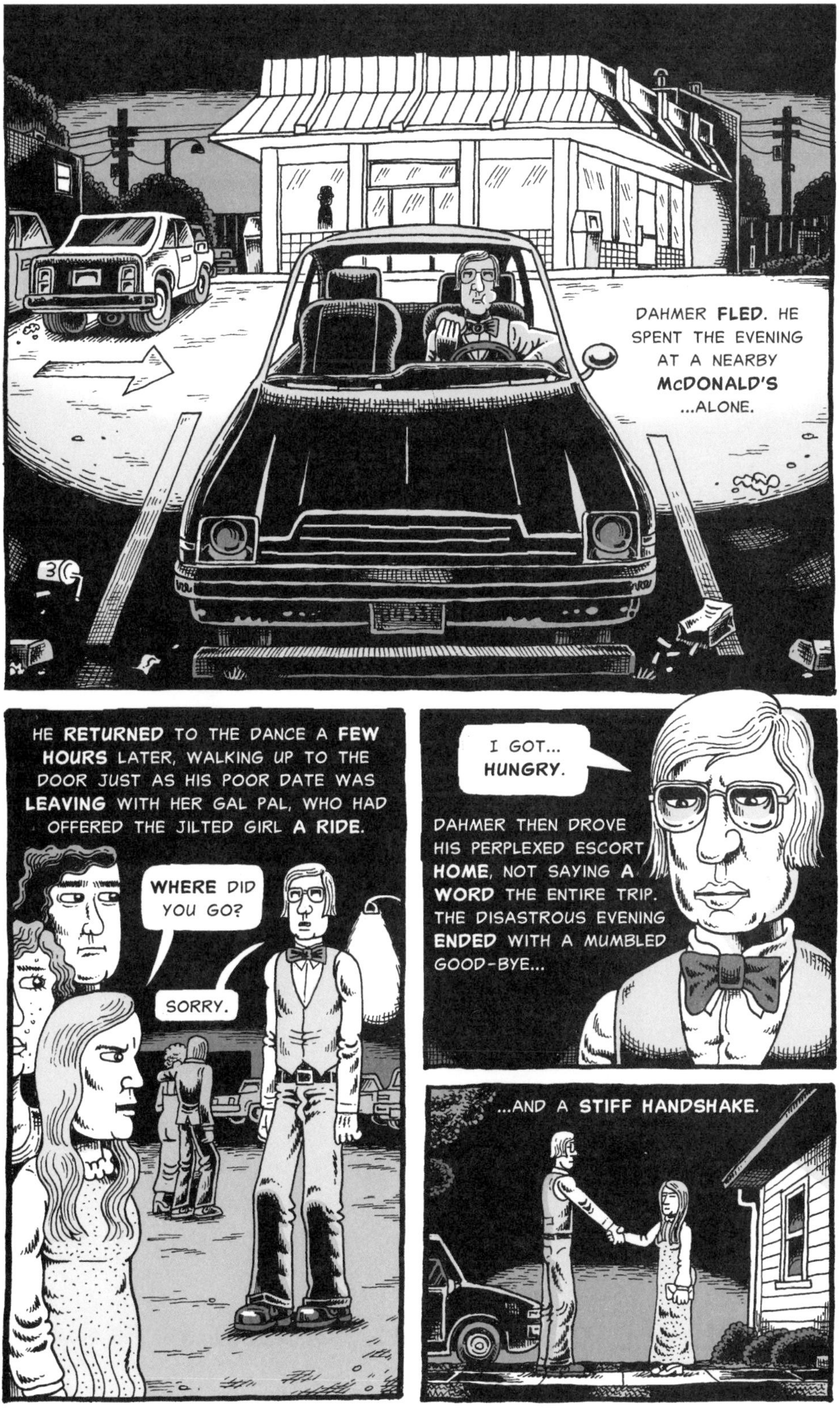
DAHMER **FLED.** HE SPENT THE EVENING AT A NEARBY **McDONALD'S** ...ALONE.
HE **RETURNED** TO THE DANCE A **FEW HOURS** LATER, WALKING UP TO THE DOOR JUST AS HIS POOR DATE WAS **LEAVING** WITH HER GAL PAL, WHO HAD OFFERED THE JILTED GIRL **A RIDE.**
WHERE DID YOU GO?
SORRY.
I GOT... **HUNGRY.**
DAHMER THEN DROVE HIS PERPLEXED ESCORT **HOME**, NOT SAYING **A WORD** THE ENTIRE TRIP. THE DISASTROUS EVENING **ENDED** WITH A MUMBLED GOOD-BYE...
...AND A **STIFF HANDSHAKE.**

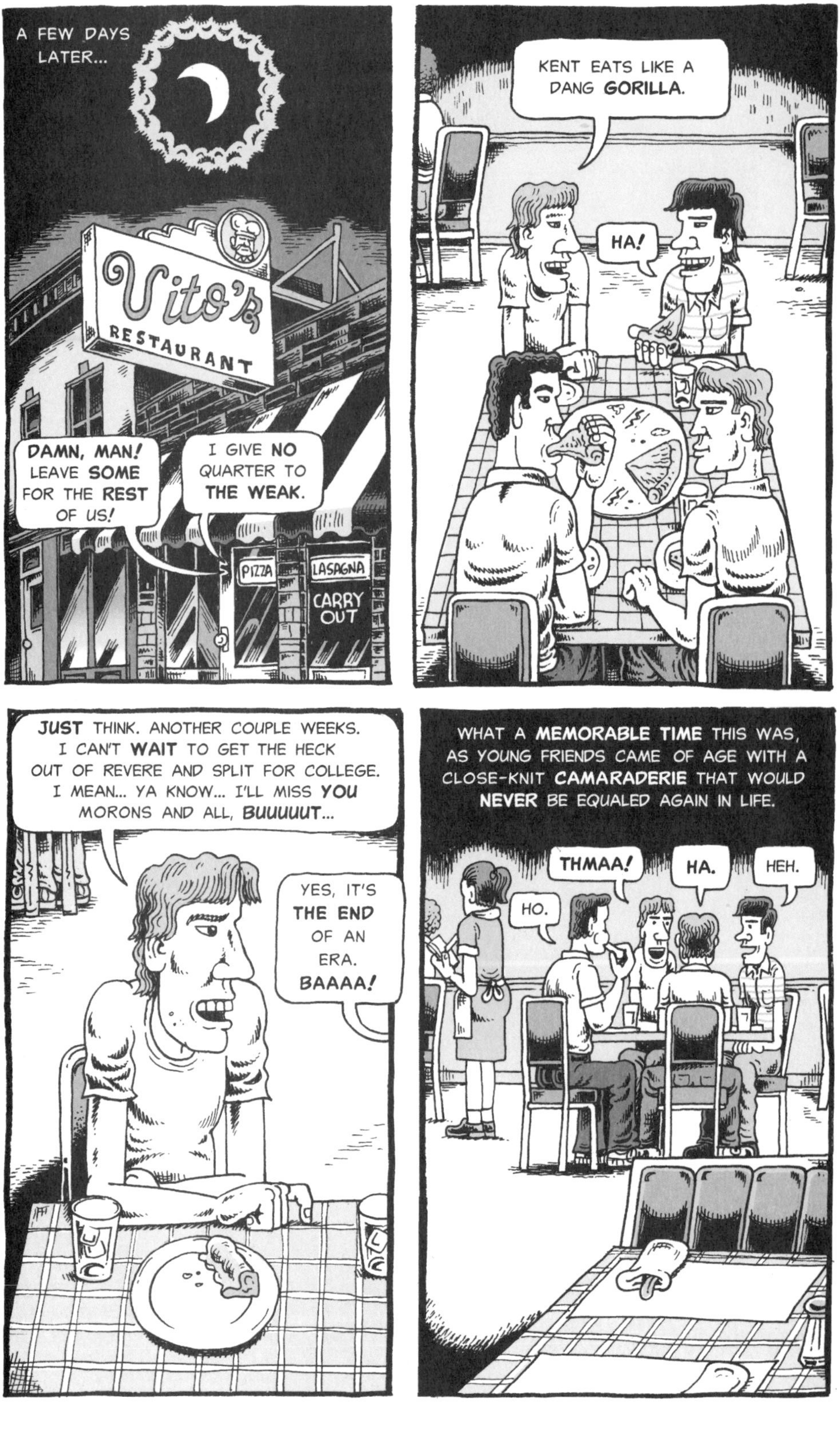
A FEW DAYS LATER...
Vito's
RESTAURANT
DAMN, MAN! LEAVE SOME FOR THE REST OF US!
I GIVE NO QUARTER TO THE WEAK.
PIZZA
LASAGNA
CARRY OUT
KENT EATS LIKE A DANG GORILLA.
HA!
JUST THINK. ANOTHER COUPLE WEEKS. I CAN'T WAIT TO GET THE HECK OUT OF REVERE AND SPLIT FOR COLLEGE. I MEAN... YA KNOW... I'LL MISS YOU MORONS AND ALL, BUUUUUT...
YES, IT'S THE END OF AN ERA. BAAAA!
WHAT A MEMORABLE TIME THIS WAS, AS YOUNG FRIENDS CAME OF AGE WITH A CLOSE-KNIT CAMARADERIE THAT WOULD NEVER BE EQUALED AGAIN IN LIFE.
HO.
THMAA!
HA.
HEH.

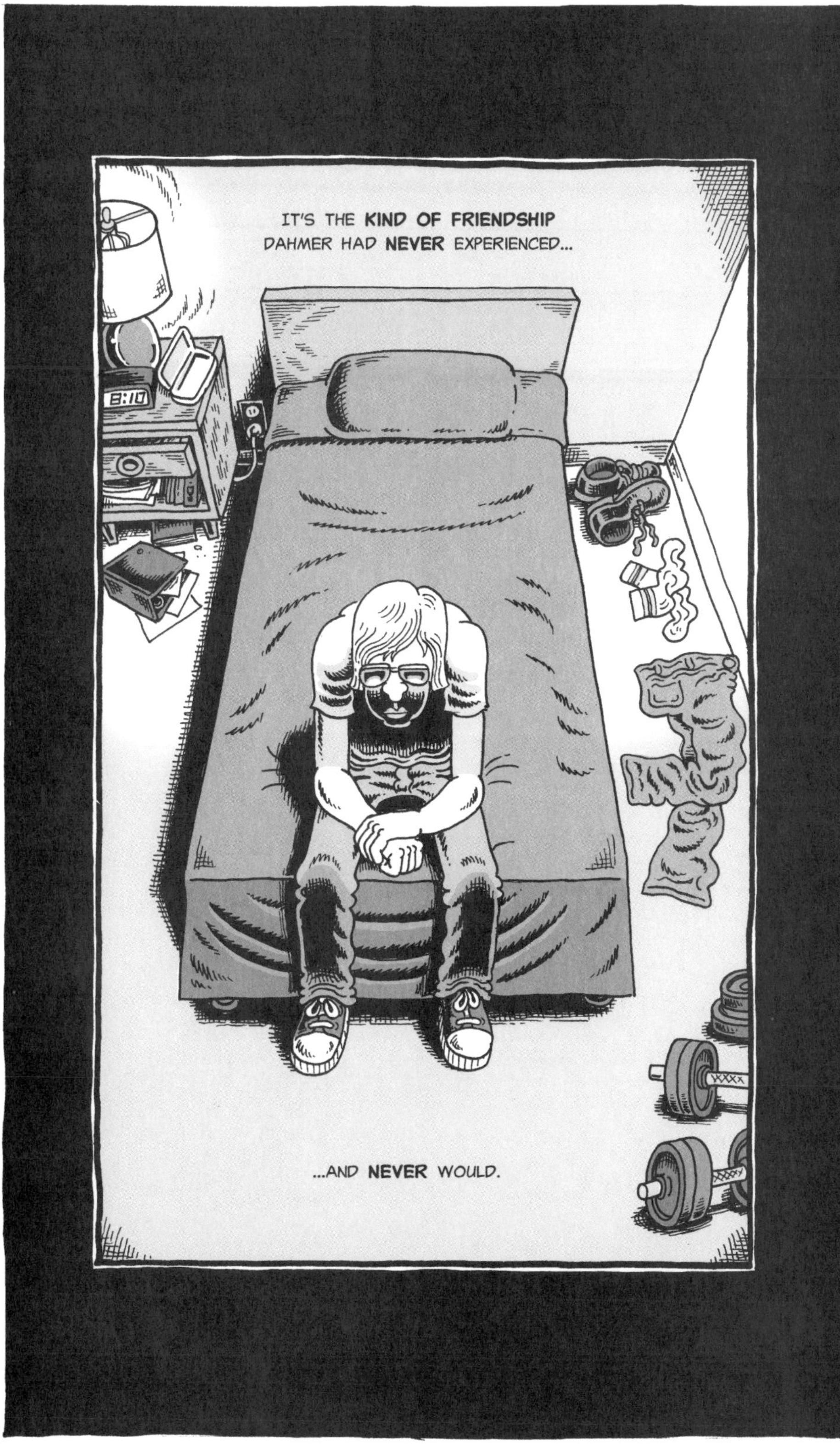
IT'S THE KIND OF FRIENDSHIP DAHMER HAD NEVER EXPERIENCED...
...AND NEVER WOULD.

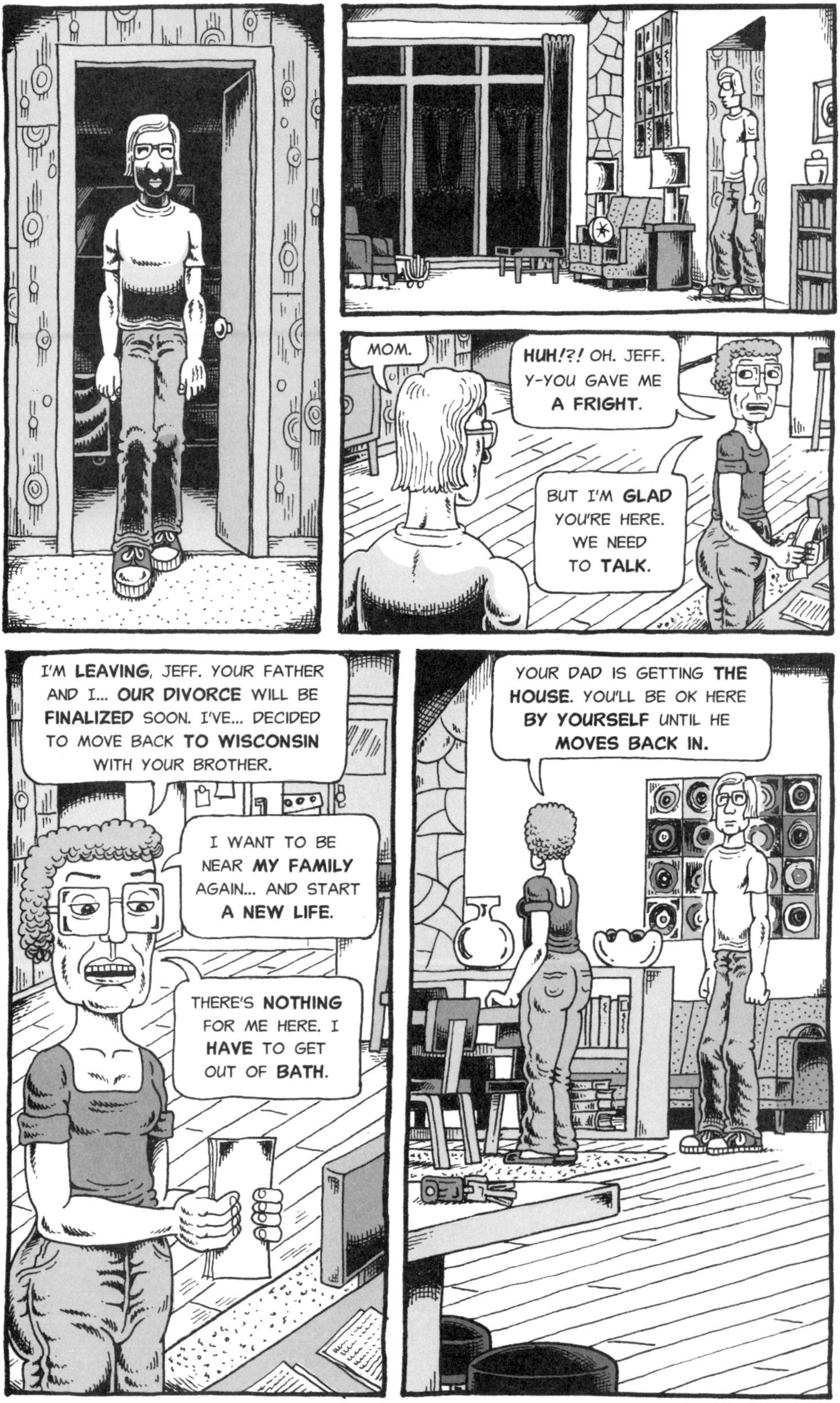
MOM.
HUH!?! OH. JEFF. Y-YOU GAVE ME A FRIGHT.
BUT I'M GLAD YOU'RE HERE. WE NEED TO TALK.
I'M LEAVING, JEFF. YOUR FATHER AND I... OUR DIVORCE WILL BE FINALIZED SOON. I'VE... DECIDED TO MOVE BACK TO WISCONSIN WITH YOUR BROTHER.
I WANT TO BE NEAR MY FAMILY AGAIN... AND START A NEW LIFE.
THERE'S NOTHING FOR ME HERE. I HAVE TO GET OUT OF BATH.
YOUR DAD IS GETTING THE HOUSE. YOU'LL BE OK HERE BY YOURSELF UNTIL HE MOVES BACK IN.

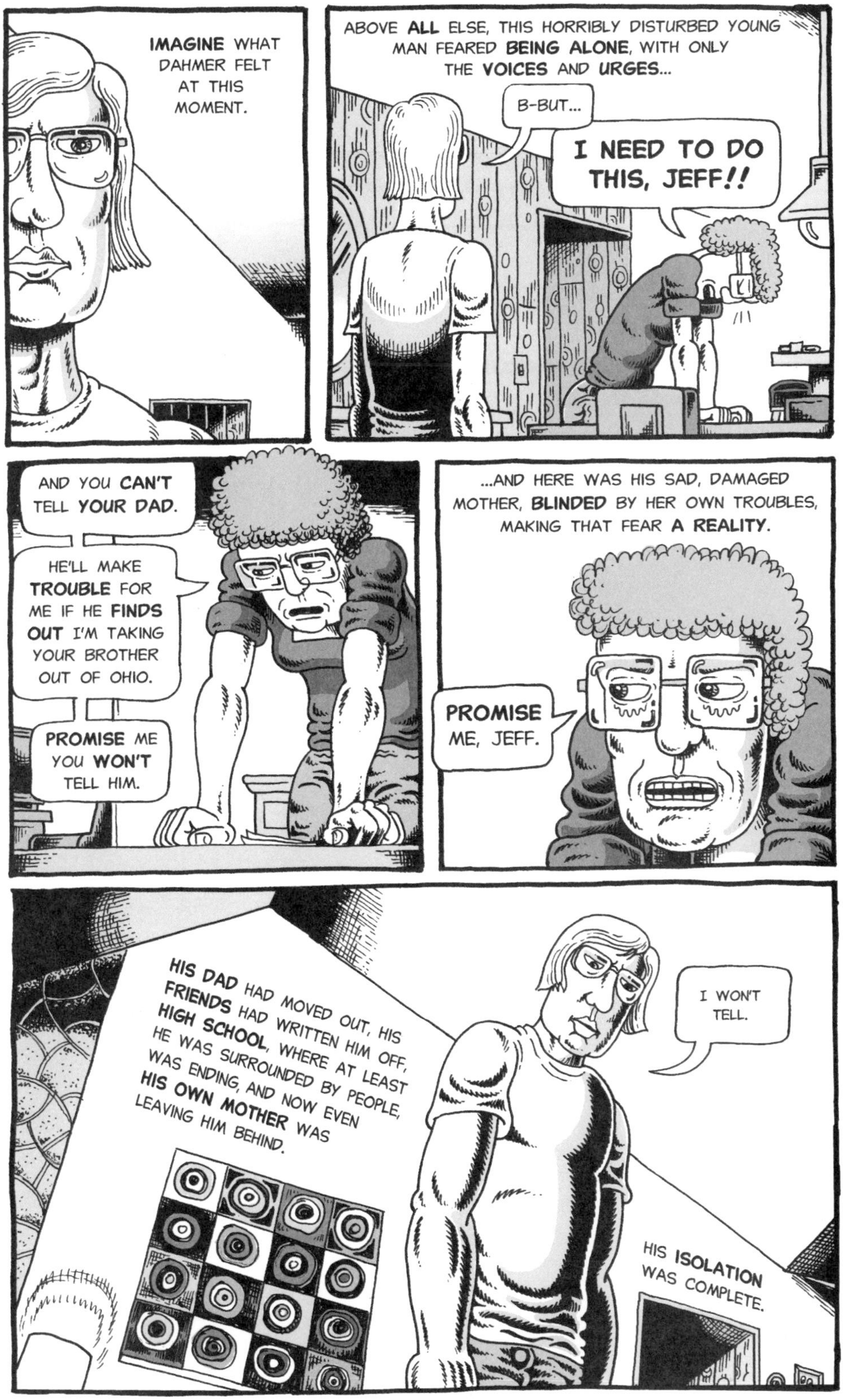
IMAGINE WHAT DAHMER FELT AT THIS MOMENT.
ABOVE ALL ELSE, THIS HORRIBLY DISTURBED YOUNG MAN FEARED BEING ALONE, WITH ONLY THE VOICES AND URGES...
B-BUT...
I NEED TO DO THIS, JEFF!!
AND YOU CAN'T TELL YOUR DAD.
HE'LL MAKE TROUBLE FOR ME IF HE FINDS OUT I'M TAKING YOUR BROTHER OUT OF OHIO.
PROMISE ME YOU WON'T TELL HIM.
...AND HERE WAS HIS SAD, DAMAGED MOTHER, BLINDED BY HER OWN TROUBLES, MAKING THAT FEAR A REALITY.
PROMISE ME, JEFF.
HIS DAD HAD MOVED OUT, HIS FRIENDS HAD WRITTEN HIM OFF, HIGH SCHOOL, WHERE AT LEAST HE WAS SURROUNDED BY PEOPLE, WAS ENDING, AND NOW EVEN HIS OWN MOTHER WAS LEAVING HIM BEHIND.
I WON'T TELL.
HIS ISOLATION WAS COMPLETE.

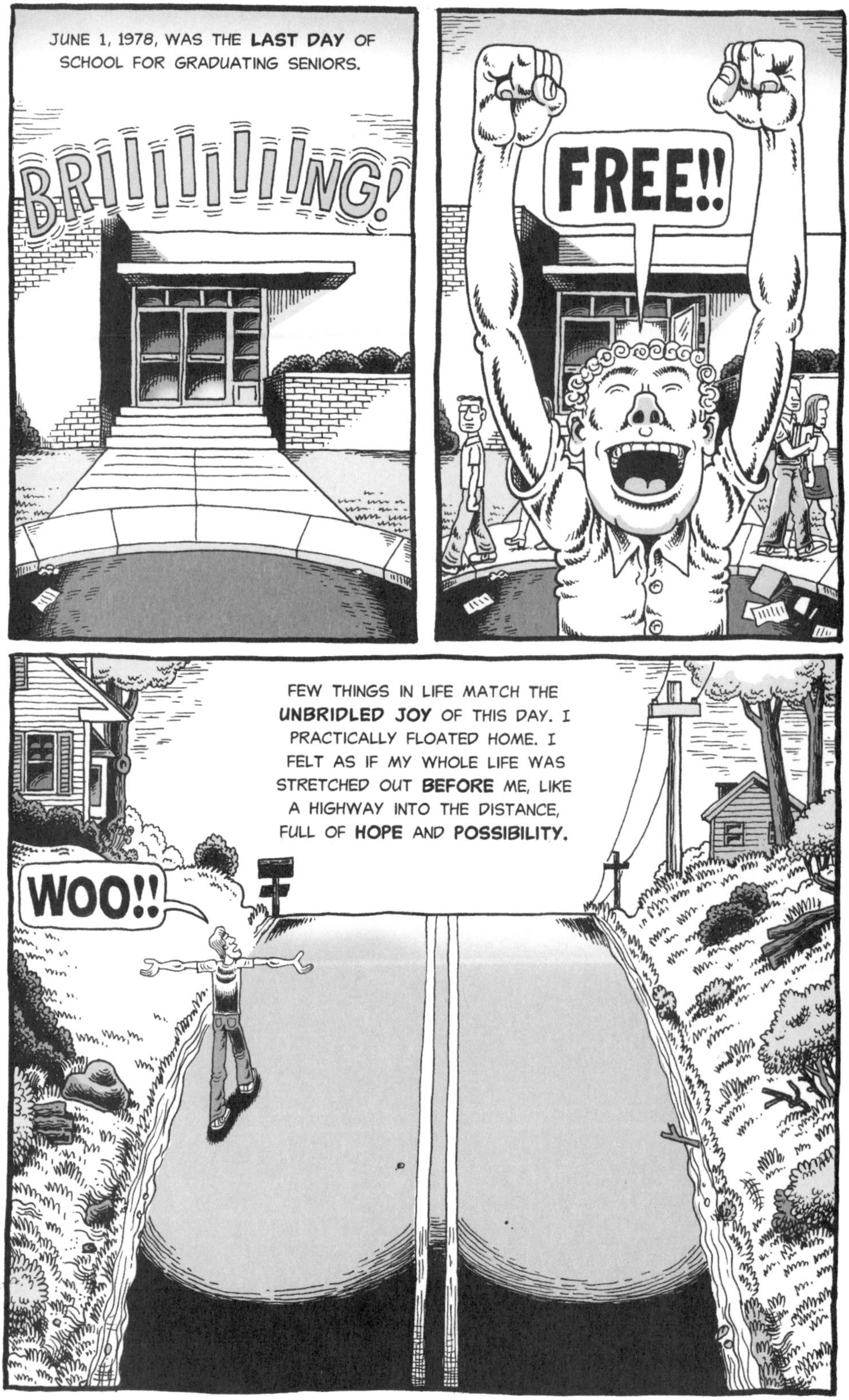
JUNE 1, 1978, WAS THE **LAST DAY** OF SCHOOL FOR GRADUATING SENIORS.
BRIIIIIIIING!
FREE!!
FEW THINGS IN LIFE MATCH THE **UNBRIDLED JOY** OF THIS DAY. I PRACTICALLY FLOATED HOME. I FELT AS IF MY WHOLE LIFE WAS STRETCHED OUT **BEFORE** ME, LIKE A HIGHWAY INTO THE DISTANCE, FULL OF **HOPE** AND **POSSIBILITY.**
WOO!!

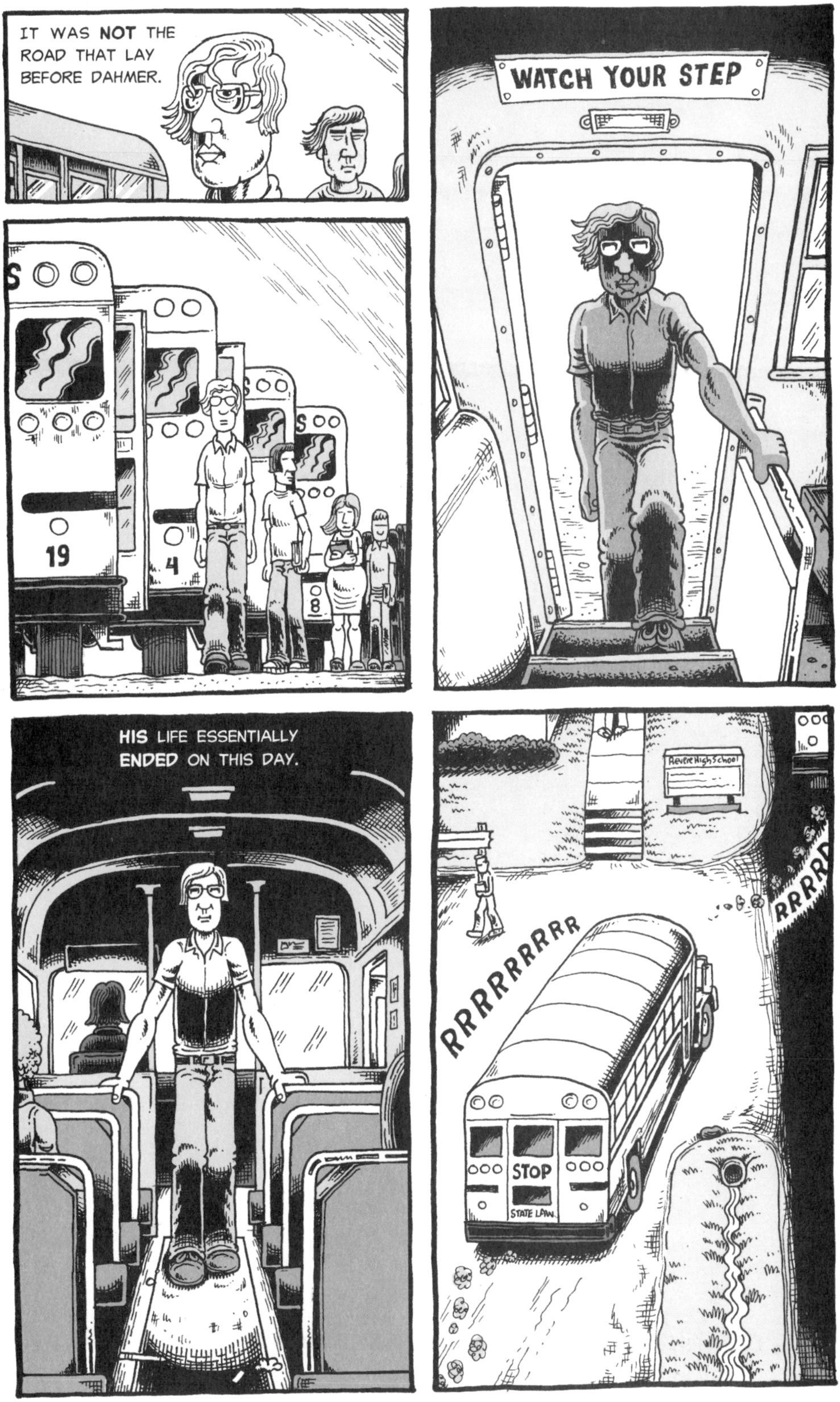
IT WAS **NOT** THE ROAD THAT LAY BEFORE DAHMER.
WATCH YOUR STEP
19
4
8
HIS LIFE ESSENTIALLY **ENDED** ON THIS DAY.
Revere High School
RRRRRRRRRR
STOP
STATE LAW

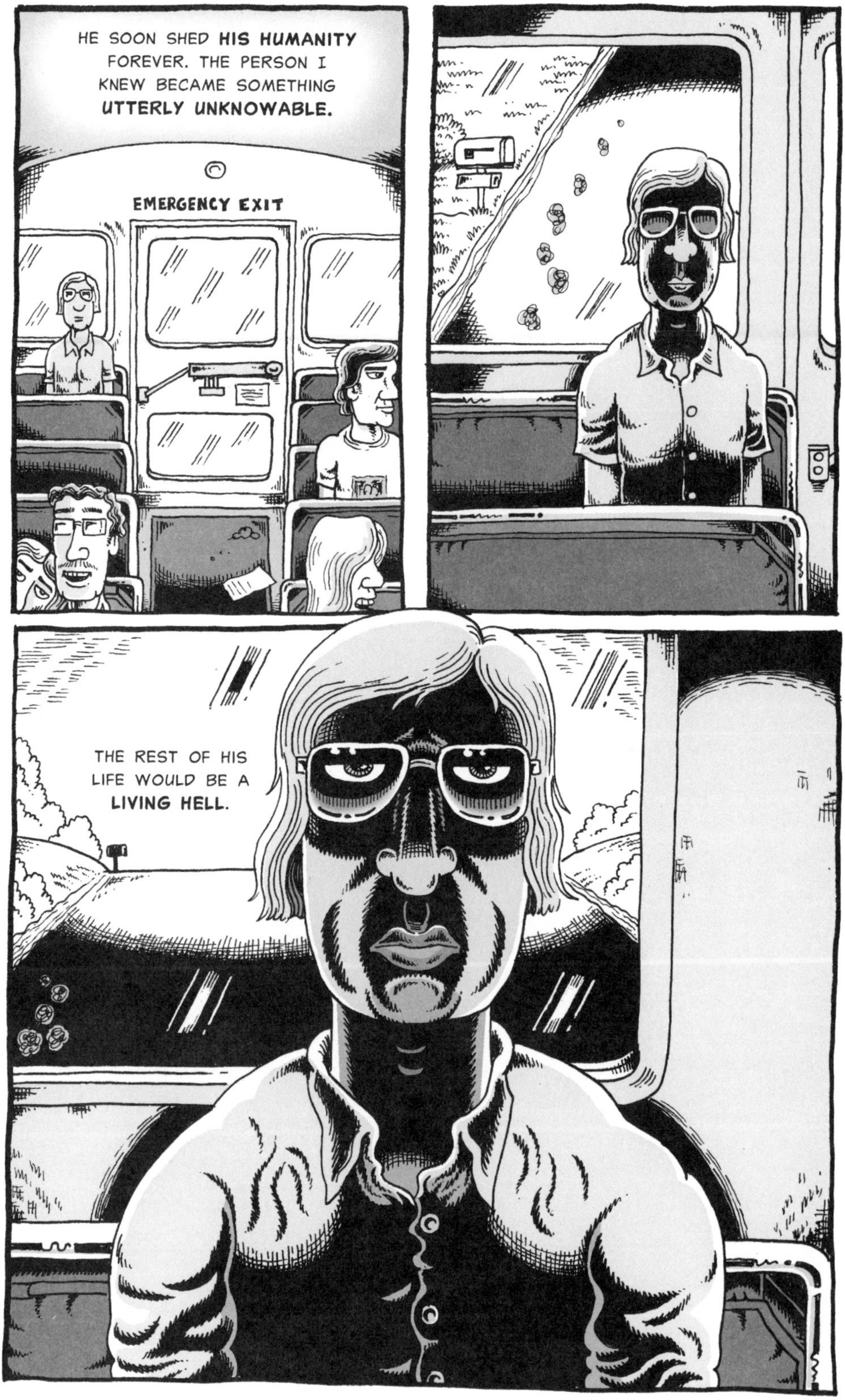
HE SOON SHED HIS HUMANITY FOREVER. THE PERSON I KNEW BECAME SOMETHING UTTERLY UNKNOWABLE.
EMERGENCY EXIT
THE REST OF HIS LIFE WOULD BE A LIVING HELL.

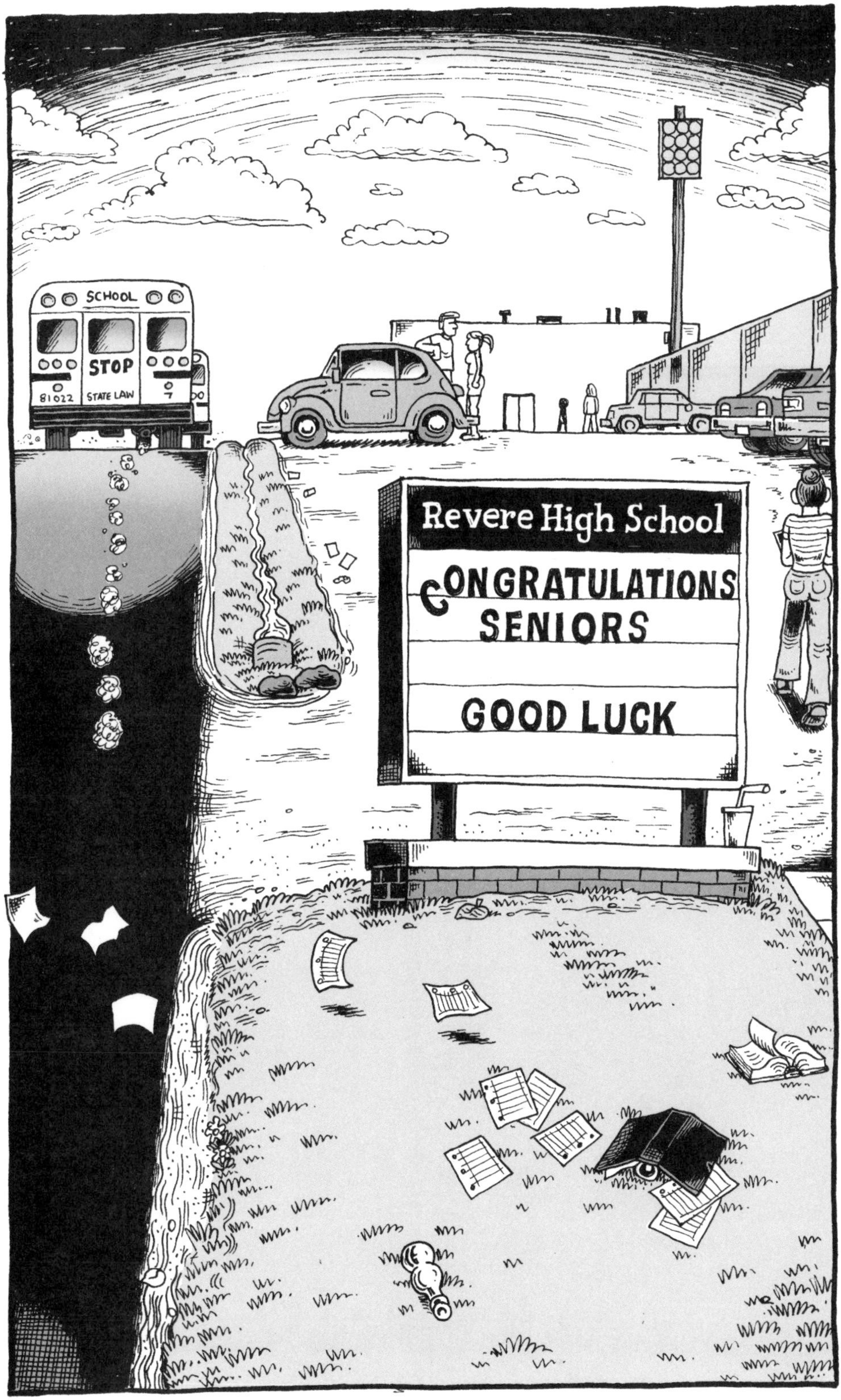
SCHOOL
STOP
81022
STATE LAW
Revere High School
CONGRATULATIONS
SENIORS
GOOD LUCK

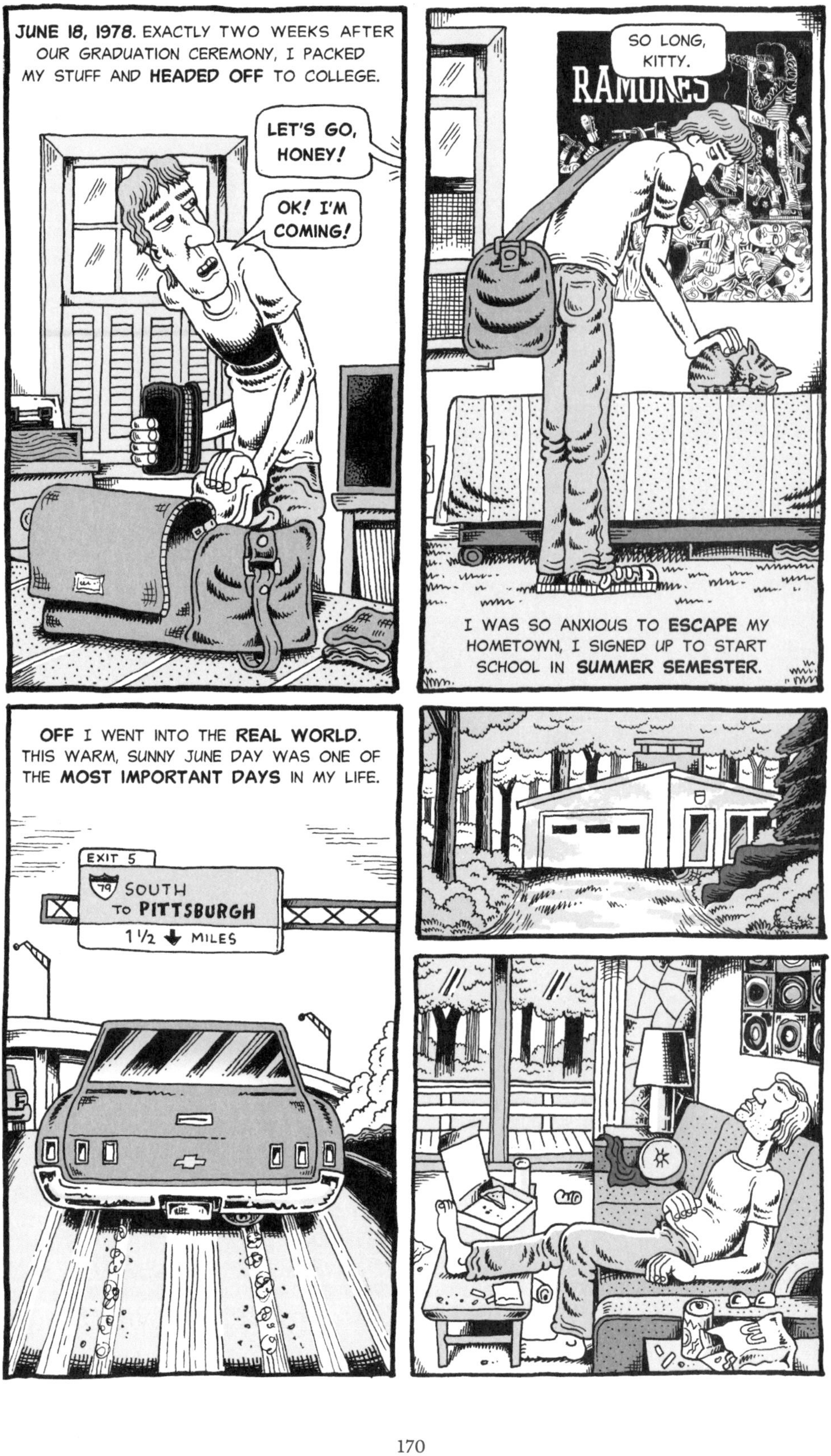
JUNE 18, 1978. EXACTLY TWO WEEKS AFTER OUR GRADUATION CEREMONY, I PACKED MY STUFF AND HEADED OFF TO COLLEGE.
LET'S GO, HONEY!
OK! I'M COMING!
SO LONG, KITTY.
I WAS SO ANXIOUS TO ESCAPE MY HOMETOWN, I SIGNED UP TO START SCHOOL IN SUMMER SEMESTER.
OFF I WENT INTO THE REAL WORLD. THIS WARM, SUNNY JUNE DAY WAS ONE OF THE MOST IMPORTANT DAYS IN MY LIFE.
EXIT 5
79
SOUTH
TO PITTSBURGH
1 1/2 MILES

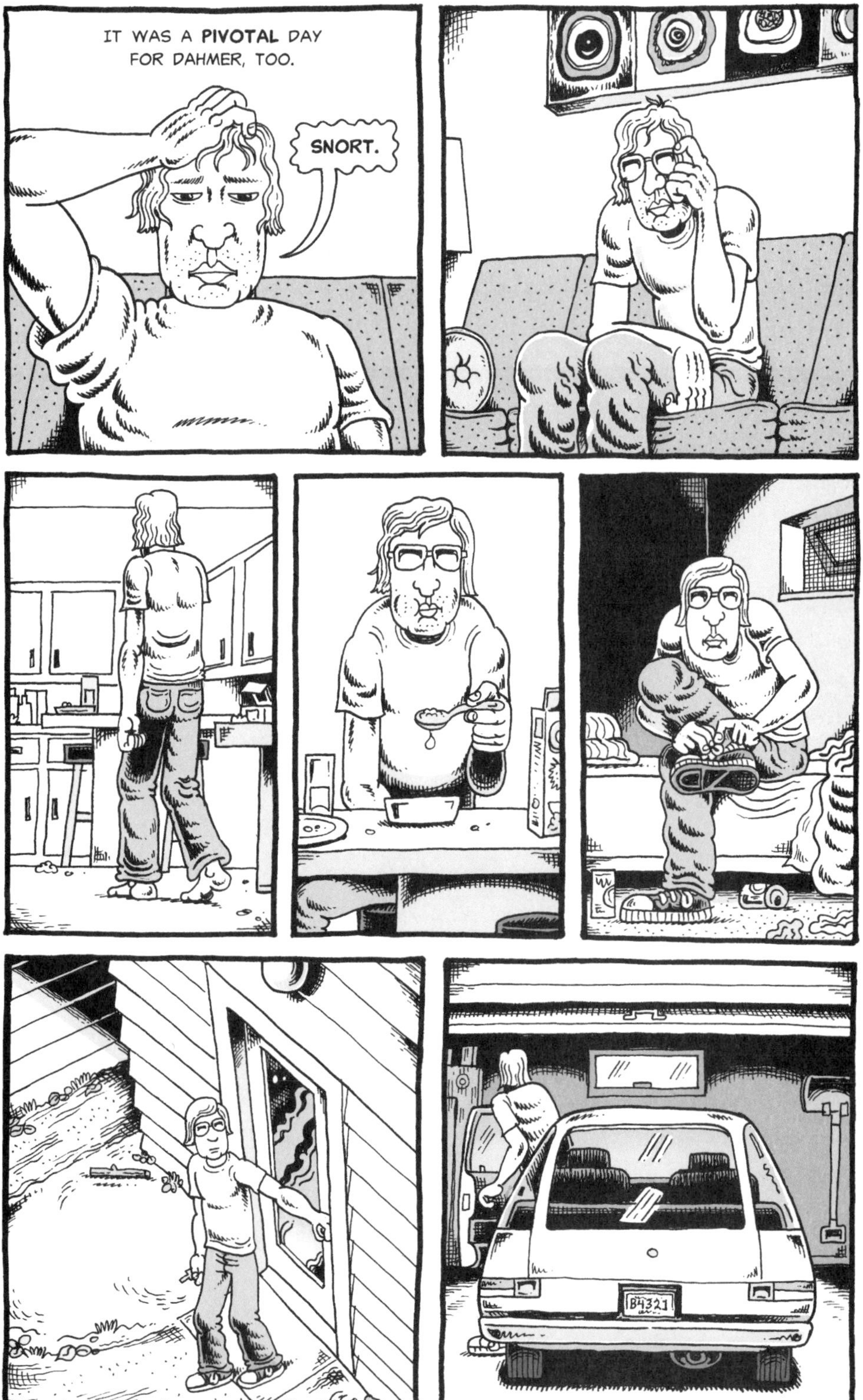
IT WAS A PIVOTAL DAY FOR DAHMER, TOO.
SNORT.
B4321

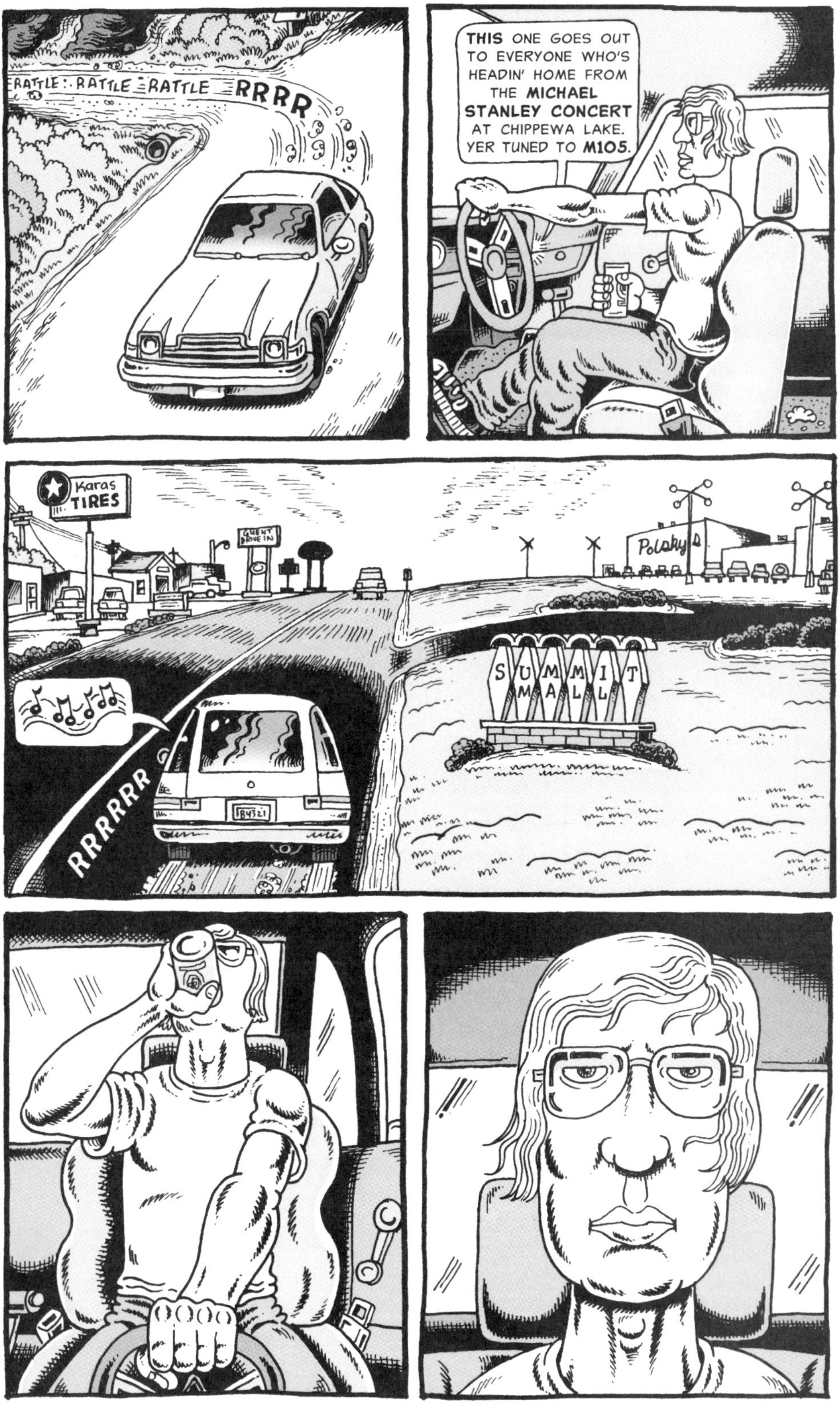
RATTLE RATTLE RATTLE RRRR
THIS ONE GOES OUT TO EVERYONE WHO'S HEADIN' HOME FROM THE MICHAEL STANLEY CONCERT AT CHIPPEWA LAKE. YER TUNED TO M105.
Karas TIRES
Polsky's
SUMMIT MALL
RRRRRR

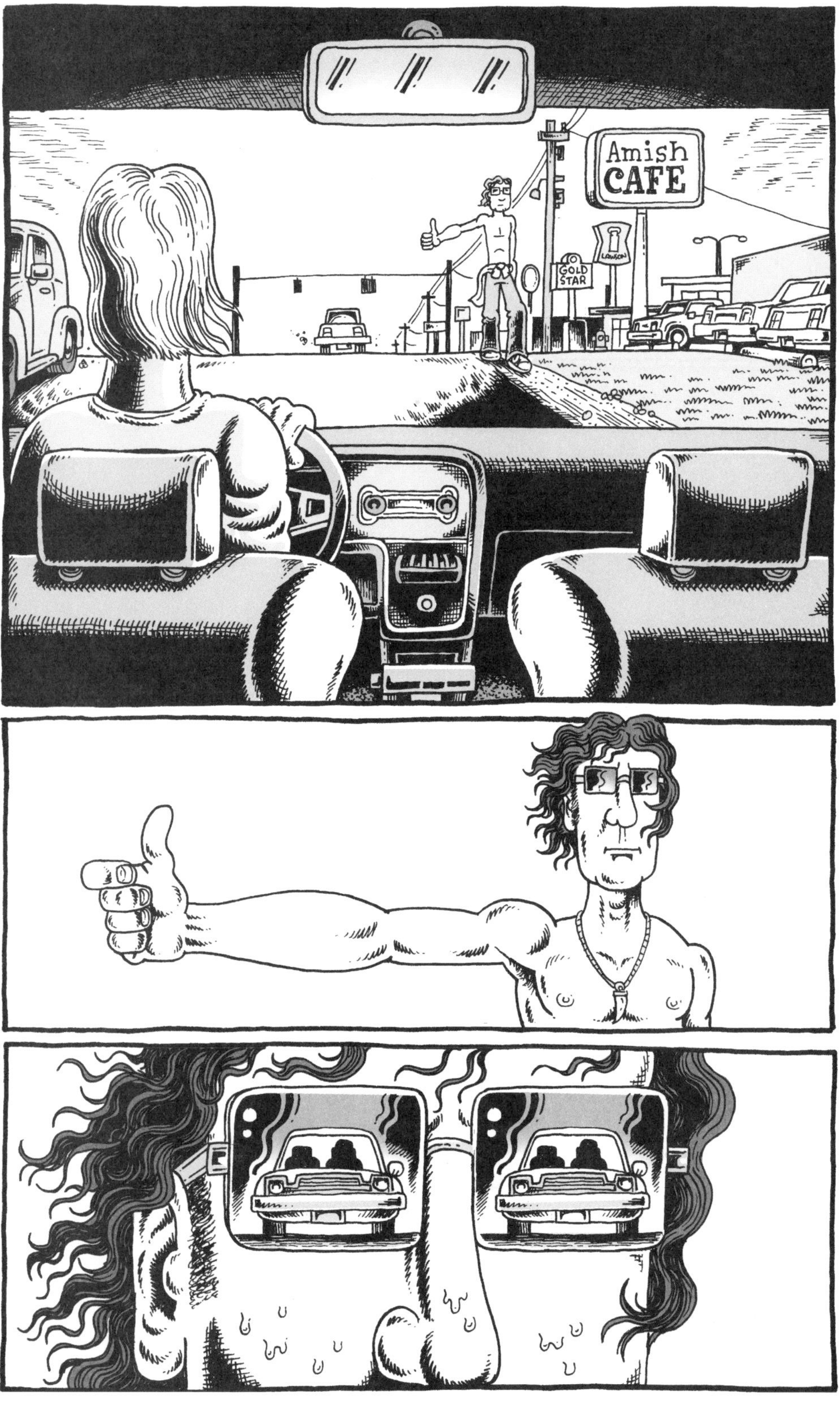
Amish CAFE
LAWSON
GOLD STAR

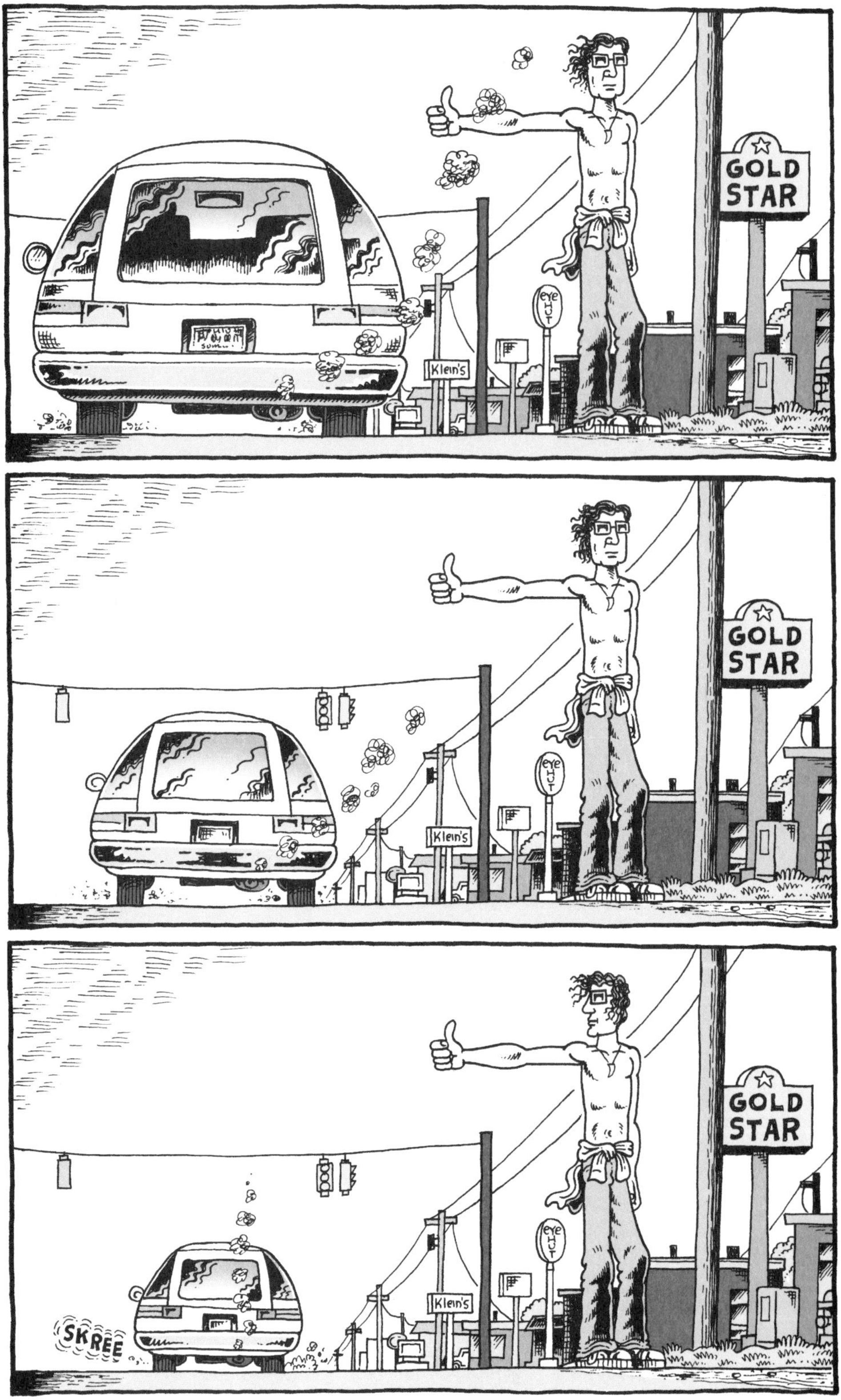
Klein's
eye HUT
GOLD STAR
Klein's
eye HUT
GOLD STAR
SKREE
Klein's
eye HUT
GOLD STAR

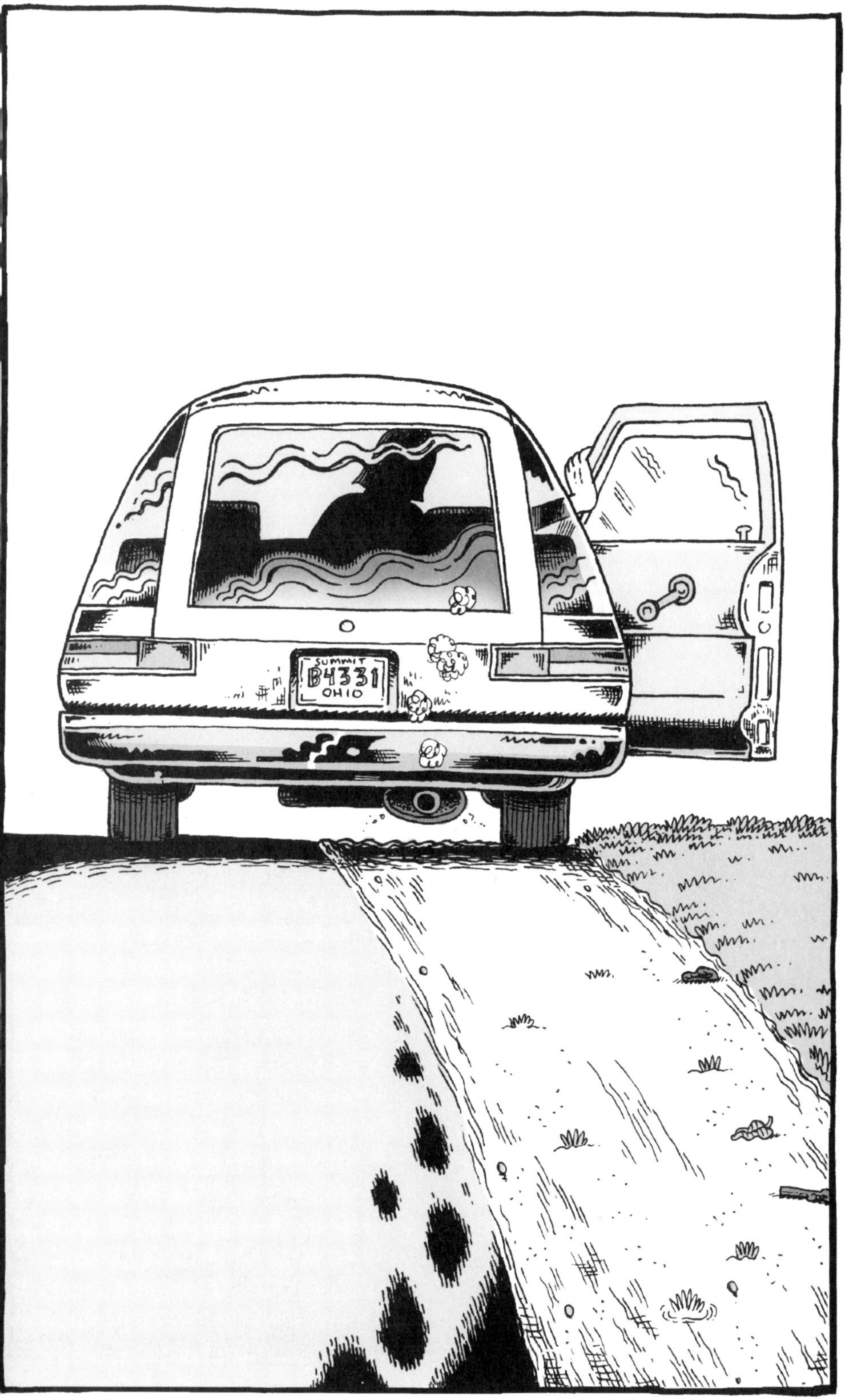
SUMMIT
B4331
OHIO

PART 5

Fade to Black

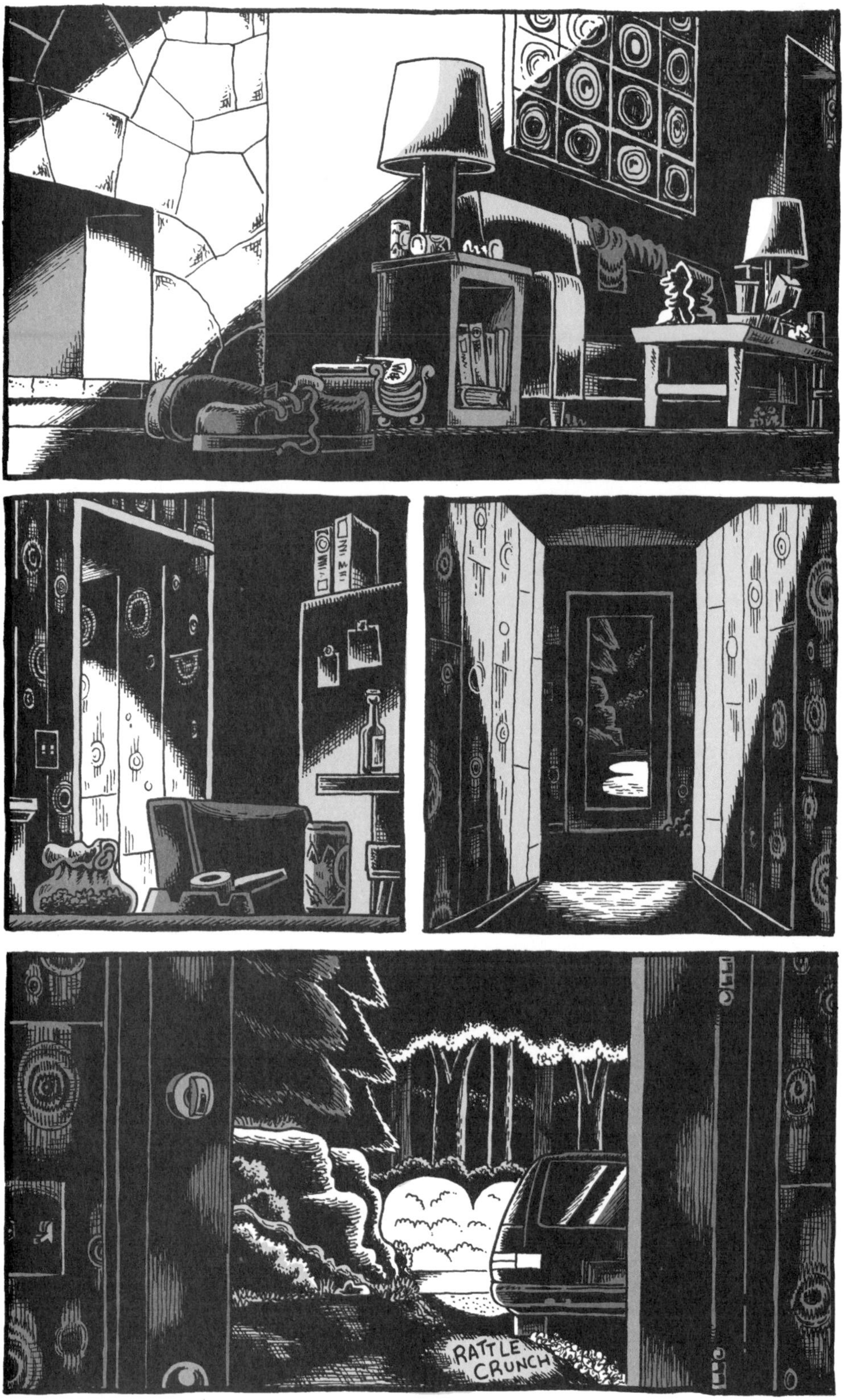
RATTLE
CRUNCH

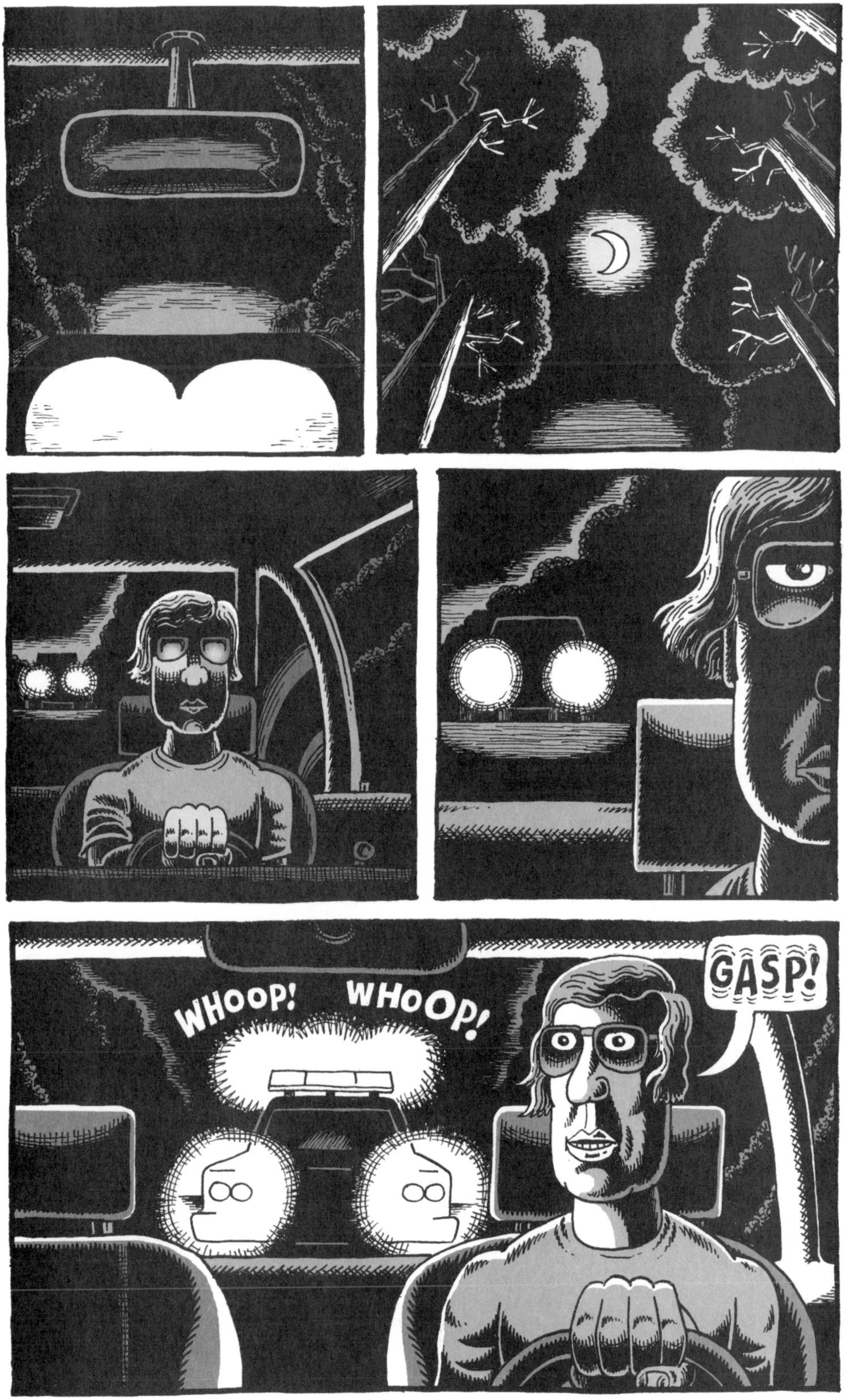
WHOOP! WHOOP!
GASP!

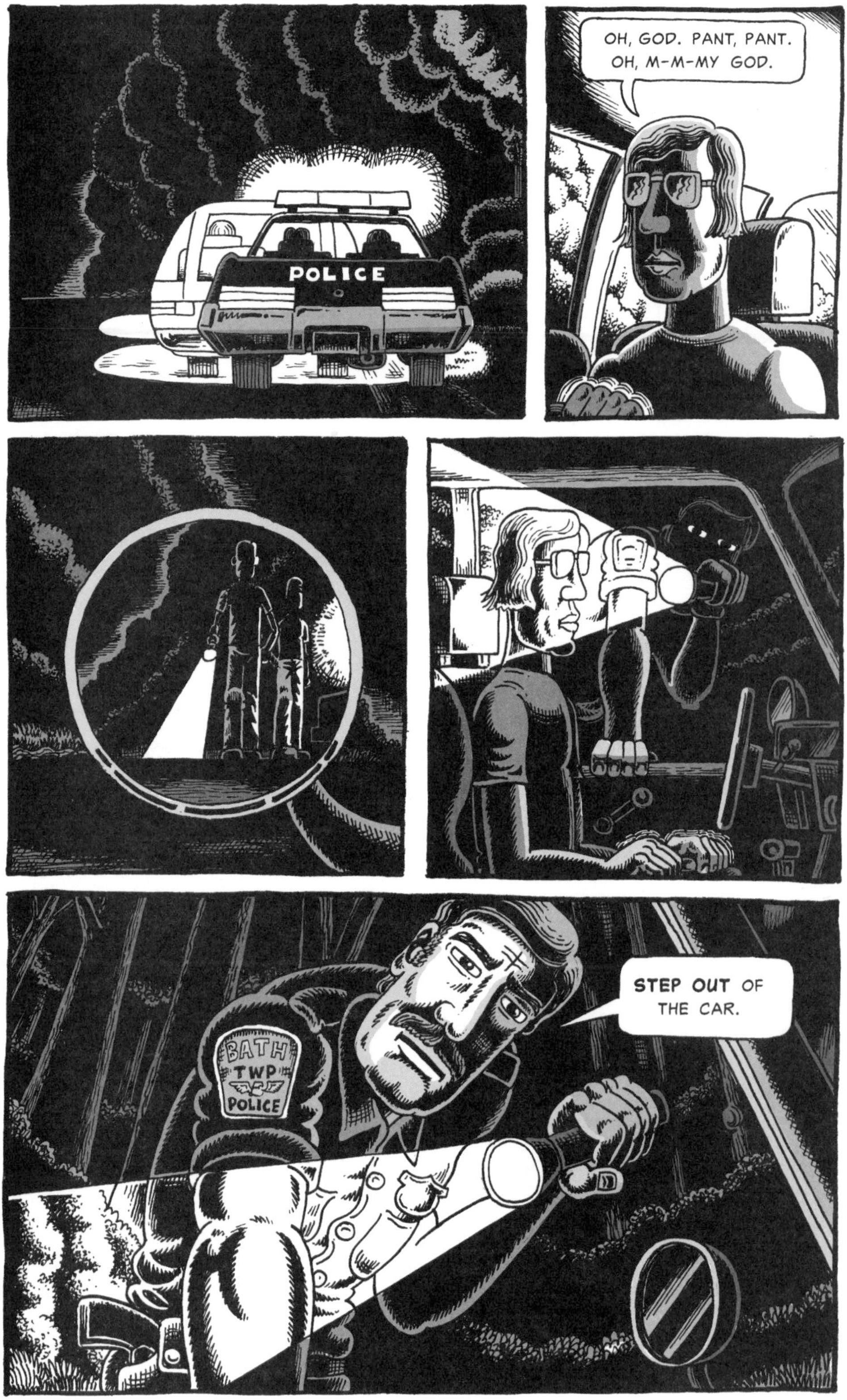
POLICE
OH, GOD. PANT, PANT. OH, M-M-MY GOD.
BATH TWP POLICE
STEP OUT OF THE CAR.

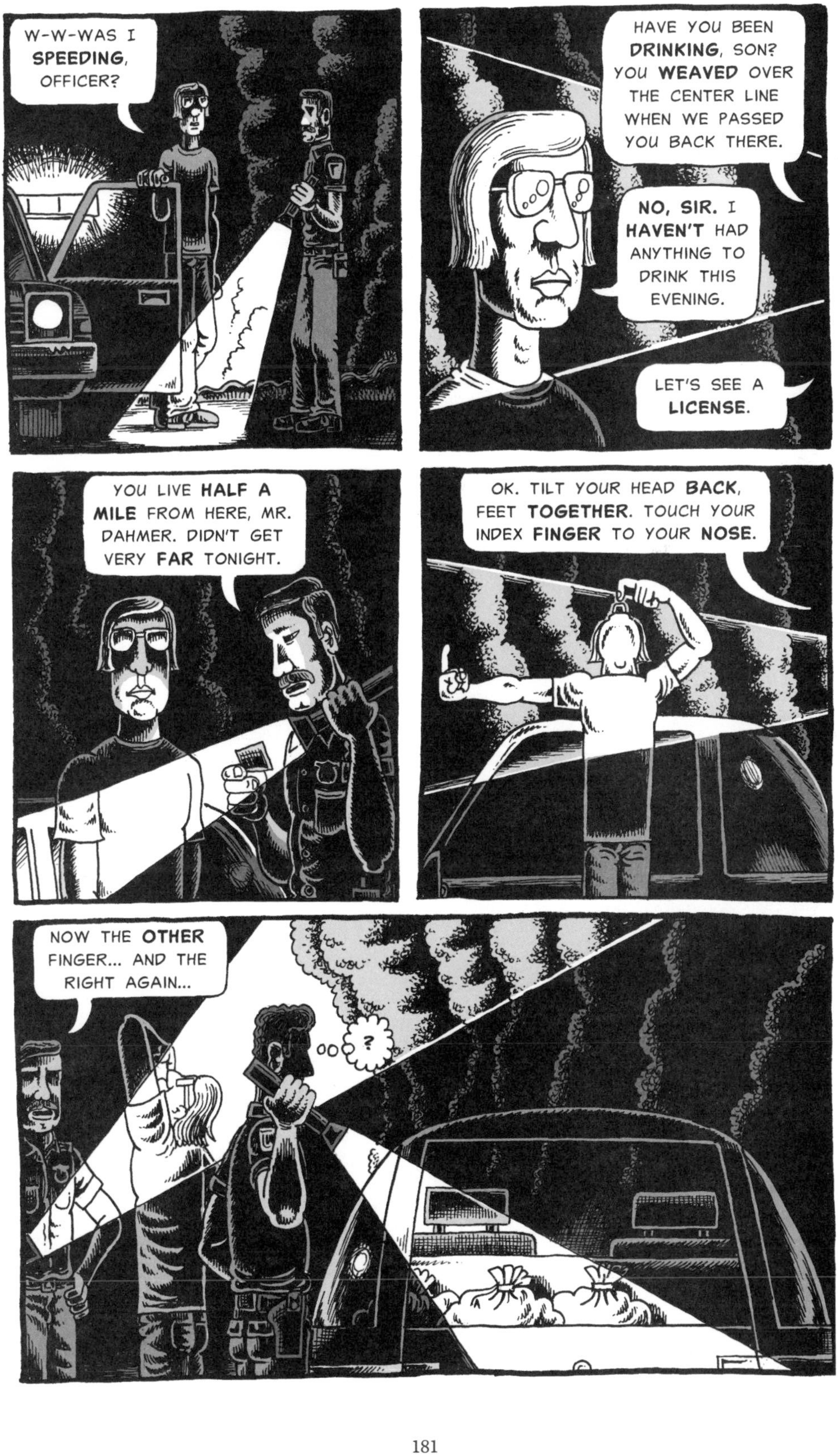

W-W-WAS I **SPEEDING**, OFFICER?
HAVE YOU BEEN **DRINKING**, SON? YOU **WEAVED** OVER THE CENTER LINE WHEN WE PASSED YOU BACK THERE.
NO, SIR. I **HAVEN'T** HAD ANYTHING TO DRINK THIS EVENING.
LET'S SEE A **LICENSE**.
YOU LIVE **HALF A MILE** FROM HERE, MR. DAHMER. DIDN'T GET VERY **FAR** TONIGHT.
OK. TILT YOUR HEAD **BACK**, FEET **TOGETHER**. TOUCH YOUR INDEX **FINGER** TO YOUR **NOSE**.
NOW THE **OTHER** FINGER... AND THE RIGHT AGAIN...
?

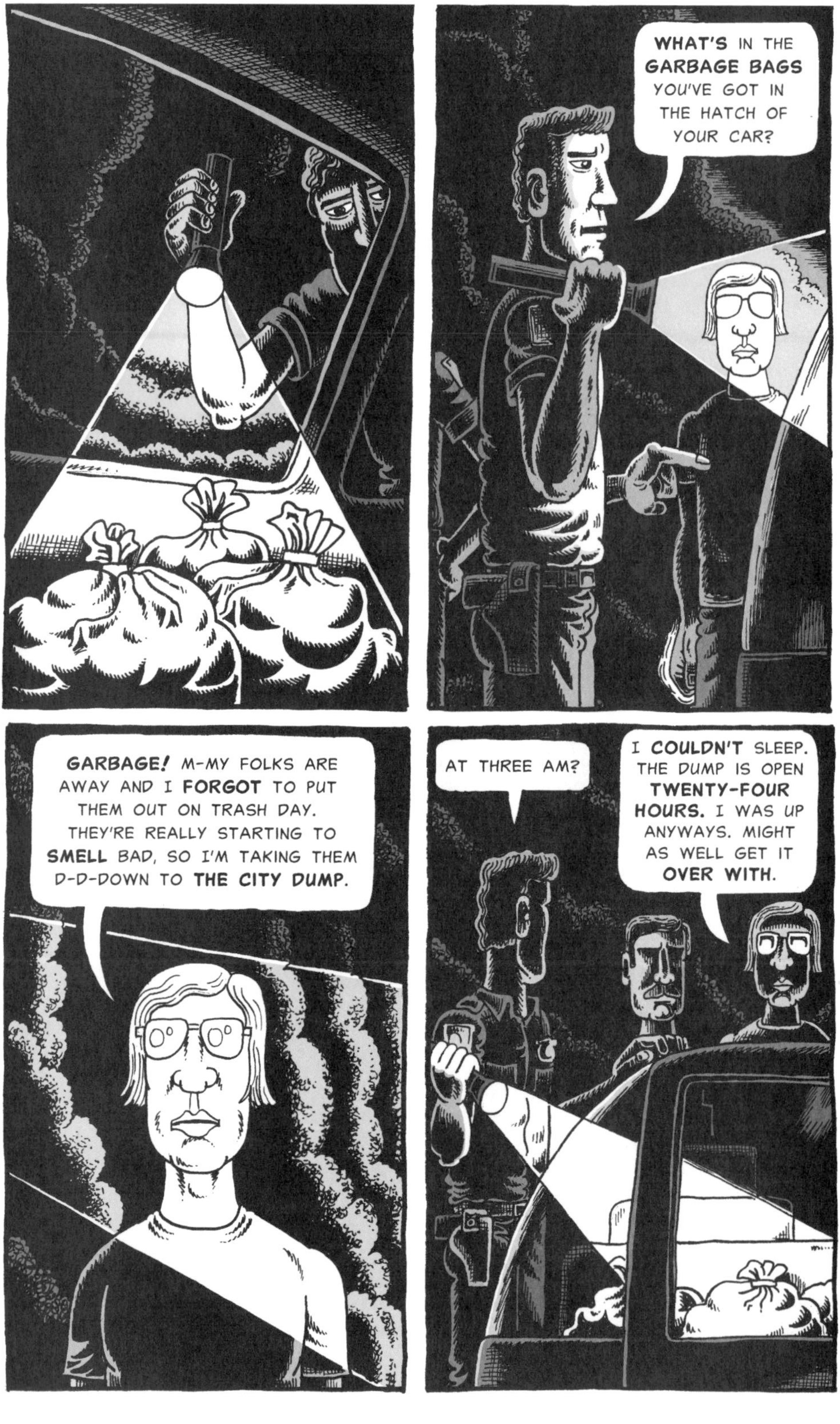
WHAT'S IN THE GARBAGE BAGS YOU'VE GOT IN THE HATCH OF YOUR CAR?
GARBAGE! M-MY FOLKS ARE AWAY AND I FORGOT TO PUT THEM OUT ON TRASH DAY. THEY'RE REALLY STARTING TO SMELL BAD, SO I'M TAKING THEM D-D-DOWN TO THE CITY DUMP.
AT THREE AM?
I COULDN'T SLEEP. THE DUMP IS OPEN TWENTY-FOUR HOURS. I WAS UP ANYWAYS. MIGHT AS WELL GET IT OVER WITH.

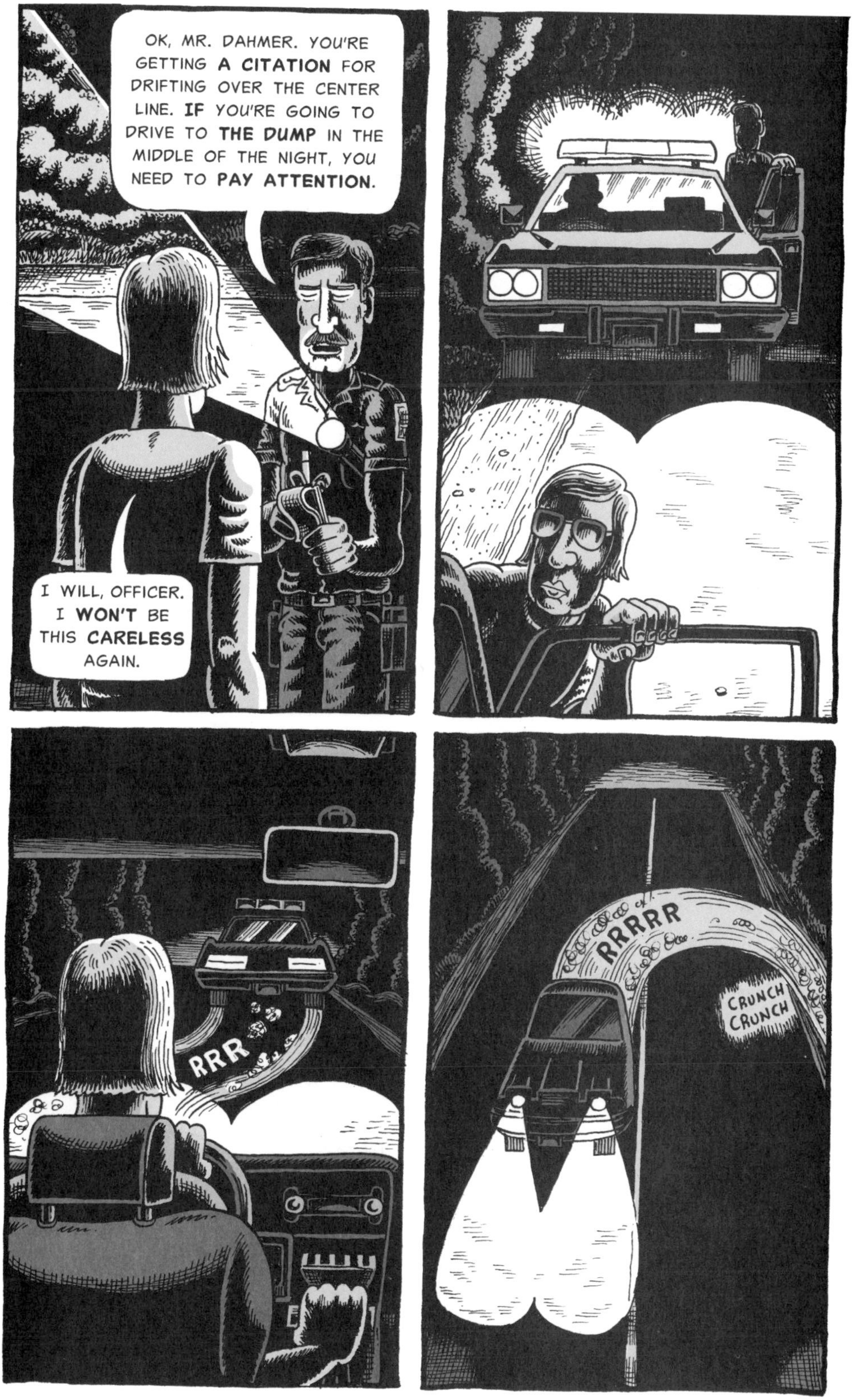
OK, MR. DAHMER. YOU'RE GETTING A CITATION FOR DRIFTING OVER THE CENTER LINE. IF YOU'RE GOING TO DRIVE TO THE DUMP IN THE MIDDLE OF THE NIGHT, YOU NEED TO PAY ATTENTION.
I WILL, OFFICER. I WON'T BE THIS CARELESS AGAIN.
RRR
RRRRR
CRUNCH CRUNCH

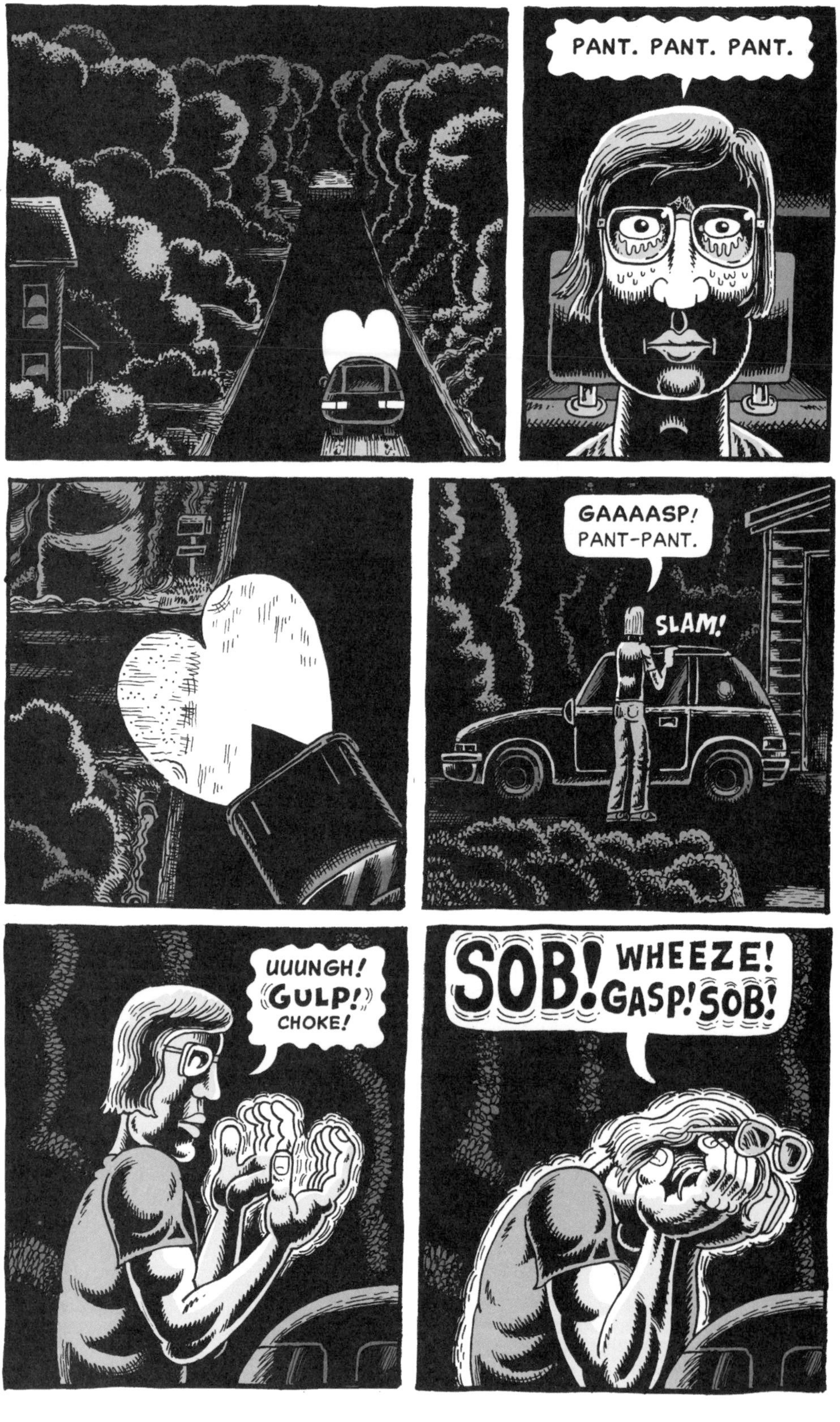
PANT. PANT. PANT.
GAAAASP! PANT-PANT.
SLAM!
UUUNGH! GULP! CHOKE!
SOB! WHEEZE! GASP! SOB!

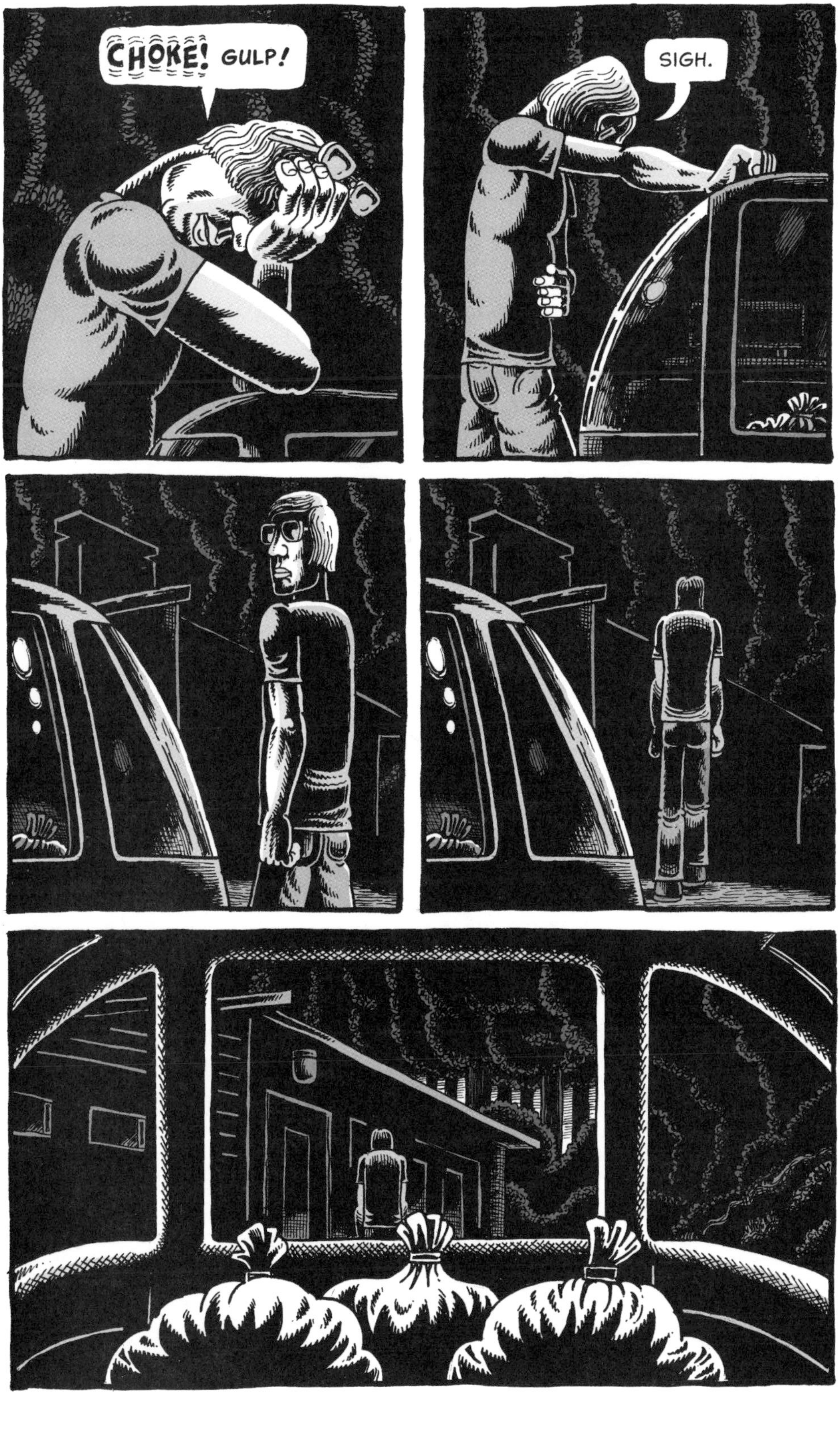
CHOKE! GULP!
SIGH.

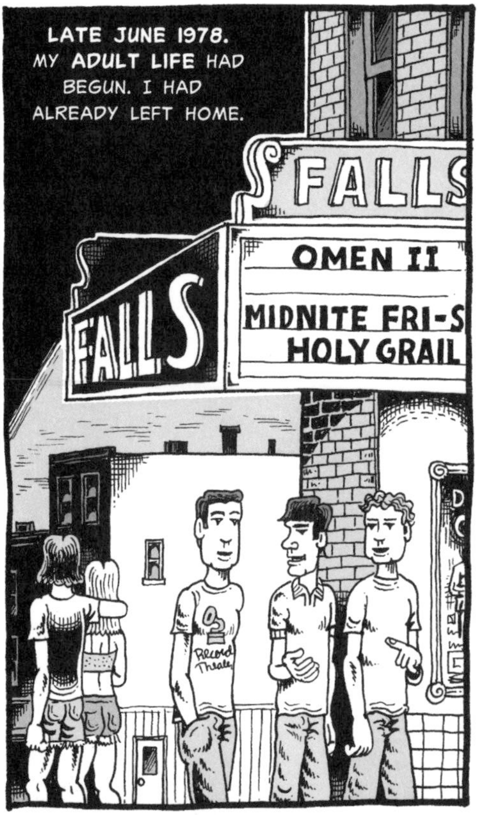
LATE JUNE 1978. MY ADULT LIFE HAD BEGUN. I HAD ALREADY LEFT HOME.
FALLS
OMEN II
MIDNITE FRI-S
HOLY GRAIL
FALLS
Record Theatre

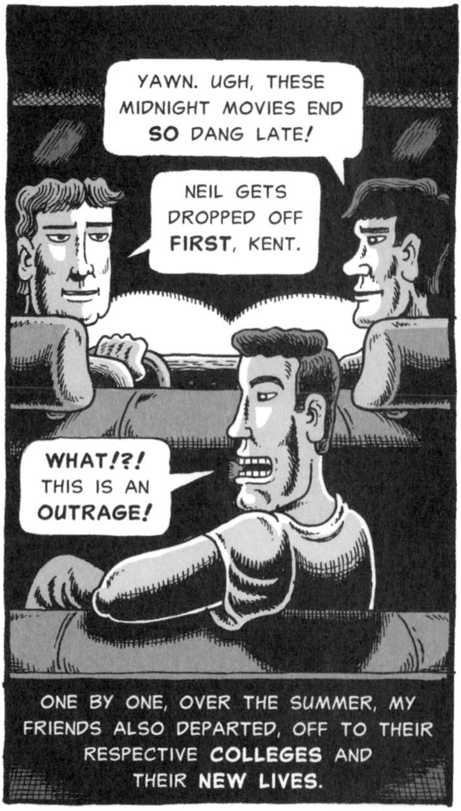
YAWN. UGH, THESE MIDNIGHT MOVIES END SO DANG LATE!
NEIL GETS DROPPED OFF FIRST, KENT.
WHAT!?! THIS IS AN OUTRAGE!
ONE BY ONE, OVER THE SUMMER, MY FRIENDS ALSO DEPARTED, OFF TO THEIR RESPECTIVE COLLEGES AND THEIR NEW LIVES.

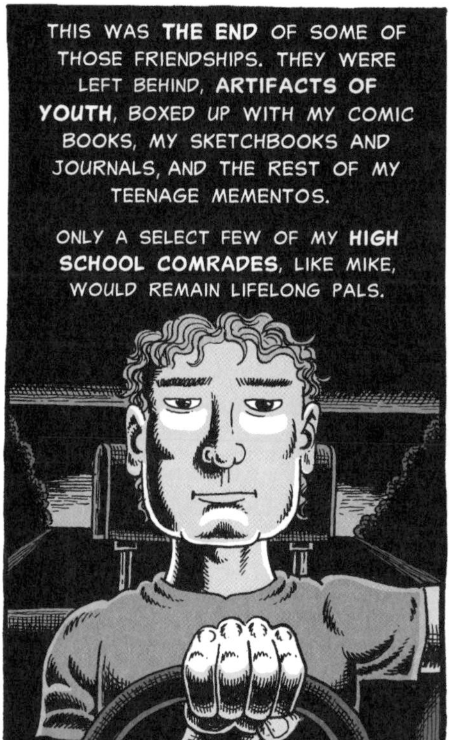
THIS WAS THE END OF SOME OF THOSE FRIENDSHIPS. THEY WERE LEFT BEHIND, ARTIFACTS OF YOUTH, BOXED UP WITH MY COMIC BOOKS, MY SKETCHBOOKS AND JOURNALS, AND THE REST OF MY TEENAGE MEMENTOS.
ONLY A SELECT FEW OF MY HIGH SCHOOL COMRADES, LIKE MIKE, WOULD REMAIN LIFELONG PALS.

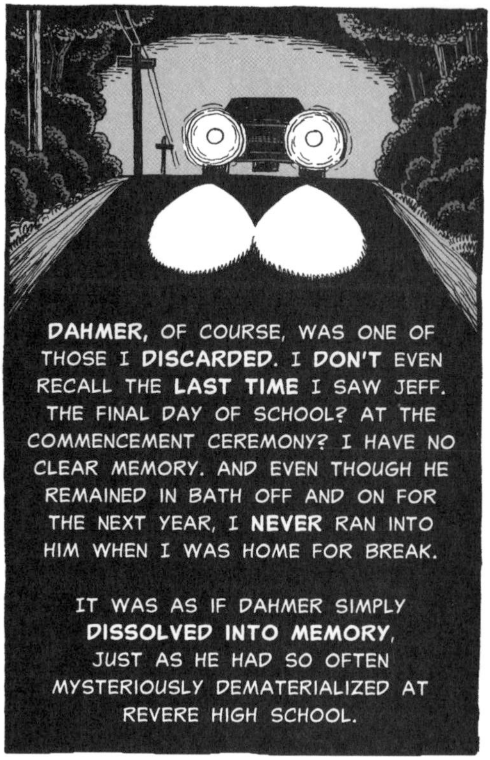
DAHMER, OF COURSE, WAS ONE OF THOSE I DISCARDED. I DON'T EVEN RECALL THE LAST TIME I SAW JEFF. THE FINAL DAY OF SCHOOL? AT THE COMMENCEMENT CEREMONY? I HAVE NO CLEAR MEMORY. AND EVEN THOUGH HE REMAINED IN BATH OFF AND ON FOR THE NEXT YEAR, I NEVER RAN INTO HIM WHEN I WAS HOME FOR BREAK.
IT WAS AS IF DAHMER SIMPLY DISSOLVED INTO MEMORY, JUST AS HE HAD SO OFTEN MYSTERIOUSLY DEMATERIALIZED AT REVERE HIGH SCHOOL.

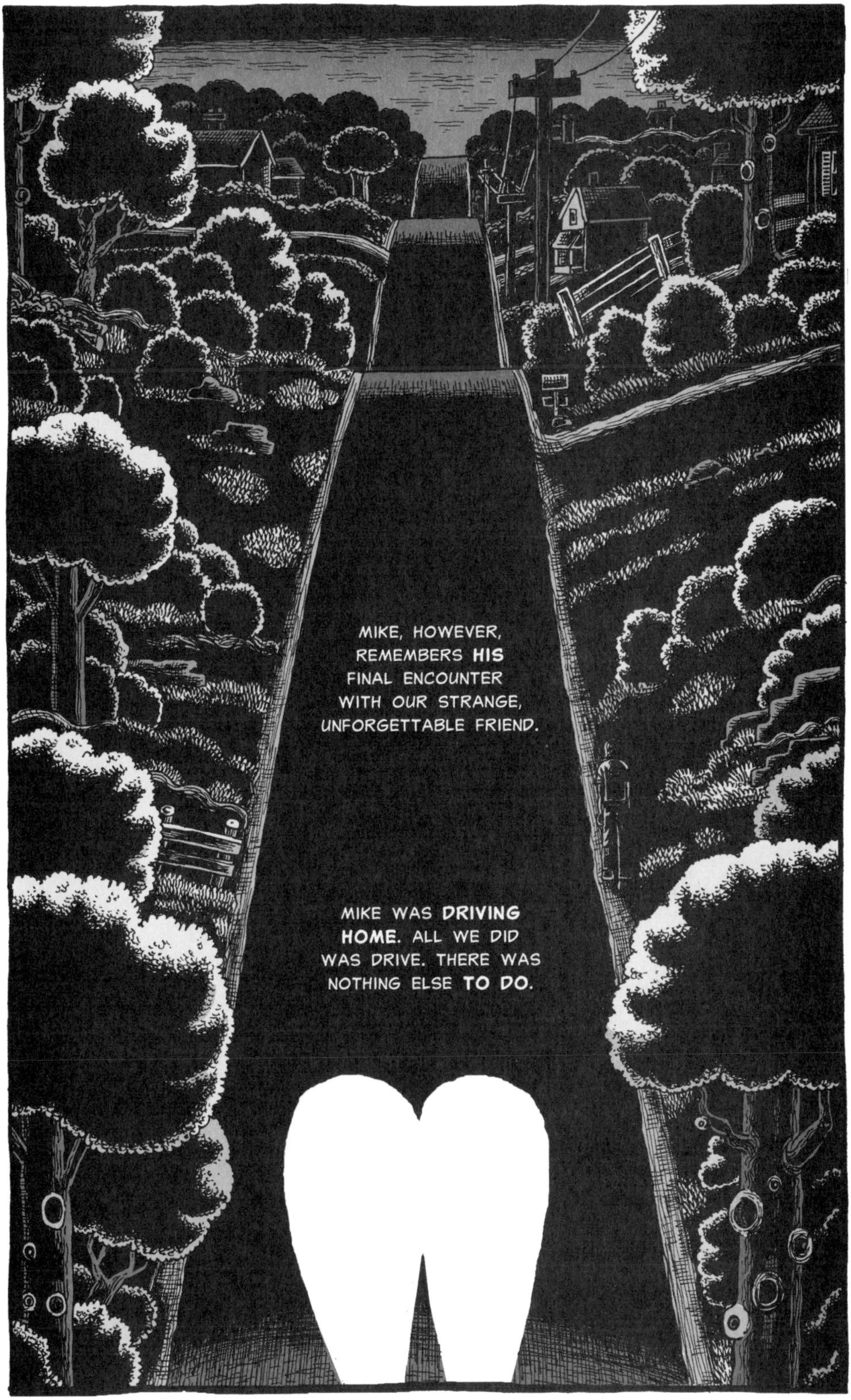
MIKE, HOWEVER, REMEMBERS HIS FINAL ENCOUNTER WITH OUR STRANGE, UNFORGETTABLE FRIEND.
MIKE WAS DRIVING HOME. ALL WE DID WAS DRIVE. THERE WAS NOTHING ELSE TO DO.

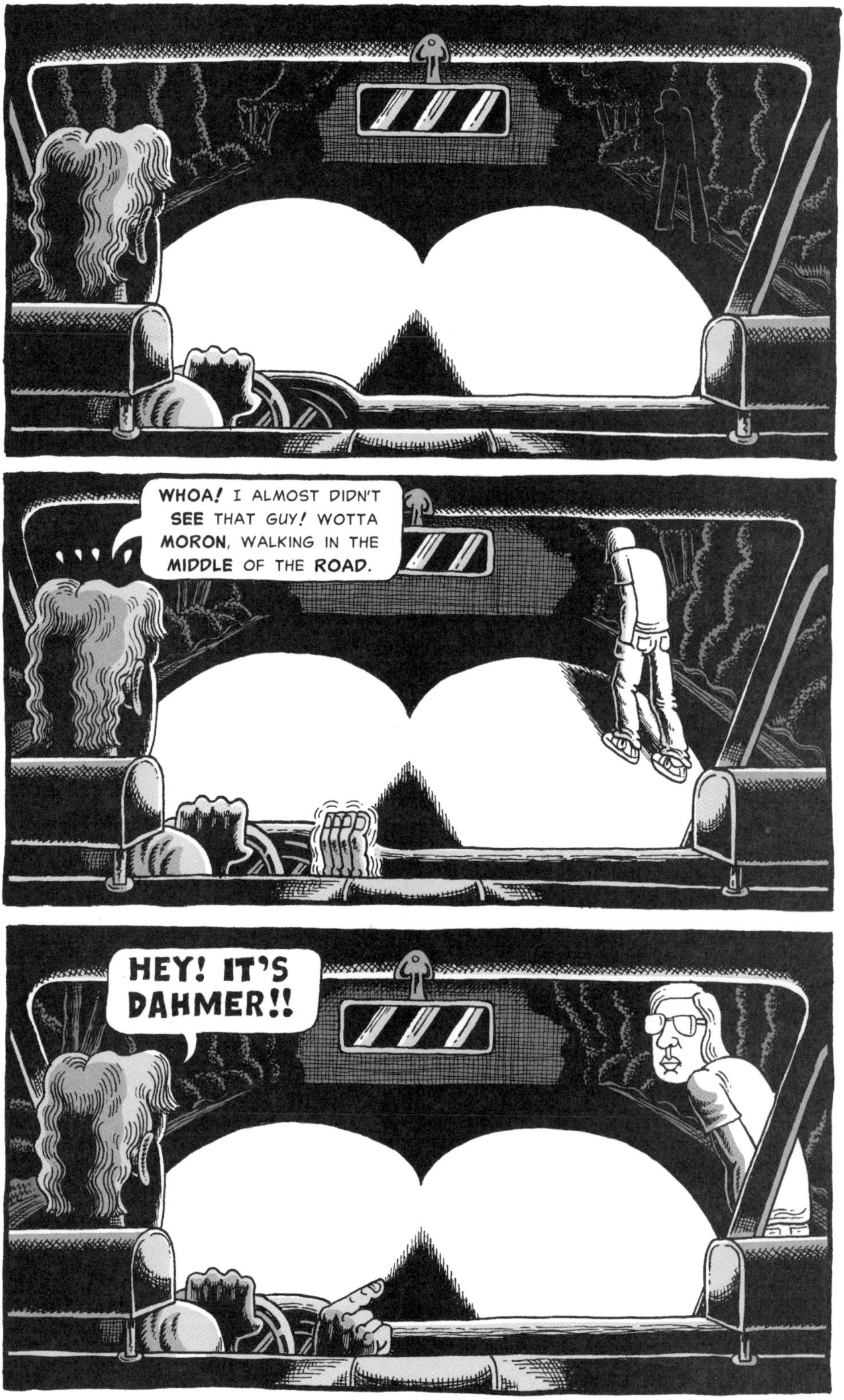
WHOA! I ALMOST DIDN'T SEE THAT GUY! WOTTA MORON, WALKING IN THE MIDDLE OF THE ROAD.
HEY! IT'S DAHMER!!

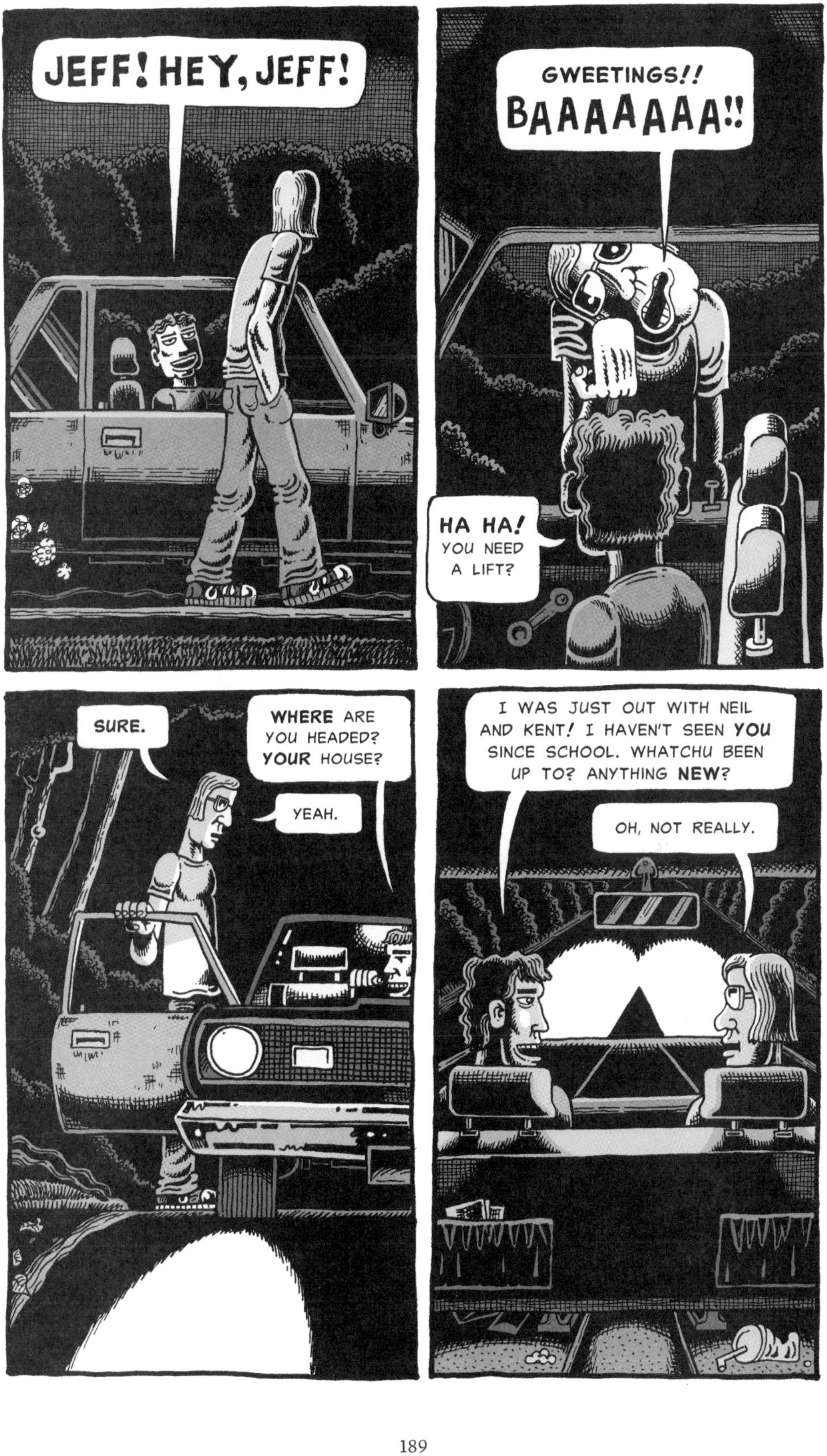
JEFF! HEY, JEFF!
GWEETINGS!! BAAAAAAA!!
HA HA! YOU NEED A LIFT?
SURE.
WHERE ARE YOU HEADED? YOUR HOUSE?
YEAH.
I WAS JUST OUT WITH NEIL AND KENT! I HAVEN'T SEEN YOU SINCE SCHOOL. WHATCHU BEEN UP TO? ANYTHING NEW?
OH, NOT REALLY.

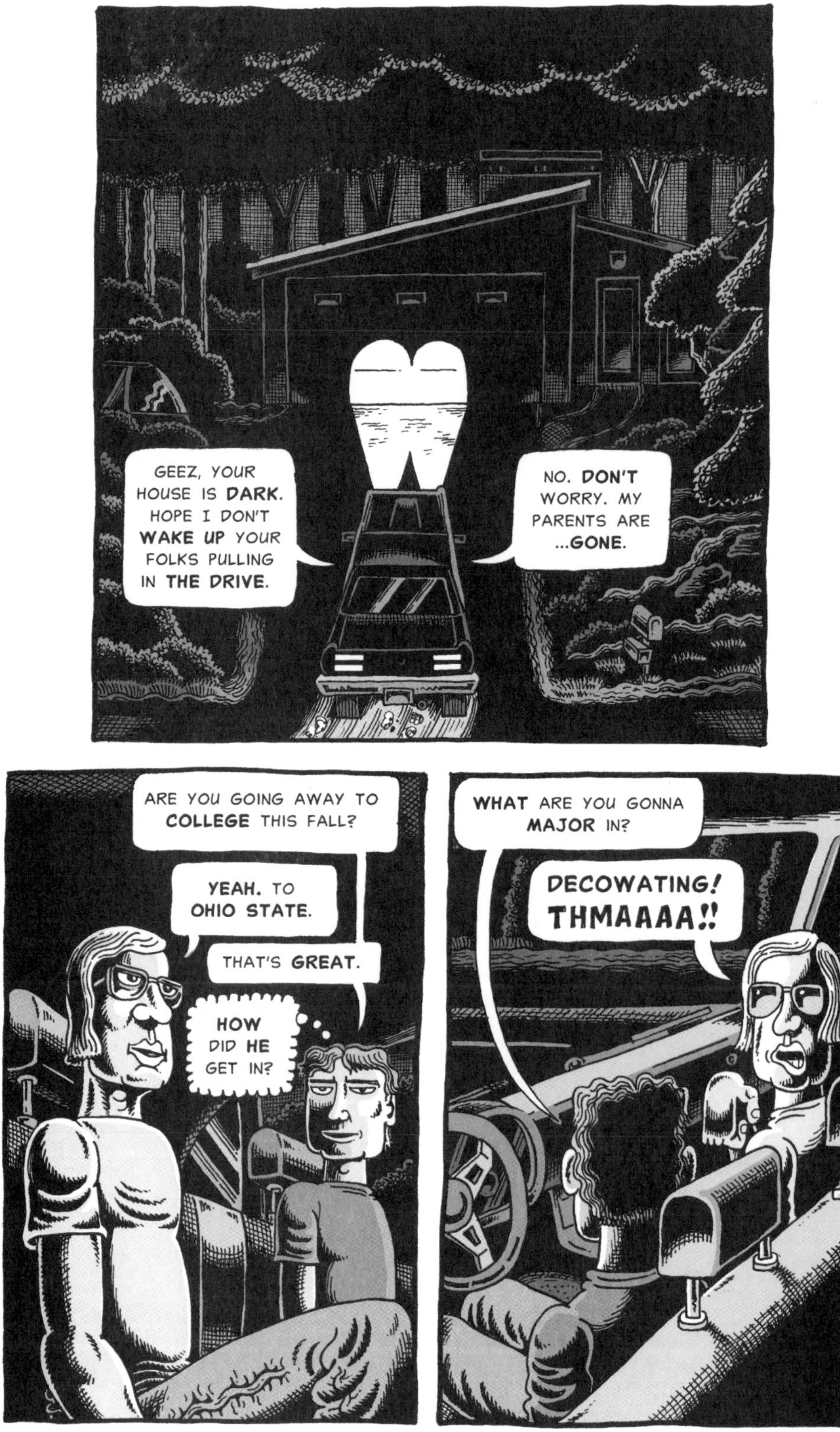
GEEZ, YOUR HOUSE IS DARK. HOPE I DON'T WAKE UP YOUR FOLKS PULLING IN THE DRIVE.
NO. DON'T WORRY. MY PARENTS ARE ...GONE.
ARE YOU GOING AWAY TO COLLEGE THIS FALL?
YEAH. TO OHIO STATE.
THAT'S GREAT.
HOW DID HE GET IN?
WHAT ARE YOU GONNA MAJOR IN?
DECOWATING! THMAAAA!!

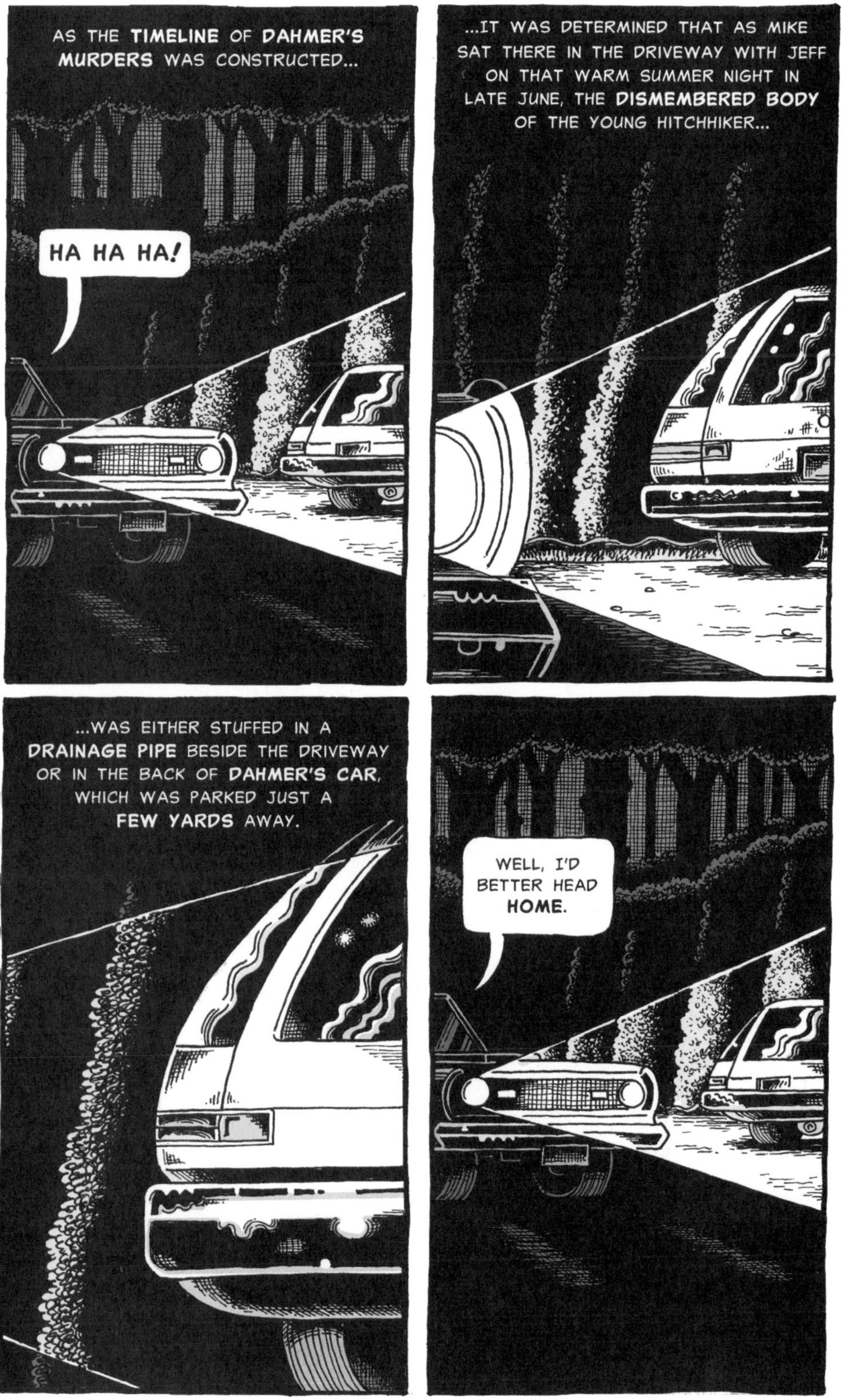
AS THE TIMELINE OF DAHMER'S MURDERS WAS CONSTRUCTED...
HA HA HA!
...IT WAS DETERMINED THAT AS MIKE SAT THERE IN THE DRIVEWAY WITH JEFF ON THAT WARM SUMMER NIGHT IN LATE JUNE, THE DISMEMBERED BODY OF THE YOUNG HITCHHIKER...
...WAS EITHER STUFFED IN A DRAINAGE PIPE BESIDE THE DRIVEWAY OR IN THE BACK OF DAHMER'S CAR, WHICH WAS PARKED JUST A FEW YARDS AWAY.
WELL, I'D BETTER HEAD HOME.

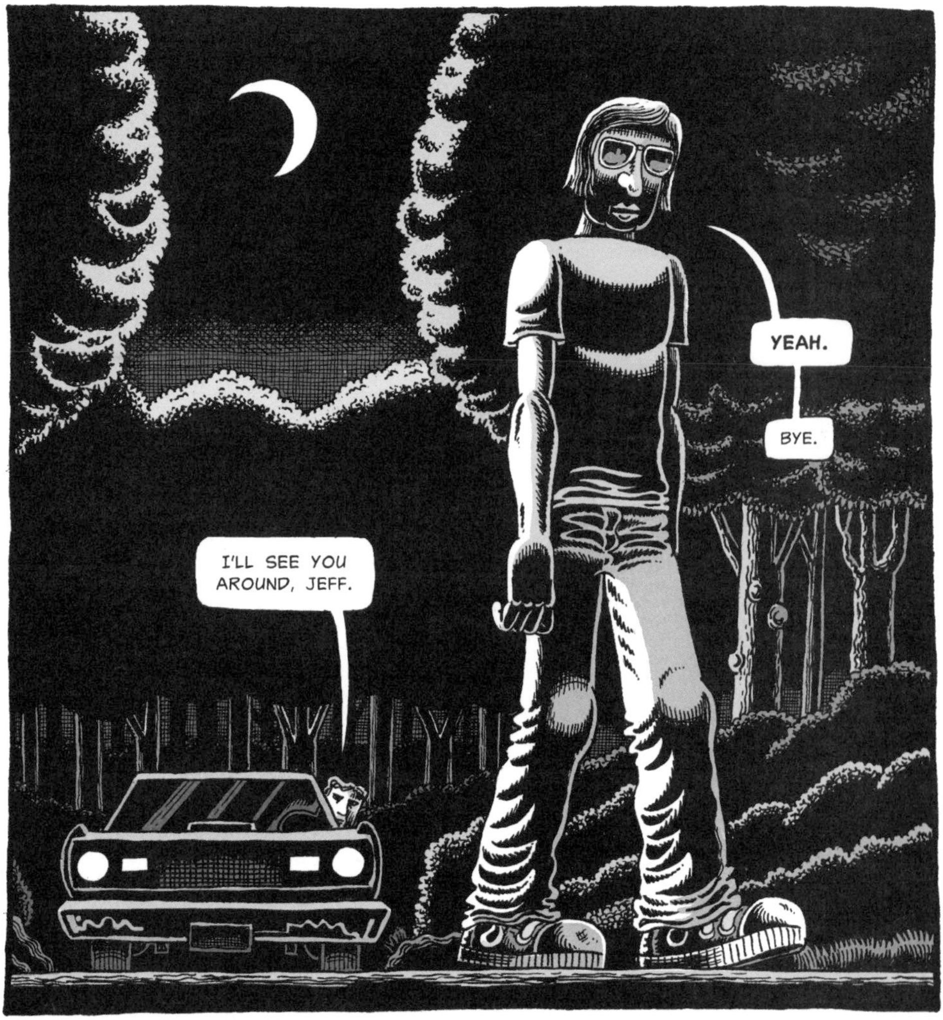
I'LL SEE YOU AROUND, JEFF.
YEAH.
BYE.

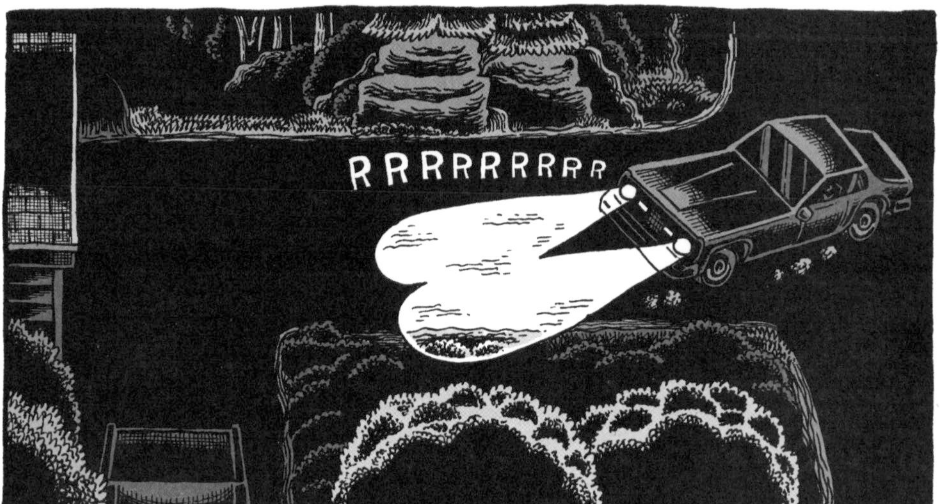
RRRRRRRRRR

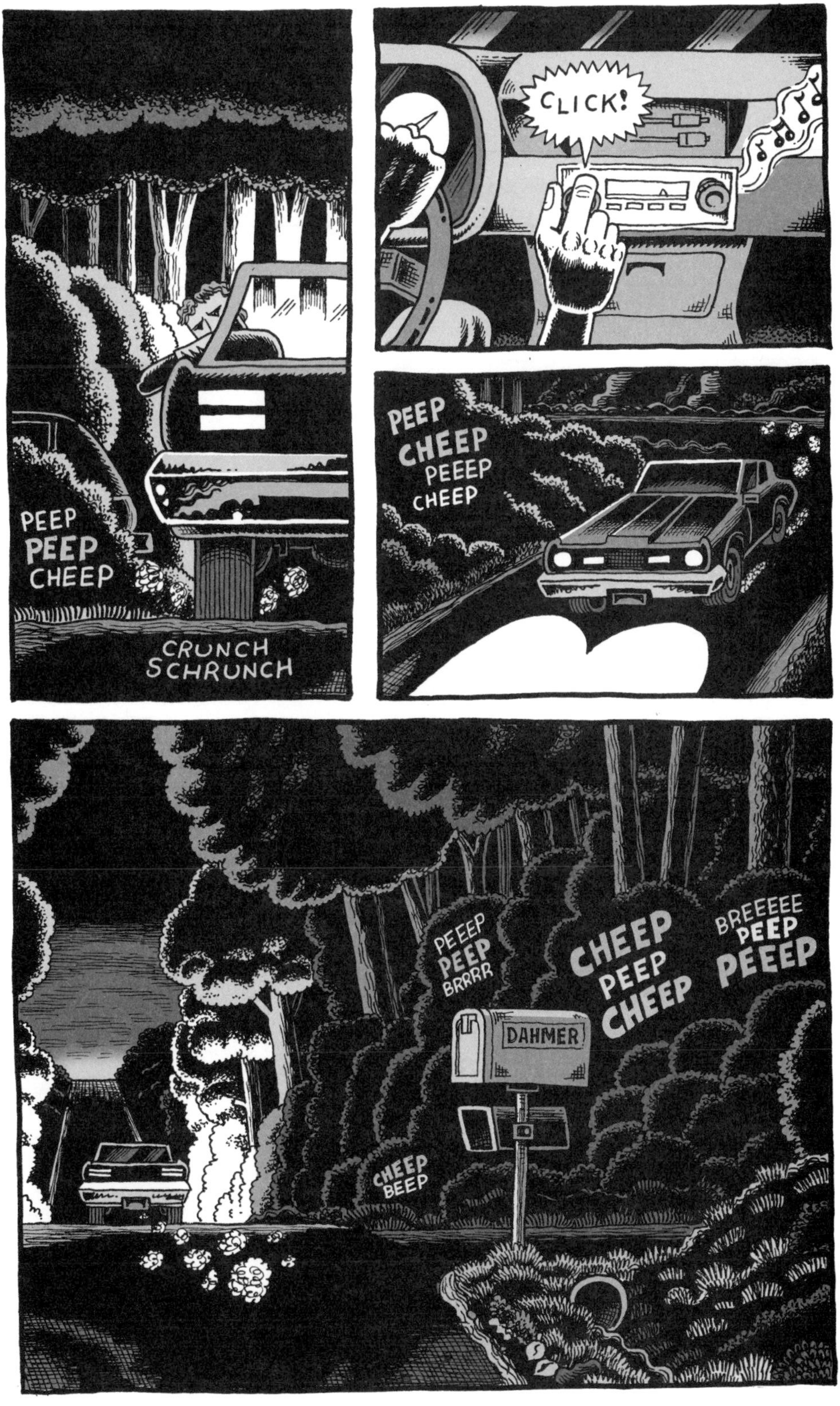
PEEP
PEEP
CHEEP
CRUNCH
SCHRUNCH
CLICK!
PEEP
CHEEP
PEEEP
CHEEP
PEEEP
PEEP
BRRRR
CHEEP
PEEP
CHEEP
BREEEEE
PEEP
PEEEP
DAHMER
CHEEP
BEEP

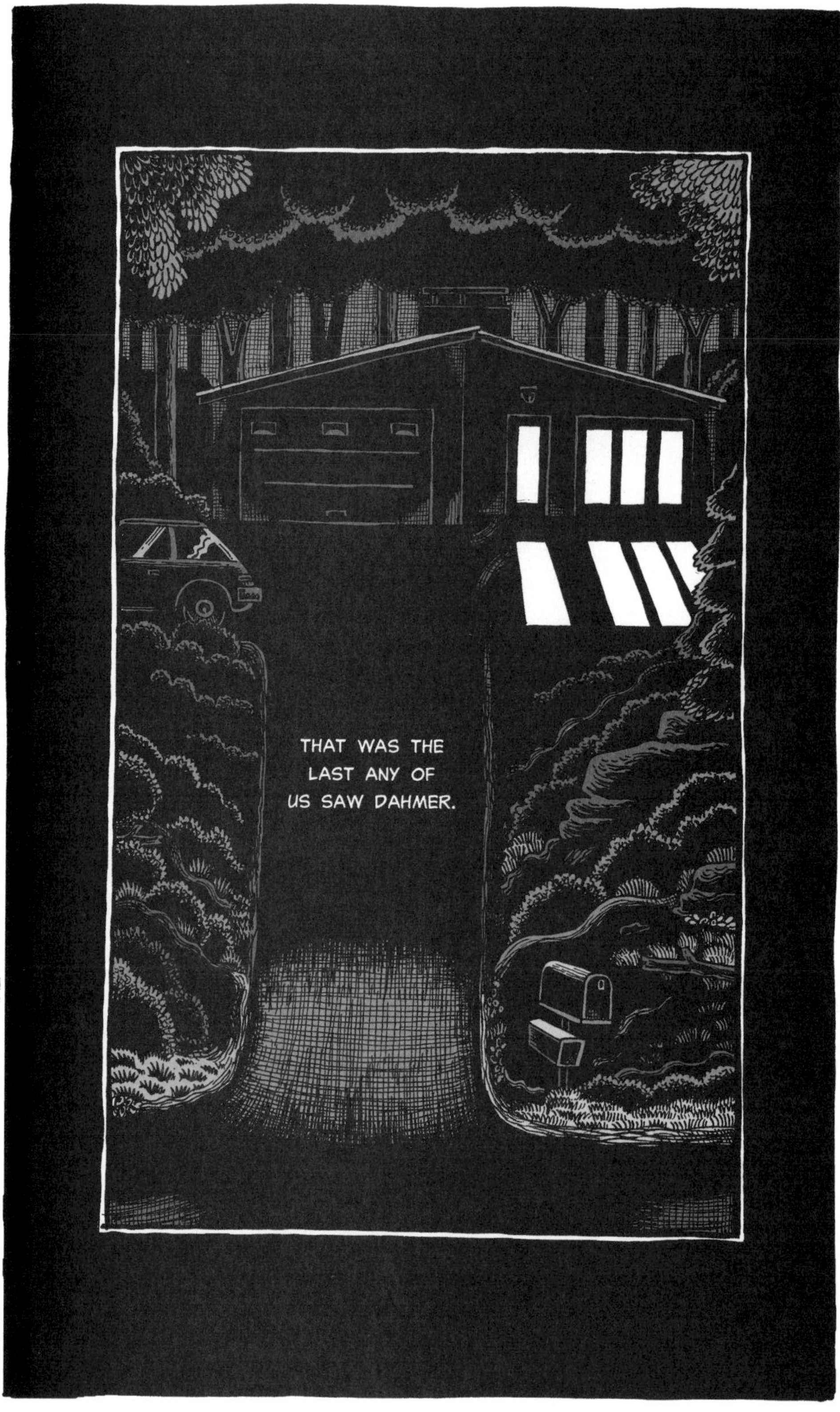
THAT WAS THE
LAST ANY OF
US SAW DAHMER.

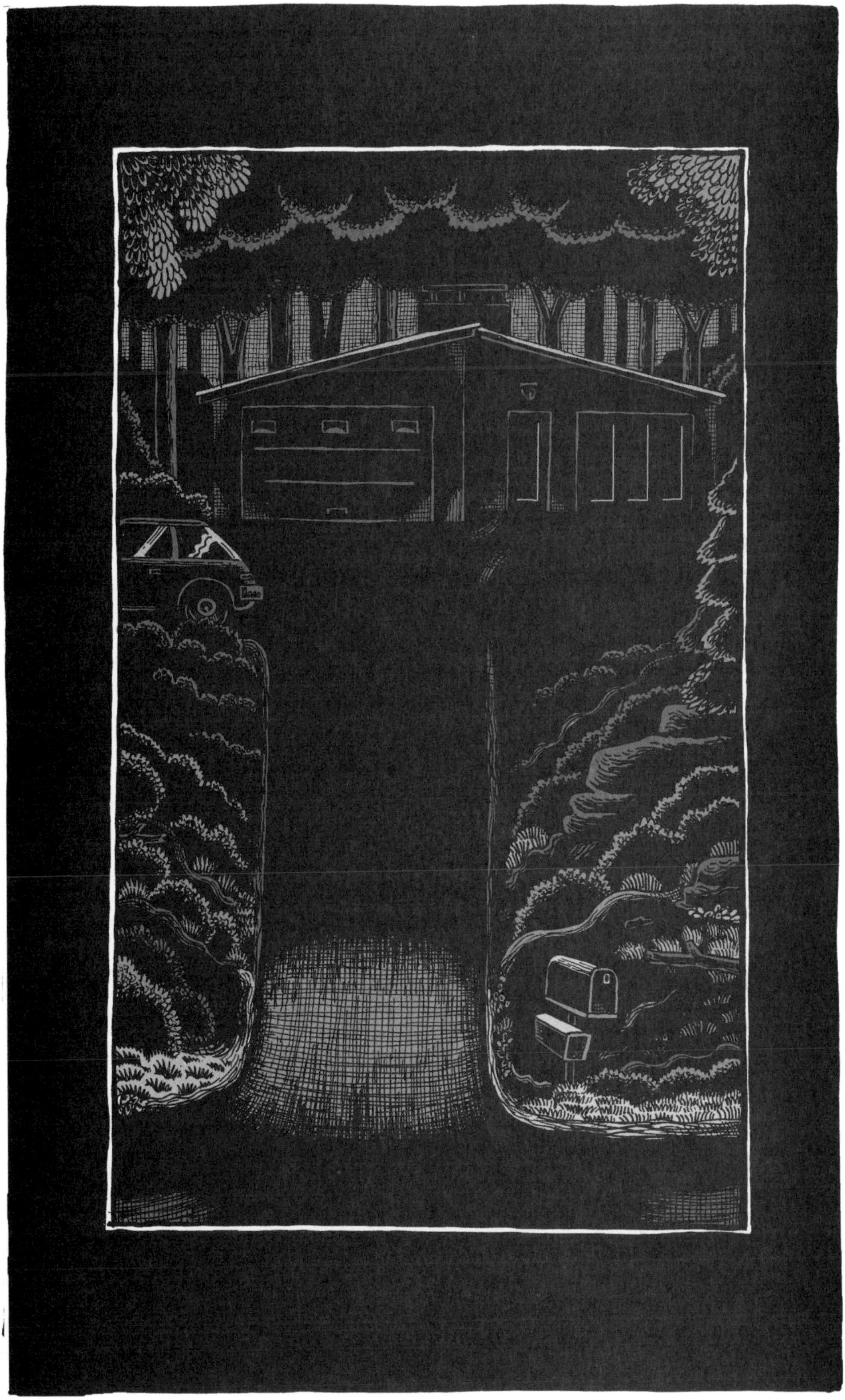

Epilogue

"That night in Ohio, that one impulsive night. Nothing's been normal since then. It taints your whole life. After it happened I thought that I'd just try to live as normally as possible and bury it, but things like that don't stay buried."

—Jeff Dahmer,
interview with psychologist Dr. Kenneth Smail,
Milwaukee Police, August 26, 1991

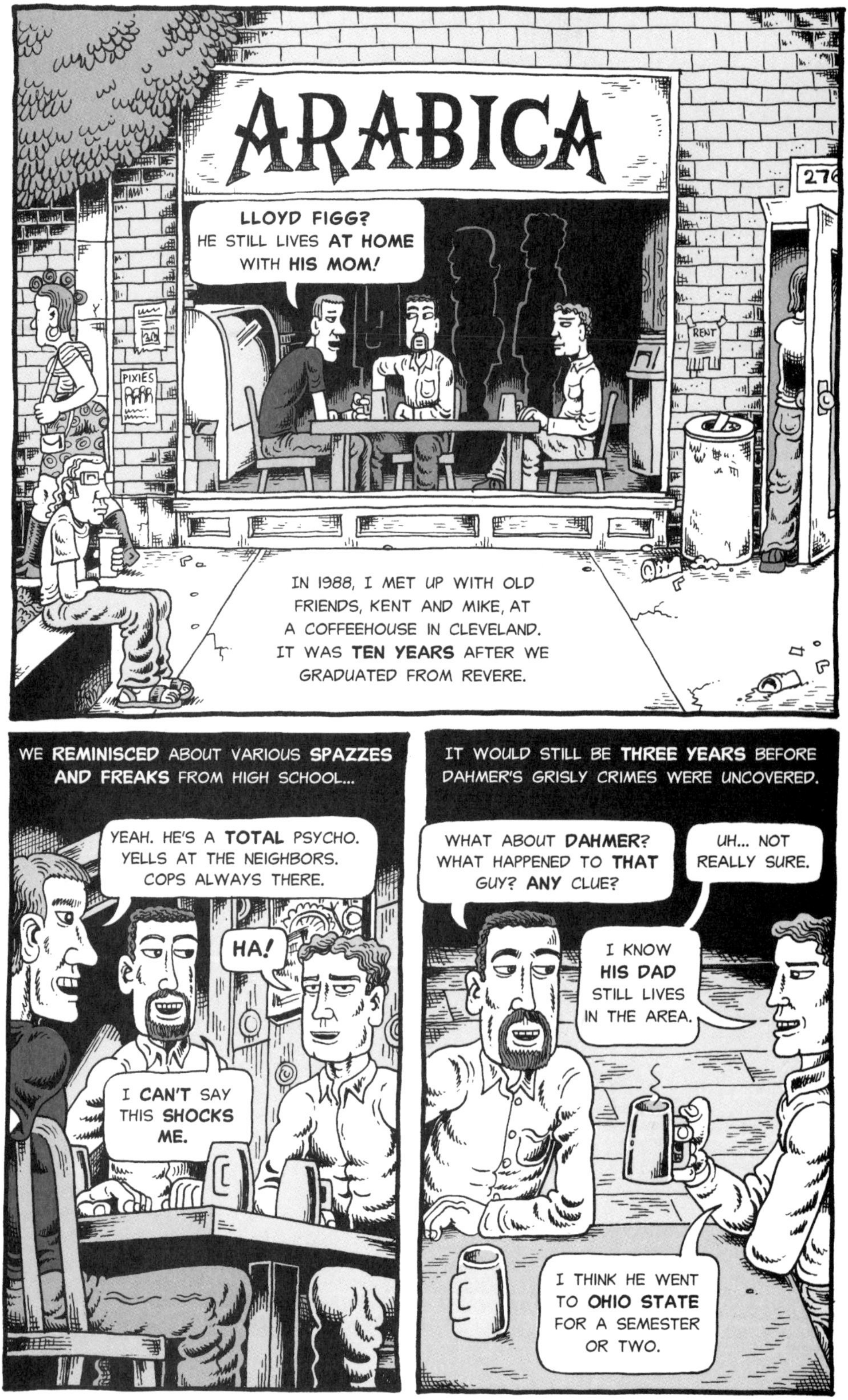
ARABICA
276
PIXIES
RENT
LLOYD FIGG? HE STILL LIVES AT HOME WITH HIS MOM!
IN 1988, I MET UP WITH OLD FRIENDS, KENT AND MIKE, AT A COFFEEHOUSE IN CLEVELAND. IT WAS TEN YEARS AFTER WE GRADUATED FROM REVERE.
WE REMINISCED ABOUT VARIOUS SPAZZES AND FREAKS FROM HIGH SCHOOL...
YEAH. HE'S A TOTAL PSYCHO. YELLS AT THE NEIGHBORS. COPS ALWAYS THERE.
HA!
I CAN'T SAY THIS SHOCKS ME.
IT WOULD STILL BE THREE YEARS BEFORE DAHMER'S GRISLY CRIMES WERE UNCOVERED.
WHAT ABOUT DAHMER? WHAT HAPPENED TO THAT GUY? ANY CLUE?
UH... NOT REALLY SURE.
I KNOW HIS DAD STILL LIVES IN THE AREA.
I THINK HE WENT TO OHIO STATE FOR A SEMESTER OR TWO.

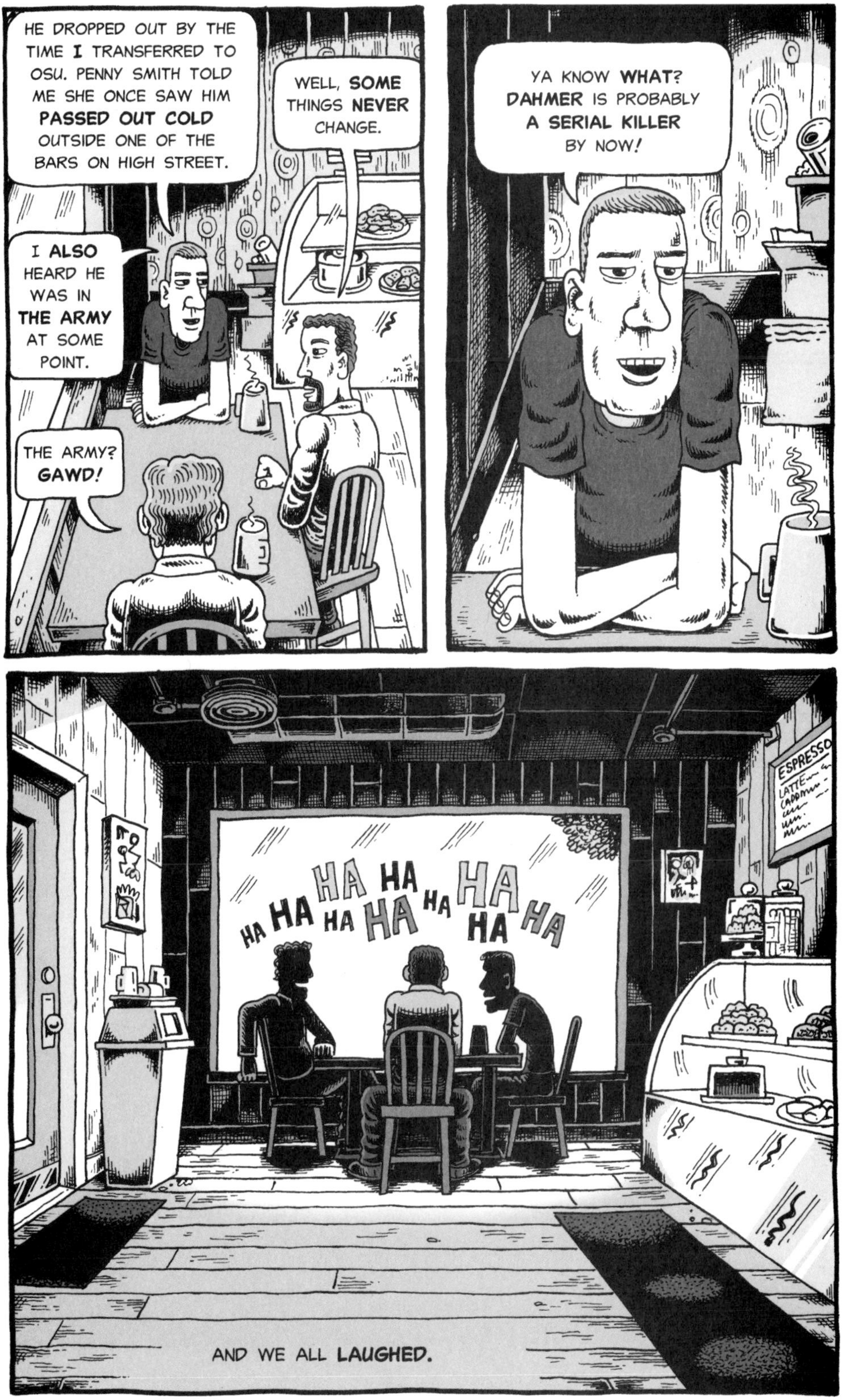
HE DROPPED OUT BY THE TIME I TRANSFERRED TO OSU. PENNY SMITH TOLD ME SHE ONCE SAW HIM PASSED OUT COLD OUTSIDE ONE OF THE BARS ON HIGH STREET.
WELL, SOME THINGS NEVER CHANGE.
I ALSO HEARD HE WAS IN THE ARMY AT SOME POINT.
THE ARMY? GAWD!
YA KNOW WHAT? DAHMER IS PROBABLY A SERIAL KILLER BY NOW!
ESPRESSO
LATTE
HA HA HA HA HA HA HA HA HA HA HA
AND WE ALL LAUGHED.

SOURCES

THE MATERIAL USED TO WRITE THIS BOOK COMES FROM THE FOLLOWING SOURCES:

Personal memories and interviews with contemporaries

This is, of course, a personal memoir—my recollections of my friendship with Jeff Dahmer—so most of this story is based on my own memories and papers, or the memories of other high school friends whom I trust. If two or more eyewitnesses described events similarly, I considered that to be fact. Most of these recollections come from the members of the Dahmer Fan Club: Kent, Neil, and Mike (their names have been changed in this book).

I also interviewed dozens of former classmates, especially those who lived in Dahmer's neighborhood, and several teachers who worked at Revere High back in the day. I gleaned a few valuable things, but to be honest, the most common answer was "I didn't know him" or "I never talked to him." In the case of the teachers, each one said basically the same thing: "I never noticed anything wrong with him." That, in itself, is telling.

My firsthand account was supplemented with material gleaned from these sources:

INTERVIEWS WITH DAHMER

Dahmer's descriptions of his youth, in his own words, are more reliable than any other source. Once caught, Jeff was remarkably forthright with the police, unlike most serial killers, who are either pathological liars, like Henry Lee Lucas, or manipulative psychopaths, like Charles Manson. Dahmer was truthful and coherent.

These are the interviews I found most helpful, even though they all basically repeat the same anecdotes and information:
 • Interview transcripts. Dahmer was interviewed extensively by several FBI agents and psychologists, and these interviews were particularly useful. The entire FBI file on Dahmer—more than ten thousand documents—was released to the public through the Freedom of Information Act and is now in the public domain.
 • *Dateline NBC* (November 29, 1994), later broadcast on MSNBC with additional material. Also available on DVD under the title *NBC News Presents: Inside Evil*. Can also be viewed on YouTube. Long interview by Stone

Phillips (conducted in February 1994 at the Columbia Correctional Institution in Portage, Wisconsin) with Jeff and Lionel, and a separate interview with Joyce. This is the only time that Jeff and Joyce were interviewed on camera (Joyce consented to one earlier print interview with a columnist for the *Milwaukee Sentinel*, which I also referred to).

NEWS ACCOUNTS

Most of the news stories I used as references were those written by the *Akron Beacon Journal*, Dahmer's "hometown" paper, and the *Milwaukee Journal* and *Milwaukee Sentinel* (then working under a joint operating agreement, but still using separate newsrooms). These three papers owned the story. The rest of the media—the national press and the bungling local TV news outfits—followed in their wake, rereporting what these newspapers uncovered. I was a staff artist at the *Beacon Journal* at the time and worked closely with the reporters and editors, discussing the emerging story and police investigation in great detail with them. I also spoke to reporters from the Milwaukee papers. As a journalist, I was surprised, and more than a little dismayed, at how sloppy the reporting by the national media was during the feeding frenzy of those first few weeks after Dahmer was arrested: names and dates were screwed up, town names were swapped, rumors were printed as fact. I'm confident, however, that the reporting from these three papers was accurate.

OTHER SOURCES

- FBI files. Available under the Freedom of Information Act, these voluminous FBI files include police reports; evidence and arrest records; confessions; transcripts of interviews with Dahmer by FBI agents, psychiatrists, and profilers; and news clippings.
- Family calendar. My mother kept and saved a very meticulous family calendar. The one from 1978 is chock-full of various events from my senior year. This was a vital resource in creating the timeline of Dahmer's own fateful senior year and in pinpointing when various events occurred.
- *A Father's Story*, by Lionel Dahmer (William Morrow and Company, 1994). Most of the incidents described in this book were known to me from other sources, but Lionel added some detail and also helped me place the dates of the Dahmers' divorce and Joyce's departure, specifically the events of May and June 1978. There were many conflicting dates in media reports, so I'm going with Lionel's recollections. He also corroborates, in detail, Joyce Dahmer's mental and emotional problems, which I knew mostly as schoolyard rumor and neighborhood scuttlebutt. (I have to say that the scuttlebutt was surprisingly accurate.) I use Lionel's memoir mainly to confirm information from other sources, since Joyce angrily disputes

almost everything Lionel writes. I tend to believe him more than her, but I still looked for corroboration.

The problem with Lionel's book is that its clarity comes in hindsight. Lionel, during the period covered in *My Friend Dahmer*, noted very little amiss with his son, outside of some social difficulties that concerned him and an overall lack of purpose. He didn't know about his son's binge drinking, the roadkill, his bizarre behavior, or the fake fits that imitated Joyce's nervous episodes. To Lionel, his son was—incredibly—a normal teen! Therefore, *A Father's Story* is a list of what Lionel *didn't* know. As such it is the best example of the adult obliviousness that Jeff so effectively exploited, first as a youth and later as a butcher. *My Friend Dahmer*, on the other hand, recounts what my friends and I *did* know.

NOTES

In the Notes below, I use the following annotations:

NBC: *Dateline NBC*, Stone Phillips interview (November 29, 1994)
ABJ: *Akron Beacon Journal* news stories
MIL: *Milwaukee Journal* and *Milwaukee Sentinel* news stories
FBI: anything from the FBI files
CAL: family calendar

PROLOGUE

Pages 13–27: This story was recounted by one of the neighborhood kids depicted in this sequence. Dahmer's "hobby" of collecting roadkill is written about in detail in virtually all my source material (ABJ, FBI, NBC, MIL). He started with a large insect collection and then around age twelve graduated to collecting roadkill.

Page 21: Dahmer always called the homemade clubhouse in the woods behind the family home "The Hut" (ABJ). The ruins of Dahmer's "Hut" were still there when the police and media descended on the property in 1991.

Pages 22–27: Dahmer boasted he used acid to dissolve his roadkill finds, but this was likely schoolboy bragging. I've found no statements from Lionel that he gave his son acid for such purposes, and it's preposterous to think he would have let his son experiment with toxic chemicals unsupervised. The liquid was likely water or some household chemical. It's possible Jeff could have pinched some acid from his dad. My father was also a chemist and kept all sorts of chemicals, including acid, for various purposes, stored (believe it or not) in the cold war bomb shelter behind our house!

PART 1: THE STRANGE BOY

Page 30: Eastview Junior High housed the seventh, eighth, and ninth grades in the early seventies, in extremely overcrowded conditions.

Page 34: The theft of the fetal pig from the biology lab was quite the schoolyard scandal. It was generally assumed to be a prank, but no one ever stepped forward to take credit. It was only when Dahmer began giving interviews to law enforcement, after he was caught, that he admitted he was the teenage thief (ABJ, FBI, NBC). Dahmer was one of my lab partners in junior high, although I can't recall which year.

Page 37 and on: Dahmer's boyhood home was purchased in 2005 by a well-known musician of my acquaintance (I tried to talk him out of it). Later that year he had a party, which I attended, and it was the first time I'd set foot in the house since high school. I used the opportunity to make quick sketches of the interior space, so the interior sequences in this book are fairly accurate. Obviously, I'm only guessing what the furnishings looked like when the Dahmers lived there.

Page 38: The Dahmers' interior decorator, Mr. Burlman (his name has been changed), from an Akron firm, had cerebral palsy. He worked off and on for the Dahmers in the early seventies, although Jeff often derisively remarked that the only thing he ever added to the house decor was a single footstool. Frequent references to this solitary footstool became part of our patter.

Page 40: Jeff's brother, David, is purposely left out of this story. David was nearly seven years younger than us. I knew of him, but didn't know him personally. When this story begins, we were in junior high, but David would have been only five years old. When we were seniors, David was twelve, and Jeff never brought him up in conversation. Obviously David played a large role in Jeff's home life, but he was a little kid and thus beneath the notice of the rest of us teenagers. The neighbors describe David as a good kid, a bit hyper, with plenty of friends in the neighborhood. Young David was not the oddball outcast his brother had been at the same age.

Likewise, Lionel is mostly off camera during this tale. I very seldom saw Jeff's dad. That's not to downplay his role, which was clearly important.

Lionel was the one big authority figure in Jeff's life, but he simply wasn't around when I was, which was usually after school. Whenever I visited the Dahmer house, it was Jeff's mom whom I saw. This is typical of the times. Dads were at work; moms were at home. Lionel admits that as the marriage crumbled, which started happening right around the time I befriended Jeff, he stayed away from home more and more. I saw Jeff's parents at school functions, mostly in junior high. I didn't hang out at the Dahmer house, like I did at Mike's, Kent's, and Neil's. The only time I really visited the house was to pick up or drop off Jeff. The vast majority of our time together was at school.

I struggled with how to incorporate both Lionel and David into this tale, especially David. Jeff himself rarely mentions his brother in any of my source material. I decided to limit David to this cameo.

Page 41: The neighborhood adjacent to the Dahmer property had around a hundred homes on one- and two-acre plots. Several dozen of our schoolmates lived here, including Neil.

Pages 41–42: The Dahmers' marital difficulties are documented at length in all my source material. Even their respective lawyers note the ferocity of the breakup. Lionel states that the marriage steadily unraveled starting in 1970. Joyce describes the marriage as "a very unhappy place" (NBC) but insists the strife and arguments were "nothing out of the ordinary" (NBC). Both Lionel and Jeff contradict this. "I never saw any real violent arguments, in terms of hitting or anything," recalls Jeff, "but there was a lot of yelling, a lot of tension" (NBC). These face-offs never resolved anything, since neither would back down. "There was no compromise," says Lionel (NBC). He describes Joyce becoming "physically agitated" (NBC). A neighbor recalls her occasionally bursting into tears out of the blue. Neil says that Lionel used to visit Neil's parents and recount the trouble he was having with Joyce.

Pages 44–46: There's no fixed date for when Dahmer began his spaz act. I first noticed it in 1975 or '76, when we were in tenth grade. Some of the Dahmer Fan Club recall it starting earlier, as far back as eighth grade.

Page 45: Mrs. Woodard (name changed) is, as of this writing, still a working librarian and well respected in the field. Revere's library, at the time of this book, was in a converted gym, thus the high ceilings.

Page 47: When the class of 1978 moved to the high school as sophomores, the freshmen came, too, as Revere expanded to a traditional four-year school. Therefore, our sophomore year was our first at Revere.

Page 48: This group of four friends proclaimed itself the Dahmer Fan Club. I am still close to Mike and Kent. I run into Neil every now and then. All three contributed many recollections to this story.

Pages 52–55: Dahmer discussed his emerging sexuality in detail (NBC, FBI).

Page 55: The quote is from the *Dateline NBC* interview. This dispels several erroneous rumors that have been repeatedly stated as fact in many books, articles, and TV reports. Dahmer was never molested by an adult relative, and certainly not by either of his parents. Nor was he sexually assaulted when he was a kid by an older teenage neighbor. He did have a sexual encounter with a neighbor boy when he was fifteen, which Dahmer described as "kissing and heavy petting" (NBC), but it was consensual. None of us knew of this encounter at the time or had any clue at all that Jeff was gay.

Page 56: Neil and I invented the Dahmer Fan Club. I appointed myself President and later changed this to the more interesting Minister of Propaganda. There were a dozen or so guys in the Fan Club at any given time, rotating in and out. In this story, I winnowed it down to the four principals for the sake of the narrative.

Page 57: I drew numerous cartoons in high school featuring Dahmer. Several were published in the school paper, *The Lantern*, and the yearbook, *The Reverie*. I came across these drawings, which I had long forgotten, shortly after Dahmer's crimes came to light, while looking through a box of high school stuff in my parents' basement for material the *Beacon Journal* could use. A very creepy discovery.

Pages 58–59: The exact date of the incident with the jogger, a local doctor, is unknown. Dahmer himself doesn't remember specifically and put it at "fourteen or fifteen" (NBC, FBI). Since Jeff was born at the end of May, if he was fourteen, that would place him in ninth grade at Eastview Junior High. Age fifteen would place him in tenth grade at Revere High. I split the difference and have the event occur at the beginning of tenth grade. But there's no way of knowing for sure.

Dahmer's plan was to knock the jogger unconscious, drag him into the woods, lie down next to him, and, presumably, fondle him while also pleasuring himself. Dahmer wasn't planning to kill the jogger (FBI, NBC, ABJ), although, obviously, a blow to the head with a baseball bat is not a precise operation. Clearly the jogger would have been seriously injured, if not accidentally slain. The desire for "complete control" was something Dahmer cited repeatedly.

Page 60: Sixteen-year-olds could obtain temps in Ohio. Upon completion of driver-education class (held at school) and successfully passing a driving test, full driving privileges were granted. My October birthday made me one of the oldest kids in my class and allowed me to be one of the first to obtain a license. Jeff, on the other hand, didn't turn sixteen until the end of the following May, almost the end of the school year.

Page 61: The vast majority of kids took a bus or drove to school. There were no sidewalks on the country roads around the high school. Dahmer took a bus. I was one of a handful who lived close enough to walk. My house was half a mile from the school. Several years ago, a high school kid was struck by a car and killed while walking home at the exact spot I picture here, a route I walked a thousand times.

Lionel was a chemist for an Akron lab. My dad was a chemist for B. F. Goodrich, the tire maker. Our parents knew each other in chemistry circles.

Pages 63–65: Joyce's seizures, nervous fits, and reliance on pills are described in detail by Lionel Dahmer (NBC and *A Father's Story*). In her only taped interview (with NBC's Stone Phillips in 1994), Joyce angrily disputes Lionel's description of the severity of her mental issues, her reliance on drugs, and that the seizures happened at all. She accuses Lionel of making it all up to fix her with the blame for Jeff's crimes. Lionel says the seizures started during the pregnancy with Jeff, as did the reliance on prescription drugs (NBC). Jeff does not dispute any of this.

It's unclear how long these issues went on. Lionel says the undiagnosed seizures continued, along with her heavy diet of pills, fits of anxiety, and various other emotional problems, right up until he finally left her in late 1977.

Joyce was in and out of therapy for most of the decade. It should be noted that she vehemently denies virtually all of this (NBC), just as she denies the loud arguments between her and Lionel, which Jeff himself recalls in detail. Her stays in the mental ward, however, are documented in court records from the Dahmer divorce (ABJ, MIL), so clearly she is being untruthful.

Given how eerily Jeff's fake fits—the shaking and twitching—mirrored those his mother was purported to suffer, I have no doubt that these, in fact, occurred. Joyce's blanket denials, even of things that both Lionel and Jeff describe, simply ring false.

I visited the Dahmer house maybe a dozen times during our high school friendship. Joyce was usually at home when I visited, and was almost always pleasant. There were several times when she seemed weird, although I was too young and naive to equate this with mental issues or depression. At the time I thought she was an odd woman (she just gave off that vibe). Some visits, she was upbeat and chatty. Other visits, she wouldn't utter a word. On several occasions, she had obviously been crying. But then, a lot of parents were odd. I knew other moms from this time period who suffered from depression and emotional issues, as well as substance abuse—mostly alcohol. I knew several abusive dads who openly slapped their kids around. And many parents had marital difficulties. Neighbors also commented on Joyce's mental issues. Neil's parents thought she was "a nut." They liked Lionel quite a bit, however.

In the Stone Phillips interview, bizarrely conducted with the coauthor of a book she planned to write but never did (tentatively titled *An Assault on Motherhood*), a combative Joyce obviously still harbors great animosity toward her ex-husband, never referring to him by name and complaining bitterly that she learned of Jeff's crimes on TV like everyone else and was "never told" of her son's excessive drinking or aimless life. This implies she knew nothing of his adult life. She also, incredibly, claims he exhibited absolutely no out-of-the-norm behavior as a teen! Jeff and Joyce were estranged for many years, perhaps as far back as June 1978, when she left Jeff behind in the family home and secretly moved back to Wisconsin. "I hadn't been in contact with Jeff, although I tried. No one had ever let me know that Jeff had ever been in any kind of trouble at all during the years." Joyce says they reconciled after his arrest and she often visited him in prison (NBC). Joyce also lashes out at all who criticized her parenting.

Page 64: Joyce was admitted to the mental ward at Akron General Hospital twice in 1970 (ABJ, MIL) for "severe anxiety," the first time for three days and the second time for a month. Jeff was in fifth grade. I and other members of the Dahmer Fan Club heard the schoolyard gossip as far back as junior high that Joyce had been in a mental ward several times. That gossip turned out to be right on the mark.

PART 2: A SECRET LIFE

Pages 70–79: The incident at the fishing hole was told to me by my friend Neil, who lived in the neighborhood bordering the Dahmer property. Neil's family also owned a large farm several miles away.

Page 80: September 7, 1976. School year starts (CAL).

Pages 80–84: Dahmer states that he started binge drinking in our junior year (FBI). My recollection, seconded by my friends, is that Dahmer started drinking heavily a few weeks into the school year. Dahmer confirms this (NBC).

I very seldom saw Dahmer drink. That's how stealthy he was. I knew he was drunk—you could smell the liquor on his breath. At the time I assumed it was beer, the alcoholic beverage of choice in high school, but I later realized it was hard booze I was smelling. Neil thought it was excessive use of mouthwash! (We were such small-town rubes.)

Page 85: Interview with the guidance counselor (ABJ).

Pages 86–87: I lifted the narration from a 1960s antidrug "scare film" made by the infamous Sid Davis Productions (YouTube). They were still showing these things at the time, even though they were hilariously out-of-date.

Pages 88–89: Ray (name changed) became a gay scholar of some renown. He died in 2007 of complications from AIDS.

Page 90: The winters of 1977 and 1978 were among the most brutal on record. The Great Blizzard of 1977 closed Revere schools for a week in January. It was described as a white hurricane over Lake Erie, temperatures plummeted to –21°F, and howling winds created ten-foot drifts. It was days before streets were cleared in our rural town, so people were virtually trapped in their homes. The parallel between Dahmer's growing social isolation and this physical one is striking.

Pages 92–93: When Jeff's parents' arguments got too loud, he fled the house (FBI, ABJ, NBC). Lionel was unaware until years later that their battles had this effect on their son.

Page 94: Lionel grew uneasy with Jeff's strange roadkill hobby and questioned its scientific worth (NBC). At that point, Jeff abandoned his clubhouse and took his roadkill to a secret spot deep in the woods across the street from the Dahmer home (NBC, FBI). These woods, beyond the few houses situated on the road itself, were completely undeveloped for miles thanks to the vast Firestone Estate—some 1,500 acres—owned by Harvey Firestone, head of the tire company of the same name. Dahmer always carried small garbage bags in his coat pocket for his roadkill finds.

Pages 95–97: A group of thirty or so juniors and seniors spent a week in Washington, DC, in the annual Close Up program, in which students from the Akron area observed the inner workings of the federal government and met with Ohio senators and members of Congress. I did not go on this trip, but my friends Neil and Mike did. The meeting with Mondale became the talk of the school and was written about in our yearbook (*The Reverie 1977*) and later reported in the media (ABJ). The visit to Mondale's office was described by several of the classmates who were there. Columnist Art Buchwald was also hanging out in Mondale's office, and he chatted with Dahmer and the others and also signed autographs.

Page 98: Dahmer was apprehended only once with booze on him, during his junior year, and was chewed out by school officials and given detention (NBC, FBI). The school may (or may not) have informed his parents. Dahmer has given conflicting accounts about this. There were a number of kids nabbed with booze every year, usually in the parking lot. As long as the booze wasn't inside the building, students seemed to avoid suspension if caught, unless they were habitual troublemakers. I know this sounds crazy when compared to today's zero-tolerance schools, but it was a different time. After this incident, Dahmer was much more careful.

There was a "smoking area" outside the cafeteria where a large group of students (and teachers!) would gather during free periods or class breaks. Stoners smoked weed, shielded by cars in the parking lot or hidden in the nearby woods.

Page 99: Dahmer often beat trees with large sticks in the woods around his house, venting his rage over his parents' loud arguments and ever-worsening marital difficulties (FBI, NBC). A neighbor I interviewed mentioned the tree beatings but didn't know the reason behind this odd behavior.

Page 100: All of us look back on our mockery of Stan Burlman with shame. There's no defense for it. We were adolescent idiots.

In August 1977, Lionel moved out of the house and into the Ohio Motel a few miles away (ABJ). Lionel says Joyce filed for divorce first and he then countersued, but the *Beacon Journal* and *Milwaukee Sentinel* both reported that the court records show Lionel was the one who filed first, charging her with "extreme cruelty and gross neglect," with Joyce then countersuing. Either way, divorce proceedings began shortly after he moved out. The suit would drag on for nearly a full year.

Page 101: Details of the Dahmer divorce are from the *Akron Beacon Journal*.

Pages 102–7: The FBI questioned Dahmer about violence toward animals, since this is a common trait in serial killers. Dahmer described this one chilling incident, kidnapping a neighborhood dog with the intent to slaughter it (FBI, NBC).

PART 3: THE DAHMER FAN CLUB

Pages 110–11: Neil concocted the running gag of inserting Dahmer into photos where he didn't belong. The rest of the Dahmer Fan Club soon joined in the conspiracy.

Pages 112–13: BYOB "field parties" were a common part of our small-town social life. Word of the day and location was spread at school, a bonfire was built, and kids gathered.

Pages 116–17: The National Honor Society photo, with Dahmer's face blacked out, is the most famous example of the yearbook stunt. This appeared in the pages of *The Reverie 1978*. After the yearbook adviser marked out Dahmer's face, she and the student editor were on to us and killed several additional photos.

Page 118: The Dahmer Fan Club registered a fictitious candidate, Al Rebo, for student council, with Dahmer as the official "celebrity spokesman" for his campaign. Rebo ran a pizza joint that Dahmer and Neil frequented a few years earlier. Dahmer would frequently bellow out "REBOOOOOO!" as part of his act. We later expanded the gag, slipping Rebo into announcements and school newspaper stories. In the 1977 yearbook, Rebo is listed as "not pictured" with the senior class. The Rebo gag climaxed with student council elections in the fall of 1977. I drew a number of large campaign posters, which we hung around school, most featuring Dahmer. Alas, none of these survive. School officials caught wind of the prank and removed Rebo from the ballot. We then started a "Write In Rebo" drive. The drawing at the top of the page is one of the actual flyers I drew. We secretly used the school copier to make hundreds of copies and passed them out in the halls. Our imaginary candidate received more votes than the rest of the field combined. The results were thrown out, and several of us got hauled into the assistant principal's office and chewed out, even though he could barely keep a straight face.

The cartoon at the bottom of the page ran in the yearbook (*The Reverie 1978*). Dahmer is at lower right, directly in front of Kent, who is holding a tuba. All the members of Dahmer Fan Club are in the drawing somewhere. The nonsensical captions are, for the most part, Dahmerisms. I also drew a cover for the yearbook that featured Dahmer as one of the drummers in the famous *Spirit of '76* painting, but the yearbook adviser shot it down.

Pages 121–23: This particular attack by school bullies is described in several taped interviews (FBI). Dahmer claims, in different statements, that he was hit by a blackjack, a billy club, or a fist. The exact date is unclear, and Dahmer himself places it at different times. I saw Dahmer hassled by bullies on a number of occasions throughout our years in junior high and high school, so consider this a reenactment of a regular occurrence.

Page 124: The drinking age in Ohio at this time was eighteen, but for beer only. You had to be twenty-one to purchase liquor, but it wasn't hard to get.

Page 125: This is a good example of how crafty Dahmer was, even when drunk. The Dahmer house was small, just one floor, and Jeff shared a tiny bedroom, about 150 square feet, with his little brother. His mother's bedroom was right next door. The bedroom doors were a foot apart, and there was only one bathroom, so there was little privacy. It seems unlikely that Joyce, even with her problems, would have failed to notice, in such close quarters, that her son was drunk. This also explains Jeff's binge drinking. He needed to consume as much liquor as he could when it was safe to do so. The Dahmers owned two cars, so Jeff had access to wheels at least some of the time. His mother only learned to drive in the seventies (FBI), so she was likely not much of a driver. Dahmer usually rode the bus or got rides home after school from fellow students, most often from Figg, who had his own car. I gave Jeff lifts on occasion, usually as I was on my way to Kent's house or to the houses of other friends.

Pages 126–27: The 1978 Revere variety show, *Acts from Our Attic*, ran for three performances, March 9–11, 1978. The comedy troupe, the Acme Ash Company, named after the local garbage hauling company that picked up the trash in Bath, was essentially the members of the Dahmer Fan Club. All the bits were written by us. The Hitler skit was the hit of the show (CAL, *The Reverie 1978*).

Page 128: Joyce took out a restraining order against Lionel, accusing him of harassing her and the children, specifically of pressuring David to leave her and move in with him (ABJ). Lionel was barred from visiting the house.

Page 129–30: This was the last time I set foot in the Dahmer household.

Pages 131–42: Everything in this chapter on Dahmer's Command Performance was based on my recollections and corroborated by my friends, in most cases by several people. No one recalls the exact date of the Command Performance. Sometime in March is my best guess.

PART 4: BECOMING THE MONSTER

Page 149: Having already met all graduation requirements, I had but two morning classes, an art class and band. I officially had "early dismissal" and could have left at the 11:30 lunch period. There was no monitoring of the seniors' comings and goings.

Pages 150–51: Figg was regarded by all as the class psycho, far worse than Dahmer. In addition to his disruptive behavior at school, he was a heavy pot smoker and was rumored to be dealing weed. This was the main element of his "friendship" with Dahmer. They were spotted smoking together several times by Neil and others. Figg enjoyed running over animals in his car and was accused of purposely hitting several neighborhood pets. Dahmer recounts an incident when he was getting a ride with Figg and Figg swerved to hit a small dog, a cruel act that enraged even Dahmer! Figg was argumentative and confrontational and was frequently smacked around by schoolmates, but he was so mammoth that he barely felt the blows.

Pages 153–57: A photo of the mutilated dog carcass has been widely published. The remains were discovered by neighbor kids. The number of kids varies in the accounts, so I went with just the one. At the time, it was blamed on some kind of cult. It was later confirmed by Dahmer to have been his doing. Neighbors also periodically found small animals—squirrels and toads—nailed to tree trunks. The exact date of this incident is unclear. I recall the cops were summoned, but it's unclear if they actually were. Dahmer said in various interviews that he was sixteen or seventeen. That could place this incident anywhere from May of his sophomore year until May of his senior year. The trees in the photo are bare, so it was sometime between November and March of any given year. I make a guess and place it in early spring of our senior year. Dahmer told FBI psychologist Robert Ressler, "I thought it would be a fun prank." Dahmer insists in several interviews that he never harmed a (living) animal, only dead ones he found (FBI). This was *not* the dog Dahmer considered killing on pages 102–7.

Pages 158–61: Dahmer's prom date, Brenda (name changed), was interviewed by both the *Beacon Journal* and the *Milwaukee Sentinel*. The prom was held on Saturday, May 27, 1978 (CAL). The date was arranged by one of the last of Dahmer's lower-caste friends who still occasionally socialized with him. That friend's date wanted her gal pal, Brenda, to accompany them, and Dahmer was suggested. Dahmer's friend may have even asked Brenda to go with Jeff, although there are conflicting recollections of this (ABJ, MIL). This male friend was also an art-class colleague of mine and would himself later come out of the closet in an unfortunate interview with the local press (ABJ). He wondered whether he could have "saved" Dahmer if they had been lovers in high school (ABJ).

Pages 164–65: Joyce secretly decided sometime in spring 1978 to move back to her hometown, Chippewa Falls, Wisconsin, with David, who was finishing seventh grade at Eastview, in defiance of the custody agreement (ABJ, MIL, NBC). Jeff states that he didn't tell his dad she had left because "I was told not to tell" (NBC). Obviously, this conversation is a re-creation, based on Jeff's recollection. It's a key moment, with such tragic repercussions that I had to include it. Again and again Dahmer explains that he killed his victims, kept body parts, and eventually cannibalized some of them so his lovers would never leave him. If this was the driving force of his spree, then his father and mother leaving him in succession would logically have been a devastating blow. Especially the departure of his mother and brother, which left him totally alone and provided Jeff the opportunity to kill his first victim.

Lionel agreed to buy out Joyce's share of the house (ABJ).

Pages 166–69: The last day of school for seniors was Thursday, June 1, 1978 (CAL). School was dismissed at 2:35. Attendance by seniors those last few weeks was pretty spotty, with many popping in just for a token appearance and others not showing at all. Most seniors attended the last day to say their farewells and participate in the joyous celebration of the final bell.

Our graduation ceremony on Sunday, June 4, was held at the cavernous Richfield Coliseum, then home of the NBA's Cleveland Cavs. It was a ridiculous place, built at the halfway point between Cleveland and Akron, making it convenient to neither. It was surrounded by cow pastures on Richfield's rural eastern edge and has since been demolished, the land donated to the neighboring national park. I recall seeing Dahmer at commencement, sitting in the row behind me, but don't remember speaking to him. This was followed that night by the traditional senior all-night party at a private recreation center in Akron. Seniors came and went throughout the evening, but I don't remember seeing Dahmer there. Several members of the Dahmer Fan Club and I greeted the dawn on the steps of the high school and taunted underclassmen as they arrived for school. Classes ended for all other grades on Wednesday, June 14 (CAL).

Joyce and her younger son, David, moved to Wisconsin sometime between the end of school for underclassmen on June 14 and June 18, although she may have returned to Bath several times after that for brief stays or to collect more possessions from the house. According to MapQuest, it's a seven-hundred-mile trip one way, which would have taken more than thirty hours round trip in 1978, so she wasn't driving back and forth a lot. Clearly, she was gone from June 18 to at least June 30, when Dahmer had the corpse of his first victim in the house or hidden outside on the property. Dahmer states in his confession to the Bath police that she had already moved by the eighteenth. Joyce was not allowed, under the terms of the custody decree, to leave the state with the still-underage David, and she instructed Jeff not to tell Lionel they had left (ABJ). Lionel, still under a restraining order to stay away from the house, did not discover that Joyce had left until early August (ABJ), although she had permanently moved to Wisconsin by then. Eventually, Lionel suspected she had returned to her home state, and he tracked down her whereabouts by calling middle schools in Wisconsin until he found where David was enrolled. There was then another long legal battle over custody of David, but the court declined to enforce the custody terms (ABJ). In 1982, David moved back to Bath of his own volition to live with Lionel (MIL, ABJ) and reenrolled at Revere.

Page 170: June 18 was move-in day at my college, the Art Institute of Pittsburgh (CAL). The summer semester began the following day.

Pages 173–75: Dahmer killed Steven Hicks on Sunday, June 18. Hicks, age nineteen, was thumbing his way home from a daytime rock concert at Chippewa Lake Park, an old (and shortly to close) amusement park in the middle of Amish country in rural Medina County, due west of Akron. Hicks's home was in Coventry Township, a small bedroom suburb on Akron's southern border. Hicks attended a kick-off-the-summer concert by the Michael Stanley Band, a Cleveland group with a huge following in northeast Ohio, although mostly unknown elsewhere. Tickets were three dollars. It's about fifteen miles as the crow flies from Chippewa Lake to Coventry, through what was then farmland, but the most likely route on well-trafficked roads would be more like thirty miles, probably along Route 18 from Medina to Akron, then south to Coventry. Dahmer picked up Hicks near the Summit Mall, at the intersection of Cleveland-Massillon Road and Route 18 on the Bath-Akron border, so Hicks had gotten a ride roughly halfway home. This was a frequent cruising strip for Revere kids, with the mall, several theaters, pizza joints, and a drive-in restaurant that was Revere's unofficial hangout. Dahmer was driving around out of boredom, passed Hicks, then, on a whim, stopped and picked him up (FBI, ABJ). Hicks, handsome and thin, with long hair and his shirt wrapped around his waist, was Dahmer's stated sexual ideal. He revealed that for years he had had a fantasy in which he picked up a shirtless hitchhiker, took him home, and had "total dominance" over him (NBC, FBI). Here was that fantasy standing before him! "I wish I had just kept on going," Dahmer later said (NBC).

Hicks was described as outgoing and well liked by those who knew him, but he struggled with typical pitfalls of the generation (FBI). "Steven was an average youth," his parents said in their only statement to the media, in 1991. "He had qualities that would make any parent proud. He also had problems not uncommon to youth of that time: drinking, smoking, traffic tickets, and the occasional rowdiness of youth." Dahmer offered Hicks some beer and pot, and Hicks agreed to accompany him to the nearby Dahmer house in exchange for a ride to Hicks's house in Coventry, a twenty-minute drive from Bath. This was not at all unusual in the stoner culture of the seventies. Total strangers, especially teenagers, often shared a bong or pipe. The stoner code was: you never turned down a chance to get high. Kids would share a joint and forge a friendship. Hicks may well have been stoned already that day, as the Chippewa Lake concerts were a well-known gathering place for potheads, and in those days concertgoers smoked openly at shows, with little or no interference from police.

Hicks was not gay and the two did not have sex—another erroneous report in the media that is repeated to this day. Hicks stayed at Dahmer's house for one to two hours and then asked for that promised lift home. When he turned away from Dahmer, Jeff clubbed him across the back of the head with a small barbell. Dahmer then strangled Hicks as he lay unconscious on the floor. The exact time of death is not fixed, just a general "early evening" (FBI). Hicks had promised to be home in time for his dad's birthday dinner (ABJ). It was also Father's Day (the poor man). The gates opened at ten a.m. for the Chippewa Lake concert, and the show itself probably started at noon (*Scene* newspaper, June 15, 1978). There were five bands on the bill, so probably three hours for the show. Hicks obviously managed to score a ride as far as the Summit Mall from some fellow concertgoers. Figure that took about an hour. So Dahmer probably picked him up between four and five p.m. Coventry is about eighteen miles due south of Dahmer's house, and Jeff had promised to give Hicks a ride home, so that's maybe a twenty-minute drive from Bath. They each had a few beers (knowing Dahmer, he probably gunned a six-pack) and smoked a joint before Hicks asked to leave (FBI, ABJ). So Hicks was probably killed between six and seven p.m.

The Hicks family wouldn't learn Steven's fate for thirteen years. He simply vanished from the face of the earth.

PART 5: FADE TO BLACK

Page 178: June 18, 1978. Dahmer touched and fondled the corpse and repeatedly masturbated while standing over it, at last fulfilling his monstrous fantasy (FBI). That night, fearing his mother would return from Wisconsin, he dragged the body into a small, wedge-shaped storage area in the lower rear of his house beneath the overhead porch. The next day he bought a hunting knife and dismembered the corpse (ABJ, FBI, NBC), taking time to masturbate in the middle of the process (FBI). The police beat reporter for the *Beacon Journal* told me that when police investigators first examined the storage room in 1991, it was covered in dried blood residue. Floor, walls, ceiling—everywhere. Jeff stashed the body in a large drainage pipe on the Dahmer property that carried a seasonal stream under the street and down the hill. The stream was bone-dry in the summer. It was late June, and the summer heat made the corpse reek; Jeff quickly realized he had to get rid of it.

Pages 178–85: June 21, 1978. Dahmer was most likely driving to the Hardy Road Landfill in the nearby Cuyahoga Valley, the main dump for the city of Akron at that time. He also claims, in an interview with an FBI psychologist, that he was planning to dump the bags in a remote ravine "ten miles away." Bath Road enters the Cuyahoga Valley National Park on its east end. The likeliest dumping spot would have been the Hampton Hills area of the park. Dahmer would have passed the township police station, just half a mile from his house, en route to either destination, and was pulled over within sight of the station. One cop pulled him over, and another arrived shortly after as backup (FBI). I put them in the same cruiser here just to make the scene less cluttered visually. The cops gave Dahmer a sobriety field test, which he passed. Incredibly, he had not been drinking that day, perhaps because there was no need to dull his urges since he had spent the last few days giving in to them completely. The police wrote Jeff a ticket for crossing the center line. Terrified at this close call, he returned home immediately (ABJ).

The Bath police chief later angrily defended his officers and their incomprehensible blunder that night (ABJ). The Bath Police Department was a typical small-town force. There was very little crime in town. Mostly they made traffic stops and harassed local hot-rodding teens. In fact, the officer who pulled Jeff over in this scene and later interviewed him in prison about the Hicks murder was notorious in the seventies for being a "hardass" for routinely ticketing students as they left the high school parking lot. It's hard to believe that the officers weren't more suspicious of Dahmer's ridiculous story and that they didn't recognize the distinctive stench of a dead body coming from the car. Dahmer's killing spree should have ended right there.

Page 186: Colleges on the semester system generally started in mid-August. Many state universities in Ohio in 1978 were still on the quarter system and started in mid-September. Ohio State, which Dahmer attended, had the latest start of all, September 18. I was the first of the Dahmer Fan Club to leave, in June. Mike, Neil, and Kent, who all went away to school, left starting in mid-August. Dahmer was the last to head off to college.

Page 187: I was concerned that stacking up three driving scenes at the end of the book would be somewhat visually monotonous. But a friend and contemporary rightly pointed out that all we did was drive around, day after day, mile after mile, so this was an accurate portrayal of our everyday lives. The school district actually included *two* rural towns, Bath and Richfield, identical in size, each about twenty-five square miles. Bath was more suburban by the seventies, especially on its southern border with Akron. Richfield, on the other hand, was still a farm town, and houses and neighborhoods were widely spaced. There was no public transportation, and most of the hilly, narrow country roads were difficult or even dangerous to bike on, so younger kids had to rely on parents for rides to go anywhere. For older teens, socializing meant driving. Only Neil lived near Dahmer, in the neighborhood behind Jeff's property. Mike and I both lived in Richfield, five miles away. Kent lived on the southern edge of Bath, near the Summit Mall, five miles from Dahmer and ten miles from me. Eastview Junior High and Revere High were centrally located, right next to each other on the Richfield-Bath border. All of us had cars of our own, usually battered hand-me-downs. Kent and I both drove Chevy Vegas, considered among the worst cars ever made. Mike had a Plymouth Duster. Usually one of us would pick up the others, one by one, and then we would drive to the Summit Mall and the nearby traditional cruising strip, or even further into Akron, looking for something to do. Occasionally we would travel all the way north into Cleveland.

Pages 187–93: This incident was related to me by my friend Mike.

Page 190: Jeff lived alone in the house for five to six weeks. He didn't have a job, so money was short, probably just what his mom had left him when she split. Jeff lived on fast food and snacks. Some reports state that the power was shut off at some point for nonpayment of bills. It is unclear if this was true, although the refrigerator did stop functioning (ABJ). It's hard to excuse Joyce's shocking selfishness here, although I'm generally sympathetic to her. I think she did the best she could with the many problems she was lugging around. But in leaving Jeff alone, she was clearly concerned more about herself and her escape from Lionel than about her son. Some contemporaries knew Jeff was alone in the house, and Lloyd Figg and a small number of fellow psychos used it as a stoner pad. At one of these gatherings, Dahmer held a séance and attempted to contact the dead, presumably Hicks. His prom date, Brenda, was at this party (MIL), reluctantly dragged along by the couple who had talked her into attending the prom with Jeff. Brenda was so freaked out she quickly left. Even the psychos soon stopped coming over, since Dahmer's behavior was so creepy and out of control.

Page 191: After the failed attempt to dump the body on Wednesday, June 21, Dahmer stashed the dismembered corpse alternately in the drainage pipe behind his house or in the trunk of his car until Friday, June 30, when he finally disposed of it. The incident I draw here occurred sometime in those two weeks. It's only conjecture, of course, but the obvious conclusion is that this was the reason Dahmer was walking, not driving his car that night. He was afraid to drive again with the body in the trunk after the terrifying close call he'd had (ABJ, FBI).

June 30: Dahmer once again took the dismembered corpse into the crawl space and stripped the decomposing flesh off the bones. If he wasn't already insane by this point, this grisly, horrific act surely pushed him over the edge. He bagged the flesh and organs in garbage bags and set them out on the curb for trash pickup. (Note: Six months later, when I dropped out of art school, I myself became a local garbageman. The stench these bags omitted would not have been all that unusual, especially in the middle of summer, although it would have been noticeably strong and foul.) According to an interview with FBI psychologist Robert Ressler, Dahmer then put the bones back in garbage bags, stashed them in the drainpipe, and smashed the front of the pipe with a sledgehammer to make it inaccessible. He burned Hicks's clothes in the built-in outdoor grill at the base of the main chimney and tossed his necklace and wrist bracelets into the Cuyahoga River (FBI, ABJ). In 1982, when home for a visit, Jeff retrieved the bags and took the bones to a large boulder in the woods behind his house and, one by one, smashed them into small bits with a sledgehammer. He then scattered them by throwing the pieces into the woods in a semicircular motion. He was so thorough he even crushed the teeth (ABJ, FBI). Lionel put the house up for sale shortly after this. That was probably Jeff's impetus for destroying the remains. By 1983, according to the *Bath Community Directory*, the Dahmers had relocated to another residence in Bath.

I was home from college the weekend of June 30 (CAL), when Dahmer was busy with this gory task, and hung out with the members of the Dahmer Fan Club at Neil's house just a few hundred yards away. I didn't see Dahmer, but recall hearing the scuttlebutt that he was alone in the house.

The Dahmers' divorce was finalized July 24, 1978. Unbeknownst to Lionel, Joyce and David were long gone. But Lionel, for some unexplained reason, stayed away from the house for two more weeks after the settlement was final, presumably waiting for word that Joyce had moved out of the house— word that never came, since Joyce was in hiding. Sometime in the beginning of August 1978 (exact date unclear), Lionel went to the house, discovered that Jeff was living there alone, and immediately moved back in. Jeff refused to reveal where Joyce had gone (ABJ).

Dahmer insisted he was haunted by the Hicks killing (FBI). Unlike the later murders, this one was an act of spontaneous violence, not a case of methodical stalking and careful planning. This may just have been the psychological shock of committing such a gruesome crime for the first time. Jeff's drinking became even more severe that summer, so much so that Lionel, for the first time, became aware of it. But even then Lionel remained clueless about just how much booze his son was consuming on a daily basis.

It would be more than nine years until Jeff killed again. And then, once he started, he didn't stop.

I was home for break the last three weeks in July and the first week in August 1978 (CAL). During this time the Dahmer Fan Club hung out in Neil's basement and made some homemade films that featured us doing our goofy shtick. We then screened the films at a big party at Neil's house. Dahmer wasn't invited.

During this break I attended a field party (bonfire and beer) in Bath with Mike and a few others. Surprisingly, Lloyd Figg showed up and, as usual, was behaving like an annoying idiot. He danced around us, babbling that he "knew a secret." Finally, one of us said, "Okay, Figg. What secret?" But then Figg clammed up and quickly vanished. Looking back now, I wonder if he knew of the Hicks murder. Did Dahmer blurt something out? Figg was the last of the lower-caste psychos (some of whom were serious drug users) with whom Dahmer stayed in contact after high school. These friendships, if they could be called that, would all peter out by the end of that summer. Lionel insists there were "several" teenagers passed out in the living room when he first discovered in early August that Jeff was living in the family home alone and Joyce had split (FBI, NBC). I doubt it was "several." My recollection, confirmed by my friends, is that no one, not even stoners, wanted anything to do with Dahmer by this time. Only Figg, who didn't live far away, maintained contact. There was also a rumor in the summer of 1978 that Dahmer and Figg had stolen a car from the Summit Mall parking lot and joyrode around town before abandoning it. Later that summer, Lionel banned Figg from the house when he suspected Figg had stolen some valuables (*A Father's Story*). This was the last friendship Dahmer would have in his life.

At the end of the fall quarter, I dropped out of art school and returned home, unsure of what to do next. It was December 1978, and Dahmer was also back in Bath, having flamed out miserably in college. It was the final time we were both home at the same time. I never saw him. A few weeks later I embarked on my career as a garbageman, and Dahmer joined the army and shipped out.

Sometime in December, just before leaving, Dahmer tried to dig up the body of a former classmate who had been killed in a car accident in July 1978. The grave was in a small, remote cemetery in the valley. But the ground was frozen solid, and Dahmer couldn't make a dent in it. Fearing discovery, he gave up and fled. Word quickly spread that someone had vandalized the grave, but Dahmer wasn't connected to the crime until he later confessed (ABJ, FBI).

EPILOGUE

This sequence took place at the Arabica Coffee House (now defunct) in Cleveland Heights in 1988. I had returned to the area in 1986 after five years in college and three years in southern Florida. Mike and Kent remain close friends of mine to this day.

Page 198: The fate of the class spaz, Lloyd Figg, was revealed to me by the Bath Township detective who interviewed me in 1991 about the Hicks murder. "Oh, he's well known to us," she said with a weary smile. All the members of the Dahmer Fan Club were called in, one by one, for interviews as the cops investigated and prepared charges.

Pages 198–99: Dahmer attended Ohio State University for one quarter, from September to December 1978. He lived in Morrill Tower, one of the infamous freshman high-rise dorms, known collectively as "the Towers." Kids were bunked four to a room, sixteen to a "pod," with a central living room, in these twenty-four-story beehives situated on the far side of Ohio Stadium. They are considered hellholes by OSU students. Jeff lived in the male-only section in the lower floors, called Ross House (which is often mistakenly listed as the name of the entire dorm). It is a long hike to the rest of the campus, and even farther to the famous High Street commercial district—a mile-long strip of bars, food joints, and shops on the campus's eastern edge that is the center of student life. Jeff seldom attended class and, according to his podmates, spent most of the quarter drunk (ABJ, FBI, *A Father's Story*). He was usually passed out cold in his room by late afternoon. His cumulative grade point average for his one quarter was 0.45 (FBI). Twenty or so Revere classmates went to Ohio State, but Penny Smith (name changed) is the only one who ever saw him on campus, passed out on the sidewalk outside a bar on High Street. I started at Ohio State a year later, in the fall of 1979, and graduated in the summer of 1983. When Lionel went to the dorm to retrieve Jeff's belongings, he writes in *A Father's Story*, his son's roommates described how Jeff drank himself into a stupor every day. This is the first Lionel knew of Jeff's shocking alcohol consumption, and he was stunned. At this point, Jeff had been binge drinking for more than two years!

Pressured by his dad, Dahmer enlisted in the army in December 1978 and served until March 1981 (ABJ, FBI). It was old-school "tough love," almost comically ill thought-out, as if boot camp would somehow straighten out a twisted young man who had already committed sex acts with, and butchered, his victim's corpse. Psychological counseling was apparently never an option, probably thanks to the bad experience the family had with the mental health profession during Joyce's decade of ineffectual treatment.

Dahmer was a private, stationed mostly in Baumholder, Germany, and was drummed out of the service for excessive drinking and a refusal to undergo treatment (FBI). He received an honorable discharge on March 24, 1981 (FBI).

Dahmer moved to the Milwaukee area in 1982. His killing spree started on September 15, 1987. He killed sixteen victims, two of whom were fourteen years old, over the next four years, until his grisly crimes were discovered on July 22, 1991 (ABJ, MIL), when a seventeenth man slipped his handcuffs, ran screaming and half-clothed from Dahmer's apartment into the street, and flagged down a passing police car.

"Dahmer is probably a serial killer by now!" I actually said this. A very clear and chilling memory.

THE PLAYERS

Jeff Dahmer returned to Akron one last time, in chains. In May 1992 he was extradited from a Wisconsin state prison to stand trial in Akron for the June 1978 murder of Steven Hicks. It was just procedure. Dahmer pled guilty, the gavel was banged, and he was stuffed in the prison van and whisked back to Wisconsin. The few steps he took from van to courthouse were the last he ever set in the outside world, and it was the last time he would see his hometown— through the windows of the prison van as it traveled on I-77 through Bath, north toward Wisconsin.

I was working at the *Akron Beacon Journal* that warm and sunny day, four blocks from the Summit County Courthouse, where Dahmer's trial was held. The paper had a squad of reporters and photographers covering the trial, but quite a few staffers walked down, as curiosity seekers, to see Dahmer arrive. One asked me if I wanted to go, but I shook my head and remained behind, working on an illustration.

Jeff became a born-again Christian in prison. "Jesus forgives all our sins," he said. "Even mine." He was a marked man and was kept in protective solitary confinement. Eventually he requested to be put into the general prison population. In July 1994 an unidentified inmate tried to cut Dahmer's throat as he exited the prison chapel after services. But the homemade knife broke and Dahmer escaped with minor injuries. Jeff was a model prisoner and was frequently interviewed by criminal psychologists and FBI profilers. He repeatedly expressed relief that the secrets and lies with which he had built his life were no longer necessary. Unlike many serial killers, who are manipulative (Charles Manson) or pathological liars (Henry Lee Lucas) or both, Dahmer was honest and forthright, although he grew testy as interviewer after interviewer asked him the same questions. Eventually Jeff only agreed to talk in exchange for cigarettes and junk food. Once muscular and fit, Jeff grew quite flabby behind bars. He was disciplined only once, for imitating a prison official with a speech impediment, just as he had imitated the interior decorator all those years before.

On November 28, 1994, Dahmer was killed by fellow prisoner Christopher Scarver, a convicted murderer and violent schizophrenic. Scarver bludgeoned Dahmer in the back of the head with a bar from a weight machine while they were on work detail cleaning toilets next to the prison gym (*New York Times*). Scarver then finished the job while Dahmer lay on the bathroom floor, his head crushed so severely that prison officials had trouble identifying him. Scarver also murdered another inmate on the same detail, convicted killer Jesse Anderson. Dahmer died of severe head trauma while on his way to the hospital in an ambulance (*Time*). Fittingly, Dahmer killed his first victim the same way, clubbing Steven Hicks with a barbell.

Dahmer's brain was retained for study; his body was cremated.

Joyce and Lionel, in one final, bitter skirmish, fought in court over their son's remains. Each received half of Jeff's ashes (ABJ, MIL).

The rest of the world was happy Dahmer was dead, but I was surprised that news of his death upset me. Certainly Dahmer deserved his brutal end, but I suppose it's understandable that I had an emotional reaction to his murder. He was only the second high school comrade, at that point, who had died, the other being a friend who was tragically killed in an auto accident while home from college during our first Christmas break in 1978, a death that absolutely devastated me.

The premise of this book is that Dahmer was a tragic figure, but that only applies up until the moment he kills. After that horrible day in June 1978, the only tragedy is that Dahmer didn't have the courage to put a gun to his head and end it. More than anything, Dahmer was a coward. He was afraid to confess to his dad—the one adult who tried to help him over the years—about what was going on in his head, terrified of being caught. Dahmer was also driven by selfishness and didn't care about anything other than his own obsessive needs. His perverse sexuality was constructed entirely of dominance and total control; his lovers' sexual desires never entered into it. They weren't even real people in his mind, merely objects for his sexual pleasure (FBI). Cowardice and selfishness—these were the two themes of Jeff Dahmer's life. We can excuse those things, perhaps, in a fifteen-year-old kid, but these were central parts of the adult Dahmer as well. And because of this fear and selfish sexual hunger, this perverse wretch spread his misery to the dozens of people who still mourn the loss of his seventeen victims.

Joyce Dahmer remarried, lived in California, and worked as an AIDS counselor. Her coworkers held her in high regard (ABJ, MIL). She and Jeff were estranged, perhaps as far back as 1978 when she fled to Wisconsin, and rarely spoke (NBC). After Jeff was imprisoned, they reconciled and, according to her, talked frequently (NBC). When Jeff was killed, she bitterly lashed out: "Is everyone happy now?" (MIL). She would never speak publicly again. Joyce Dahmer died of cancer on November 27, 2000, at age sixty-four (ABJ).

Lionel Dahmer, now in his eighties, remains in the Akron area. According to an interview with Larry King on CNN on June 17, 2004, all of the profits from *A Father's Story*, which Lionel had planned to share with the victims' families, were gobbled up in legal fees to fend off lawsuits by those families. A film adaptation of *A Father's Story* was released in 2006, titled *Raising Jeffrey Dahmer* and starring Rusty Sneary (it is not a good film). Lionel has since become a strong proponent of intelligent design, the creationist pseudoscience (NBC)—a belief also adopted by Jeff before his murder.

As for the **Dahmer Fan Club**, Mike is a professor at a small Midwestern college, Kent is working in the public sector, and Neil is a successful businessman.

"This is the grand finale of a life poorly spent and the end result is just overwhelmingly depressing. . . . A sick, pathetic, miserable life story, that's all it is."

—Jeff Dahmer

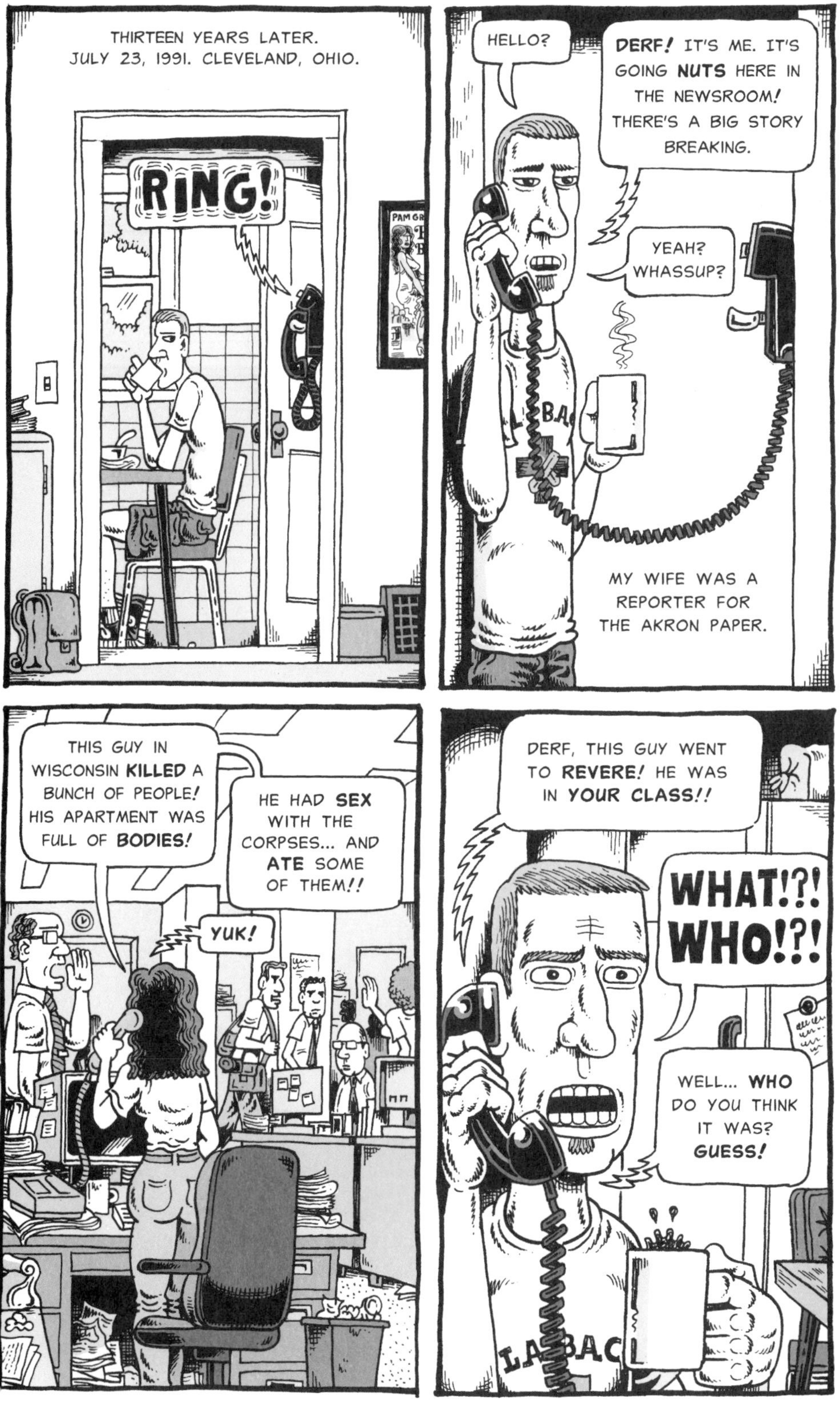
THIRTEEN YEARS LATER.
JULY 23, 1991. CLEVELAND, OHIO.
RING!
HELLO?
DERF! IT'S ME. IT'S GOING NUTS HERE IN THE NEWSROOM! THERE'S A BIG STORY BREAKING.
YEAH? WHASSUP?
MY WIFE WAS A REPORTER FOR THE AKRON PAPER.
THIS GUY IN WISCONSIN KILLED A BUNCH OF PEOPLE! HIS APARTMENT WAS FULL OF BODIES!
HE HAD SEX WITH THE CORPSES... AND ATE SOME OF THEM!!
YUK!
DERF, THIS GUY WENT TO REVERE! HE WAS IN YOUR CLASS!!
WHAT!?! WHO!?!
WELL... WHO DO YOU THINK IT WAS? GUESS!

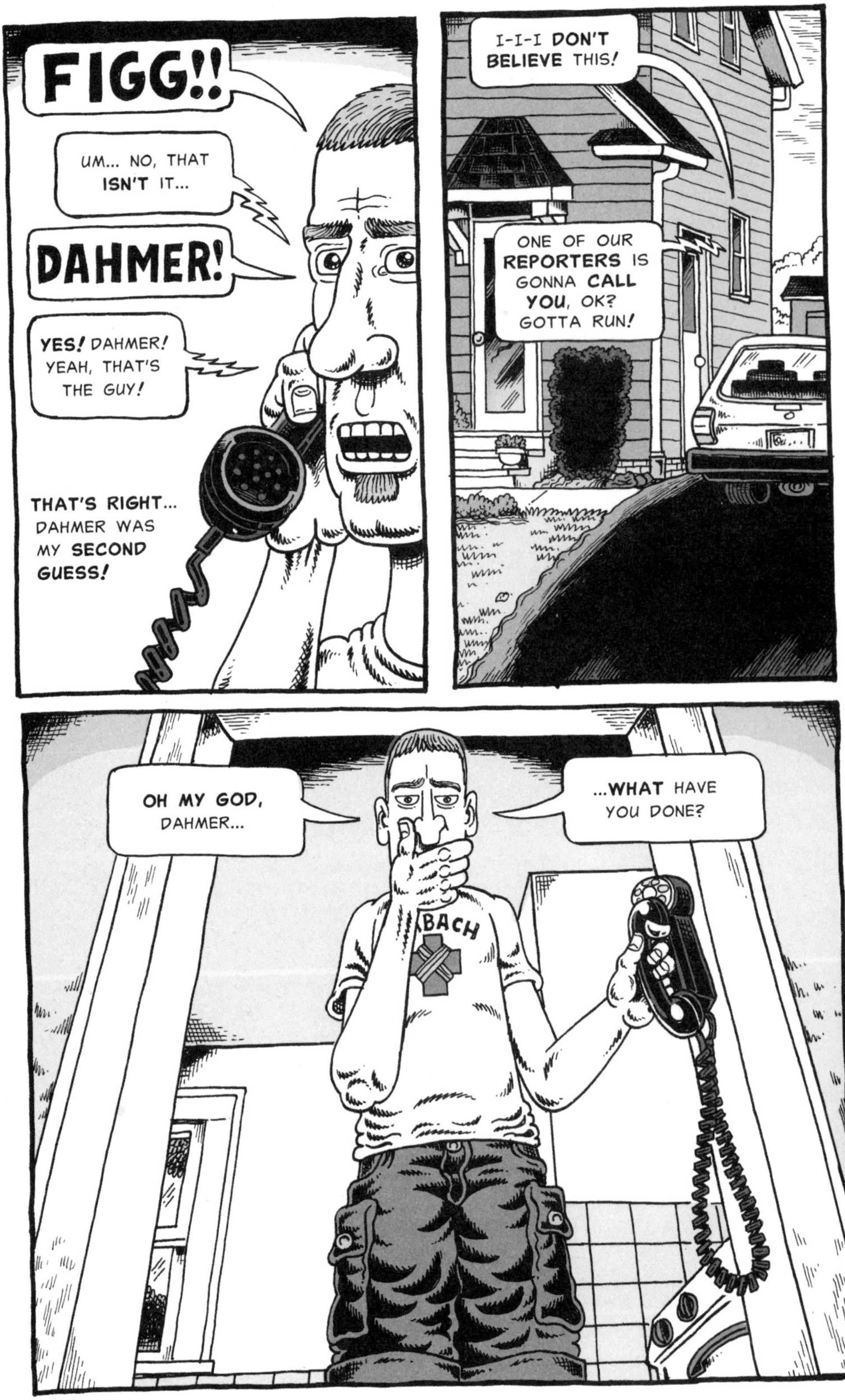
FIGG!!
UM... NO, THAT ISN'T IT...
DAHMER!
YES! DAHMER! YEAH, THAT'S THE GUY!
THAT'S RIGHT... DAHMER WAS MY SECOND GUESS!
I-I-I DON'T BELIEVE THIS!
ONE OF OUR REPORTERS IS GONNA CALL YOU, OK? GOTTA RUN!
OH MY GOD, DAHMER...
...WHAT HAVE YOU DONE?

MY FRIEND DAHMER MOVIE PHOTO GALLERY

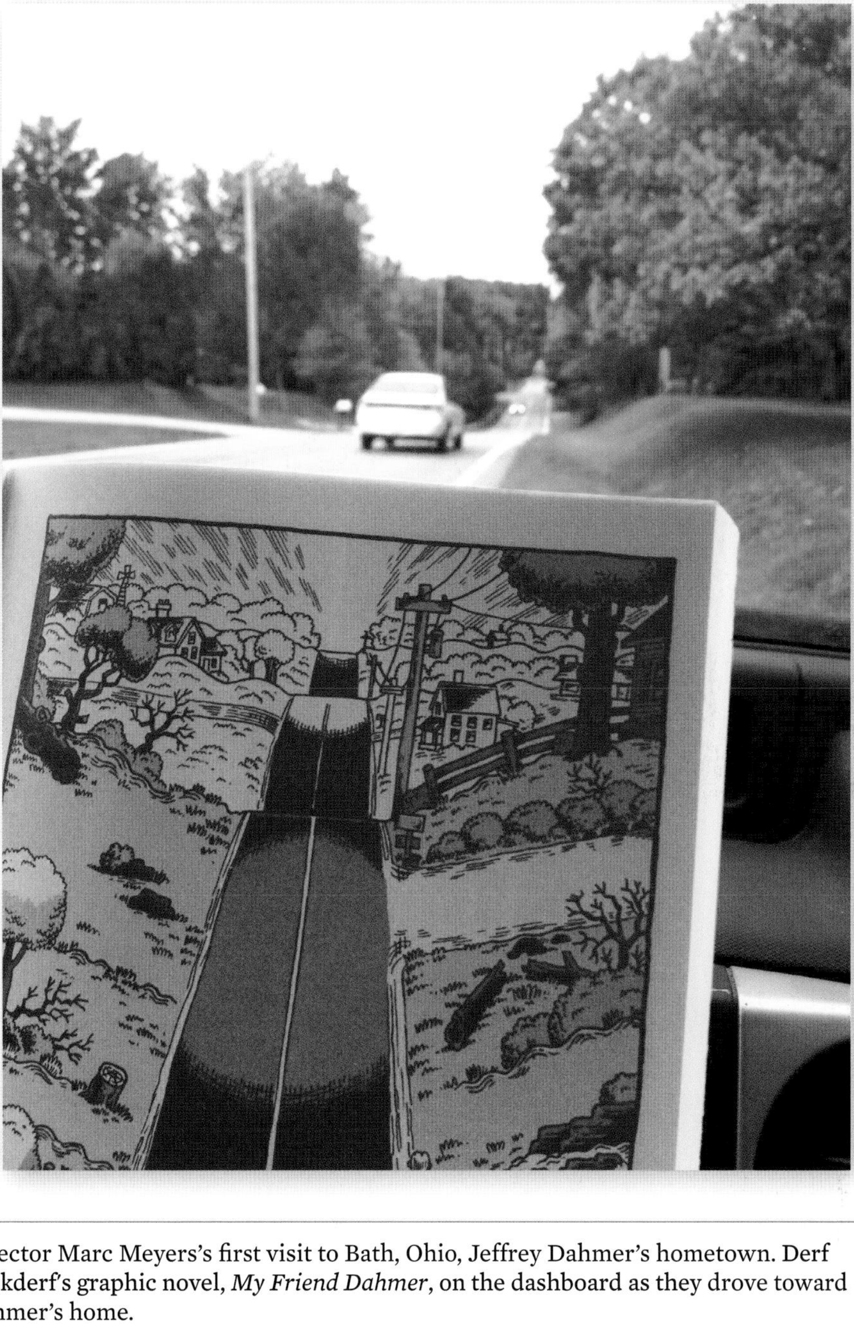

Director Marc Meyers's first visit to Bath, Ohio, Jeffrey Dahmer's hometown. Derf Backderf's graphic novel, *My Friend Dahmer*, on the dashboard as they drove toward Dahmer's home.

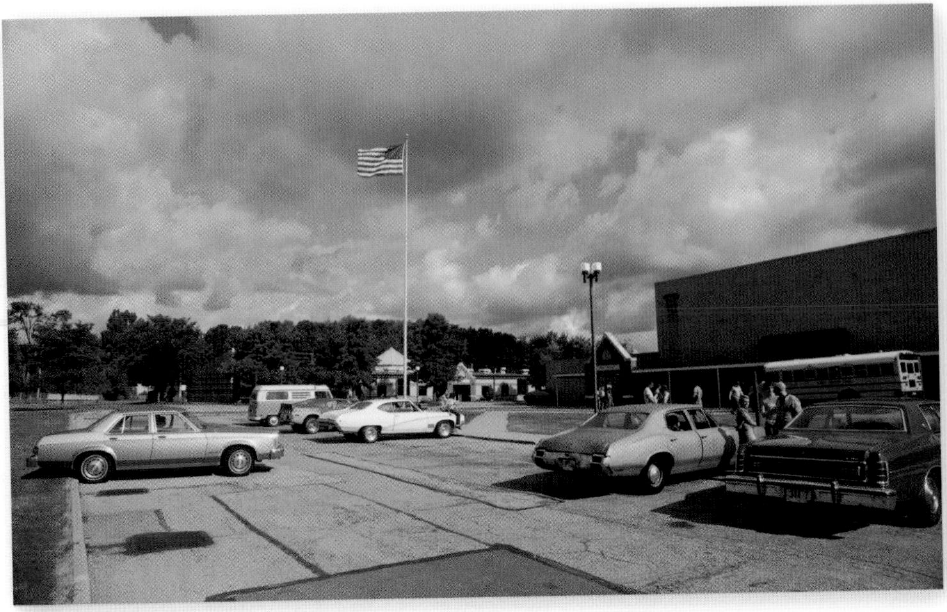

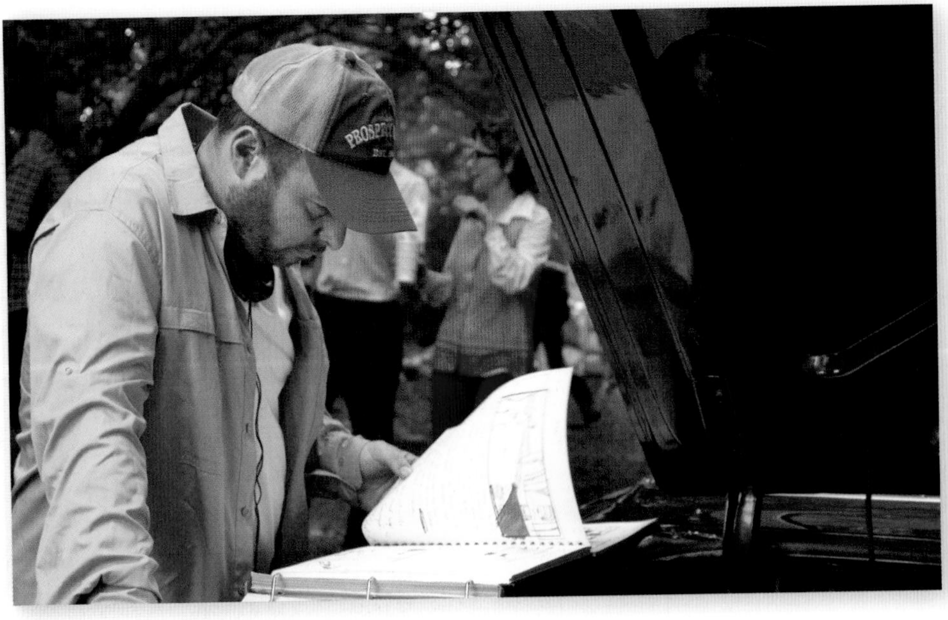

TOP: Period vehicles parked on location at Middleburg Heights Junior High School (standing in for Revere High School) in Ohio, where filming took place.
BOTTOM: Marc Meyers looks over his storyboards while on set.

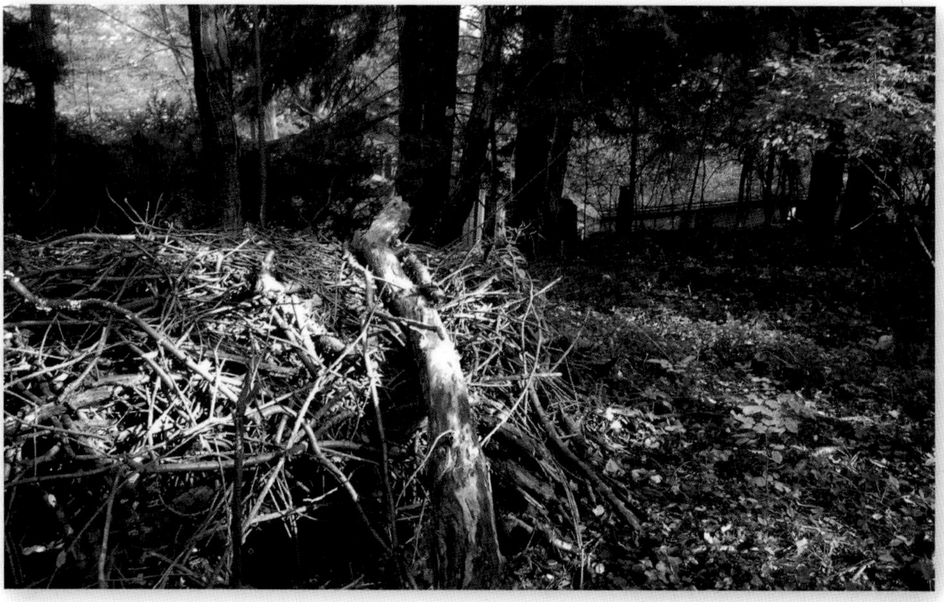

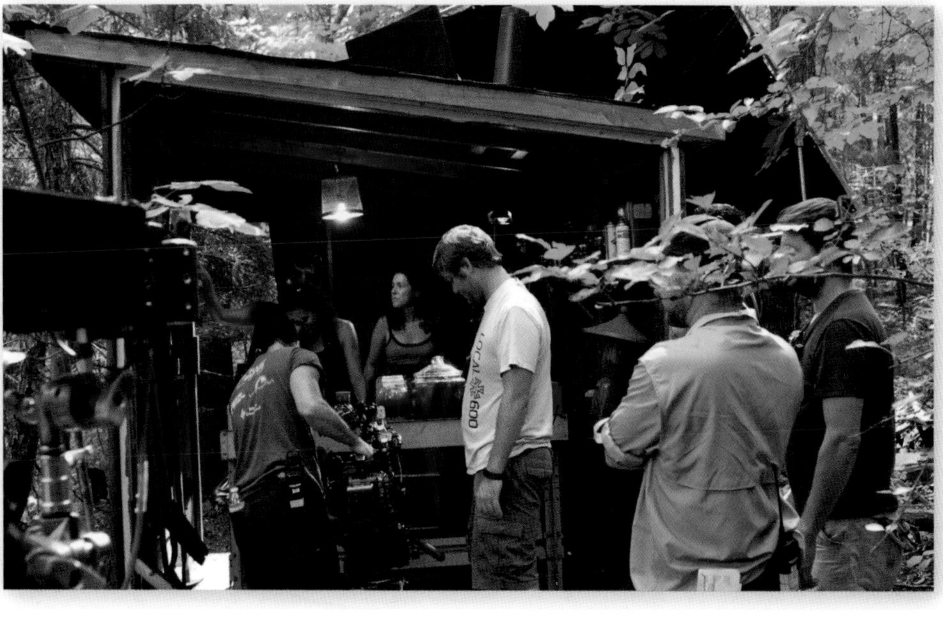
LOCAL 600

TOP: The actual spot where Dahmer's homemade clubhouse once stood on his family's property. Its rotting roof is under these branches.
BOTTOM: The crew prepares a shot set in the interior of Jeff's re-created clubhouse, which he referred to as "The Hut." The hut was built on the exact same spot as the original.

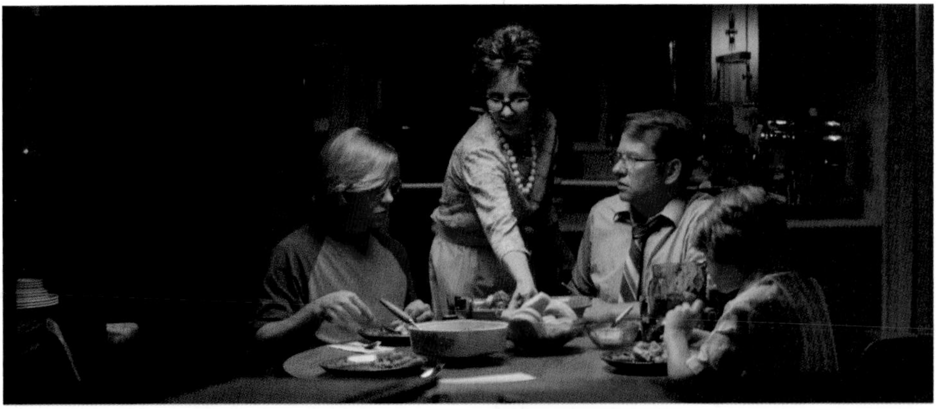

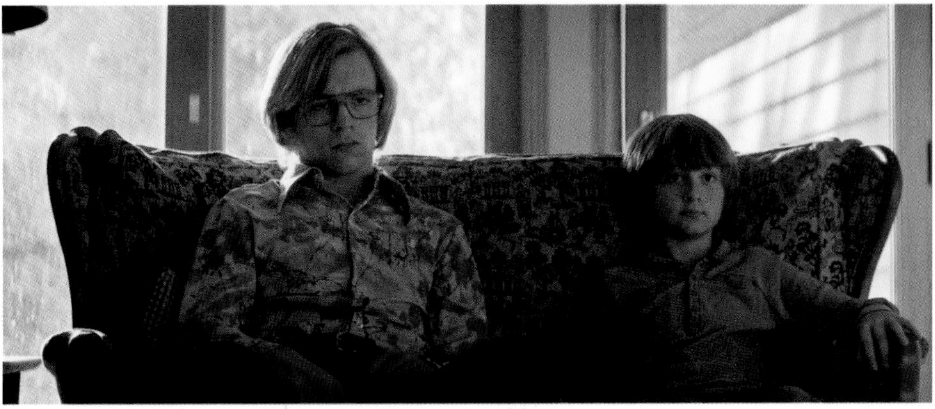

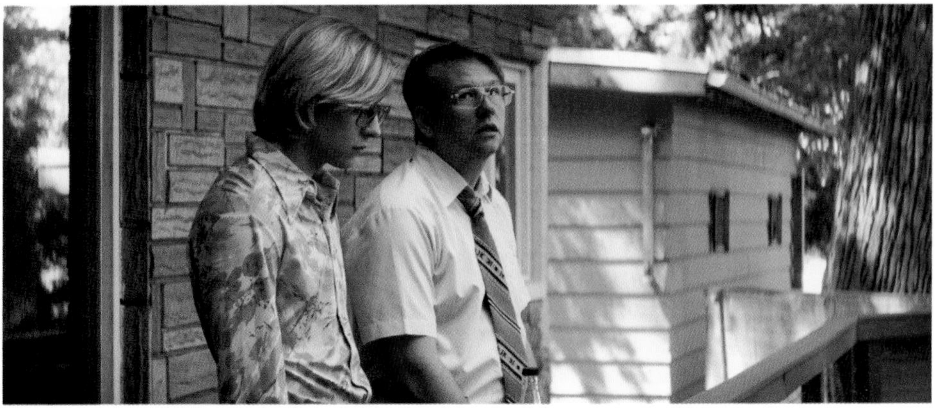

TOP: Dahmer family dinner scene with Jeff (Ross Lynch), Joyce (Anne Heche), Lionel (Dallas Roberts), and Dave (Liam Koeth).
MIDDLE: Jeff and his brother, Dave, watch TV in the living room as their parents argue in the kitchen.
BOTTOM: Jeff and his dad, Lionel, have a heart-to-heart.

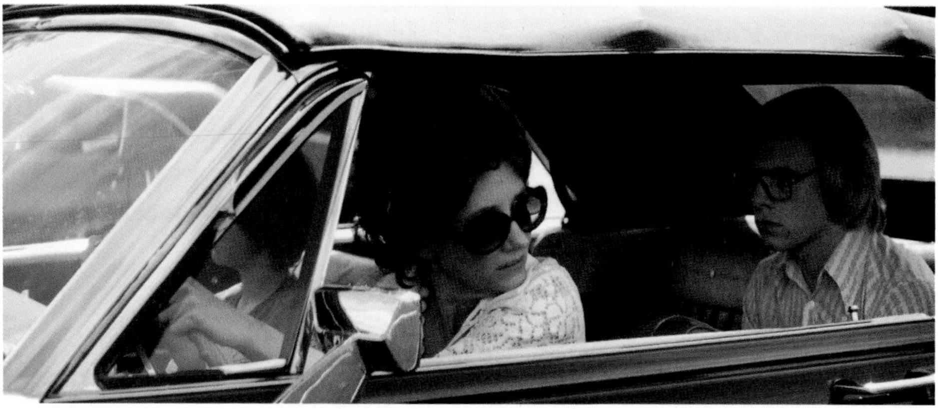

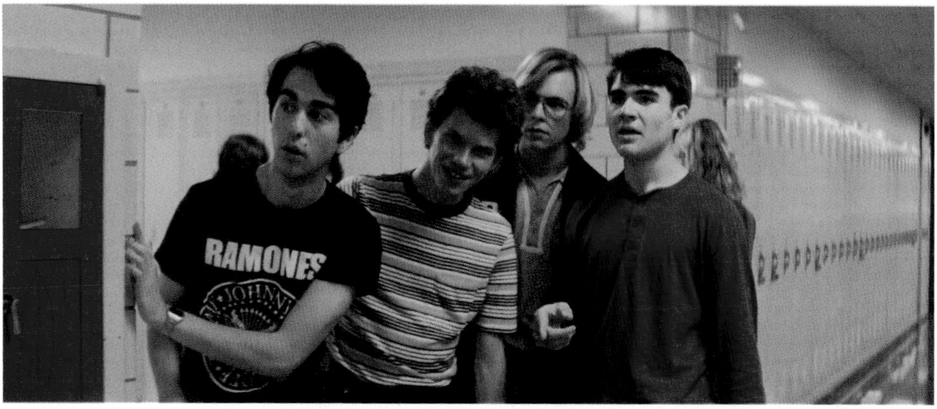

RAMONES

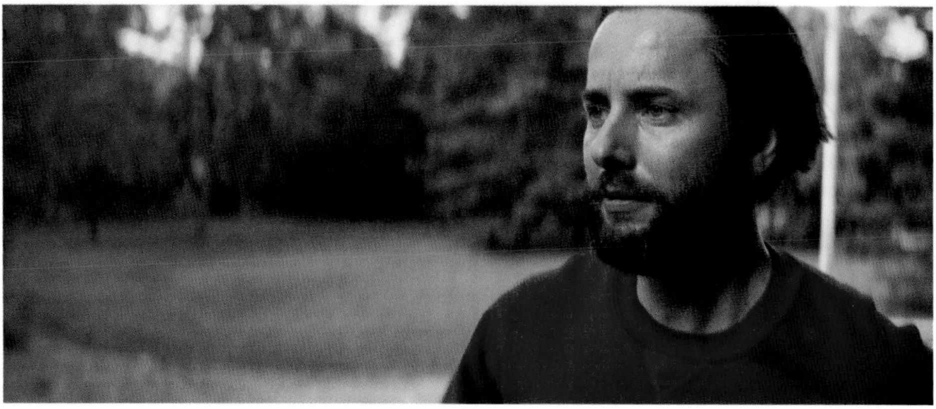

TOP: Joyce takes Jeff and Dave to meet Lionel in a parking lot after the parents' separation.
MIDDLE: The Dahmer Fan Club plots another hallway stunt, with Derf (Alex Wolff), Neil (Tommy Nelson), Jeff, and Mike (Harry Holzer).
BOTTOM: The neighborhood jogger (Vincent Kartheiser) passes by Jeff's home.

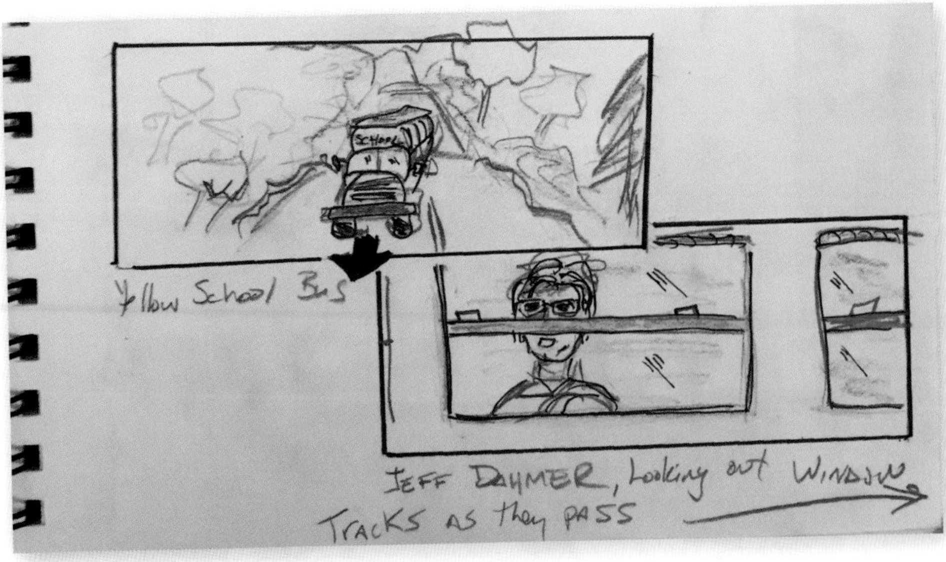
Yllow School Bus
JEFF DAHMER, Looking out WINDOW
TRACKS as they PASS

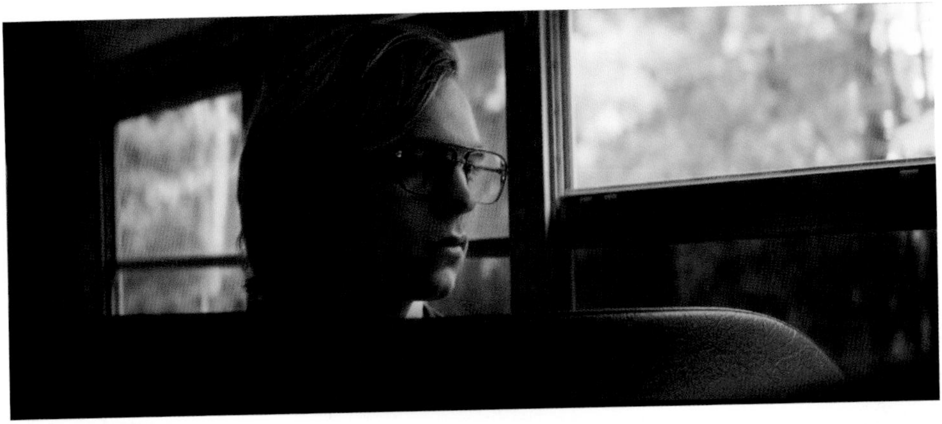

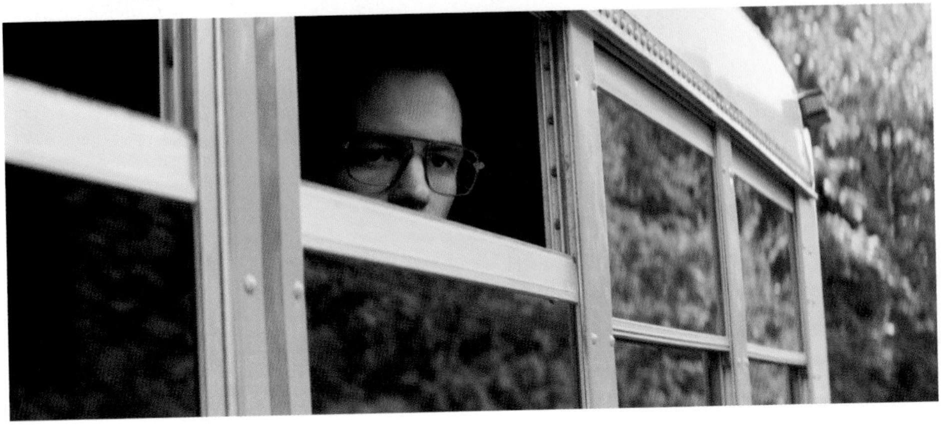

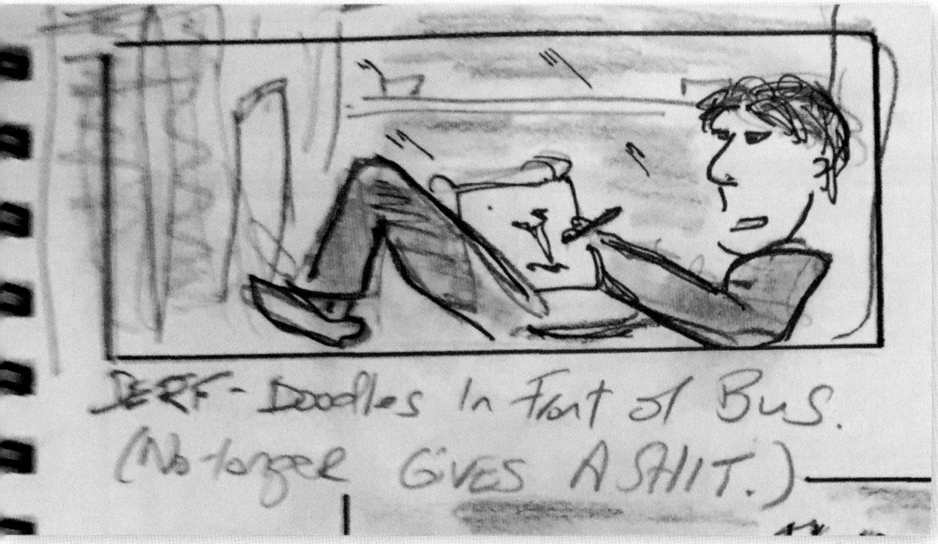
DERF - Doodles In Front of Bus.
(No longer GIVES A SHIT.)

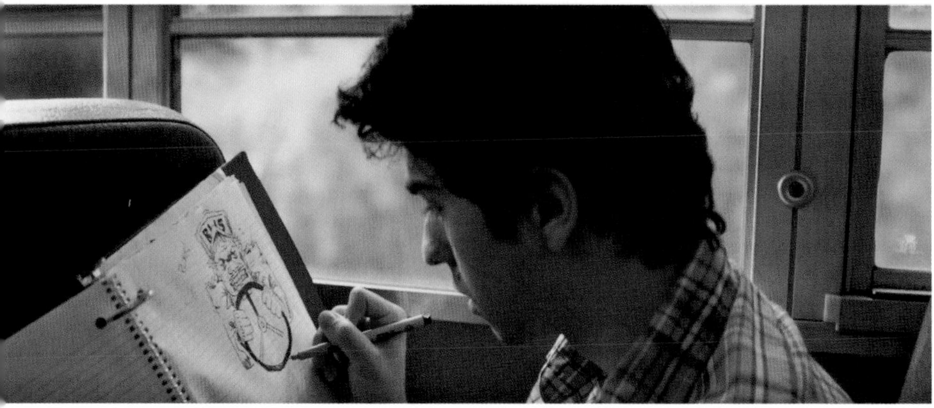

OPPOSITE LEFT TOP: Portion of storyboard for the opening scene.
OPPOSITE MIDDLE: Jeff spots the neighborhood jogger from his seat.
OPPOSITE BOTTOM: Different angle of Jeff as he spots the jogger.
ABOVE TOP: Storyboard panel introducing the character of Derf.
ABOVE BOTTOM: Derf doodles an angry bus driver.

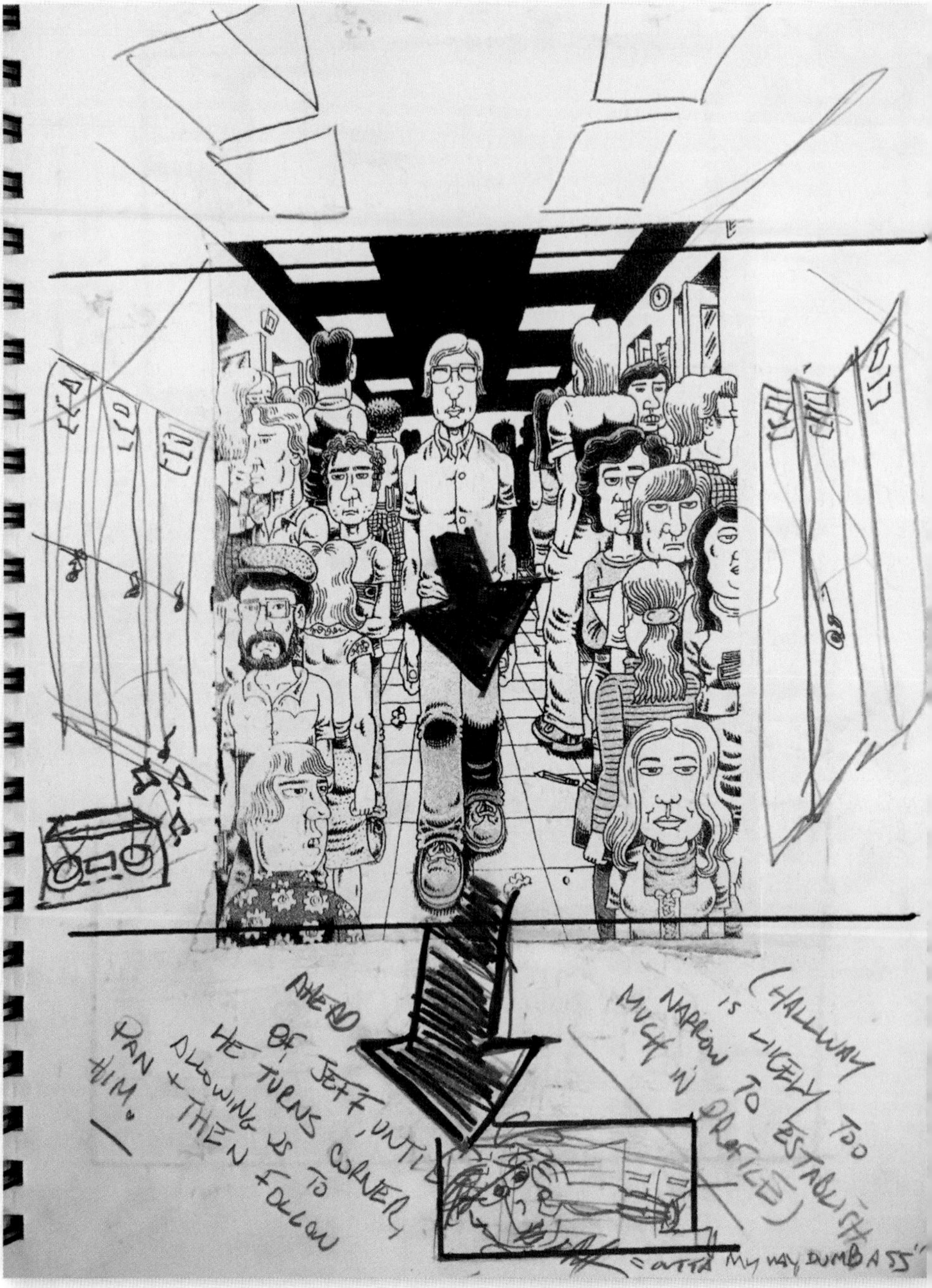
AHEAD OF JEFF, UNTIL HE TURNS CORNER, ALLOWING US TO PAN + THEN FOLLOW HIM.
(HALLWAY IS LIKELY TOO NARROW TO ESTABLISH MUCH IN PROFILE)
"OUTTA MY WAY DUMBASS"

OPPOSITE: Storyboard for the shot in which we first see Jeff walk through the high school hallway. Incorporated into the storyboard is author Derf Backderf's panel from his graphic novel.
ABOVE TOP: Jeff is about to throw his first hallway spaz.
ABOVE BOTTOM: Jeff on the first day of his senior year.

WS of CLASSROOM

CUT OUT TO A WIDER VIEW OF SCENE CLASS ROOM

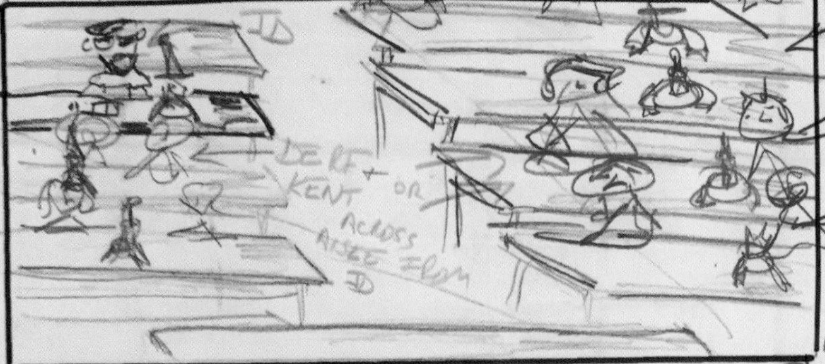

JD
DERF + KENT OR ACROSS AISLE FROM JD
Streams Sunlight IN

CAMERA: WS is ASKEW to THE SIDE, PLACING JEFF FAR TO ONE SIDE of FRAME TO SUGGEST HOW HE'S PUSHED ASIDE, WORKING ALONE, ODD MAN OUT is A THEME, VISUALLY.

SET UP

* DON'T PLACE DERF + KENT FRONT ROW THERE'S GIRLS AHEAD, HE'S DOODLING THEIR BUTTS.

DERF

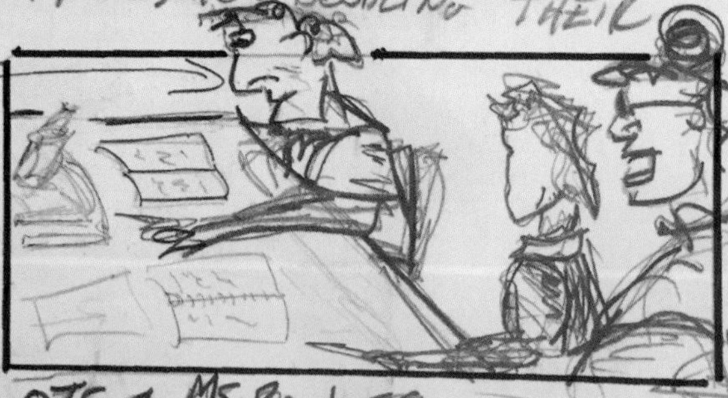

OTS of MS. BOWLES

* OTHER TIGHTER SHOTS COME INTO PLAY AS DERF IS FORCED TO SIT & WORK WITH JEFF.

OPPOSITE: Portion of the storyboard for the biology class scene in which Derf is caught goofing off and is moved to sit with Jeff and share his microscope.
ABOVE TOP: Jeff offers to draw classmate Penny (Katie Stottlemire) during English class. Derf looks on while Neil remains focused on his assignment.
ABOVE BOTTOM: Derf doodles in history class.

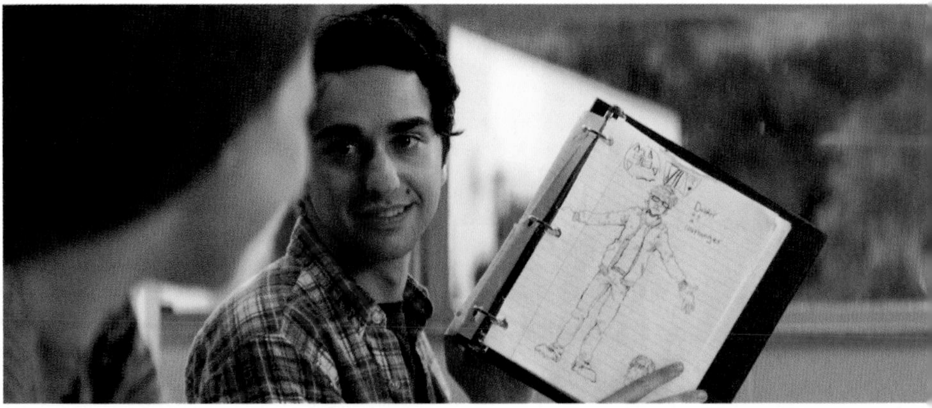

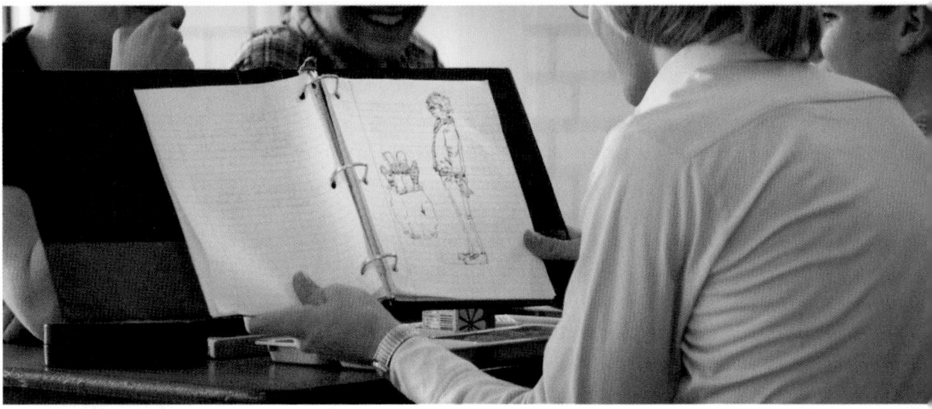

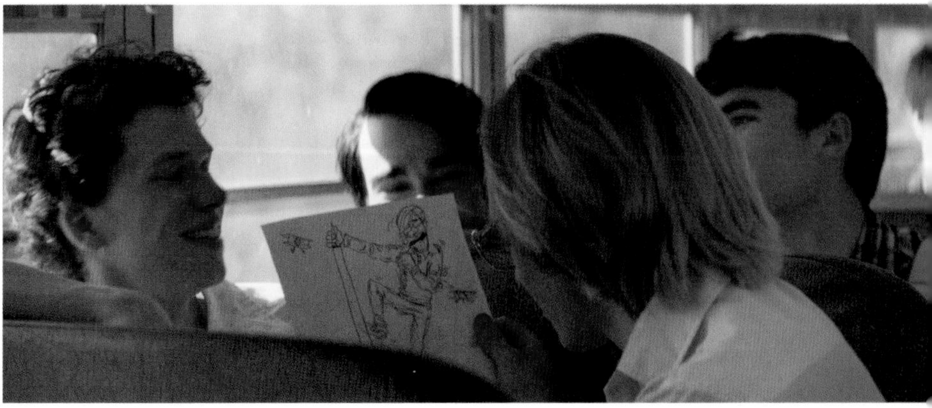

TOP: Derf shows Penny his cartoon of Dahmer as a coat hanger.
MIDDLE: Jeff looks at Derf's drawings of him as a bag of groceries and a telephone pole.
BOTTOM: During their school trip to Washington, DC, Derf shares his sketch of Jeff as King Kong on the Washington Monument.

TOP: The Dahmer Fan Club is born, with Neil, Derf (as the Minister of Propaganda), Jeff, and Mike.

MIDDLE: Jeff explains the inspiration for his hallway spaz.

BOTTOM: Derf in his bedroom packs to leave for college. The drawings on the walls (by young artist who attended Firestone High, Lucie McCoy) are exact re-creations of Derf's childhood bedroom, based on photographs he provided. McCoy also re-created the illustrations on the opposite page.

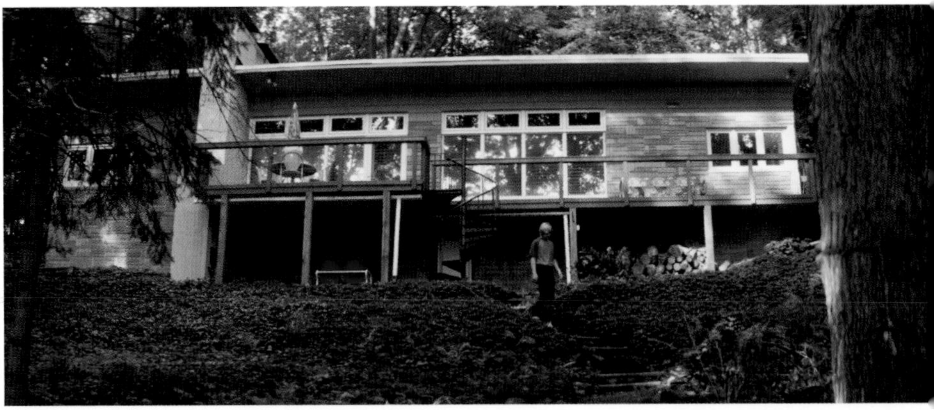

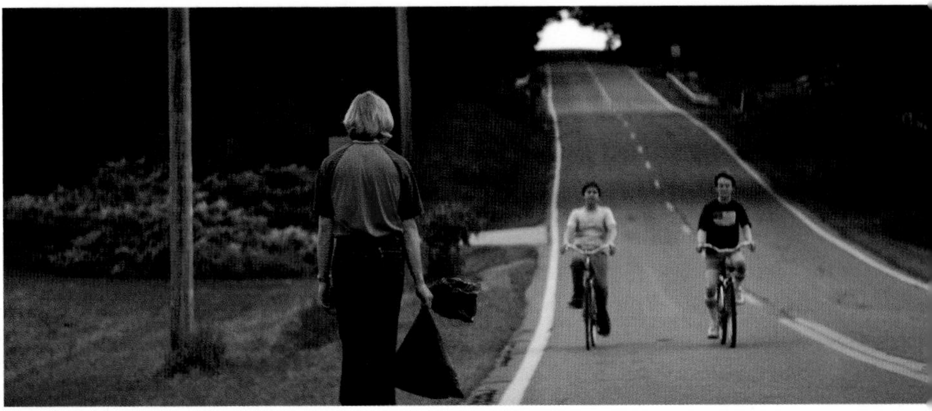

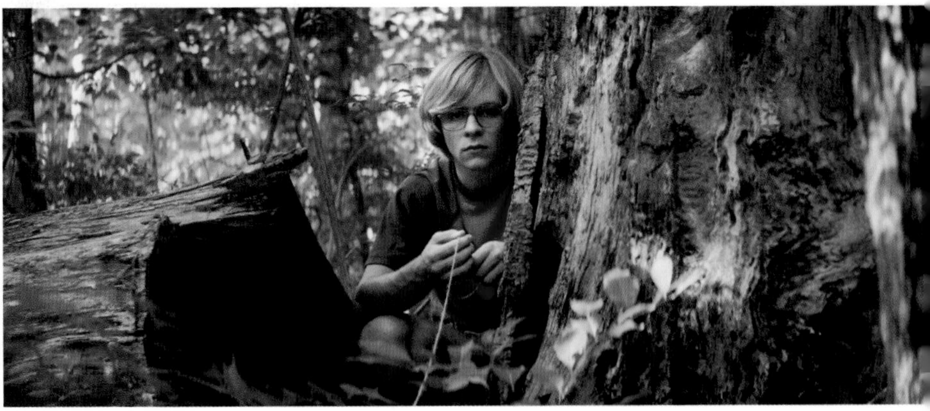

TOP: Filming took place at the location of the actual Dahmer family home.
MIDDLE: Jeff on the way to his hut with roadkill, only to be stopped by two curious teenagers.
BOTTOM: Jeff traps a squirrel during his summer break between junior and senior years of high school.

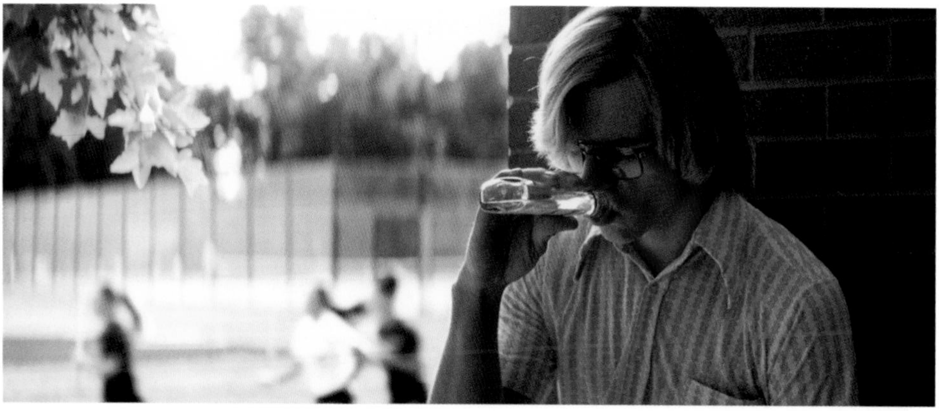

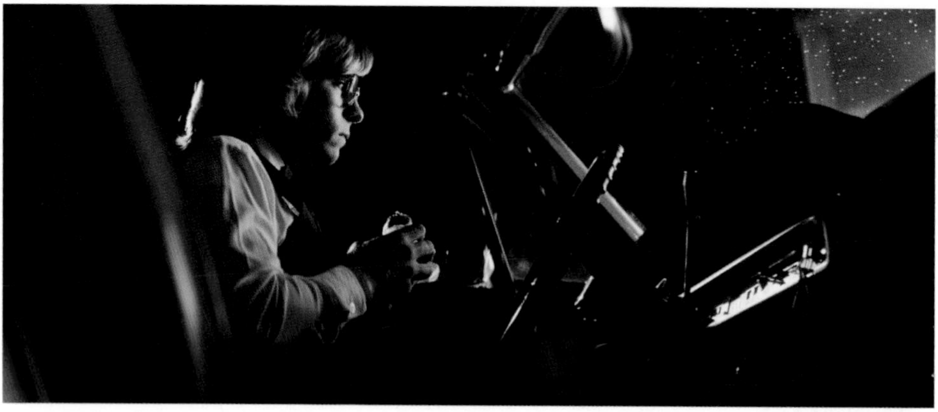

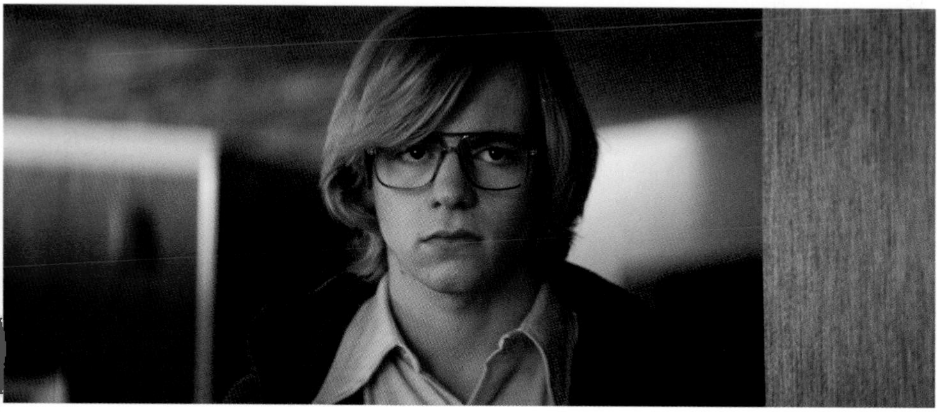

TOP: Jeff gets drunk on school grounds.
MIDDLE: Jeff eats a hamburger in his car after abandoning his prom date.
BOTTOM: Jeff waits at home to get his mother's attention, as his humanity slips away.

TOP: Actual Revere High yearbook club photo from 1977 glued into the director's storyboards—taken from the e-book of the graphic novel.
BOTTOM: Jeff in one of the many yearbook club photos he placed himself into. This image became the first promotional still for the *My Friend Dahmer* movie.

FILMRISE presents an IBID FILMWORKS and APERTURE ENTERTAINMENT production a film by MARC MEYERS "MY FRIEND DAHMER"
in association with NOVOFAM PRODUCTIONS STRANGE CAVERN ATTIC LIGHT FILMS SECTION PERSPECTIVE
ROSS LYNCH ANNE HECHE DALLAS ROBERTS ALEX WOLFF TOMMY NELSON and VINCENT KARTHEISER
casting by STEPHANIE HOLBROOK, CSA music by ANDREW HOLLANDER music supervisor JONATHAN LEAHY costume designer CARLA SHIVENER
production designer JENNIFER KLIDE edited by JAMIE KIRKPATRICK co-producer WILLIAM K. BAKER director of photography DANIEL KATZ, ISC
executive producers MIKE NOVOGRATZ GIORGIO ANGELINI producers MICHAEL MERLOB MILAN CHAKRABORTY
produced by JODY GIRGENTI, p.g.a. MARC MEYERS, p.g.a. ADAM GOLDWORM, p.g.a.
based on the book by DERF BACKDERF written & directed by MARC MEYERS